FIRST DEGREE RAGE

THE TRUE STORY OF 'THE ASSASSIN,'
AN OBSESSION, AND MURDER

PAULA MAY

WildBluePress.com

FIRST DEGREE RAGE published by:
WILDBLUE PRESS
P.O. Box 102440
Denver, Colorado 80250

Publisher Disclaimer: Any opinions, statements of fact or fiction, descriptions, dialogue, and citations found in this book were provided by the author, and are solely those of the author. The publisher makes no claim as to their veracity or accuracy, and assumes no liability for the content.

Copyright 2020 by Paula May

All rights reserved. No part of this book may be reproduced in any form or by any means without the prior written consent of the Publisher, excepting brief quotes used in reviews.

WILDBLUE PRESS is registered at the U.S. Patent and Trademark Offices.

ISBN 978-1-952225-06-2   Trade Paperback
ISBN 978-1-952225-05-5   eBook

Cover design © 2020 WildBlue Press. All rights reserved.

Interior Formatting by Elijah Toten
www.totencreative.com

FIRST DEGREE
RAGE

"For jealousy is the rage of a man: therefore he will not spare in the day of vengeance"
(Proverbs 6:34)

CHAPTER ONE

"...the law is not made for the righteous man, but for the lawless and disobedient, for the ungodly and for sinners, for unholy and profane, for murderers" (I Timothy 1:9)

Never have my feet been so cold. I marveled at the fact that my lower extremities could be simultaneously numb – and painful. I looked down at the snow that clung to my slacks from the hem to the knee, well above the tops of my slick leather loafers. My vision blurred with another gust of the arctic wind in my face, and the frozen mascara on my upper and lower eyelashes were causing them to adhere together when I blinked. I squinted into the wind and trudged forward; wiggling my toes to assess them with each step I took.

The last crime scene I had been to outdoors – an attempted arson – was not in the snow but the rain, resulting in mud that caked my boots so completely that I had left them in my garage where I had removed them, and where they still remain, dried hard as concrete. The insulated coveralls I had worn but had not yet had time to launder were hanging on a nearby hook. I had planned to clean both my boots and my coveralls tomorrow, then repack them in the trunk of my unmarked Crown Victoria, taking the chance all week that I would not need them before the weekend. Just one more day and I would have been in the clear.

This being a wintry Friday, I had planned to work inside the office all day. But after twenty-seven years of living in the Blue Ridge Mountains of Appalachia I should have known better, particularly when for the past six years I had been dispatched to a variety of crime scenes in every sort of weather imaginable. Yet here I was, plodding through several inches of snow, on a major crime scene for who knew how many hours without my insulated coveralls or boots.

A good investigator is always prepared, said a voice from my past. I promptly ignored the voice.

Despite the wintry conditions, I could not deny that the scene around me was breathtaking, both literally and figuratively. Nothing less than the creative hand of God could have rendered a painting so resplendent. When the sun peeked through the heavy cloud cover, the snowy ground shimmered like a field of diamond dust. I took a mental photograph of the peaceful scene, despite my disdain for the bone-chilling temperature and the immediate tasks that lay before me. The only visible movements other than that of law enforcement officers were the billowing of pines and pin oaks and the occasional whirling columns of snow stirred by increasing gusts of wind. Sadly, it was a place not untouched by evil, and it was that thought that drew me back to the purpose of my present station.

Just an hour ago I was working at my desk in my warm little office in the Criminal Investigations Division of the Watauga County Sheriff's Department in Boone, North Carolina. I was catching up on some reports for the upcoming session of the grand jury. I had hoped to finish my paperwork and drive home to my family before dark. I lived in a rural area a good thirty minutes out of town. The snow-covered roads were slick and getting worse by the hour. I had just finished a prosecution summary on a domestic violence case when the phone on my desk rang. It was our dispatch center.

"Sergeant May?"

"Yes," I answered.

"Are you the lucky one on call this evening?"

"I am. Now why do I get the feeling that my plans for the evening are about to change?"

"You *are* a good detective," he said and laughed.

"I'm just a bran muffin in a world of Krispy Kremes," I said. "What do we have?"

"Dead body," he said. "…and on such a lovely day."

"Legit?" I asked.

"Afraid so."

"Outdoors?" I asked.

"Yes, in the woods, east side of the county. A land surveyor found a body in the snow."

"Is it the body of an adult?" I asked.

"I believe so. You know where the Parkway crosses Highway 421 in Deep Gap?" he asked me.

"Right at the top of the mountain," I confirmed.

"Right." The dispatcher said and provided a few more details, including the fact that Deputy Patrick Baker, who had just arrived on scene, said it looked like the body had been there for several days at least.

"…I'll be on my way in just a minute or two then," I said getting up. I grabbed my coat and briefcase.

I met Ray Halle in the hallway, one of the hard-working detectives I supervised.

"Sarge, you hear about the DOA?" he asked.

"Yes, I just did hear. That's where I'm headed. You coming?" I asked.

"Yeah. …Do you have snow tires yet?"

"On order."

"Okay, I'll drive. Idol's Tire just put mine on yesterday. I'm parked right out front."

"Okay, I'll meet you out there. No huge rush; the body isn't going anywhere. Deputy Baker's on the scene and said it's been there for a while," I said.

"We're probably gonna be there for a while too," he surmised.

I grabbed a couple of fresh legal pads, tossed them in my briefcase, and headed outside to get some things that I would likely need out of my Crown Vic.

It was nineteen degrees and dropping; I shuddered to think what the wind chill might be. I got into the passenger side of Ray's burgundy unmarked Crown Victoria. I began making notes as he carefully navigated the partially clear, partially snow-covered roads.

"What other details do you have?" Detective Halle asked.

"A land surveyor, working with a private crew that was contracted to the state highway department – the D.O.T. – was in the woods above the Blue Ridge Parkway entrance off 421 at the top of the mountain. The surveyor was apparently searching for a property marker in the ground when he saw it – him or her – in the snow."

"You know my brother worked for the D.O.T.," Detective Halle said, deliberately off topic.

"No, I didn't know that," I said.

"One day they told me he was stealing from the state. I didn't want to believe it, but when I went to his house, all the signs were there," he said, and we laughed at his joke.

"Ah, good one," I said. Ray Halle was good natured and enjoyed humor as long as it was clean. I appreciated both the attributes.

"Just trying to lighten the mood," he said soberly. "It could be a long night."

"Wouldn't be the first time," I agreed.

"Or the last. Now, if the body out there today is covered with snow, and the man who found it did not get a good look at it, it could be another mannequin, like the Halloween prank by the boys in the frat house...Remember that mannequin they hung in the tree?" I recalled that it had greatly upset a jogger passing by. She thought it was a real person hanging by a noose from the tree limb. She was not even remotely amused by the prank. However, a few of the deputies had some fun afterward with the frat's old life-size mannequin, placing him in variety of unsuspected locations and scenarios for another officer to happen upon.

"I remember. I'm thinking this one's real, since Deputy Baker's already on scene. But... it could be on federal property – since it was found apparently close to the Parkway – and then it would fall under the jurisdiction of the U.S. Park Service and the FBI."

"Right," he said. Then he added, chuckling, "No need to make a federal case out of it yet though."

As we neared the scene, Ray eased the Crown Vic off the partially cleared Highway 421 and onto the snow-covered ramp that led to the Blue Ridge Parkway.

Thankfully, it seemed that news of a body being found had not yet reached public ears. Although the immediate area where the body was located was uninhabited, it was close to a major throughway. US Highway 421 is the direct route up what locals call Wilkes Mountain, the main thoroughfare connecting the towns of Wilkesboro and Boone, located in northwest North Carolina in the heart of the Appalachian Mountains, elevation about 3,000 feet above sea level.

Perpendicular to the heavily traveled US 421 is the Blue Ridge Parkway, where commercial vehicles are prohibited. The Parkway is a scenic route taken primarily by slow-moving tourists meandering around on a warm spring morning when the mountain laurels are in bloom, on a hot summer day when a mountain breeze is most appreciated, or in autumn when the mountains burst with fiery color. But rarely do any travelers attempt to drive on the Parkway in the dead of winter where little or no road maintenance is performed. In fact, many sections of the Parkway are closed during the winter months. At present, the Parkway was covered with a thick blanket of snow and ice, and the main public roads were only in moderately better conditions.

The access ramp leading to the Blue Ridge Parkway is a short portion of paved road approximately one quarter of a mile long. At present, the ramp was currently snow and ice covered as well. To the right of the access ramp is the short incline leading into a densely wooded area. At the base of the incline is a wooden sign identifying the property as that of the U.S. Park Service. The body lay somewhere in the dark woods beyond the sign.

When Ray parked, I opened the passenger side door automatically, but the burst of arctic wind made me delay exiting the warm car immediately. I closed the door and took a few minutes to jot down some observations and the names of the officers I could see already present at the scene while I was still inside the warm car. I make an effort to record even the seemingly insignificant details, which I knew from experience could potentially become significant issues later.

I glanced over at the two brown and tan patrol cars marked with gold star badge emblems on the doors that read "Watauga County Sheriff's Department," which were barely visible under a whitish film of salt from the treated mountain roads. The patrol cars were idling on the paved access ramp, and were parked closely together as if trying to keep warm. Both cars had snow chains on their rear tires. The blue bubble lights atop the cars were spinning silently. A white Chevrolet Blazer adorned with the Blue Ridge Park Service logo was parked just beyond the unmarked vehicles. White smoke poured from the exhaust of the running Blazer, hovering close to the ground before dissipating into the wintry atmosphere.

I quickly filled the first and second page of a yellow legal pad with notes while Ray searched the interior of his car for gloves. He came up with a thick pair for each of us, although I did have a thinner pair in my coat pocket. "God bless you," I told him.

"He already has, many times over," he said as he had many times in the past. Then he added, "But we could freeze to death in this weather if we're out here too long…and before you say it, it has nothing to do with my being from the Sunshine State."

"Hey, I love Florida," I countered. "In fact, Florida sounds *really* nice today. But, right here and right now – well, this is what we signed up for – weather notwithstanding – so let's do it."

"I'm ready," he said.

At the time, I directly supervised our three other investigators – Ray, who was nearly twice my age but much newer to criminal investigations, another male detective who had been promoted to investigation from patrol a year or so prior but was currently on another assignment, and an undercover narcotics investigator – they came and went frequently – who was working on a task force at present, in another jurisdiction. My direct supervisor was Lt. Allen Stout, an experienced officer, a decade my senior. Lieutenant Stout was respected among the team. He had a dry sense of humor and a sharp wit, but tended to internalize his stress, and I was worried about him. I was concerned about his health especially in light of the excess weight he carried and his increasingly high blood pressure, which his smoking habit did nothing to mitigate.

The five of us made up the entire Investigations Division. Lately we had been especially busy. We were still investigating a homicide that occurred over a month ago – a domestic violence case in which the victim refused to leave her abusive boyfriend despite numerous pleas and warnings – a case that Detective Halle and I were working together, and a number of other felony cases assigned to each of us individually. Because our division was small in number, we did not have the luxury of specializing. We were required to investigate every significant incident from break-ins to rapes to frauds to illegal drugs and everything in between. As time permitted, we investigated minor crimes as well. Nevertheless, we rarely experienced more than one homicide case per year in rural Watauga County; having two unrelated murder investigations going at once was, up to that point, unheard of.

Ray and I walked carefully up the icy ramp toward two uniformed deputies standing on our side of the wood line, bundled in brown from head to toe like toddlers in snowsuits. No one else was visible. The usual crowd of onlookers was missing, most likely due to the extreme cold.

"Sergeant May, Deputy Baker is waiting in the woods for you. He's up there with the surveyor who found the body and the surveyor's supervisor. I can walk you back up there," the first deputy said, "or you can just follow the tracks in the snow." A clear path had been made by officers tromping back and forth.

"No need," I assured him, "I'd rather you stay here and keep the scene secure. I can follow the tracks. Do I assume correctly that the only tracks here are yours and the surveyors'?"

"Mine, Deputy Miller's, and two surveyors," he reported. "The snow must have accumulated sometime after the body was left here. There were no signs of any tracks in the snow when we got here, except for a few animal tracks here and there. But nothing larger than perhaps a coyote."

"Got it; thank you," I said. "And I know you will, but just as a reminder, please keep anyone away from the scene who doesn't have a legitimate reason to be here."

"You got it," he said, and held up the notebook on which he had already begun a crime scene log. I smiled and nodded my approval before following the human foot tracks into the woods.

"Ray, are you coming now?" I asked.

"I'll be on in a few minutes," he answered. He wanted to record the observations of the first officers on the scene while the details were fresh in their minds.

It was only 2:00 in the afternoon of Friday, January 7, 1994, but already it seemed to be growing darker. Very little light peeked through the ceiling of tree branches over my head. As I trudged through the snow, my own body growing colder by the minute, I prayed that the decedent's body lay within the boundaries of federal jurisdiction. But my prayers apparently did not rise above the lower pine tree limbs, which brushed across my face, dumping snow on my hair and coat as I climbed further up the wooded incline, following the footprints in the snow that would lead me to Deputy Baker and the two surveyors.

The trail was a bit longer than I anticipated, or maybe it was just the frigid weather that made it seem so. As I walked up the incline through the snowy woods, the wind cut across my face, making my eyes water. Long strands of blond hair had already escaped from my loose French twist and now slapped across my cheeks when I turned my back to the wind. I stopped to pull my hood onto my head, tucking my notebook between my knees while I tied my hood tightly around my face. I was standing in a spot where the snow did not look quite as deep, but turned out to be the perfect depth for seeping down into the sides of my loafers and coating my thin socks. My ankles were already starting to tingle in a pre-frostbite kind of burn. In a small clearing, I bent down in a futile attempt to brush the bulk of the clingy snow off my socks and pant legs.

Glancing upward I saw that the darkening sky carried the promise of more bad weather. I knew that more snow would only continue to conceal whatever existing physical evidence pertaining to this case might be on the ground in the woods. I continued on, considering the implications of a deceased person having been discovered at this particular location.

It was not uncommon for serene wooded areas of our beloved mountains to be sullied by those who, through violent means, leave the corpses of their enemies behind, lifeless and alone, in hopes that they will not soon be discovered. Over the years several murdered bodies had been discovered in remote areas along the Blue Ridge; only God knew how many others had not been found nor ever would be. Others came to the mountains to die intentionally through self-inflicted means. Still others died here accidentally, taking too many chances at the edge of a slippery rock cliff or merely stumbling over a root and smacking their head on a rock. Twice I knew that a lone hiker had gotten lost in the unfamiliar terrain and never made it out alive, one expiring from a heart attack and the second from hypothermia following a broken leg. I wondered if an accident could possibly have caused the demise of the present victim. Still, my gut instinct said no, not this time.

"Detective Sergeant May, we're over here…" Ahead and to my right, Deputy Patrick "Pat" Baker was waving at me. The two men standing near him looked toward me, one of whom in particular wore a slight expression of surprise as he realized I was the responding investigator. Over the past six years, I had grown somewhat accustomed to curious stares directed toward me from those who had not assimilated a female detective into their cerebral classifications of the proper social order, particularly here in Appalachia with its patriarchal societal structure. Inwardly I rolled my eyes. Outwardly I made professional eye contact with each of them, smiled politely and turned my attention to Deputy Baker.

Cheerily, he said, "Good afternoon, my lady," and gave a slight chivalrous bow. Pat was a robust strawberry-blond man with a matching thick mustache, as jolly as old Saint Nick, no matter the circumstances. He and I had worked together since 1986, and he had always treated me with the utmost respect.

After brief introductions, Deputy Baker stated, "Sergeant May, these dedicated gentlemen were working here, surveying the property for, ah, future highway improvement projects. This gentleman here was searching for an iron marker, when he happened on a most disturbing sight…"

"And what was that specifically, sir?" I asked.

"A pair of bare feet sticking up out of the snow, with the victim lying flat on his back it appears," said Deputy Baker, "just over that little ridge there."

"*Bare* feet?" I asked for clarity, scrunching my own cold toes involuntarily.

"Yes ma'am," he answered. "An adult, probably male. The rest of the body is covered in snow, but this poor guy's bare toes are pushing up daisies – er, snowflakes – pretty as you please… Well, you'll see for yourself."

I briefly questioned the surveyor who had found the body about his findings.

"Would you mind taking me on the same route you were walking when you found the body?" I asked him. I could tell from his facial expression he was less than anxious to go back there, but he agreed. His supervisor remained behind with Deputy Baker.

I estimated that we were still on federal property at that point, but I began to lose my jurisdictional optimism as the surveyor and I tread deeper and deeper into the woods. I followed closely behind him, through the snowy woodland with its scrub brush, leaves frozen in mid-decay, around a large thicket of tangled mountain laurels, and finally to the base of a once-towering mountain pine that now lay horizontal. The pine tree appeared to have been blown over by the wind or perhaps had fallen over due to the soft earth in which it was once anchored. The collapse of the tall pine had pulled its root ball out of the ground as it fell, leaving a significant indentation just beneath its protruding roots.

The surveyor stopped and pointed toward the root end of the fallen tree. I could see that he had no desire to get any closer.

"I almost stepped on them!" he said nervously.

"You almost stepped on what?" I asked.

"His feet!" he exclaimed.

"I can certainly see why you would," I replied. "I don't see them yet." The ground was uneven, variegated with tree limbs and saplings, items partially or fully covered with snow.

"Just step on over that way," he said, pointing, "where you can see under those roots that are sticking out from that fallen tree there..."

It took me a moment longer to find and focus on the two objects. One was undeniably a bare, left human foot. Approximately twelve inches separated the left foot from the right, which was not a complete foot, but rather a foot with only the phalanges, or bones of the toes, exposed. I leaned closer. The soft tissue, nails and skin that make human toes recognizable, were missing. It was a fact I attributed to woodland wildlife creatures, no larger than a coyote, as indicated by small teeth marks visible on the outer dermis of the foot itself.

Although only the tops of the feet rose out of the snow, the silhouette of an adult body was clearly visible under the blanket of snow north of the feet. *Definitely an adult; has to be male*, I thought, as I noted the heavy dark hair growth on the big toe of the left foot, the only big toe that remained.

"Well, if you don't need me anymore, I'll just go on back," the surveyor said, seeming to pause for my permission. I noticed that in spite of the biting wind, he looked a bit pale.

"Sir, you did not touch the body or anything around it?" I asked.

"No ma'am," he responded. "I backed away as soon as I realized what it was." I noted that there were no tracks in the snow within about five feet of the body.

"Sure, that's all I need for now," I said. "Deputy Baker has your initial statement and all of your contact information, in case we need to talk with you again. Thank you very much." He nodded, turned, and walked back the way we came.

I turned back to the lonely sight before me. I wondered about the identity of this body and potentially its clues that lay before me, beneath the pristine blanket of snow.

I was reminded of the last body found in a wooded area nearby, the body of Miss Jeni Gray. On the morning of Sunday, September 21, 1989, the smart young journalist was on her way to attend church in the town of Boone with her father when she was abducted by a stranger on the street who ordered her into his vehicle at gunpoint. She endured several subsequent hours of torturous assaults and heinous rape before dying of strangulation at the hands of her abductor, Daniel Bryan Lee, a local young man who kept to himself, and had, ten years prior, been in the same homeroom with me in high school. I had well learned that we cannot know the thoughts and intents of those with whom we brush elbows from day to day. I had also learned that the heart of humankind is desperately wicked. Thankfully, not everyone acted out their sinful thoughts as Daniel Lee had done heinously.

Daniel Bryan Lee had left Jeni Gray's mutilated body, discarded like an unwanted rag doll, in a similar wooded area in Deep Gap a few short miles from this location. He had acted alone but with inexplicable rage toward a stranger. Following his conviction in court, Daniel Bryan Lee died in prison of a brain aneurism while he awaited execution by lethal injection. Even with reliable information that Jeni Gray's body was left in the woods within a particular area, it took days for law enforcement to locate her in the densely wooded mountain terrain. It was a case that would not soon be forgotten in Watauga County, North Carolina, but it was not the case for which I was in the area to investigate today.

If not for the members of the dedicated survey crew with the gumption to work diligently under extreme weather conditions, it could have been weeks or even months, if ever, that this body would have been discovered. Because the decedent was situated under the protruding roots of the fallen tree, in all likelihood it *would have been* overlooked but for the precise spot where the surveyor needed to be. Divine intervention alone accounted for the discovery. I had learned that much at least in my chosen field. When human efforts have been exhausted, that is seemingly when God steps in.

Regardless of the precipitating event(s), it was unlikely that the decedent accidentally fell into his final resting place. I searched my mind for possible scenarios this could account for that did not involve murder, but I was still coming up empty when Det. Ray Halle approached me quietly from behind. He tapped me on the shoulder, and I jumped involuntarily, startled. He laughed. I took a deep breath.

"It isn't looking accidental or suicidal," I commented.

"It certainly isn't," Ray agreed.

But who was the individual whose body now lay before us? I knew we did not have any active reports of missing persons in Watauga County, but surely a person whose body had been left here for any extended length of time would be reported missing in a jurisdiction perhaps not very far away.

This body had been here for some time, so there would be no fresh leads. I ran through the usual possibilities in my mind. A domestic incident, a drug deal gone badly, and so forth. But none of those readily seemed to fit the current circumstances.

"It is *seriously* cold," said Ray, stating the obvious.

"I concur," I replied, and rubbed my gloved hands together in an attempt to generate some friction heat. I was fast losing feeling in my hands as well as in my feet.

"But you know," I added, "the freezing temperatures most likely preserved the body from decay thus far, which should be a help to us." Ray agreed.

Only a few moments passed until the two of us were joined by Chief Park Ranger Gene Redmon, a gray-haired man with a military build who was nearing retirement. He was short in stature but long in experience. At the moment, he was smiling, a very bad sign in my opinion.

"Chief, I bet you're here to inform us that this body is on federal property and we are hereby relieved of our duties," I said. "So we will just move on out of your way."

"Nope," he answered, grinning like a possum. I expected as much. "It's all yours."

"How long did it take?" Ray asked him.

"How long did *what* take?" he asked.

"How long did it take you and the rest of your Rangers to drag this body out of your jurisdiction and into ours?"

"Quite a while," the chief teased back. "No, seriously, I just heard from our dispatch about this," he chuckled, "but I came up here to make sure you didn't move him from your jurisdiction onto federal park land." Then Chief Redmon grew serious. "Any idea yet what happened, Paula?"

"No," I responded. "But I'm fairly certain we have a homicide victim here, Chief."

"I figured as much," Chief Redmon said.

I later learned that Chief Redmon almost had jurisdiction over the case, as the body was a mere thirty-nine feet outside the property of the U.S. Parks Service. But even if it had been, we still would have helped him, and I believe the Chief knew that. It was shaping up to be a long day.

Lieutenant Stout, at lunch when the call came in, was next to arrive on the scene. He emerged from the trees and walked over to us. He was noticeably out of breath and his cheeks were pinker than usual. He wore a coat over his short-sleeved shirt but had not bothered to zip it up. He was the warmest blooded person I knew. He stood, taking in the scene. Sheriff Lyons was a few steps behind Lieutenant Stout.

Sheriff James C. "Red" Lyons was a naturally charismatic leader, a tall, compassionate man with a commanding presence. I had worked for him since I was nineteen years old and admired him most for his integrity and secondly his ability to communicate with people. But I also knew that he was not one to waste time. I briefed Lieutenant Stout and Sheriff Lyons to the extent I knew at the time, which did not take long. Neither did it take Sheriff Lyons long to make a decision.

"Let's get the SBI out here to help us with this one," Sheriff Lyons announced, and my spirits lifted. I was one local detective who appreciated rather than resented the aid of an "outside" agency. I had worked with several agents in the past on various cases, and had found them helpful and resourceful. On this particular afternoon, however, I had no idea just how much work lay ahead and how much assistance we would need from multiple resources in order to investigate this case sufficiently.

Sheriff Lyons made the call. While we waited for field agents and the crime scene unit to arrive from the North Carolina State Bureau of Investigation, Lieutenant Stout began taking photographs. While the SBI agents undoubtedly would take a plethora of photographs as well, it seemed to be growing darker in the woods by the minute.

Special Agent Jeff Sellers from the SBI arrived next. He was a tall, dark-haired and clean-cut man in his forties. "It's good to see you again, Paula," he said as we shook gloved hands. We had worked on occasion together on previous cases.

"It's good to see you too, especially here. We're grateful for the help, especially in this weather. I'm sure you'd rather be someplace else on a day like today."

"I'm glad to help," he stated politely, and zipped his coat further up his neck.

I watched Agent Sellers bracing against the freezing weather as he spoke to Sheriff Lyons and Detective Halle. Agent Sellers explained that our resident SBI agent, Steve Wilson, was out of town, and until he could return, Agent Sellers was covering our area. He began taking his own photographs of the scene with a 35mm camera.

Crime scene technicians from the SBI arrived next. Following a general briefing, they began processing the scene, taking samples, measurements, pictures, and making sketches. When the scene had been documented adequately as it was, the next step was to move the body.

We cautiously and meticulously began removing small portions of snow from around the body, practically by the spoonful, ensuring that we did not discard anything more than just the snow. We soon discovered the body of an adult white male, partially decomposed, and partially frozen. His mouth was gaped open, revealing straight white teeth. The skin, or rather the remaining skin that had not slipped away, was dark complexioned but in some areas had decomposed to a moldy green pallor. One of the eyes appeared to be missing, but likely had lost its moisture and fallen back into the head cavity or had been perhaps consumed by an animal. A large portion of the right ear was missing too, as well as the lower half of the nose. Without the blanket of snow, the body – for certain now a man – was completely nude.

Almost immediately I observed what appeared to be a bullet entrance wound on his left temple, just at the edge of his dark hairline. My weekend plans further dissolved into the snowy fog that now hung densely in the treetops. I had seen enough to know that I would be working for many hours to come before I could crawl into a warm bed.

While we waited for the county medical examiner and the transport team from the local funeral service to arrive, Steve Wilson arrived. Agent Wilson was not dressed much more warmly than I, in his dress shoes and long trench coat that was too thin for this type of weather. After the handshaking rituals, Lieutenant Stout and Agent Sellers shared what limited information we had with Agent Wilson. Agent Wilson relieved Agent Sellers then, apparently taking over as the primary field agent assisting us on the case.

As they talked, Lieutenant Stout walked over to where Sheriff Lyons was combing through the snow with a stick. He spoke to the sheriff briefly and then motioned for me to come over.

Lieutenant Stout looked at me then and stated, "Detective Sergeant May," he began formally, "since this is your weekend on call, this will be your case. I've got faith in you; you can handle it," he added.

"Yes, sir," I responded. I had mixed feelings about the directive. Ray and I still had work to do on the domestic homicide, and I already had a heavy caseload. But Lieutenant Stout was well aware of both of those facts. On the other hand, I preferred working crimes against persons over property crimes like break-ins, and I truly believed that violent crime investigation was my calling. Lieutenant Stout knew where my passion lay.

"You'll want to go ahead and initial the tag when we bag him, so there will be one less link in the chain of custody. Then there's the autopsy..." he added. I nodded.

Agent Wilson offered to attend the autopsy that would occur sometime over the weekend, and there was no need for two investigators to attend. I needed to search the databases of missing persons. As fascinating as autopsies were, it was my least favorite task in a homicide investigation. Someone had to attend to observe and collect the physical evidence, including bullets, directly. The sights and sounds did not bother me at all, but the noxious odors that emanated from an opened body cavity still caused me to take a few steps back from the examining table when certain organs were removed and examined.

"Are you sure you don't mind attending the autopsy?" I asked Agent Wilson.

"Nah, they won't do it until tomorrow anyway, as late as it is, and I have no plans. I'll call you right after," he assured me. "Besides, I remember autopsies are not your favorite thing."

"They are my *second* favorite thing," I told him, "second to a chunk of hot coal in my eye." It was a gross exaggeration, but it got a laugh.

"Will you be available by phone in the morning?" he asked.

"Yes. I'll be in the office tomorrow, researching what I can in the meantime. I'll start running missing person searches this evening."

Dr. Brent Hall, local pathologist and medical examiner for the northwest region of North Carolina arrived then to examine the body briefly at the scene and officially pronounce the victim dead. I had worked with him on several death cases in the past. Dr. Hall worked long hours in the morgue, which happened to be located on the basement level of the old section of our regional hospital. It was a creepy walk down the long hall past the boilers from the elevator to the morgue, the stuff of which bad dreams were made.

I had called Dr. Hall out three times in the last few weeks during the wee morning hours, first for an overdose death, second for the domestic violence homicide, and third, for an accidental autoerotic death. I attended the autopsies of the latter two that he had performed.

He was up working late all three times when we had called him out.

"So, Doc, you actually come outside in the daylight?" Lieutenant Stout directed the question to Dr. Hall.

"I do," he answered, and turned to me. "I'm not *really* a vampire," he said to me conspiratorially.

"Good to know," I responded, matter-of-factly, "It will be dark soon."

"I'm leaving on a family vacation first thing in the morning, though," he added.

"Where ya headed…Transylvania?" Ray asked, joining in the teasing.

Dr. Hall laughed. "Florida," he said, "The Sunshine State." He walked over to the body and became all business.

The task that followed Dr. Hall's cursory examination of the victim was the removal of his body, which we ultimately had to pry from the frozen ground with a couple of shovels we covered with plastic not only to avoid contamination of the body but also to protect the skin, of which the majority remained perfectly intact on the victim, thanks to the winter's freezing temperatures. I wondered briefly if the perpetrator had thought of that in terms of evidence preservation. I wondered how many days, or even weeks, the body had been there. Having just come through the Christmas holidays, I hoped it had not been even longer that someone was missing a friend, a brother, a husband, or a father. Regardless, it was a life that had been snuffed out too soon. He appeared to be about middle-aged, if even that old.

Regardless of the number of deceased bodies I have seen (and there had been many already) in various conditions, prior to being prepared by an undertaker for viewing, I never cease to be struck with a keen awareness that a lifeless human body, without its spirit, is but a shell, a temporary home for a person whose spirit is far, far away. The essence of the person, the very soul that *IS* the person, is absent when life is absent.

Notwithstanding one's religious beliefs, the fact remains that the life of any living person is in the blood, specifically the circulation of oxygen through the blood, a scientific fact that cannot be disputed. Leviticus 17:11 came to mind: "For the life of the flesh is in the blood: and I have given it to you upon the altar to make an atonement for your souls: for it is the blood that maketh an atonement for the soul." The man's blood had stopped flowing in the not too distant past. I hope that he had made preparation for his soul that would live on outside this battered shell of a body.

I thought of the Quakers and how in the late nineteenth century, they practiced excessive public displays of mourning over a deceased person. In 1892, a British Quaker periodical entitled *The British Friend* published an article on the common practice of excessive mourning at funerals. The writer contended that overly strong mourning made people forget that their loved one had the hope in Heaven. The writer included a quote attributed to Mr. George MacDonald, a Scottish author, poet, and Christian minister. "Never tell a child," said MacDonald, "you have a soul. Teach him, you *are* a soul; you *have* a body."

"As we learn to think of things always in this order," the writer said it should be realized "that the body is but the temporary clothing of the soul…"

This truth was articulated by the Apostle Paul in his epistle to the Corinthians when he wrote, "Know ye not that your body is the temple of the Holy Ghost which is in you, which ye have of God, and ye are not your own? For ye are bought with a price: therefore glorify God in your body, and in your spirit, which are God's" (I Corinthians 6:19-20).

The temple of this unknown man had been seized, assaulted, and killed. But the soul of the man himself had departed. Whether his eternal destination was Heaven or Hell I could not say, but there was no question his soul was gone from this cold, desolate place. The body that remained behind was, to us, evidence. It was evidence of some awful act committed by another person or persons, and it was our job to uncover the facts.

We had to move the body. As it was loosened from the frozen ground, more snow fell away from his muscular arms, revealing that the body was adorned with two items of jewelry. On his left wrist was a man's watch that appeared to be an imitation gold piece, and on his left ring finger was a man's gold signet ring bearing the initials "RMR." The unique ring and watch together should be easily identifiable, and hopefully they would help us to determine the victim's identity quickly. We lifted the body gingerly onto a clean white body bag spread open on the ground beside him.

As we scoured the area for evidence precisely where the body had lain, Sheriff Lyons drew our attention to his location a few feet away. He had uncovered from the snow what appeared to be a strip of tape made up of a combination of several layers of both black electrical and beige masking tape. The adhesive side of the tape was covered in black hairs averaging an inch to an inch and a half in length, and tiny droplets of blood. There was one noticeable hole surrounded by black powder near the end of the tape. We all recognized it to be a bullet hole. The victim had apparently been bound with the tape when he was shot.

"Why *two* kinds of tape?" Dr. Hall asked me.

"I have no idea," I admitted, "unless maybe he ran out of one kind and had to find another. Or maybe the masking tape wasn't strong enough and he opted for the electrical. Maybe we will find out eventually for certain."

No other items of significance were found at the scene, though we searched the general area and beyond, not only that afternoon but also in the days that followed. I figured whomever had killed the man had removed all other pieces of evidence including the victim's clothing and most likely additional tape used to bind him in order to prevent the discovery of trace evidence that could connect the suspect to the crime.

If it was dark when the murder took place, the killer could easily have dropped the one length of tape without knowing it, particularly if he was alone and had his arms full of items such as clothing in these dark woods. We had not collected a lot of evidence to go on, but at least the tape was *some*thing.

With Ray holding a flashlight for me, I scribbled my initials along with the date and time on the body bag, and our John Doe was loaded into the ambulance. Agent Wilson informed me that the body would be transported to Chapel Hill, where the Chief Medical Examiner for the State of North Carolina, Dr. John Butts, had already scheduled the autopsy for the following morning, Saturday, January 8, 1994.

We all left the scene then, finding our way through the woods, back to our respective vehicles, both literally and figuratively in the dark.

CHAPTER TWO

"A good name is better than precious ointment; and the day of death than the day of one's birth" (Ecclesiastes 7:1)

My feet were stinging. Burning sensations prickled in my feet as Ray's car's heater blew hot air onto my damp stockinged feet. The warmth was simultaneously heavenly and hellish.

I sniffled, and Ray handed me a Kleenex box out of the back seat.

"You're probably gonna catch cold," he said.

"Maybe. But noses just run in my family," I responded. He laughed.

My tired bones ached for a warm bed and a soft blanket. But first there were more important needs to be met.

At the office I quickly drafted a message for our dispatch center to broadcast to law enforcement agencies in the region informing them that we had discovered an adult male victim of an apparent homicide. I also ran an inquiry for reports of all missing adult males in North Carolina and surrounding states. Meanwhile, I phoned my husband, Randy, to let him know I was back at the office. I would fill him in more when I got home.

When I left the office another two and a half hours later, it was pitch dark and snowing again. But I left with optimism, confident that an agency would respond soon with a missing person report that would fit the general description of our victim.

The thirty-minute drive home took over an hour, due to slow moving traffic on the dark snowy highways. I mentally planned my next steps in the investigation and spent the remainder of my time alone thinking about – and praying for – the family members yet unknown to me who would soon learn of their loved one's untimely death. When I finally made it home and walked inside, I was counting my blessings as my two-year-old daughter, Katie, ran to me in her new Christmas pajamas, arms outstretched. I hugged her tightly.

Not ten minutes later my pager went off. Randy handed me the cordless home phone.

"Sergeant May?" the on-duty dispatcher asked when I called in.

"Yes? Do you have news for me?" I asked.

"Several missing person reports came in that I can see already could not be a match, but I did receive a message from Salisbury PD requesting that you call a Lieutenant Harrison there." I pictured a North Carolina map in my mind and placed Salisbury somewhere in the middle of the state, a couple of hours southeast of Boone, between the cities of Winston Salem and Charlotte.

"Can you patch me through?" I asked the dispatcher. She put me on hold while she transferred the call to the number provided; I reached for my notepad and pen. Lieutenant Harrison introduced himself, and I listened carefully to what he had to say.

About three weeks earlier, in mid-December of 1993, the Salisbury Police Department took a missing person report on a Swedish national who was living in an apartment in the city of Salisbury. Lieutenant Harrison described forty-one-year-old Viktor Ake Lennart Gunnarsson as a Caucasian male, six feet, two inches tall, and 225 pounds, with black hair, mustache, and blue eyes. I took notes as Lieutenant Harrison spoke. In a month-old photograph attached to the report, Gunnarsson wore a gold ring and a gold watch. I told him about the watch and ring I observed on the body that had been covered by snow at the scene.

"It sounds promising," I told him. "I will know more tomorrow after the autopsy. ...What else can you tell me about your missing person?"

"A great deal, I'm afraid... Gunnarsson is very well known in Sweden," Lieutenant Harrison stated, "and not in a good way, it seems."

"Really?"

I listened with growing interest. Viktor Ake Lennart Gunnarsson was officially reported missing on December 15, 1993, by his apartment manager at Lakewood Apartments, a large, busy complex in Salisbury. As it turns out, however, Gunnarsson had actually been missing for several days prior to December 15. The police officers in Salisbury had found Gunnarsson's only registered vehicle, an older model Lincoln Town Car, parked in its usual space in front of his apartment. Salisbury officers had found Gunnarsson's keys, passport, and wallet lying on a coffee table just inside his apartment, and the front door was closed but unlocked.

"We believe he was kidnapped."

I wondered how Viktor Gunnarsson, or any man, could have been kidnapped without detection from a busy, heavily populated apartment complex. While it seemed unlikely in one sense, I also knew that people could be oblivious to their surroundings.

Whether or not Gunnarsson's spirit was the one who had once occupied our snow-covered body, his story was fascinating. According to Lieutenant Harrison, Gunnarsson was arrested in Sweden in 1986, charged with the assassination of Prime Minister Olof Palme that occurred on February 28th of the same year. Gunnarsson was held in custody for questioning for several days without bail. Because an eyewitness to the assassination subsequently failed to identify him in a photo lineup, Gunnarsson was released and the assassination charges against him dismissed.

However, many Swedes still believed Gunnarsson to be the assassin, and because he found life too uncomfortable in Sweden, Gunnarsson came to the live in the United States, seeking political asylum. I had to consider the possibility that an international hit of some kind had been carried out against Viktor Gunnarsson.

"I don't know the details of the assassination investigation, but I'm sure if it *turns out your DOA is Viktor Gunnarsson, you will learn all about it soon enough,*" he said.

Interesting though it was, I was not particularly enthused about investigating a case of international intrigue, as the logistics alone would be difficult, at best. But if Gunnarsson was killed at the location where the body was found, it would be my responsibility. I had primary territorial and subject matter jurisdiction as a sworn deputy sheriff of the county. I would begin researching the assassination of the Prime Minister immediately.

"Before you hang up, there is one other thing I should make you aware of," Lieutenant Harrison said.

"Ok, I'm listening," I told him, picking up my pen again.

"If Gunnarsson was murdered, there is one other possible scenario, than the assassination motive, I mean."

"Really? What is that?" I asked.

"There is a man… actually a police officer… excuse me, a former police officer who is also under investigation right now."

"Under investigation for what?" I asked.

"Well, he is apparently one of those extremely jealous types, and there was a woman we believe was dating both Gunnarsson and this police officer, Underwood. I understand there was some stalking going on by Underwood," he informed me.

"Ah… same old story, different faces," I said. I scribbled down the name *Underwood.* "But a cop? That's awful."

"Yes," he agreed, "It's not right if he was doing that." But he did not volunteer any further details with me in that first phone conversation, presumably since our victim's body had not even been identified yet. I thanked Lieutenant Harrison and just before we hung up, I had one more question.

"Lieutenant Harrison, where did he work?"

"Pardon?" he asked.

"The police officer you said was so jealous..." I glanced down at my notepad. "*Underwood*. What agency did he work for?" I waited for what seemed like a moment too long.

"Salisbury," he said, sighing. "Salisbury PD... He worked for *us*."

The next morning, Saturday, January 8, 1994, I woke early and phoned SBI Agent Steve Wilson. I informed him of the missing person report from Salisbury, providing him with the physical descriptors on the report so that he could compare them with the body during the autopsy.

I got dressed and then bundled Katie up in her furry pink coat; then Randy, Katie, and I went next door to my parents' house for breakfast, our Saturday morning routine. My mother was a traditional southern cook, and her homemade biscuits and sausage gravy were unmatched. But I preferred her biscuits with her homemade chocolate gravy or hot strawberry jam to sausage gravy. Today it was the hot strawberry jam, perfect for a winter day barely above freezing. Katie wanted to stay and play with her "Memaw Gail" and "Papaw Allen," so I drove on to the office. Randy and Katie would meet me later in Boone for dinner if the weather did not worsen. I was glad I did not need to return to the crime scene today.

In all likelihood, it could take some time to obtain Viktor Gunnarsson's identifying information such as a copy of his fingerprints and any available dental records he had from Sweden, so I made the request, with some assistance from Interpol. I also made some contacts and requested information regarding the assassination of the Swedish Prime Minister.

Shortly before lunch Agent Wilson called from Chapel Hill. "Dr. Butts just finished the autopsy. Two gunshots. Two entrance wounds, no exits."

I recalled the position of the body as we found it and the location of the obvious wounds we had observed.

"Where was the second shot?" I asked.

"It was on the right side, on his neck."

"Right side of the neck and left temple?" I asked, to be sure.

"Yes."

"Small caliber?"

"Yes, pretty sure it's a .22."

"Other injuries?" I asked. "Any blunt force trauma?"

"That's more difficult to tell due to the decomposition, but…" He went on to discuss the details of Dr. Butts's autopsy findings and told me he had custody of the watch, the ring, and the spent bullets from the body. Both he and Dr. Butts took a number of photographs. Blood and other samples were taken from the body to aid with identification. Agent Wilson had also taken rolled impressions of the victim's fingerprints for identification purposes.

I shared with Agent Wilson a summary of the information I had already gained about Viktor Gunnarsson and the Swedish Prime Minister's assassination.

"I don't mean to interrupt you," he said, "but I don't think our victim is gonna be the missing Swedish man."

"Really?" I asked, disappointed. I had hoped to identify the body quickly. "I thought the physical descriptions were a decent match."

"The hair and eyes maybe. But the body is three inches shorter than the missing person's height, and the body also weighs about fifteen pounds less."

"Hmm… Don't you think the person who made the report could be off that much in their estimation? And maybe the weight is off because of decomposition or who knows what other factors?" I suggested.

"Three inches are a lot to be off on a man's height. I just don't think it's the same guy," he said. I was not convinced, but Agent Wilson had viewed our body all morning, so perhaps he was right.

"What about the watch and the ring?" I asked.

"Lots of men wear a watch and a ring," he responded.

"Let's compare the fingerprints anyway," I said.

"Of course," he agreed. "We need to be sure. We can at least eliminate the possibility."

We had to wait until the following Friday, January 14, 1994, to prove conclusively our victim's true identity. SBI Laboratory Analyst Joyce Petzka compared the known rolled impressions of Gunnarsson's fingerprints with the actual fingerprints of our victim. They were a match.

"Aren't you gonna say *I told you so?*" Agent Wilson asked.

"No point," I said.

Church services were cancelled the next morning due to the weather, so I spent Sunday at home making notes and reviewing the information I had obtained thus far about both Viktor Gunnarsson and Prime Minister Palme.

At 11:20 p.m. on February 28, 1986, Prime Minister Palme was fatally wounded in central Stockholm by a single .357 caliber gunshot while he and his wife, Lisbet, were walking home after seeing a movie, an outing they planned spontaneously that evening, after they had released their security team for the day. It was one of several occasions when they were out in public with no bodyguards. They were approached by a man who shot at close range. Following the shot striking the Prime Minister, Lisbet Palme was slightly wounded by a second gunshot.

Viktor Gunnarsson, age thirty-three at the time, was known to have connections to various extremists groups, and some literature from the European Workers Party that was hostile toward the Prime Minister was found in his home outside of Stockholm. Gunnarsson loosely fit the description of the assassin. He was arrested on March 12, 1986, but was released after just a few days when eyewitnesses failed to identify him as the shooter in a photo lineup. Gunnarsson sued the Swedish government and in light of the overwhelming media attention on himself and his family, upon receiving a monetary settlement, Gunnarsson fled to the United States. The Prime Minister's wife, Lisbet Palme, subsequently identified a man by the name of Christer Pettersson as the shooter, who was actually convicted of the assassination in 1988. Pettersson already had a criminal conviction history of murder, as well as being a known drug and alcohol abuser. However, Pettersson was acquitted on appeal, due to failure of the prosecution to produce the murder weapon; errors by the police in the lineup procedures; and the lack of a clear motive for the assassination. The prosecution, learning of even more evidence against Pettersson including a possible confession, filed a petition for a new trial, but the petition was denied by the Supreme Court of Sweden.

A number of other theories for the assassination emerged, including motives of revenge against Social Democrat Palme's outspoken opposition to the Apartheid regime in South Africa, Palme's links to arms trades in India in the Bofors Scandal, and Palme's granting of asylum to leftist Chileans in the early 1970s following a coup that overthrew the President of Chile in 1973. Another theory was that the assassination was a result of a conspiracy among Swedish right-wing extremist police officers. Another was that it was the work of the Kurdistan Workers' Party or PKK. Yet another theory is that a CIA operative carried out the deed. The assassination remains an active investigation officially classified as unsolved to date. Viktor Gunnarsson, born March 31, 1953, in Jämjö, Blekinge, was unlike most of the other potential suspects in that he had no known history of violence. He was a lover, not a fighter.

According to one of the several Swedish Police Investigators I spoke with over time, he was not at all surprised that Gunnarsson could have died at the hand of a jealous man.

"Viktor Gunnarsson was, what you call in America, a real ladies' man. He was handsome, and he used his looks to his advantage. He bedded more women than any man I have ever known," said one Swedish investigator with a heavy accent. "He had no discretion whatsoever, and no discriminating taste. Any woman was fair game to this man Gunnarsson. He loved them all."

The investigator went on to describe numerous incidents of Viktor Gunnarsson's love life, and how he had a passion for meeting people everywhere he went. He would encounter a person riding on a bus, for example, and by the end of the trip, he would have arranged to spend an entire season with them. He knew no strangers. His friends came from all walks of life, unrestricted by age, gender, social or economic status. Viktor was quite the charmer, a natural magnet instantly attracting people to him wherever he went. He openly shared his right-wing conservative beliefs with anyone he met, hence his many contacts that included a few extremists who were known for being disgruntled with the Prime Minister's liberal political agenda. But the Viktor Gunnarsson I was learning about struck me as more of a big talker than an actual threat. I knew that I was only beginning to scratch the surface in this investigation.

On Monday morning, January 10, 1994, I met Agent Wilson at the sheriff's office. He had been officially assigned by the Special Agent in Charge to assist me with the investigation. Together we compiled a list of initial tasks to complete and prioritized them. We divided many of the responsibilities and decided which ones would be best completed together. One of the first tasks to complete was to conduct a more thorough search of the crime scene. We returned to the crime scene at 4:00 that afternoon, arriving with five other SBI agents, primarily crime scene technicians, and two other deputy sheriffs.

It was almost as cold as it had been on Friday, but I had dressed much more warmly this time. We had brought with us two gasoline powered space heaters at Lieutenant Stout's suggestion, thinking we might be able to melt some of the snow in one small area at a time where the victim's body had been found in case there was more physical evidence to be found. It was so cold, however, that the heaters were of little effect. They did give us a place to warm ourselves briefly as we searched, which made them worth the trouble, in my opinion.

The only significant items found and seized that day were several clumps of frozen dirt that had some hairs visible. Later we learned, unfortunately, that each of the sixty hairs belonged to the victim. Thus far we had found nothing that would link a suspect to the scene. No gun, no shell casings, nothing except the length of electrical and masking tape the sheriff had uncovered the day the body was found.

We returned to the scene on many occasions during the following weeks and months when the snow was gone, searching without success for any clues left by the suspect to give us a lead. We searched using a line of about twelve officers in a grid fashion. We searched with a metal-detector expert. We searched with the use of high-powered lighting equipment. Finally, Agent Pam Tulley, an SBI crime scene technician arrived. I had met Pam before and knew her to be top-notch when it came to crime scenes. After a brief discussion, Pam was about to conduct a luminol test.

In recent years, crime scene investigators had learned to use blood visualization enhancing chemicals, and luminol was the chemical of choice. Luminol can be applied to crime scenes to indicate the presence of blood not otherwise visible to the naked eye. Luminol reacts to as little as one part of blood per million. The process involves spraying a combination of chemicals in total darkness, typically at night, because the reaction is displayed as a glowing light. The luminol reaction can display wipe marks after a clean-up attempt, handprints, footprints, shoe prints, and even cloth texture marks.

A disadvantage in using luminol is that it is only a *presumptive* test for blood. If the blood can only be visualized with luminol, no further analysis can be performed to confirm the presence of blood. Although a potential reaction is not specific to blood (other oxidizing agents such as bleach may cause luminescence) it is a good test for locating potential blood evidence not otherwise detectable, that might show the path of a bleeding body, drag marks, or such helpful aids to reconstructing the series of events in a crime.

For crime scene purposes, luminol should only be used as a last resort to test for the presence of blood. A bloodstain must be present in sufficient quantity to perform conclusive testing and testing for genetic markers (such as DNA testing). Blood that can *only* be seen with luminol cannot be collected and compared in a laboratory. In our wooded crime scene, no blood whatsoever was visible to the naked eye, and luminol testing was indeed the only practical method for detecting the presence of blood.

Critics of luminol are quick to point out that the substance can give false reactions, and indeed it can. In addition to reacting with blood, luminol can also react with copper ions, copper compounds, iron compounds, and cobalt irons, as well as potassium permanganate (found in some dyes), and hydrated sodium hypochlorite (bleach). When a "positive" reaction is made, then the investigator must determine if the reaction could be caused by a substance other than blood. In our case, the crime scene was a wooded area where no copper, potassium permanganate, or bleach substances were present (Schiro, George. "Collection and Preservation of Blood Evidence from Crime Scenes." Louisiana State Police Crime Laboratory, Baton Rouge, Louisiana).

The basic process used for crime scenes involves combining substances into a plastic spray bottle. The typical solution used is one-part luminol, one-part sodium hydroxide, seven-parts water, and one-part hydrogen dioxide. The combined substance is then sprayed all over the crime scene to be examined. The luminol reaction can be photographed but must be done quickly as the reaction fades after a few minutes.

Agent Tulley sprayed the luminol mixture on the ground in and around where the body was found. The reaction was instantaneous, and the place glowed like midday. The positive reaction indicated that some type of substance, in this case blood, was once present in profusion. Most likely, the victim was shot, stripped of his bindings and clothing, and left to bleed to his death in this very spot.

An unnatural chill spread across my body as I thought about what happened and what kind of person could kill another human being in cold blood.

I met Don Gale for the first time by phone. As the resident agent for Rowan County, he was Steve Wilson's counterpart in Salisbury. He also happened to be the criminal field agent assigned to investigate the murder of an elderly lady in Rowan County, which occurred a month earlier, on December 8, 1993. As he described the murder scene there to me, I had not yet seen the relevance to ours.

"Murdering a little old lady in her home is just awful," I said to Agent Gale, "but what does that case have to do with our investigation?"

"A lot. You see, your victim Viktor Gunnarsson was dating Kay Weden, who happens to be the daughter of *my* murder victim, Catherine Miller."

"You're kidding."

"No, I'm not."

Agent Gale gave me the *Reader's Digest* condensed version. Catherine Miller was a 77-year-old woman who lived alone in a brick ranch-style house, with a private security system, in a nice Salisbury neighborhood near her daughter Kay Weden. Mrs. Miller had worked full-time in accounting at W.A. Brown, a refrigeration company in

Salisbury for many, many years and almost never missed a day of work. She was a pleasant grandmotherly type who doted on her only daughter, Kay, and grandson, Jason. She was quick to offer a helping hand to a neighbor or friend and volunteered to serve frequently in church activities, but otherwise minded her own business.

I wondered what kind of monster would kill such a harmless lady.

"Let me start with Kay, the victim's daughter…" Agent Gale said.

Agent Gale informed me that Catherine Miller's daughter, Kay Weden, had recently attempted to end a three-year relationship with an insanely jealous man by the name of L. C. Underwood.

"Underwood… the police officer," I realized.

"Yes. L. C. Underwood is a suspect in the homicide of Catherine Miller."

"The main suspect?" I asked.

"You could say that."

"Do you have enough evidence to charge him?" I asked.

"Not yet," he answered honestly.

"I understand he worked for Salisbury PD?"

"He has been with the Salisbury Police Department for eight years, but he worked for other law enforcement agencies for eleven years before he was hired by Salisbury PD."

"He isn't still working as a cop, though, correct?" I clarified.

"Not now. He retired last month, allegedly on disability."

"Allegedly?"

"Well, he got into some trouble with the Police Chief over stalking Kay Weden."

"Underwood was stalking her, not the Chief?" I clarified.

"Right. Kay reported him to the Chief, and, well, a Disability Retirement was simplest way to get rid of him."

"You know, I talked with a lieutenant at Salisbury PD."

"Yeah I know. You talked to Lieutenant Harrison. But did he tell you that he is a personal friend of L.C.'s?"

"No, he didn't."

"Well he is. So be careful who you talk to and what you say." I thought about that. I was anxious to meet everyone involved in the investigation in person because at that point, I had no idea who to trust.

I wanted to talk with Kay Weden as soon as possible, but I also wanted to get as much background information as I could first.

"Do you know Steve Wilson, the case agent here in Boone?" I asked.

"I do."

"Would you be willing to meet with the two of us soon so that we can put all our heads together on these cases?"

"Yeah. Steve is a good guy. And we need all the help we can get. I'm sure that we have a lot of information that you all need as well."

We made plans to meet, and meanwhile Agent Gale gave me a great deal more information to digest. The investigators in Rowan County had already conducted a number of interviews, so Agent Wilson and I had some catching up to do, although over the phone Agent Gale summarized, as best he could, what they had done already.

A series of events began to unfold in my mind. I had investigated more than enough tragedies to grasp that a man could easily kill an ex-girlfriend's new boyfriend in a fit of jealous rage. But for a man to murder his ex-girlfriend's elderly mother in cold blood seemed to require something more, something …sinister.

CHAPTER THREE

"Even a child is known by his doings, whether his work be pure, and whether it be right" (Proverbs 20:11)

Lamont Claxton Underwood was born at 1:24 a.m. on Monday, September 10, 1951, at City Memorial Hospital in Winston Salem, North Carolina. His original birth certificate spelled his first name Lamounth, but he changed it to Lamont in 1968. The handsome dark-haired, dark-eyed boy was born to Floyd Claxton Underwood and Ethel May Underwood.

Floyd Underwood was known to his friends and family as "Rass." He was described to me as a 1950s he-man, a drinker who wore his dark hair slicked straight back, dirty straight leg jeans and T-shirts with a pack of cigarettes rolled up in the sleeve. He carried his rough and tough reputation proudly, and Ethel reportedly did little to hide her own reputation as a loose partying woman who could not be bothered to care for her children properly.

Rass and Ethel Underwood had three children in all: another son, Richard, Lamont's older brother; and a daughter, Margo, Lamont's little sister. Unfortunately, as I was told, good parenthood proved too burdensome and inconvenient for the Underwood couple.

Agent Steve Wilson and I interviewed the few Underwood family members we could identify and locate. We gleaned as much information from Lamont's early years as we could. While the Underwood family members were not the most objective of sources, they were certainly the most knowledgeable. The first family member who agreed to speak with us was Lamont's uncle, George Underwood, Rass's brother.

According to Uncle George, Ethel Underwood would bring her three children, Richard, Lamont, and Margo, to George's house for George and his wife to care for during the day "while Rass worked and Ethel was out gallivantin' around town."

"Was that a frequent occurrence?" I asked George.

"Sure was. And when she didn't bring them to our house, she would set the three of them out on a street corner while she traipsed off to meet other men... At least that's what I was told," George added.

As the forty-year-old rumors were told to me, Rass and Ethel parted ways when Rass caught her with another man. Ethel then allegedly "took up with some man on the east side of Winston Salem." A short time later Ethel's neighbors reported to Rass that Ethel and the children were living in a car and that the children were being neglected. George boasted that he reported her to "the Welfare Department" himself.

Then one day in January of 1957, Ethel showed up on George's doorstep, pleading with him and his wife to take the children. Ethel moved in with a new paramour in the town of Yadkinville, according to George. George found Rass, who came to George's house and picked up Richard, Lamont, and Margo. Rass kept the children with him for about three months, living at his parents' home. Then Rass, too, abandoned the three children. It seemed there was no room in the lives of either parent for three little innocent dark-eyed children.

On July 9, 1957, George and Delzia Underwood were granted legal and physical custody of five-year-old Lamont and three-year-old Margo. Richard, the oldest at age six, was placed in the custody of both his aunt Ruby Underwood,

Rass's and George's sister, and Annie Underwood, Richard's paternal grandmother.

"Three of them were just too many to take on," George explained. "We already had our own son. But we took the two youngest."

Richard the oldest, as was reported, thrived in the home of his aunt and grandmother. Although the situation was not ideal, it was functional, stable, and caring, all the things Richard lacked from his own parents. Richard was encouraged to work hard and complete his education. He did so and managed to stay out of trouble. As an adult, Richard had a successful career in the firefighting service. He had little contact with Margo and practically none with Lamont.

Margo and Lamont reportedly did not fare so well in the home of Uncle George and Aunt Delzia. From the many stories we were told, George may not have been mentally stable. He was a strict disciplinarian, at least when it came to Lamont and Margo. When Lamont turned six, for instance, Uncle George's idea of punishment for one of Lamont's infractions was to make Lamont wear a dress and suck a pacifier as he swept the front porch, while his young friends looked on and laughed in derision. I cringed involuntarily.

George laughed aloud to himself as he bragged about keeping little Lamont under control. I was not smiling, and neither was Steve. But that did nothing to dissuade George once he got started sharing anecdotes.

"One time he was so out of control, kicking and screaming, I told him if he didn't straighten up, I'd tie him up in a sack. I did it, too, when he wouldn't stop throwing his little tantrum."

"You put him a sack?" I asked, to be sure I understood correctly.

"Yeah, I told him I'd bind him up and put him in one if he didn't straighten up, so I had to keep my word," he said. I thought of Viktor Gunnarsson and how he was bound with the tape.

"I did make him walk the chalk-line," George said arrogantly as he leaned back in his chair and inhaled deeply, causing his chest to protrude. "The first five years of his life already ruined him," George added. My heart ached for the unwanted little boy.

"How long did you keep Lamont and Margo?" I asked, trying to maintain my professionalism in the face of the blatant child abuse.

"Well after nearly three years, Ethel came back to Winston Salem, 1960, it was. Ethel claimed she was gonna take care of them, but we knew it wouldn't last. She couldn't handle the responsibility and took off. Lamont said he hated her and never wanted to see her again. All that woman did was mess the kids up," George said.

"Could you elaborate on that please?" I asked.

"Well for one thing, you couldn't leave them alone," George explained. "Both of them – Margo and Lamont – were scared to death of being left alone. They had to be right underfoot all the time." *No wonder*, I thought sadly.

"Lamont said more than once that when he grew up, he was going to kill Rass." Little Lamont was surely crying out for help. Unfortunately, no one seemed to hear his piteous cries.

Uncle George tolerated Lamont and Margo, or rather they tolerated *him*, for a total of five years. During that time, Lamont's name was shortened to "Mont." Then later "Mont" turned into "Mookie," the reason lost in time.

"It's just that we would get Mookie out of one thing and he'd get right into something else," George continued. "He had sticky fingers."

"Sticky fingers? As in he took things that didn't belong to him?" I asked.

"Yeah. I don't know what in the world prompted him to do the things he did. He was a selfish, possessive boy, and he refused to share anything that he had with anybody. And he and Margo both were prone to telling lies," George added.

"And he was three? Three, four years old?" I clarified.

"I suppose," he said.

George was quick to point out that he took Lamont and Margo to the Holiness Church he and his wife attended every Sunday. One Sunday morning, however, Lamont bucked. He told George unequivocally that he was not going to go to church. George told him as long as he lived under his roof he would indeed go to church. Without elaborating on the means and extent of the punishment he inflicted on young Lamont, George told us that Lamont did go to church that day and every Sunday thereafter. But George added that he doubted the depth of Lamont's religious convictions. I rather doubted the depth of George's.

"I didn't have that kind of trouble out of *my* son," George shared. George and Delzia's son was about the same age as Lamont.

"How did Lamont and your son get along?" Steve asked.

"Okay, for the most part," George said. "Like I said, I never had any trouble hardly out of my boy." I never heard that George ever made his own son wear a dress or suck a pacifier in front of his friends, but then again Lamont was not the son but the orphan.

George said he reached the end of his rope when Lamont began setting fires in the house.

"That would be a problem," I said. "What were the circumstances?"

"That boy was up in the attic pouting about something," George recalled, "and he had a pack of matches he stole from me. He lit those matches in the insulation up there! The insulation was smoldering. He nearly burned the house down! Right after that, a caseworker from the Department of Social Services came out to conduct one of her monthly home visits with Margo and Lamont. My wife, Delzia, had about all she could take. That caseworker lady got an earful."

George said the caseworker listened to Delzia describe the problems they were having with the children. It was the caseworker who suggested that they place Margo and Lamont in The Children's Home, an orphanage in Winston Salem. George and Delzia agreed.

The Methodist Children's Home was founded in 1909 by Methodists from the western part of the state. They took over the Glenwood Avenue property of the former Davis School Military Academy, which operated throughout the 1800s. The Children's Home was an orphanage and offered a residential program for children.

It was not George but other family members who told us that when little Lamont was about to be sent off to the orphanage, he cried for days. He readily admitted that he had been "bad" and insisted that he was "really sorry," and begged not to be sent away. Once again, his cries fell on deaf ears. Lamont and Margo were admitted to The Children's Home in June of 1961, and each remained wards of the Domestic Relations Court of Winston Salem, North Carolina, until reaching the age of eighteen.

Interviewing Uncle George made me all the more anxious to talk with Margo. I had no idea of the shape we might find her in, but when Steve and I finally located her, we were pleasantly surprised to find that she was nothing like Lamont. She lived with her son and daughter in a modest but neat mobile home on a quiet street in Winston Salem. She was recently divorced and worked at a local bank. Margo was home alone when Steve and I knocked on her door.

We were met by a petite dark-haired woman, polite but apprehensive. Steve and I introduced ourselves and displayed our respective badges. She looked genuinely puzzled as to why we wanted to speak to her. In spite of her hesitation, Margo invited us inside.

Margo had the same dark-brown eyes as her brother but without their hardness. She said she had not seen Lamont since 1984. She heard from someone that he was working as a private detective in Lumberton.

"Well, that's close," I responded. "He was working as a Sheriff's Detective in Lincolnton. But he left there and has been working for the last several years as a police officer in Salisbury." The city of Salisbury was less than an hour's drive from where Margo lived.

"Oh. Well we don't stay in touch with each other," she said as she looked down at the carpet.

"And you have another brother as well?" Steve asked her.

She looked up then. "Yes, that's Richard. I haven't talked to him in a long time either. I think he got married. Annette or something like that is his wife's name. ...But they're divorced now. Richard is a police officer in Winston Salem," she added.

I did not correct her this time, but Steve and I exchanged glances. No need to tell her Richard was a fireman, not a police officer. It was obvious she was out of touch with her family.

"Since you haven't been in touch with Lamont recently, is it safe to assume that you are not aware of Lamont being a possible suspect in a homicide case?" I asked Margo.

"He's *what*?" she asked, wide-eyed.

"Yes ma'am. That is why we are here. I am sorry to have to tell you that," I said.

"He does have a history of being in trouble with the law," she stated.

"What do you mean?" I asked.

"Well, he had to go to court over this girl... Maybe it was two girls..."

"When was that?"

"Let's see... It had to be in the early 1970s. Lamont was just a teenager. He represented himself; he did not want a lawyer." I know how *that* scenario usually goes. He who represents himself has a fool for a lawyer and all that... It was an accurate adage.

"What happened with the case?" Steve asked.

Margo thought for a moment and then said, "Lamont was found guilty of something. I just don't remember what exactly. I know they placed him on probation."

"What else can you share with us about his background?"

"I heard that he was married, but that his wife died of some... natural cause."

Steve explained gently, "That is not entirely accurate. He has been married, but his marriages ended in divorce."

"Oh," she replied, without emotion. "Like I said, we don't stay in contact. We're not a close family." That was obvious enough. "I'd like to see him again, though, but I don't know what I'd say to him."

She needed to be able to visit him in a controlled environment, I thought. Like prison.

"What kind of personality did Lamont have? While you were growing up together, I mean."

The first word she uttered was "possessive."

"When we were born – Richard, Lamont, and I – we lived with our natural parents, Floyd and Ethel May Underwood. Our mother left first. Our father tried to raise us, but he just couldn't. You know how it is, with three small kids to tote around and feed… Lamont and I went to live with father's brother, Uncle George, and Aunt Delzia. We always called her Del. Del was the closest thing to a mother that Lamont and I ever had. Richard went to live with our grandmother and Aunt Ruby."

"What was it like living with George and Del?" I asked.

After some hesitation, Margo answered and then couldn't seem to stop remembering. "…Well, I was two years old when Lamont and I went to live with them. I could not talk plainly then, so George made me suck a pacifier, even though I was too old for one. Of course, that didn't help my speech. George made Lamont wear little girls' dresses and pick up trash outside, in front of his friends. …George would whip me and Lamont by holding us upside down by our ankles, and he beat us with his belt. Oh, and he also made us stand for hours – literally for hours – on one leg when we did something bad. We couldn't put our other leg down or we'd get whipped again."

"I, I'm so sorry," I told her, meaning it. "You were only two years old?"

"Yes, but I remember it very well. George did that kind of thing all the time we were staying there. He had an awful temper. You didn't have to do much to make George mad. …One night when we were older and were staying there, Lamont came in drunk, and George busted Lamont's head on a towel rack. …When Lamont was placed on probation in that court case, I was talking with his probation officer, who told me that I had adjusted and would continue to adjust much better to life than Lamont. The probation officer knew what kind of childhood we had."

I had a pretty good picture of Uncle George's personality, but I wanted to know more about Lamont.

"What do you remember most about Lamont as a child?" I asked.

"Well, before we ever went to The Children's Home, Lamont stole a locket of mine and gave it to one of his girlfriends. I've never forgotten that. …Lamont was cruel, and he was violent too. He would just walk by me and hit me for no reason. Lamont told me several times that he hated me. …When we went to The Children's Home to live – The Methodist Children's Home – we both received counseling. But Lamont always had a lot of anger inside him, and I don't think the counseling did him any good."

"So Lamont was mean to you too. I'm sorry," I said.

"He was just mean, in nature. And not just to me. It was his makeup and his, his character. He would butter up to you and then almost want to slash your throat, and you wouldn't know why. …And he was always such a liar." I thought that sounded pretty harsh coming from a sister.

"Was Richard like Lamont?" I asked.

"No. Richard did not go with us to live in The Children's Home. I didn't know him as well as I knew Lamont, but I don't think he was mean and cruel like Lamont. He was probably better off with Grandmother and Aunt Ruby. Lamont probably resented Richard because of that. Richard was taken better care of than we were."

"How did Lamont get along in The Children's Home?"

"Okay, I guess. But like I said, he always seemed to be angry on the inside. Once I heard about him taking a cat and slinging it by the tail against the barn wall until he killed it. When I first heard about that, I didn't want to believe it. But later, I heard other stories about him killing animals, so I guess it was true about the cat too."

"Do you recall a couple there whose names were Barbara and John, who worked at The Methodist Children's Home?" I asked her.

"Yes. They worked on the farm. As far as I know, they lived at The Children's Home with their kids. Lamont was closest to Barbara. They had an, uhm, an odd relationship. She was not much older than him, in any case too young to be a mother figure. But I don't know what really went on between them, if anything. Maybe it just *looked* odd."

Steve asked Margo, "So you both stayed at The Children's Home in Winston until high school graduation. When did you graduate from high school?"

"I graduated from high school in 1972; Lamont graduated in 1969. But we still stayed with George and Del some too, like on the weekends. Then George told Lamont he had to move out completely after he graduated… as in the very day he graduated. Sometimes Lamont would call me and ask me to call Del for him. He wanted to talk to her, but not to George. Lamont knew George did not want him around, so he didn't want to talk to him. So, he had me call, you know, in case George answered the phone."

Margo told us that in one of the last conversations she had with Lamont he said, "I never want to lay eyes on George again." I couldn't much blame him.

Margo told us that she had married in May 1973. Lamont came to her wedding, and Richard, being the oldest, gave her away. She had some contact with Lamont during 1976 and 1977, but did not hear from him again until 1987 or 1988 when their father Floyd Underwood died of bone cancer.

Then Margo suggested to us, "I really think you ought to interview Richard. He's the oldest, so he can tell you more about our parents and what it was like when we lived with them. ...The last time I heard, Richard was living on Peach Tree Street in Winston Salem. ...I'll do whatever I can to cooperate with you people, but I really don't want to ever have to testify in court against Lamont."

Steve and I located Richard Underwood shortly thereafter, but we did not get a chance to interview him until May of 1994, almost two months after we talked with Margo. But she had been right; Richard had a much more vivid recollection of their childhood years.

Richard Underwood agreed to meet with us and invited us to come by his place of work, a fire station in the Winston Salem area where he was a command level officer. Richard welcomed us into his office and was not hesitant to answer our questions, even after we informed him that we suspected his brother of murdering both Viktor Gunnarsson and Catherine Miller. I sensed that Richard was no more involved in Lamont's personal life at present than was Margo. I also sensed that Richard was not entirely surprised to learn about his brother's troubles.

"Do you remember living with your biological parents?" I asked him.

"Yeah, some." He seemed to be lost in thought for a moment.

"Would you mind to share with us the things that you do remember?" I asked.

"Well... I remember one Christmas Eve, for instance. Our mother and father were fighting. ...Of course, they were always fighting... Both of them were drinking, I guess. They were always drinking. And we – Margo, Lamont, and I – we were all upset because they were fighting with each other. I guess we were screaming and hollering too. So, our father took the three of us and shut us up in the barn. My father went back in the house, and we could still hear them shouting at each other. Margo covered her ears, but she could still hear them. That was probably the worst Christmas I ever remember. I just kept wondering why Santa Claus never came." I could feel my eyes misting, and I looked out the window of the fire station.

I thought about my own daughter, Katie, three years old now. The very thought of a parent – or any caregiver for that matter– depriving children of Christmas was simply beyond my comprehension. I did not want to dwell on it, though, and neither, apparently, did Steve, who redirected the interview.

"When did you last talk with your brother?"

"When our father died," Richard said, matter-of-factly.

"Margo told us that would have been in 1987 or 1988?"

"Our father died December 21, 1989. I knew Lamont was working at the Salisbury Police Department then. I called him there and left several messages before I finally reached him. I told him our father had cancer and was dying. Lamont told me in no uncertain terms, he said, 'I don't care if the son-of-a-b*tch dies. Don't call me anymore! So, I didn't. And he never came."

"When did you see Lamont last?"

"Probably twenty years ago. It was in 1973 or 1974, when I was a police officer in Winston Salem."

"Oh, so you *were* a police officer?" I asked.

"Yes. I was a police officer for the City of Winston Salem for ten years, but then I transferred to the fire service. I like it a lot better."

We discussed the pros and cons of each career, then Richard said, "I was working one night on patrol when I found Lamont drunk in a car on Miller Street. I took him home to his apartment on Augmon Drive, at his directions. That's the last time I ever saw him. ...Lamont always carried a grudge against me and against the world, for that matter."

Richard continued, "When he and Margo were in the Children's Home, I visited about every Sunday. But I don't think Lamont cared whether I came or not." Richard did believe, however, that he is the reason Lamont became interested in law enforcement.

"Lamont liked authority," Richard explained. He liked to exert authority. He was a mean person. He wanted to get on at Winston Salem PD. But I could not recommend him. Lamont was very possessive and liked to control people. ... By the way, I heard that Lamont got in trouble while he was working at the Sheriff's Office in Lincolnton for mistreating a prisoner. Do ya'll know if that's true?"

"It could be, but we aren't aware of any specific use of force complaints," Steve answered.

"Not that I'd be surprised," Richard continued.

"Do you know of any problems Lamont had with women?"

"Hmm... not specifically, but he had such a temper. Wait – I do recall that he got arrested over some girl when he shot into an occupied vehicle. He went to court and later got his record expunged. That was before he applied for a job as a cop."

Richard felt that although Lamont is his brother by blood, he only knew him as a young boy. When Richard read Lamont's wedding announcement in the newspaper, Richard noticed that Lamont named some people as his parents of whom Richard had never heard.

"I thought that was really weird," Richard commented. I agreed.

Richard told us he had not seen his mother Ethel Underwood for a long time, but he thought that she was living in California. From the time she left Richard when he was six, it was twenty-nine years until he saw her again. When Richard was thirty-five years old, his mother came back and visited him. She told him at that time that she would stay in touch, but thus far she had not even contacted him. Richard said Lamont and Margo never wanted to see their mother. I could not stop the wave of sympathy that came over me every time I thought about those children growing up without even one parent who loved them.

I commented to Richard that he seems to have made it through some tough times very well. He agreed without hesitation. He said he believes that he can make it through anything because of what he went through as a child. "I guess it either destroys you or makes you stronger," he said.

Before we left Richard that day, he had one final comment. "You know, Lamont seemed to have so much going for him. He was always the better-looking man too," he added, and smiled at me. No way, I thought. Lamont's eyes were cold and hard. Richard's eyes were rimmed with laugh lines and smile crinkles, embedded features that were sadly missing from the faces of both his brother and sister.

A few days after we talked with Richard, Steve and I located another relative of Lamont's in Winston Salem, an uncle by the name of Jim. Jim was married to Lois, whose sister Ruby was the Aunt Ruby who raised Richard Underwood. Jim and Lois were listed on the old visitor's log at The Children's Home. We had no trouble locating an address for Jim in Winston Salem.

"My wife passed away," Jim told us. "She and I both always felt sorry for Lamont and Margo. There was just no sense in them being in that orphanage when they had parents living."

Jim recalled one day when he and Lois visited The Children's Home, they saw Lamont walking by himself with his head hung down. Jim thought he looked so sad for a little boy. He looked at his wife and said, "I hope I live long enough to see your brother (George Underwood) regret this." Lois agreed. I refrained from telling him that George did not seem to regret the decision yet.

Jim said he and Lois visited Lamont and Margo often. They took them places regularly. Once while they were out, Lamont got sick. They were required to call The Children's Home, and they were told to bring back the children immediately. But when they did so, the staff put Lamont in a room by himself and would not allow Jim or Lois to check on him. "We should never have taken him back," Jim said. I wondered why Jim and Lois didn't try to adopt Margo and Lamont.

However, as with all the rest of the family, Lamont eventually disowned them as well.

"You know, Lamont would not even go see his own father when he was dying," Jim told us. "Lamont's father worked at Roadway. His wife ran around on him, and after a while he decided he would have himself a big time too. That's how they ended up losing their three children."

"How long has it been since you've heard from Lamont?" I asked.

"Oh, it's been years," he said. "I was surprised that Lamont never visited. Me and Lois tried to befriend him, but he would never let us get close to him."

"Did you stay in touch with Richard?"

"Not really. Richard was spoiled by his Aunt Ruby. He didn't need us."

"What do you know about George Underwood? He took care of Margo and Lamont for a while, didn't he?"

"George thought he could make some money by raising Lamont and Margo. But he never did treat them like his own children. His son always had the best of everything. …George was hotheaded, too, and mean to Lamont. He'd make Lamont wear a dress and suck a pacifier on the front porch in front of his friends. I didn't see it, but I heard about it. I heard about a lot of abuse that went on, but I never saw it myself. I know George was always getting on to them about something, though. ...Lamont always said that if George came to the town where he worked, he would put his butt in jail and figure out a charge later." I did not like to think about Lamont and me sharing the same profession.

"You knew George pretty well then?" Steve asked.

"Yes. But he doesn't have anything to do with me now that Lois is dead. ...Did you know that Lamont's father left $2,000 to Ruby to buy him a grave marker, and when he died, Ruby kept the money herself and did not even buy a grave marker?" Jim shook his head and went on. "Lamont's father once agreed to donate his body to a college – I think probably he did that once when he was drunk – and nobody knows where it went from there." Lot of places, I thought.

"What about Lamont's mother?" I asked.

"I haven't had any contact with Ethel. She married a man by the name of Jack Gentry – twice her age and a cousin to George. But Jack died. Jack was from Yadkinville, and they had kids of their own."

When we brought up the subject of the homicide investigation, Jim said that he had already heard about it. "But I haven't heard from Lamont since he got out of The Children's Home, so I don't know anything that would help you with that. I know when Lamont left that he still hated George. I don't hear from Margo either. I know she married some boy from The Children's Home, but they later divorced. I do hear from Richard occasionally. He's a captain or something with the fire service. Richard will lick his way up to any position he wants. He's married now for the third time I think, and he is the biggest liar in the world. As for Lamont, I just don't know. Murder is a serious thing. I can't say whether he'd be capable of killing someone or not. I guess anybody can, under the right circumstances. Lamont sure had a lot bottled up inside him. No doubt about that."

As hard as I tried, I could not understand how a mother could abandon her small children. I just had to ask her myself. After months of investigation, Steve and I finally succeeded in locating Lamont Underwood's biological mother, Ethel. She was living in Simi Valley, California, where she owned her own business, a business she inherited from her late husband. I called her as soon as we found a phone number. I half-expected her to hang up on me, but she didn't.

Ethel said, "I would like very much to tell my story of what happened all those years ago and why I had to give up my children. I bet if I wrote a book about it, it would be totally different from what you all may have heard from people in North Carolina. I hoped that her version would be an improvement over what we had been told thus far.

I summed up for her as tactfully as I could what the Underwood family members had told us about her and about the circumstances, wherein she gave up her children. It still sounded pretty rough, listening to myself telling the story.

"I'm not surprised at all by what they told you," she said, not sounding terribly hurt by their opinions of her. "But I have my own version of the story too. I could tell you things about Lamont's father and how he treated me that you would not even believe. And in those days, there was no talk about domestic violence – it was a secret thing. Women couldn't just walk out on their husbands, take their kids, and make it on their own. It just didn't happen. But I would like very much to come back to North Carolina. I always thought that someday I'd have the chance to come back and tell my side of the story…"

She would not go into detail, but she did not sound like the irresponsible harlot that the Underwoods made her out to be. Perhaps she had made mistakes in the past and now regretted them, but she had remarried and raised other children, remained in a healthy marriage until her husband passed away, and was successfully operating her own business on the west coast.

"I don't know if Lamont could be involved in the murder of those people or not," she commented. "But if he is, then he ought to be held responsible. That's the way I believe it should be."

I thanked her for talking with me and hung up.

Not long afterward, Steve Wilson and I traveled to The Children's Home Orphanage in Winston Salem, with a court order in hand to obtain copies of their records pertaining to Lamont and Margo Underwood. I left the orphanage with a heavy heart for the two children and their lack of a loving family.

After Margo and Lamont were placed in the orphanage, they continued to visit their Uncle George and Aunt Delzia's home once or twice a year, usually over Easter weekend at least. George did not seem to know a lot about what went on in the Children's Home, other than the fact that the staff there, in George's words, "ran a tight ship." George said he never heard of Lamont getting into any fights there. I asked George if he and Delzia had stayed in close touch with Margo and Lamont at The Children's Home, and he awkwardly answered, "Well, we visited some, but… well, not really." I could not help but picture my own daughter, who was just learning to read her favorite Christmas book, *The Baby in a Manger*, spending Christmas and holiday after holiday in an orphanage. I hurt for the little boy and girl that no one wanted.

Lamont and Margo resided in The Children's Home until they graduated from high school. Lamont was a resident at The Children's Home from June 1961 until June 1969. While Lamont seemed to have a hard time making friends, he did take a liking to John and his wife Barbara. In fact, Lamont referred to them as "Mom" and "Pop," in spite of the fact that Barbara was only eight years his senior. Lamont spent quite a bit of time with John and Barbara and their family when they worked on the orphanage-operated farm. It was during that time that Lamont allegedly began to take his frustrations and anger out on the barnyard animals – cats, dogs, chickens, and so on. We were told by several individuals that Lamont was an especially cruel boy.

I thought of the MacDonald Triad, a phenomenon I had been taught years earlier, in which three childhood components being present in the same young person was indicative of a sociopathic or psychopathic personality, as in serial murderers. The three components were setting fires, cruelty to animals, and bedwetting. No one recalled specifically whether or not Lamont had a history of bedwetting, but I wondered.

In 1970, John and Barbara left The Children's Home. Lamont remained in contact with them, but when they divorced in 1980, Lamont gradually decreased contact with John. Shortly after Lamont moved to Salisbury, John stopped by for a visit. John parked his truck in Lamont's driveway, and found Lamont washing his patrol car. Lamont took him inside the house and gave him a brief tour. Lamont's house was immaculate. They walked back outside, and Lamont looked at John's truck. He told him, "Pop, you're going to have to move your truck; it's leaking oil on my driveway." John, offended, told him, "Well, if you feel like that, Lamont, I'll just go on." John left and did not initiate further contact with Lamont. The last time John saw Lamont was on Father's Day 1991, when Lamont gave him a pair of shoes as a gift.

Lamont did, however, stay in regular contact with Barbara. Barbara told us that she has always loved Lamont "as a son," and that she and her husband John would have adopted him years ago if they had been able to locate both of his parents to obtain legal consent. Barbara left Winston Salem in 1981 and moved to Ohio, where she met Burl Childress, whom she married in 1986. Burl Childress had four sons by a previous marriage, and although Lamont rarely communicated with them, he occasionally referred to them as his "brothers" when he talked to friends he made later in life.

After high school graduation, Lamont was no longer allowed to live at The Children's Home. He and Margo moved in together for a short while with George and Delzia, but hardly no time passed until George forced Lamont to leave again. In a subsequent conversation with George, he related to us the following vignette:

One summer in the early 1970s, Lamont began dating a particular girl. One evening, two guys came over to George's house to "whip up on Lamont for something Lamont had done regarding this girl. Lamont retaliated by shooting at them in their vehicle with a .22 rifle. George never got the whole story from him, but Lamont was charged and convicted, and sentenced to probation. Lamont only told George that the thing that got him into trouble, according to the judge, was that Lamont had shot once at a vehicle and then ran to another vehicle and shot again, and these facts indicated the second shot was not made in self-defense. George recalled that Lamont later got the conviction removed through an order of expungement from his criminal record. No one could recall any other incidents where Lamont got in trouble with the law except for several speeding violations.

When Lamont graduated from high school, he began working at R. J. Reynolds Tobacco Company in Winston Salem, where he worked from December 22, 1969, until April of 1976. Lamont enlisted in the National Guard on May 17, 1970, ultimately reaching the highest rank of Specialist 4 with an honorable discharge on May 17, 1976.

As tragic as his childhood was, Lamont Underwood was not without ambition. While he did not find military life to his liking, he held onto his dream of becoming a law enforcement officer. As soon as he reached the minimum age limit, he set out to reach that goal, all the while longing for a family he was not equipped to have.

CHAPTER FOUR

"Husbands, love your wives, and be not bitter against them" (Colossians 3:18)

The number one family vacation spot in the Carolinas is Myrtle Beach. The hub of the Grand Strand, Myrtle Beach, is both a city and a vacation destination on South Carolina's Atlantic coast. Never having experienced a real family vacation, with friends, or a vacation of any kind for that matter, Myrtle Beach held great appeal to Lamont. He could not wait to see what all the hype was about. In his late teens, Lamont finally got the opportunity to go with a group of other teenagers.

It was the summer of 1973 when Lamont finally found himself on vacation at Myrtle Beach, and it was there that he met a pretty young woman who had recently separated from her husband. Her name was Karen. Lamont was still living in Winston Salem, and she was living in Charlotte.

Lamont and Karen began to date. Lamont would drive to Charlotte to see Karen on the weekends. In retrospect, Karen believes that she was dating Lamont on the rebound, and that he was in an emotionally vulnerable position as well.

Steve and I had some trouble locating Karen. When we finally did, she was more than a little reluctant to talk to us. When we showed up on her doorstep one summer evening and introduced ourselves, she stepped out on the porch and quickly shut the door behind her. She stood defensively with her arms crossed, and kept glancing over her shoulder at the door. She had a new family, and they were obviously present inside the house. She had long since made a new life for herself, and was quick to inform us that her husband and children had no idea that she was once married to Lamont Underwood, and she was adamant that they not find out, not under any circumstances.

"Ma'am, we aren't going to disclose anything to your husband or your children. We are just here to get some background information on Lamont's life during the time you knew him. You are just one of many people that we are talking to, and we are simply trying to be as thorough as possible."

Karen admitted that she married Lamont Underwood on July 29, 1973, after only dating him for three months. Basically, the marriage was a flop. Communication between the two of them was minimal. The marriage ultimately deteriorated to nothing, and she filed for an annulment, which was granted the following March, 1974. The annulment was really a simple matter since Karen had mistakenly assumed that her lawyer had completed the divorce proceedings between her and her first husband. Because she was still legally married to Fredrick, she was not legally married to Lamont anyway.

During their brief marriage, Karen and Lamont lived with Karen's mother in Charlotte. Lamont continued to work in Winston Salem at R. J. Reynolds as a materials handler. He commuted from Charlotte to work and back every workday. When Fredrick came to visit a few weeks after Karen and Lamont were married, he informed Karen that the two of them were still legally married. Lamont moved out and Karen never heard from Lamont again.

"How did Lamont treat you while you were married?" I asked Karen. "Was he jealous at all? Possessive?"

"He, uh, uhm, no."

"Pardon?" Steve asked.

"Well ...we weren't married very long," she answered vaguely.

"...and?" I prompted.

"Well, I suspected, I mean I thought he might be gay," she said, uncomfortably.

"What made you think that?" I asked.

"We couldn't, uh... well it was just a, a gut feeling I had. ...I'm sorry, but I really need to get back inside the house. They will come looking for me any minute."

"All right," I told her. "But if there is anything else you can share with us, please contact me," and I gave her my business card.

"There's nothing else to tell," she said. "Please don't get me involved in this. Lamont was a part of my life that is over now, and I want to keep it that way." Karen walked back inside her house, and Steve and I left, more concerned with what Karen had not told us rather than what she had.

After his first failed marriage, Lamont moved to back to Winston Salem. He met and began dating a popular coed named Brenda, who was attending Elon College. Again, Lamont proposed after a short dating period, and he and Brenda were married on August 17, 1974, in Winston Salem. From all accounts, Lamont's second marriage was no better than his first.

Steve and I had an even more difficult time locating Brenda than we had locating Karen. After we finally persuaded her family to tell us how we could reach her, they gave us her phone number only under the condition that we call and interview her by phone instead of visiting her in person. As much as I wanted to meet her and as easy as it would have been to use her phone number to obtain her address, I would not break my word. I dialed the number and identified myself to Brenda. She had been expecting my call but was not particularly eager to be involved in the investigation.

"Ma'am, are you in contact with Lamont Underwood anymore?" I asked her.

"No. I'm not," she answered.

"Is it true that the two of you were married?" I asked her.

"Yes, it's true. I was eighteen when I met Lamont. He was twenty-two. That would have been in 1973. I was living in Winston Salem then. We got engaged when I was in college. We had planned to get married at the orphanage where he grew up, The Children's Home, but at the last minute, Lamont changed his mind."

"Do you know why he changed his mind?" I asked.

"No... I really don't. But we did get married at my parents' house."

"Where did the two of you live?"

"Lamont encouraged me to continue my education. So, through the week I lived on campus and Lamont lived with my parents. But that didn't work out. So, Lamont moved out and lived alone during the week. On the weekends I came home to be with him."

"How long did your marriage last?"

"Only eight months. The distance between us caused the relationship to deteriorate. I was too young and immature, and we made a mistake by getting married while I was still in college. After a while, I quit coming home from college on the weekends. I preferred to spend time with my friends rather than with Lamont. ...Lamont and I had a mutual agreement. I waited for him to get a lawyer and divorce me, but he never did. Finally, after about a year and Lamont had never contacted me, I got a divorce from him in Graham, North Carolina."

"You never heard from him while you were separated?"

"Not once."

"What was your marriage like when you were together? How did Lamont treat you?"

"Oh, he treated me well. But... all he ever *really* wanted was to be a cop."

"Did you find anything particularly unusual about Lamont after you married him?"

"Well, one thing I found strange was that he alienated himself from his family."

"How so?"

"I tried to encourage him to visit with them or just call them. But he didn't want anything to do with any of them. But after we split up, Lamont quit working at R. J. Reynolds and moved away from Winston Salem. I know before he moved, he worked some as a reserve police officer in North Wilkesboro, you know up in Wilkes County? Then he moved up there. ...But that's all I really know about him."

I was looking over the brief notes I had taken when she asked, "I won't have to testify in court against him, will I?" and she genuinely sounded scared.

"No reason that I know of at this point," I answered. I tried to assure her without making any promises.

"You really don't have any knowledge about anything having to do with the murders, so I wouldn't worry about it unless you hear from me again."

"Well, no offense, but I hope I don't."

"I understand," I told her. Even on the phone I sensed that she was not giving me the whole story.

A few days later, Steve and I located two of Brenda's friends, a husband and wife couple who knew Lamont when he and Brenda were married. The four of them often went out for dinner together. They shed a bit more light on the relationship between Lamont and Brenda.

"Lamont was quick-tempered and often lashed out at Brenda. My wife and I saw him hit and slap Brenda a couple of times. Lamont was extremely jealous over Brenda. ...He was mean. And he had a chip on his shoulder."

"You actually saw him strike Brenda?" I asked the husband.

"Absolutely. Both of us saw it," he said. "I didn't know what to do. Domestic violence was not the hot issue it is today. We talked about it and figured it was their business, and that Brenda ought to have enough sense to leave him, which she finally did."

"Why would Brenda tell me he treated her well?" I asked.

The wife responded, "She's embarrassed probably. But I doubt that she wants to dredge any of that back up after all this time." I thanked both of them for their candor, wondering if Lamont had been abusive to Karen as well.

As we returned to my office, I shared my gut feeling with Steve, that somewhere there was a record of Underwood abusing someone.

"I (cough) know a place we can start looking," he said, and coughed again.

Steve and I had completed a number of interviews into Lamont's personal life, so we began to examine his employment history. Lamont began his law enforcement career, as his second wife Brenda had recalled, working as a reserve officer with the North Wilkesboro Police Department. He took the oath of office on December 1, 1975. North Wilkesboro is a town located about half an hour's drive southeast of Boone, located in Wilkes County, which borders Watauga County. The county line separating the two counties on Highway 421 is only three miles from the location where Gunnarsson's murdered body was discovered.

Lamont Underwood worked for the North Wilkesboro Police Department mainly on the weekends, while he was still working full-time at R. J. Reynolds in Winston Salem. Prior to his acceptance as a reserve officer, Lamont disclosed to Chief Kyle Gentry that he had been charged with assault in the past. After checking both the Winston Salem Police Department and the Forsyth County Clerk of Court's Office, we could not find a record of an assault arrest against Underwood.

Underwood worked as a reserve officer until he was hired as a full-time police officer with the Newton Police

Department in Catawba County, North Carolina. He worked at Newton from March 4 through August 14, 1976. After the excitement of full-time police work wore off, Lamont reportedly suffered from bouts of depression. He was reported to have some issues relating to his failed marriages and occasionally entertained thoughts of suicide.

About that same time, Lamont met Jeannie, a tall, slim young lady with a pretty face. Jeannie was attending the nearby Kings College. She lived alone in an apartment in the city of Newton. She and Lamont dated for two months. They went out on the weekends, and according to Jeannie, Lamont was a gentleman at first.

"He was really polite. And super neat," she described.

Yet Jeannie got the feeling that Lamont harbored some deep-seated anger for reasons unknown to her. Lamont told her that he was an orphan and had grown up "in a boys' home," but he did not provide any other details about his background to Jeannie.

Shortly after they started dating exclusively, Lamont began to accuse Jeannie unjustly of seeing other men. He was quite jealous, she recalled, and his jealousy worsened toward the end of their relationship. Jeannie began to see what she described as "the other side of Lamont."

Certain incidents really disturbed Jeannie. The first of such incidents occurred when she realized that Lamont had a key to her apartment. She had never given him a key. But she came home one day to find him asleep on her couch.

On another occasion, Jeannie had visited an older lady she knew and did not get back to her apartment until 10:00 p.m. She found Lamont waiting for her in the parking lot of her apartment building. He jumped out of his car and started accusing her of seeing another man. Lamont ranted and raved until she was finally able to explain where she had been.

Jeannie realized that their relationship was not normal, and she needed to end it. When she said as much to Lamont, he threated to kill himself.

"I'll just shoot myself," he told her.

Despite Jeannie's protests, Lamont got into her car, drove a few blocks away, and then Jeannie heard the unmistakable sound of a gunshot. She ran down the street, heart pounding, trying to locate him, but could not find him in the area where she heard the gunshot. She returned to her apartment sick with worry but not knowing what else to do. A couple of hours later, Lamont showed up with her car. He apologized for scaring her, but never explained about the gunshot or where he had gone. She was relieved to see him but angry with him for pulling such an awful trick.

On another occasion, Lamont broke into her apartment one night when she was home alone. He had knocked on the door, and when she answered it, she saw that Lamont had torn the screen door open. He rushed in, irrationally angry and threatening to kill her, all the while waving around a revolver. They scuffled, and she was finally able to get the gun away from him. She realized again that she was going to have to do something to end their relationship for good, but Lamont was very persuasive in seeking her forgiveness and was very manipulative.

One weekend, Jeannie and Lamont took an overnight trip to Winston Salem. They went to a popular nightclub, Mother Fletcher's, and later returned to their motel room. An argument ensued between them, and Jeannie attempted to leave the motel room. Before she could reach the door, however, Lamont grabbed her, and she struggled to get free, causing her to fall. Someone heard them fighting and called the police. Jeannie does not believe that a report was made, but the officers responded to see if everything was all right and left shortly thereafter. The officer had not even asked their names.

A few days later, however, Lamont brought a copy of a police report to Jeannie and told her that he had gotten the report from his brother who was a Winston Salem Police officer. The report reflected that Jeannie was intoxicated and responsible for the altercation between Lamont and her that night in the motel. The incident report stated that Jeannie was "drunk and disorderly." Jeannie said that she had only drank a couple of beers that evening and could not possibly have been intoxicated.

Fortunately for us, Jeannie had kept the copy of that police report. I recognized the form as an official police incident report form. However, several fields on the form had been marked incorrectly, and not all required fields were filled in. The narrative portion of the report read as follows:

> At approximately 1:30 a.m. on the first day of August 1976, I received a call to go by the Holiday Inn on Silas Creek Parkway in response to an Assault on a Female... Both parties had been drinking heavily and was very intoxicated. The parties had checked in as man and wife on Friday, July 30, 1976. ...I then took Mrs. Henson to the front where she was given another room. At one point Mrs. Henson and I were walking up the sidewalk and almost fell to the ground. She had a very strong odor of some type of intoxicating beverage on her breath."

Jeannie told us that Lamont threatened to use the police report to embarrass her. She had no idea that Lamont had created the fictitious report himself.

At that point, according to Jeannie, she, her brother, her sister, and brother-in-law went to see Newton Police Chief Mike Harrell about Lamont. At the Chief's request, Jeannie provided him with a copy of the police report Lamont had brought her. Chief Harrell told Jeannie, "The form the report was written on came from our forms here at the Newton

Police Department. Lamont has falsified these records." The Chief was justifiably upset with Lamont Underwood.

"I also gave Chief Harrell copies of some letters Lamont wrote to me," Jeannie added.

"Letters? Do you still have copies of them by chance?" I asked, hopeful.

"I do."

> *Dear Jeannie,*
>
> *Please believe me when I tell you that I will never hurt you in any way. No threats can ever hold you and I know that. And I'll control my temper. I promise. Just please give me another chance to prove to you I mean what I've said in my last couple of letters. Darling, I will get out of this job if it bothers you and get a job that will make you happy. Jeannie, you are the best thing that has ever happened to me. I don't want to ruin that again if you will please give me another chance. Please Honey, take me back. I promise I will love you like I should have done all along. I'll respect you and try very hard to do what you want. Just please take me back so I can prove that to you. I wanted to take you in my arms tonight when I saw you so bad I didn't know what to do. Honey please take me back. No more threats, fussing and fighting with you. I swear to God. I'll never even raise my voice. I don't want to hurt you. I only want to love you. Darling, I miss and love you so much. I can't stand this being without you. Please let me come back into your life. Call me tomorrow please. Please. You are more important to me than anything. I miss you, Jeannie. Please call or write or something. Let me know you still care. I want to come back to you.*

Lamont

His tone and his attitude varied greatly, as I saw in the next letter he gave Jeannie, written after she refused to trust him again.

Jeannie,

The damage has already been done. I have sent copies of that report to your Personnel Dept., your mother and sister. You could have prevented all of this by coming back to me. But now you are going to hurt like I've been hurt, you d*mn b*tch. I'll run you out of this d*mn town if it is the last thing I do. I have nothing to lose any more. You have hurt me more than anyone in my whole life has. So now it's your turn to suffer. Every time I see you I'll start talking loud enough to where everyone can hear what kind of person you are. You will not be able to hold your head up in this town. I'll ruin you, Jeannie, if it is the last thing I do. If it takes me the rest of my life to get you out of this town I'll do it. You can bet your *ss on it. I got hurt so why shouldn't you. The letter will be mailed if you call me or not. You could have bought them from me, but no. You were too proud! So let's see you hold your head up now. Everyone is going to know what you have done to me and with me.

Lamont

"Jeannie, what did Chief Harrell do about Lamont?" I asked her.

"I don't know," she replied. "He just said he'd take care of it."

Jeannie did not hear from Lamont for a few days. But then he called her from a friend's house in Winston Salem and asked again if they could try to work things out. Jeannie refused and never heard from Lamont directly again.

Lamont Underwood resigned from the Newton Police Department on August 14, 1976. On the mandatory separation form that was submitted to the North Carolina Department of Justice Training Standards Division, Chief Harrell indicated that he could not recommend Lamont for employment elsewhere as a criminal justice officer. Further, Chief Harrell added a recommendation that the state officials review Lamont's law enforcement certification. Unfortunately, Lamont's background was not reviewed thoroughly enough to prevent his being hired at other law enforcement agencies.

Some months later, Jeannie received a call from a woman by the name of Patty Lewis. Patty explained that she had been dating Lamont, and asked Jeannie if she had had any problems with Lamont when he and Jeannie dated.

"I did have problems with him, and you better stay away from him. He's dangerous," Jeannie told Patty.

Patty told Jeannie, "Well, Lamont actually has a list of everyone who has done him wrong, and your name is on it. I just thought you ought to know."

"I'm not surprised," Jeannie told Patty, and she wasn't. But her stomach tightened with the anxiety caused by the mention of Lamont's name.

"He's a cop here," Patty told her.

"Where?" Jeannie asked.

"He's working for the Lincoln County Sheriff."

"I can't believe another law enforcement agency would hire him. He got in trouble at Newton PD."

"Well he is… And now he's a detective."

Lamont began working for the Lincoln County Sheriff's Office in Lincolnton, North Carolina, in 1976, just after he resigned from Newton PD and was honorably discharged from the Army National Guard. Lincolnton is a small town located near Newton and about an hour-and-a-half drive from Watauga County. Lamont started as a jailer. Within months, however, he was transferred to the Patrol Division and was sworn in as a deputy sheriff. In October of 1978, Lamont was promoted to a supervisor's role as sergeant. On April 2, 1979, the extremely neat and smooth-talking young man was promoted to detective. A perfect storm was brewing.

Lamont was hired by the elected sheriff of Lincoln County at the time, Harvin Crouse. Sheriff Crouse was an old-school Andy Taylor–type sheriff who basically made his own rules. Elected sheriffs in North Carolina are politically powerful and autonomous. They hire and fire at will.

When Steve and I interviewed the seventy-two-year-old retired sheriff on the front porch of his brick ranch home one warm sunny morning, Harvin Crouse had long since retired. We drank lemonade as we listened to the white-haired sheriff recall "the good old days."

Twenty years had passed, but Sheriff Crouse remembered Lamont Underwood well.

"Oh yes," Sheriff Crouse recounted, "I put that boy on as a jailer, a job he did not particularly care for. You see he thought he should start right out in the Patrol Division. But I made everybody start out in the jail, and I thought it would be good experience for him too."

Sheriff Crouse further explained that Lamont did not work as a jailer for very long, though, and it was not long until he had an opening on Patrol into which he transferred Lamont.

"Eventually he was promoted to the Detective Division," he told us.

"Do you recall any disciplinary action you may have taken against Lamont?" I asked.

"Let's see… There was this one incident when some girl accused him of writing something ugly about her on the sidewalk, or maybe it was the wall of a church…"

Sheriff Crouse recalled that he confronted Lamont about the incident, but does not recall now Lamont's response or whether Lamont admitted or denied the allegation.

"I warned him to stay away from that girl."

"Was this incident documented? Did you make any notes about it?" I asked.

"Oh no, nah, I didn't – there's nothing on paper, I'm sure. I just counseled Lamont about it, and that's the last I heard of it." I didn't say anything for a moment, and he continued.

"I never wrote anything down when there were complaints against my employees unless there was a good reason." Malicious damage to property is a crime, I thought. He was tormenting a young woman. I wondered what Sheriff Crouse considered to be a good enough reason to document Lamont's behavior if this situation did not constitute it.

Although I tried not to show a reaction, Steve made eye contact with me, and I gave him a subtle look of disgust.

"I preferred to confront the employee and deal with it in person," Sheriff Crouse commented.

"Sheriff, do you recall any other details about the vandalism incident?" Steve asked him.

"Not really," he responded. "Best I can recall there was just something spray-painted on the sidewalk in her neighborhood. I don't even recall what it said, to be honest with you. Something derogatory. But the girl was convinced that Lamont had done it."

"Do you recall other complaints against Lamont while he worked for you?" Steve prompted.

"Not that I can recall. I did tease him quite a bit, though, about all the speeding tickets he wrote. Too many speeding tickets ain't good for an elected sheriff, you know. They don't buy votes, he said, grinning. "I had a fond spot for that boy, because of his background, his being raised in a 'home' and all. He even called me *Pop.*"

"Have you seen him or talked with him since he left Lincoln County?" Steve asked.

"Oh, he did come to visit me on occasion. But after he hurt his back, he didn't visit as often. Even his personality seemed different after that. He just wasn't himself. He was... uptight. And he didn't cut up and have fun like he used to."

"Sheriff, do you remember what kind of weapons your officers carried back then?"

"Why, they could carry whatever kind of gun they wanted. In those days, the Sheriff's Department did not provide their officers with weapons. They carried whatever they had."

"Mr. Crouse there is a record in Lamont's personnel file that shows that he received a weapon in a court case once while he worked for you."

"Yeah? Well that was fairly common. A judge would sometimes award a gun in a case to the investigating officer. All the Sheriff's Department ever did was document the transfer to the officer. Let's see... When Lamont was a detective, I believe he carried a short barrel revolver. Most all of them did."

"What else do you recall about Lamont?"

"Well, that boy was very neat. I know he'd even clean out an ashtray the minute somebody put their cigarette out. Everybody used to kid him about being so particular about his car and the way he dressed. And he'd take the kidding in a good manner. I kidded him a lot myself. And he never had any dust or dirt in the trailer where he lived. He was probably the neatest officer I ever had." He chuckled.

"Was his work meticulous as well?" I asked.

"Well, as a detective he was very conscientious. His cases were well worked and well documented. Lamont was quite adept at crime scene sketches, almost like he was an artist. He was very dedicated, you see."

"I could see that," I said. "Do you recall any specific homicide cases that Lamont investigated?"

"No, not specifically. But he probably worked a few."

"Sheriff Crouse, would you be surprised to learn that Lamont had committed murder?"

"Yeah I would. ...But, if he did, he ought to be held responsible like everybody else."

We thanked him for his time and left him sitting on the front porch with the remainder of the lemonade.

We had already learned a great deal more about Lamont's life while he worked at Lincoln County Sheriff's Department than Harvin Crouse was able to recall. But the lack of documentation was frustrating, forcing us to rely on the recollections of those we interviewed.

The next person to be interviewed was James "Jim" Ingle, who supervised Lamont Underwood when he worked at the Lincoln County Sheriff's Office. Jim had retired in 1988 and was operating his own business when we approached him.

"I remember Lamont well. He was a good officer. He knew at least as much as the other patrol officers, or at least I thought so," he shared. "But he sure was hot-headed. But hell, so am I." Jim described Lamont as being argumentative to his commanding officers and resentful of their authority when they told him what to do.

"Did he make a good detective?" I asked.

"He was average, I guess. Nothing special. He did write good reports and expressed himself well."

"Did you supervise him closely?"

"I usually got the cases each morning, and I would assign them to individual detectives. Then I'd review the cases they worked every week or two. But I generally knew what they were doing on a daily basis. It wasn't that big of an office." I was familiar.

"Did Lamont work alone most of the time? Or did he partner up with other investigators?"

Jim was thoughtful for a moment. Then he said, "I think he and K. B. Crouse were pretty tight. K.B. might remember some more about Lamont than I do. But I knew he had girlfriend problems."

"What do you remember about them?" I asked.

"He gave this one girl Patty Lewis a real hard time. Patty is a good friend of mine, and I've known her father for years. Lamont had dated her for some time. He even had a trailer parked near her place at Iron Station. But Lamont stalked Patty, followed her every d*mn where. Back then, of course, there was no law against stalking. Lamont threatened her in some way, and Patty came in and talked to me three or four times, complaining about Lamont. I finally confronted him about her, but I don't remember exactly what he said. I know he didn't think it was none of my business, though. I casually told him to back off. Since it was not a work-related problem, I didn't take any disciplinary action against him. But I did talk about him to Sheriff Crouse and to Barbara Pickens who was the Chief Deputy at the time. The whole thing was resolved about a month later, but I don't know how. I never heard anything more about him, and Patty never mentioned it to me again."

"Did you make any notes at all about those events?"

"No, I don't think so."

"Do you recall any other incidents in particular involving Lamont and any other women?"

"Not that I can recall… But now that I think about it, though, Lamont did get some psychological treatment when he had those problems with Pat. I think he went to the County Mental Health Department, but I'm not real sure. I always thought it was odd that he was so neat. He dressed neat, and he kept his home, his desk, and his car all very neat."

"Did you visit Lamont in his home?"

"Yeah, some. He lived alone. And his place was always as neat at could be."

"Do you know what kind of gun Lamont carried as a Detective?" I asked.

"Yeah I do. It was a Colt Detective Special as I recall."

"Do you know if he turned that gun in when he left the Sheriff's Office?"

"I don't know for sure, but that was the loosest d*mn department about personal equipment getting turned back in. I wouldn't be surprised at all if he still had that Colt."

"Did you stay in contact with Lamont when he left the Sheriff's Office?" I probed.

"The last I heard was that he left the Sheriff's Department to go to Salisbury PD. Lamont said he met some girl in Salisbury who worked at a hospital. They got married, and that's why he moved, I reckon. ...Love will make you do any d*mn thing," he added.

"Including killing somebody?" I asked.

"Even that, I guess," Jim responded.

I wanted to find K. B. Crouse next. He was still working in law enforcement when we located him. He was working at the Catawba County Sheriff's Office. Catawba County borders Lincoln County to the north. K. B. remembered Underwood well.

"We worked together," he told me. "I transferred first from the road into Investigations, and Lamont came a little later.

"Did you investigate cases together?" I asked.

"Usually we'd be in the office together doing paperwork or what have you, but then we'd go out in the afternoons and do our separate things – you know, interviews and so forth."

"What about after hours? Were the two of you friends?" I asked.

"Yeah. We'd go to the Viking Lounge at the Ramada with a bunch of people on Friday or Saturday nights. Lamont liked to drink, and he liked to dance. Disco was his big thing then."

We all chuckled.

"Oh, you should have seen him then... He had this white jumpsuit. I guess he thought he was John Travolta or something." Now that was a mental image.

"How close of friends were you?"

"Well, we got along fine. But I knew he had problems. With the women, I mean. There was one time I got onto him about it. He was going out with Patty Lewis. She worked for D.S.S. at Lincoln County, and the two of them dated for a while. Then she started dating some other guy named Jeff, and Lamont and Jeff got into it. Lamont wrote letters to Jeff's supervisors at work and did everything he could against Jeff, to cause him problems. He accused him of smoking pot and all kinds of things that weren't true. And he wouldn't leave Patty alone. He called her and followed her, and they argued. But it was getting out of hand. So, I figured I'd better talk to Lamont about it before he got into trouble. I called both Lamont and Patty into the office one day, and I told them to straighten up. Patty told me Lamont had slapped her, and he didn't deny it. Then I talked to Patty by herself, and she said Lamont was threatening her in person and over the phone, and that he would not leave her alone. So, I went back and talked to Lamont by himself, and he kind of acknowledged that all she said was true. But I could tell my lecture to Lamont was going in one ear and out the other. He was steaming mad that I was butting in on their business. I wouldn't let them walk out of the office together. I made him wait until Patty was gone. I think that was the last I heard about the two of them."

"What about other women he dated?" I asked.

"There was another woman who lived on the west end of the county. Lamont dated her until she tried to break it off. He spray-painted graffiti in red on the outside wall of the church she attended."

"Do you remember her name?"

"Hmm, no I don't. It's been too long now."

"Do you remember what the graffiti said?"

"I think he called her by her name and said she was a wh*re. It was written in red spray paint, and she reported it. I was sent to photograph it and investigate. ...You know, as soon as I looked at that wall, I knew it was Lamont's handwriting! Even in paint I could tell. He made a *Y* in Patty just like he makes all his *Y*'s."

"Did you confront Lamont about that?" I asked.

"Yeah, I did. Right after I found a can of red spray paint in the trunk of his patrol car."

"You're kidding."

"No, I'm not. He denied doing it, and I told him I could get a sample from the church wall and compare it to the paint he had. He told me there was no way I could do that, and I told him yes, I could. He backed off then, and I told him to leave her alone. As far as I know, he did."

"Did Lamont ever talk to you about his past marriages?"

"He talked about his first wife. He said it was all her fault though. Everything that went wrong in Lamont's life was always somebody else's fault."

"I see."

"You want to know the weirdest thing about Lamont?"

"What's that?" I asked.

"He was the neatest guy I've ever met in my entire life. He kept his car, his house, his desk, everything just immaculate. On his days off, he spent his time washing his car. I thought I was neat, but I can't hold a candle to Lamont Underwood."

Officer Crouse did not have much more to add than what I had already learned. But a few others did.

I called a friend of mine, Terry Burgin, Police Chief for the City of Lincolnton. I had heard that Terry had been a detective at the Lincoln County Sheriff's Office at the same time Lamont was employed there.

"We did work in investigations together," Terry told me.

"What do you remember about him?" I asked Terry.

"I always thought he was too aggressive. I thought he used too much force on duty."

"Why do you say that?"

"Well, one night when I was off duty, I drove to a 7-Eleven in Lincolnton to get something to drink. The 7-Eleven was closed, but as I drove around it, I saw someone holding up a cement block like they were getting ready to throw it through the window. I called for backup on my radio, and when I drove back around, I saw that the glass in the door of the 7-Eleven was broken. I saw the guy inside the 7-Eleven trying to hide in the aisles of the store. I got into a scuffle with him, and we were sliding around on the safety glass, which was broken and all over the floor. The guy got away from me and headed toward the front door. I ran out the front door and shot up in the air a couple of times to let my backup officers know that we were up front. But the guy had run out the back door. He laid down on the ground because he thought I was shooting at him. The officers thought I killed the guy. One officer was on top of the suspect, who was still struggling some. I grabbed the bad guy's arm to cuff him when he raised his head up for some reason. Then out of the corner of my right eye, I saw a sweeping motion and then a hit..."

"What happened?" I prompted.

"Underwood had swung the butt of his shotgun like a golf club and hit the guy in the head as hard as he could. We had to take him to the hospital before we took him to jail. I thought Underwood had killed him. I told him that was unnecessary force. Underwood didn't like what I said about it. But that was just wrong, and I don't stand for such abuse, and I know you don't either."

"That's right. ...Was that the only time you saw him lose his temper?"

"That I saw personally, yeah. But one of my officers told me about Underwood threatening some girl in Catawba County that he had been dating. Underwood threatened her and her family too."

"Do you remember her name?"

"No, I just remember all the talk about him and her. I did know another girl he dated though, where there was some violence going on."

"Who was that?"

"Monica. She used to work for the finance department in the City of Lincolnton. But there were always rumors floating around about domestic violence in Underwood's personal relationships."

"How well did you know him personally?"

"Well, I know he is different. He loves himself. He was always sharp dressed, very neat, and very preppy. He was a ladies' man, but when he got turned down, he couldn't take the rejection. ...He loved to drink alcohol. He smoked too. I don't know if he ever used drugs, but I wouldn't be surprised. I also wouldn't be surprised if he killed someone. But that's about all I know about him."

It was time to talk to Lamont's ex-girlfriends.

Patty Lewis told me that she met Lamont Underwood in 1976, when he was working as a jailer and she was a social worker in Lincoln County. She was at the jail on business, and Lamont introduced himself in an unusual way.

"Do you know that n*gger on that TV show *Sanford and Son* ...the son Lamont? Well that's my name. Lamont." Patty admitted that she laughed, and the two of them ended up talking for three hours that evening.

"He was very charming," she explained.

"Sounds like it," I said, sarcastically.

"No, he really was. He had this tough-guy cop image, but he also seemed like he had his crap together. He was funny. And he was pretty good looking too," she added.

Patty said that Lamont was a total gentleman at first. The problems began to surface when Patty headed out on her annual beach trip with her girlfriends. It was Easter week of 1976. Lamont pouted about her beach trip before she left, but shortly after she got to the beach, he called her.

"That's it!" Lamont told her. "You've abandoned me. You're not coming back!" I thought about Lamont and Margo as children, so afraid of being abandoned.

"That's ridiculous, Lamont," she told him. "I'll be back in a few days."

When Patty returned, things were not the same between her and Lamont. He seemed to resent everything positive in Patty's life. The same things that appealed to him when they began dating suddenly seemed to infuriate him: her looks, her job, her income, her education, her strong family support. Lamont liked Patty's stability but liked to have his fun also.

"He liked to go to bars, but he wouldn't allow me to go to bars. His idea of a date was to come to my apartment for me to cook supper for him while he watched TV. And he'd see these women on TV and then ask me why I didn't look like Jacqueline Smith or some other model or something."

I was taking detailed notes and avoided eye contact with her. I was afraid my expression would give away my thoughts.

"He complained about my clothes. They were either too sexy or not sexy enough. There was no pleasing him… Oh and his gifts! They were also an insult. He was so cheap."

"For instance…?"

"For Christmas he kept on until I bought him this gun he wanted. It was $150. You know what he got me? A blender! A $19.95 blender!" Next to a good case of food poisoning, a cheap boyfriend is my second favorite thing.

"I can't tell you how many cigarettes I bought him."

Patty said it did not take her long to discover Lamont's temper.

"Little things would set him off. One evening he got super mad at me because I didn't have any cigarettes in my apartment for him to smoke."

"Did you smoke?" I asked.

"No, I've never smoked," she said.

"I don't understand."

"That bum expected me to buy cigarettes to have for him just in case he ran out," she explained. "And matches too."

Give a man a match, and he will stay warm for a day, I thought. *Set a man on fire and he'll stay warm for the rest of his life.*

"When Lamont got angry," she continued, "he would curse and start shaking. He would throw things. I mean he was just out of control. He didn't like me talking on the phone with anyone but him. Once when we were watching TV, I got a call from a client. Lamont took the phone away from me and started cursing my client for calling me at home. I got in trouble at work because I was on call, plus I was so embarrassed."

On another occasion, Lamont and Patty went to visit a friend of Lamont's who happened to be an attorney. The attorney passed out beers for everyone, and even though Patty did not normally drink alcohol, she accepted the beer so as not to appear rude. But Lamont grabbed the beer out of her hands and told her loudly enough for everyone to hear, "Sluts drink." He embarrassed her on multiple occasions.

Their relationship continued to worsen, and Patty finally told Lamont it was over. But it was not over for him.

On April 5, 1979, long after Patty broke up with Lamont, she was invited to dinner by another young man. She liked him but was so afraid of Lamont that she could not bring herself to invite the young man to her home. Instead, she arranged to meet him at her friend Pam's house in case Lamont was stalking Patty. She went on her date, and afterward he took her back to Pam's place. Patty got into her car and drove home to her apartment, alone. But her efforts to be discreet failed, and her fears were realized.

At the time, Patty was the sole occupant of an apartment building at the end of a dead-end street. As she drove up to her apartment, she noticed the reflection of another pair of headlights parked at the side of her building. She tried to turn her car around and flee, but was rushed by the other car and blocked in. It was Lamont's personal car, and he was driving. He jumped out of his car, and Patty saw that Lamont was in his police uniform, complete with his badge and gun, even though he was off duty. Lamont marched over to her car and slung open her door. He grabbed Patty by her shirt.

"You slut!" he screamed. "You are so drunk you can't even find your way home! You didn't even know where your own driveway is, you stupid b*tch!"

"I'm not drunk! I have not been drinking! I was trying to leave!" she told him. He ordered her into her apartment, and his temper was out of control the second they got inside.

Then in a fit of rage, he grabbed a heavy potted plant and smashed it on top of Patty's head. Dirt went in her eyes and all over her clothes. He tore her sweater, yanking at it while he was screaming at her. He shoved her down onto the floor, straddled her, and began to choke her.

"I went black for a minute, and he would let up. Then he would start choking me all over again, and I'd black out again. He kept doing that!" Tears ran down her face as she recalled what Lamont did to her. I could see that she still trembled with fear at the memories, even after all these years. I felt my own body tensing with anger at a man who simply refused to take no for an answer.

"He... he took his .38 revolver from his holster and stuck the barrel between my eyes... He said, 'B*tch, you are doing to die!' ...He demanded to know where I had been and who I was with. I finally told him I had been to dinner with a man I met at Pam's. Lamont said Pam was a 'fat *ss b*tch' and he hated her. I never told Pam all the things Lamont said about her. He didn't even know her and he hated her."

"What happened with the gun?" I prodded.

"He kept it there for a while, against my forehead, and just kept cursing. He finally put it back in his holster and got off of me. I tried to get up, and Lamont grabbed a wooden chair and hit me with it. I turned away to protect myself, and he hit the chair over my back, my arms and legs, and when I tried to defend myself, he hit me in the head and face. He punched me with his fists, and I couldn't do anything to stop him. He was just too strong..."

I hoped above hope that this incident was documented somewhere.

"And then?" I prompted gently.

"Lamont finally left that night, but he told me he was riding along with another officer all night, and that if I called the police, he would hear it on the radio. He said he would kill me. I didn't know what to do, and I was in so much pain I could hardly move. I just laid there crying and in pain till the next morning."

When she looked in the mirror the next morning, her left eye looked horrible. She had a burst blood vessel that made her eye look even worse. She saw marks on her neck where Lamont had choked her. Her head was so sore she could barely stand to touch it. Not wanting to involve anyone else, she drove herself to the hospital.

"Which hospital?" I asked.

"Lincoln County Hospital."

After obtaining her permission, I reviewed two medical reports dated April 6 and April 9 of 1979. The symptoms were listed as "headache, nausea, vomiting, contusions and abrasions with secondary headache…. Was beaten last night; hit by fist and chairs and tables… several abrasions to the neck and got lumps on the back of her head… Alert. Oriented. Emotionally upset… Contusions head and eye… Blurring of left eye…"

Patty was out of work for the next couple of days. She attempted to disguise her black eyes with sunglasses, and the dark bruises on her throat with turtleneck sweaters. Her parents were not fooled. Patty's father took matters into his own hands and paid a visit to Sheriff Harvin Crouse. No charges were filed, but Sheriff Crouse said he would deal with Lamont. He verbally counseled Lamont, who promised never to misbehave again.

Patty told me that after that night Lamont kept coming back around, and she was so scared she did not know what to do. She would involuntarily flinch when he got close to her, and this angered him. She finally told him at the risk of him killing her, "It has to be ended for good, Lamont." But he refused to accept it, saying that if he allowed her to break up with him, people would think something was wrong with *him*. Patty assured him he could tell everyone that *he* broke up with *her* in order to save his pride. Lamont was satisfied with that arrangement, and ultimately left her alone. Understandably, Patty was not anxious to get involved in this case for fear of inviting him unwillingly back into her life. I certainly understood, but I also knew that sooner or later Lamont Underwood's victims were going to have to testify to the things he had done. Otherwise, he would never be held accountable, and the number of his victims would continue to increase.

Lamont could not leave the women alone. The next of his catastrophic relationships I learned of was with a petite blonde named Monica, the girl Terry Burgin had told me about. Monica was working in an administrative capacity for the City of Lincolnton when she met Lamont in 1980.

"He told me he went by L. C., not Lamont," she informed me when I met with her inside her well-kept mobile home near Lake Norman.

"L. C. was a perfect gentleman, in the beginning. He was extremely neat. A perfectionist about everything. When he cleaned his house, he would even take up the metal plate that separated the carpet between rooms, you know in the doorway, so he could clean thoroughly." Monica said he was every woman's dream to have around the house, but only "very, very briefly."

"He bragged about himself all the time. He told me over and over that he was the best detective around. When I asked him to tell me about some of the cases he worked, he said they were 'top secret,' and he couldn't tell me about them. ...The funny thing was that although he talked about himself all the time, he never told me hardly anything about his background. I don't know anything about his family. He never talked about them. I just knew he was from Forsyth County."

L. C. did tell Monica about his relationship with Patty Lewis.

"He talked about her like she was a dog," Monica said. "He called her a 'trashy wh*re' and he even told me that he broke into her apartment one night. He said he kicked the door in and found other men there with her. I had no reason to believe he was lying then, but that was before I got to know him. Now I don't know if *any*thing he ever told me was true."

Monica believes that once L. C. realized she was "hooked on him," he began to treat her poorly. He often came to her apartment, expecting her to cook dinner for him.

"I remember Christmas that year. I got him all these nice gifts he wanted, but he only got me one thing. He handed me this box like he was all proud of it and all. But when I opened it, I was really disappointed. It was a blender, and not even a good one. I didn't even need a blender. I certainly didn't want a blender. But I thanked him for it and then put it away. I don't think I ever even used it once. But no matter what I did for him, he always acted like I disappointed him. He pouted like a child."

"What kinds of things disappointed him?" I asked.

"Well he got mad easily, over just nothing. And his mood would change in an instant. When he saw me talking to anybody else, he demanded to know what it was about and every word that was spoken. He had to know every place I went. I hardly went anywhere except work, the grocery store, that kind of thing. When I went anywhere, the phone would be ringing by the time I got back here and walked in the door."

"So, your relationship was exclusive?" I asked.

"We hadn't been dating but a few months when he started talking marriage," she said. "But I was afraid."

"What made you afraid, specifically?"

"His temper, for one. One night when L. C. wasn't working, we got into an argument. I can't remember what it was over. But he got so mad so fast. Since he was a detective, he wore, like, plain clothes, ya know?" I nodded. "Well he always wore his loaded revolver on his belt. We got to arguing and he shoved me down on the floor, and he pulled his gun out and pointed it at my head! He sat on top of me down on the floor and pressed his gun against my forehead... I can still remember the feel of it right here [touching her forehead]... and he said 'I'm going to kill you! Then I'm going to kill myself!'"

I saw that Monica's hands were balled into fists and her knuckles had turned white.

"I know it's not easy reliving those memories, but it's very important," I encouraged her.

"I know... I begged him to please stop, to please put the gun away, and when he finally did, I begged him to leave me alone." He just stayed on top of me – it seemed like hours although I'm sure it wasn't that long – and he finally rolled off of me. He started crying and then tried to apologize. I was just... shocked... I couldn't believe that had just happened, that he had just done that to me."

"Did your relationship end that night?" I asked, doubting that was the case.

"Well, no. He could be very persuasive. I tried to break up with him, but he kept saying how much he loved me and didn't want to lose me, and ...well I guess you know how that goes." I nodded.

"No matter what I said, he kept following me and harassing me. ...One afternoon I was getting home from the grocery store after work, and like usual, the phone was ringing as I walked in the door."

"L.C?" I asked.

She said it was L. C., but he did not say hello.

"What do you have in those bags, Monica?" he demanded of her.

"My bags? Groceries! I had to buy groceries."

"Monica… you live alone. You don't need FIVE bags of groceries!"

"How do you know how many bags I have?" she asked him, a bit freaked out.

"I know every move you make," he informed her calmly.

On another occasion, L. C. called Monica and described to her what she was wearing at the moment.

"You know I don't like for you to wear short skirts, Monica," he said. She apologized, although she did not think her skirt was all that short. But in fact, L. C. didn't like for her to wear anything remotely attractive. Monica did not know how to respond to L. C. or what to do about him.

On yet another occasion, Monica ran into a friend in a public parking lot in town. L. C. spotted her and ran the friend's license plate number. Monica did not see L. C. and had no idea he had seen her.

"Who were you talking to today, Monica?" L. C. asked her later.

Monica told him the friend's name.

"You just better be glad you told me the truth," L. C. said.

Monica realized he was following her everywhere she went. Even when she stopped for gas, L. C. would be there. At first, she was agitated, wishing he would eventually give up. But she became increasingly frightened of him when he stalked her more and more. She dreaded even to talk to him.

"Several years ago, my aunt gave me a gold-leaf picture frame for graduation. When L. C. and I started dating, I put a picture of myself in it and gave it to L. C. Later when I asked him for the picture frame, he told me if I wanted it to come to his house and get it. So, I got into my car and started driving toward L. C.'s. But I had this really uneasy feeling, and I just turned around. Somehow, I knew that if I went there that night, he would beat me or even kill me. I didn't get my picture frame back. It wasn't worth it to me."

"...L. C. kept getting worse, and I got more and more afraid. So, I went to my parents' house to stay for a while. I stayed for a few days and had to come back to my apartment for some things. My parents came with me and spent the night. After dinner the three of us went for a walk to get some exercise. There was a mill nearby. We saw these footprints in the sawdust where someone had been standing for a long time. There were cigarette butts there too, cigarettes like L. C. smoked. You could see my apartment as clear as a bell from right there. I have no doubt that's where L. C. watched me from."

"How did you finally get away from him?" I asked.

"I was at the end of my rope. My family was worried about me. Nothing I said to L. C. did any good. He just refused to leave me alone. So, my dad went to see the Sheriff of Lincoln County, Harvin Crouse. I don't know what he did, but L. C. left me alone for a long time after that."

Still, Monica was reluctant to start dating again. She moved into a small white frame house outside the city after a few months. About that time, she heard that L. C. was dating a girl named Linda, who lived near Monica's new home.

In 1982, Monica met her future husband Tim, and they began to date. Suddenly L. C. reappeared in Monica's life. One night when Monica and Tim returned to her house after a date, they found the word "wh*re" spray painted in red on the side of Monica's house. It was shortly thereafter when Monica learned that Linda had something similar spray painted on the exterior wall of Linda's church.

"Right after that, I heard that L. C. got some type of psychiatric treatment at Baptist Hospital in Winston Salem," Monica told me. But we were unable to access any of L. C.'s psychiatric records there, if they existed.

"I won't have to testify in court against L. C., will I?" Monica asked. "I never want to see him again."

Linda felt the same way. She was also an attractive woman who was glad L. C. was only a bad memory. I knew her story even before she told me, but I listened sympathetically.

"He was the perfect gentleman when we first met. He was extremely neat and super courteous. But then he became insecure and unreasonably jealous. He wanted to control everything I did," she explained.

Ultimately L. C. became violent. When Linda tried to end the relationship, L. C. begged her not to leave him. Then he stalked her, threatened her, and basically terrorized her. Linda was horrified to discover the words "Linda is a wh*re" spray painted in red on the outside of the church she had attended all her life. Although L. C. denied doing it, she recognized his handwriting, even in spray paint.

"...and he could not explain away the empty spray cans of red paint that K. B. Crouse found in the trunk of his patrol car."

"What happened then?" I asked her.

"I think all they did was warn him to stay away from me."

"He should have been charged," I couldn't help but remark.

In January 1982, L. C. met the woman who would become his third wife, Marcia. I was especially anxious to talk to her since she lived with L. C. most recently. Like the others, Marcia was not especially looking forward to talking with us. But she did invite Steve and me into her condominium, which was located in an attractive neighborhood in Salisbury.

Marcia was a pleasant woman with a friendly face. She was dressed in a modest blouse and skirt. She told us that she had battled with her weight for some time, but she was by no means what I would call obese, not really even overweight. She struck me as having a less than healthy self-image, but she seemed to have a lot going for her at that point in her life, with a nice salary as a nurse and a nice home.

L. C. and Marcia met in Lincolnton when Marcia was working at a hospital there. They began dating, and the only thing Marcia learned about L. C.'s background was that his parents ran off when he was small and he grew up in The Children's Home in Winston Salem. L. C. also told her that he enlisted in the Army after high school and afterward went into law enforcement.

They married only five months after they began dating, in July.

"L. C. said he didn't believe in prolonged courtships," Marcia offered.

L. C. resigned from the Lincoln County Sheriff's Office on November 30, 1982, when he was hired by the Salisbury Police Department. Marcia and L. C. moved to Salisbury where Marcia was originally from. Marcia began working in the larger hospital there.

Marcia recalled that L. C. brought with him a small revolver with a wooden grip, which he carried while working at the Lincoln County Sheriff's Office.

"I asked him if he didn't have to turn that gun in," Marcia explained, "but he told me Sheriff Crouse had given it to him since he used it when he worked there as a detective. ...He didn't carry it at Salisbury PD though, because they issued him a gun to carry. He kept the revolver at home, in a holster in the dresser."

"Do you know where that gun is now?" Steve asked Marcia.

"He still has it, as far as I know," she replied. "He had it when we separated anyway."

"How long were you and L. C. together?" I asked her.

"We lived in an apartment in Salisbury for about two years. Then we bought the house on Lake Drive where L. C. lives now. ...When we separated, I told him to keep the house and that if he ever sold it, we could settle then. I... I just wanted out," she added.

Marcia's marriage to L. C. was, not surprisingly, dysfunctional.

"Was L. C. ever violent toward you?" I asked Marcia. She looked away, and a flash of some kind of pain crossed her face.

"No," she said, not meeting my eyes. "I didn't see him that much. I worked second shift."

"Did you argue?"

Marcia said they argued over typical issues such as house cleaning and credit cards.

"We just weren't very compatible," Marcia offered. She did say they separated once for about six months during their marriage, but Marcia did not disclose the reason. They got back together but separated again later, permanently.

"Were there any instances of unfaithfulness in your marriage, by either of you?" Steve asked.

"No," said Marcia.

"You were never unfaithful to L. C.?"

"Never."

I pressed on. "Marcia, others have told us that L. C. was not very nice to you, and that he talked ugly to you in front of other people. Is that true?"

Her face reddened as she responded, "Well, we would argue, and he would… say things. But I knew when to be quiet. I knew not to push him."

"How did you learn when to be quiet? How did you learn not to push him?" I challenged.

"There was this one time when L. C. grabbed my arm, and it left bruises. But I do bruise easily. So, the marks stayed blue for days…because I bruise easily," she repeated.

"Everyone knows he has a temper," she continued, as if that were reason enough for the bruises. "He'd fuss over anything. I think a lot of it had to do with the stress of his being a police officer and his back injury."

"Was he jealous?" I asked.

"Uh, no," she answered, looking away.

"How did your marriage end?" Steve asked Marcia.

"We just kind of went our separate ways," she said noncommittedly.

"Marcia, you said you were never unfaithful to L. C. But was he unfaithful to *you*?" I asked.

"By the end of our marriage, I knew he had girlfriends. But by then, it didn't really matter. I hated to see him be alone," she said. I looked up from my notes at that comment. Marcia admitted that she even hoped L. C. would get involved with another woman so that she could get out of the marriage as quickly and easily as possible. They separated for good in 1992 and were divorced in June 1993.

"Did you see L. C. after your final separation?" I asked.

She looked guilty all of a sudden. "A time or two," she answered.

"When was that?"

"November, no, December of 1993. He called me one night. He was upset and crying. I felt sorry for him. He always had a way of making people feel sorry for him. He told me he had a lot of problems with his back and that he was in a great deal of pain. He also told me he wasn't with the Police Department anymore…"

"So, you were concerned for him?" I prompted.

"Yes."

"Did you go to him then?" I asked.

"Well, it was right after Thanksgiving, the night I talked to him. I was afraid; he sounded like he might try to commit suicide. So, I met him."

"Then what happened?"

"He asked me to drive him to Westcliff – you know that subdivision in Salisbury? He wanted me to pick up a table that this man by the name of Wayne Whitman was giving to him. Wayne was his supervisor at the Police Department and always thought a lot of L. C."

"What were you driving at the time?" I asked her.

"My Honda Prelude."

"Do you know the exact house you went to?" I asked.

"No."

"Did you know that Wayne Whitman lived next door to a woman named Kay Weden?"

"I know it now, but I did not know at the time."

"Can you describe the house you went to that night?"

"It was dark, but it was a brick ranch."

"And what did you and L. C. do when you got to the house?"

"We pulled into the driveway, and the lights were all out. L. C. said he didn't see the table sitting outside and that Wayne must have taken it back in the house. So, we just turned around and left."

"Ma'am, about how long were you at that house?" Steve asked her.

"Just a few minutes."

"And did you see him again after that night?"

"Yes, about three or four days later. We went out to eat," she explained.

"Why did you go out with him again?" I asked.

"He asked me to because his nerves had been bothering him. He said he just stayed home a lot. He said he never went out and he was bored. He just asked me to go out to eat with him one night. So, I did."

"When was that?' Steve asked. I could tell his adrenaline was pumping.

"Around the first of December."

"Where did you go?"

"Bogarts. We ate and talked, and then I drove him back to his house. That was all." I didn't ask what happened at his house. I doubted she would divulge it anyway.

"Was that the last time you went out with L.C?" he asked.

"Yes, it was."

"You said L. C. makes people feel sorry for him. How did he make *you* feel sorry for him?" he asked.

"It was easy for him to do that. He was my husband, and he had a rough time growing up, I think. I don't like to see anyone hurting," she explained genuinely.

I was curious about something. "Marcia, did L. C. tell you he had been married before?" I asked.

"Yes. I knew he'd been married once before."

"Once?"

"Yes. Why?"

"He was married twice before you. You were his *third* wife."

"I didn't know," she said without emotion.

"Don't feel bad," I told her, "I'm not surprised he wasn't completely honest with you. But I am surprised that you have not described him as being very jealous. He has a terrible history of jealousy…and violence."

Marcia looked at the floor and did not reply.

CHAPTER FIVE

"There is no fear in love; but perfect love casteth out fear: because fear hath torment" (I John 4:18)

One of L. C.'s supervisors at Salisbury Police Department was Wayne Whitman, Kay Weden's neighbor. Wayne Whitman was also the person who introduced L. C. to Kay. L. C. began calling Kay, and when he asked her out on a date, she accepted. Like the women that preceded her, Kay was impressed by L. C.'s initial charm, his neatness, and also by his police persona. They moved rapidly into a monogamous relationship.

I had not been investigating the case long when Rowan County Detective Terry Agner phoned and asked me to meet him in Salisbury so that we could interview someone who could share some insight into L. C.'s previous relationship with his ex-wife as well as his early relationship with Kay Weden. We met at the Rowan County Sheriff's Office, and Terry drove the two of us to the City Garage in Salisbury. There he introduced me to a city employee by the name of Joel Greer.

"L. C. and I became friends when I started working for the City of Salisbury in September of 1986. I was responsible for repairs and upkeep of the city vehicles, which included the police cars, and the first thing I learned about L. C. Underwood was that his car was about the neatest, cleanest one I ever worked on. L. C. was meticulous – more so than any man I have ever known."

Mr. Greer shared the following encounter with Detective Agner and me. "Sometime shortly after we met, L. C. came by my office and asked me if I wanted to get together, to go out for dinner and go to a club. I told him okay, and we went to Ivan's and ate. We met two girls there who wanted to go out with us. We left Ivan's and went to the house of one of the girls to pick them up. We took them to Twister's."

"In Cornelius?" I asked, familiar with the popular beach music club.

"Yes. Afterward we let one of the girls out at her house, and we both spent the night at the other girl's house. But one of the girls had lit a cigarette and burned a hole in L. C.'s car seat. He didn't see it until the next morning, and then he raised all kinds of hell. He just wouldn't drop it. He insisted on getting it repaired right away."

"What else do you remember about that night?" I asked Joel.

"I think it was that same night that L. C. told me about finding his wife with another man in a hotel in Concord. He said both of them were naked. He said he made the man leave the hotel room naked. L. C. took the man's wallet that he left behind and removed all his credit cards and ID and threw all of it out across the parking lot."

Terry gave me a look. The contents of Catherine Miller's wallet were strewn along a street following her murder, but none of her credit cards or ID were missing.

"...But L. C. had started coming in and talking to me while he was still married to Marcia. One day, he asked me to come to his house at lunch to talk. L. C. was kind of in a bad way, all emotional. Said he needed to talk to somebody. His wife was leaving him. He told me they had been living separate lives, which I had already gathered. I personally found it hard to believe that L. C. was just opening up to me like that, though, because I hadn't known him very long. I thought maybe he didn't have many friends."

"And did you go talk with him?" Terry asked.

"Yeah. Well, mostly I let him talk. I wasn't surprised that he and Marcia had a bad marriage, though. About three months before, L. C. had met Kay Weden, and I could tell he had a thing for her then."

Terry asked Joel Greer how well he knew Kay Weden.

"Oh, I've known Kay since high school. I always thought she was a fine girl. I met her a couple of times out at Rascals. She called me at my house and wanted to go out with me, but I wasn't interested in her in that way. It wasn't long after that when L. C. called and asked me if I knew her. I told him yeah, I knew her, and he started asking questions about her. L. C. and Kay got together right after that. ...One day L. C. called and asked me to deliver his car to them at the West Rowan Grill. I had worked on his car at my garage at home. I took his car to him – it was a Saturday morning – and I made the comment that they made a fine couple. But something was wrong. They both had long faces, but I don't know why."

"They continued dating after that?" Terry asked.

"Apparently so, because about three or four weeks later, I heard from L. C. again. He came to my office and said he was gonna give Kay a diamond ring. I asked him if he was sure about that because I knew they hadn't been going out very long. He said he was sure. But then after he gave her the ring, he told me several times that he wanted it back because he had 'given up on her' or something like that."

"Did L. C. share with you any details with you about his and Kay's problems?"

"Well, he came by my office when they were having problems and said he needed to get out of town. I agreed, and we went out to eat and then went to Twister's. We hadn't been there ten minutes when Kay and her friend Vicky walked in and sat down at a table. L. C. went to their table, and I followed. L. C. started giving Kay a hard time. I turned my attention to Vicky, and we tried to ignore Kay and L. C. But Kay got enough of L. C.'s mouth and turned to Vicky and said, 'Let's go.' They got up and started walking out, and L. C. followed them. I think that's the point he cussed Vicky out. A few minutes later, L. C. came in and said he was going to leave and asked if I was ready. I said, "No, I'm staying." I stayed, and L. C. left. I saw right then that L. C. could not control himself in public."

"You said you've known Kay for years. Do you know her son Jason?" Terry asked.

"Yeah."

"Did L. C. ever talk about Jason?"

"Yeah. I got the impression L. C. didn't have a good relationship with Jason or the exchange student that was staying at Kay's. L. C. said Jason was hanging around with the wrong crowd and that there were some drug dealers after him. He said Jason's girlfriend was involved too."

"When did he tell you that?"

"Just before Kay's house was shot into. After the shooting, L. C. said he thought it was the kids that were after Jason who shot into their house."

"Did L. C. ever tell you about an incident between him and Kay at Bogarts Restaurant?" I asked.

"Oh yeah. L. C. was very, uh, emotional when he told me about it. He told me the same time that his mother was real sick. Anyway, he said he went to Bogarts and saw Kay in there with another man. He said he went to Kay's table and accidentally knocked over her drink glass."

"He told you it was an accident or you just assumed it was accidental?" I asked.

"He told me."

"Did he also tell you about an incident at the Quality Mart the next morning?"

"I don't think L. C. told me, but I did hear about it. L. C. called me later and asked me to call Kay for him. I called her, and she told me that L. C. had dumped tea in her lap at Bogarts – intentionally – and that L. C. said he had people that would help take care of her date. Then Kay said L. C.

saw her at the Quality Mart the morning after, and that L. C. pushed the car door on her and jerked her necklace off and took it. Then she said L. C. had followed her to school – where she teaches – and left a note on her car that same day."

"Did you talk with L. C. again after that?" I asked.

"Yes ma'am. The next time I spoke to him was on the phone. I got onto him about what happened with Kay. He got mad and hung up on me. I talked to him again from my office about 9:00 the next morning. He asked me to take the dog Kay had given him back to Kay's house. But I told him no. He got real mad then and said he was going to take the GD dog out to the park and shoot it and throw it in the bushes. Then he hung up again. ...Then that afternoon Kay called me when she got home from school. She played me a recording of a voicemail message L. C. left her and fired a gun on the phone. ...I told her I'd call her right back. I told my boss, and he called the police. I believe my boss talked to the city manager about it too. That night L. C. called me and apologized for getting mad that morning. He asked me if I'd talked to Kay, and I told him I had. He didn't say much more, though."

"Have you talked to L. C. recently?" Terry asked.

"No, not since Mrs. Miller was murdered. I've thought about whether or not L. C. could have killed her."

"Do you think he was capable?" I asked.

"I think L. C. was jealous of anything or anyone that stood between him and Kay. He wanted complete control over her." No one said anything for a few moments.

"Do you know what kind of guns L. C. had?" I asked.

"The only guns I ever saw him with was a Remington 100 and L. C.'s service weapon. I was wanting to buy the 100, but he said his mother gave it to him and he wouldn't sell it."

"You said L. C. told you that his mother was sick? How sick? Did he say she was dying?"

"I don't think so. But I think something was bad wrong with L. C. Right after L. C. and Kay got engaged, Kay called me one night about 10:00. She asked me to meet her at her house and go with her to L. C.'s. She said she had spoken with his doctor and that he told her to get L. C. to the hospital. When I got to Kay's house, Wayne Whitman was there. Wayne didn't know what was going on either. Me and Wayne went to L. C.'s and talked to him. He first said he wasn't going to the hospital, but we finally convinced him to go. Kay and Vicky came in later and spoke to the doctor. Kay spoke with L. C.'s mother, and L. C. got mad at her over that. Kay stayed at the hospital, and me and Wayne left."

"What was it that prompted her to call his doctor?" I asked, confused.

"The reason she called me was that something had happened – L. C. had done something – that worried her and she called his doctor. That's when he told her L. C. needed to go to the hospital. But I don't know what he did that made her call."

"Is there anything else you think we should know about L. C. Underwood?" I asked.

"I don't think so. It's just that L. C. was so jealous over that woman. Bad jealous." He looked disturbed, worried. I needed to learn more about Kay Weden.

When I met Kay in January of 1994, I found a pleasant, pretty lady with short blond hair, a thin smile, and sad blue eyes. She was a forty-year-old divorcee with a teenage son, Jason. In the early 1990s, when she met L. C. she was teaching English and Drama at a high school in Salisbury. I imagined her to have more sparkle in her blue eyes when she first met L. C., all those months before she suffered such unexplained loss. Now there was a subtle but undeniable air of grief about her person. I really sympathized with her. I could not imagine what it would be like to be in Kay's shoes. I still had my own mother and a husband. She seemed just… lost.

I doubted if she felt like answering questions, but she endured many hours with me that day at the Rowan County Sheriff's Office. It was exhausting for us both, but critical for nailing down her history with L. C. Since that day, Kay and I have talked many, many times, far too many to count.

Kay was born in Rowan County. She attended Western Carolina University in Cullowhee, North Carolina. She married Matthew Weden, and they lived in northern Virginia where Kay began teaching school. In 1977, Kay gave birth to their only son Jason, the absolute love of Kay's life. Kay and Matthew divorced after thirteen years of marriage, and Kay returned to Salisbury with Jason.

Kay purchased a brick ranch-style house in Westcliffe, a nice upper-middle-class subdivision only a few blocks from her mother's residence. Kay and Jason seemed to be doing okay after the divorce. She worked through the week and spent her weekends attending Jason's soccer games, visiting her mother, or going out with friends.

Kay's house was located on a quiet street in suburbia between a nice vacant lot and another neat middle-class home. To the right of her house was a paved driveway, wide enough to park two vehicles side by side, and probably long enough to park three vehicles end to end. To the right of the driveway was a small but nicely landscaped area with a firepit surrounded by patio chairs. Kay and her son Jason often sat by the fire in the evenings, chatting with their friends when they visited. The first time I drove by Kay's house, I tried to picture it as L. C. did the night of December 3, 1993. After all I had learned about his personality, I imagined him looking on with contempt and loathing at the sight of Kay's home where he had once been welcome, where he had made love to her, and where he was no longer invited. I envisioned his fury at seeing another man there with Kay, especially a really good-looking man like Viktor Gunnarsson.

Shortly after Kay met L. C., they began to date. Like so many times before, L. C. was described as a perfect gentleman... in the beginning. He did the traditionally chivalrous things such as opening doors for Kay and pulling out her chair. He took her to nice restaurants and paid for her meals. He was extremely neat, and kept his home neat. In fact, Kay described him as meticulous about everything, from keeping his ashtrays empty and clean to keeping a clean and empty liner in the garbage can at all times. Kay said sometimes she felt like L. C. would vacuum her "right out the door" because when she walked through the house on the plush carpet, he would vacuum behind her to fluff up the footprints. Such idiosyncrasies were curious to Kay at first, but later began to irritate her.

Yet L. C. was romantic and attentive. He expressed concerns about her safety. But much like the other women in L. C.'s past, only a short time passed before Kay learned that L. C. was not the person he had presented himself to be. L. C. was tightening the reins.

"If things didn't go L. C.'s way," Kay told me, "he became a different person, and not for the better. He was very possessive. He resented my friends and my son. He always complained that he was second best. I told him he had no reason to feel that way, no reason to feel threatened by my son, my friends, or anyone else, but it did no good. I encouraged him to go out with his own friends. But he'd just say all he wanted was to be with me." What L. C. really wanted was for Kay to want to be with him, and him alone.

"If you love me, you should feel the same way," he told Kay repeatedly.

"But I don't have to be with you *all* the time," she told him. "And that doesn't mean I don't care about you. It's just that everyone needs their own space sometimes." It was like arguing with a tree.

"A relationship is not about being apart!" he screamed in her face. L. C.'s fears of abandonment continued to echo throughout his entire life.

Not surprisingly, Kay found it difficult to cope with L. C.'s insecurities constantly and the pressure he exerted on her. Kay tried to end the relationship from time to time, but the harder she tried to free herself from L. C.'s control, the more he tried to hold her. The victim of a recently failed marriage, Kay was torn between wanting the relationship to work and her own instincts urging her away from him.

Kay's mother Catherine Miller pointed out some of L. C.'s bizarre behaviors to Kay when the opportunity arose. Although Kay did not recall the precise nature of the conversation, she does recall that Catherine was tactfully admonishing L. C. for something he said or did. Instead of responding verbally to Catherine, L. C. put his hands over his eyes, as if shamed, as if he could not bear it. It was difficult for Kay to explain.

"It was just like a child who covers their eyes and thinks you can't see them then..." Kay tried to describe much later. "... My mother asked me behind his back, 'What was *that?*' She and I kind of laughed about his behavior at the table that day. It was bizarre..."

During the late summer of 1992, L. C. invited Kay on a weekend getaway with him to the mountains. L. C. had been on his best behavior in recent weeks and seemed to care genuinely for Kay, and she agreed to the trip. When they walked into the room that L. C. had reserved for them at the Cliff Dwellers Inn, Kay was surprised to see a large bouquet of summer flowers on the dresser. Attached to the flowers was a card that read, "Will you marry me?" L. C., anxiously awaiting her response, presented Kay with a ruby and diamond ring. She accepted both the ring and the proposal with an enthusiastic new optimism for the future.

They spent the weekend in the quaint, touristy town of Blowing Rock, shopping, dining, and driving around in the mountains. I was familiar with all the places Kay described. In fact, the Cliff Dwellers Inn was just a few minutes' jaunt across the Blue Ridge Parkway from Deep Gap where

Viktor Gunnarsson's body was discovered. Kay got the impression that L. C. had stayed at the Cliff Dwellers at least once before. He commented that it was nice to go there and not have to argue with Marcia. Marcia was the name of his ex-wife. The weekend was so pleasant that, in fact, they returned for another stay a few weeks later. Not once on either trip did L. C. have to consult a map or stop and ask for directions. He knew all the good restaurants and attractions in the area.

L. C. could not maintain his good behavior indefinitely, however. *From the sublime to the ridiculous is but one step.* I think it was Napoleon that said that. Out of the blue, the green monster of jealousy inside L. C. would rear its ugly head, and Kay would retreat. She gave L. C. back the engagement ring and tried again to end the relationship, but L. C. would not be so easily dismissed.

It was later that same summer of 1992, just after Kay had tried to break up with L. C., that Kay and Vicky decided to go out dancing, so they went to Twister's Shag Club. Kay's recounting of the incident was practically identical to Joel Greer's. But I listened to Kay without interrupting her. She told me that Vicky drove them in Vicky's car, and they had a pleasant drive to Cornelius. They knew the crowd that hung out at Twister's was older, and the beach music they played was great for shag dancing. Kay knew that L. C. had been to Twister's before, but she thought it unlikely that he would be there that night. L. C. had developed quite a reputation for Carolina shag dancing, despite his alleged back problems.

Kay and Vicky found an empty table when they got to Twister's, and they sat down with an empty chair between them. It was an unfortunate coincidence that L. C. and Joel walked into Twister's that night. L. C. came over first and sat in the empty chair between Kay and Vicky. He completely ignored Vicky as he talked to Kay. Kay asked L. C. to leave her alone. The music was loud, the lighting was low, and

Kay had a hard time communicating with L. C. He didn't seem to hear anything she said.

"Let's dance," he said to Kay, ignoring her request.

"No," she said firmly.

"You *are* going to dance with me," he demanded.

"NO," she repeated, a bit louder. He pulled at her arm beneath the table.

L. C. glared at her and threatened, "If you don't dance with me, Kay, I am going to say something you won't like to your fat friend Vicky!"

Kay could not prevent the tears that welled up in her eyes from frustration and embarrassment. Angrily she responded, "L. C., if you don't stop it, I'm leaving!"

Joel, L. C.'s friend, was talking to Vicky, presumably trying to distract her so she would not hear L. C.'s ugly comments about her.

Kay turned to Vicky then. "Are you ready to leave? I am."

Kay and Vicky picked up their things and walked outside. L. C. stood quickly and followed them out the door. Kay fumbled for Vicky's car keys, which she was carrying in her purse for Vicky. She found the keys, unlocked Vicky's car door for her and walked around to the passenger side.

L. C., desperate for something to stall Kay, turned to Vicky and said loudly, "You're a fat b*tch!" Kay fumed with anger and humiliation for Vicky, who wisely chose not to respond to L. C.'s insult.

Kay and Vicky sat in Vicky's car for a few moments with the doors locked, afraid to leave and not knowing what else to do. L. C. walked away, got into his car, and pulled out ahead of them. Kay and Vicky waited a few more minutes and then decided to leave, in case L. C. came back. They drove away from Twister's and turned down a side road, hoping to avoid L. C. She did avoid him for a short while, but Kay could not lose him for good.

In October of 1992, Kay was approached by a nice man with no obvious hang-ups, insecurities, or personality disorders. His name was Johnny Deaton, and he invited Kay out for a nice quiet dinner date. By this point, Kay had lost all interest in having any type of relationship with L. C. Underwood. Though she was still afraid of L. C. lurking in the shadows, Kay agreed to go out with Johnny.

They were enjoying a nice friendly date, and Kay found herself beginning to relax. But when Johnny drove Kay home at the end of the evening, L. C.'s Monte Carlo was backed into Kay's driveway. As Johnny was turning into her driveway, L. C. exited his car and started walking toward them.

"Back up, back up," Kay told Johnny. "Let's go." Kay was shaking.

"Where would you like me to go?" Johnny asked, getting the picture.

"Just take me to Vicky's," Kay told him. At Vicky's, Kay phoned Jason and told him what happened.

"Lock the doors, Jason," she instructed. "L. C. is outside." Jason locked the doors, but assured Kay that neither he nor Mikkel, their exchange student, was afraid of L. C. Underwood.

Johnny drove home shortly after dropping off Kay at Vicky's. L. C. later accused her of allowing Johnny to spend the night with her at Vicky's, but that simply did not happen.

The next morning, Kay called Jason first thing to let him know she was coming home. But it was not Jason that answered the phone at her house.

"Hello" L. C. said. Fear and shock coursed through Kay's body at the sound of his voice.

"Where's Jason?" Kay demanded. "I want to talk to my son!"

L. C. had entered her house during the night without Jason's or Mikkel's knowledge. Kay's fear intensified in direct correlation to L. C.'s audacity.

When Kay got to her house, L. C. was gone. But so was Kay's driver's license, she discovered, as she picked up the purse she had left lying on the kitchen table the night before. She also discovered that a bill from her lawyer in Virginia was missing from the kitchen countertop. Kay picked up the phone and dialed L. C.'s number.

"Where is my driver's license and my mail?" she demanded.

"I don't know what you're talking about," he said nonchalantly.

"I know you took them," she insisted. But he maintained ignorance, and she gave up, not feeling the conflict was worth pressing him about.

L. C. continued to call Kay daily, whining and pleading, until he finally persuaded her to see him again "just to talk," he said. "All I want is a chance to apologize. That's all."

Kay agreed to meet L. C., and as he had said, he immediately began to apologize. "I promise that I will change, Kay. I will give you your freedom if you will just let me back in your life… I have truly seen the error of my ways, and I love you so much! I love you unconditionally. Please let me prove it to you. Please, Kay. I don't want to live another day without you. I can't live without you. I love you so much."

L. C. had gotten good at this speech by this point in his life. He had learned what worked and what didn't. He gradually wormed his way back into Kay's good graces.

A few days later, Kay was inside L. C.'s house when she found the bill from her lawyer lying inside a trash can. L. C. had stolen her mail, just as she suspected. But she opted to leave the issue alone. She told herself the letter was of no importance, and she did not want to bring the issue up again after they had agreed to start over and put the past behind them. *If I had learned anything in my law enforcement experience, it was that the human mind can justify just about anything.*

L. C.'s good mood, however, triggered by Kay's renewed commitment to give him another chance, was ephemeral.

On the Wednesday before Thanksgiving, 1992, L. C. was particularly depressed. No matter what Kay did or said to cheer him, his mood only seemed to regress. After speaking with L. C. briefly on the phone, Kay decided to check on him in person. She drove by his house, and both his vehicles were parked in the driveway. Kay knocked on the door, but there was no answer.

More concerned than ever, Kay walked around the house to the window of L. C.'s master bedroom. She could see through the space between the blinds that L. C. was sitting lifeless in his recliner. No matter how loudly she knocked or yelled, he didn't move.

"Oh, dear God!" Kay prayed, "He isn't moving!" Kay thought L. C. was dead.

She ran back around to the front of the house which faces Lake Drive and flagged down the first car that drove past. Coincidentally, the driver of the car was a police officer, Rick Hillard, who also happened to be a personal friend of L. C.'s. Kay quickly explained the situation, and Officer Hillard got out of his car and banged on L. C.'s front door until L. C. finally answered.

"What are you doing here?" L. C. asked Officer Hillard, clearly agitated.

"Well, Kay was getting worried. She said you wouldn't come to the door."

"My God, I was taking a crap!" L. C. told him.

When Officer Hillard left, L. C. glared at Kay and demanded, "Why the hell did you get Rick to come up here?"

"I was worried that something had happened to you, L.C! I saw you sitting in the chair! You were not in the bathroom! Why didn't you answer the door?"

L. C. turned and walked away.

Still concerned about L. C.'s depression, Kay invited him to share Thanksgiving dinner with her and Jason at her mother's home.

"Your mother hates me, Kay," L. C. told her.

"My mother doesn't hate anyone, L. C. She'd really like for you to come."

He finally agreed. "All right, Kay, if you're sure."

"I'm sure," she said.

The next day, on Thanksgiving morning, Kay called L. C. at home. He did not answer, and she knew he wasn't scheduled to work. She again drove by his house. This time Jason was with Kay. Turning in L. C.'s driveway, Kay saw that both of his cars were there. She knocked on the door, to no avail.

She had a key, and this time she decided to use it. She let herself in the house, and Jason followed on right behind her. At the end of the hall, Kay walked into L. C.'s bedroom. He was in bed asleep. She tried to wake him, but could not. Her heart started racing. Knowing L. C. hated MTV, she turned the TV on and switched the channel to MTV and turned the volume as loud as it would go. L. C. still did not move. Kay watched to see if his chest was rising and falling; it was. Then she sat down in a chair in his bedroom to wait. After a few minutes, L. C. squirmed and opened his eyes. He seemed disoriented, but he looked right at her.

"Get out," he told her coldly. It was a voice that was unfamiliar to her – a dark, vibrato voice. Kay swallowed.

"L. C., I am not leaving until I see that you are okay," Kay did not understand his reaction.

L. C. reached over to his nightstand, pulled open the drawer, and took out a handgun, without getting out of bed. He held it in his hand without pointing it.

"I said get out. Get out or I'm calling the police. You broke in here. I will call the police."

"Go ahead," she said, now angry with him.

L. C. apparently did not realize that Jason was also in the room. L. C. was lying partially on his side, facing Kay, with his back to the wall where Jason stood. Jason cleared his throat, and L. C. turned and looked him straight in the eyes.

L. C. raised the gun and pointed it directly at Jason, looking him dead in the eyes. Kay gasped.

"Go ahead and shoot!" Jason told him.

"Jason!" Kay screamed.

L. C. dropped the gun to his side, but Kay was terrified. She tried to speak calmly to Jason. "Get out, son. Get out! Go get in the car right now and drive home." Jason was only fifteen years old and had no driver's license, but Kay knew he could drive. She was terrified that L. C. would turn on him.

"Come on, Mom, you come too!" Jason pleaded, almost childlike, but Kay told him she would be home soon. Jason left in the car.

"You stayed there alone with him?" I asked Kay, incredulous.

"I thought he was going to kill himself," Kay told me. I refrained from giving voice to my thoughts.

Kay tried to talk to L. C. but could not reason with him. Finally, she gave up and decided to leave. Jason was just returning for her when she walked out. Kay got into the car and drove herself and Jason to her mother's house, still perplexed at L. C.'s irrational behavior.

She did not hear from L. C. until a couple days after Thanksgiving. L. C., back to his usual tactics, apologized for his bizarre behavior and made excuses.

"It's the medicine I was prescribed for my back pain," he claimed. He tried to convince her that medication caused his depressed state. "I need you, Kay," he pleaded.

"You didn't seem to need me the other day," she responded hotly, still furious that he had pointed a gun at her son.

"I wasn't myself. I haven't been able to sleep. I haven't been able to work. It's those d*mn pain pills they gave me. But I'm fighting it. I just can't do it without you."

"L. C.," she said, "I really think you need some psychological help."

"I've, uhm, thought about it," he admitted.

"You really should. In fact, I can't go on if you don't, L. C. I never know what kind of mood you're going to be in, or how you are going to react, and I may never forgive you for pulling a gun on Jason."

"I didn't know it was him, Kay! Hell, I didn't know anyone else was in the room! It was an involuntary reaction, instinct. It probably comes from all my police training," he argued.

"I don't know, L. C., but I think you still need some help."

"If I get some help, will you stick with me? I can't bear it if you leave me, Kay." *Master manipulator,* I thought.

"I don't know, L. C. We've had such a hard time trying to make it work."

"I love you, Baby. We've been through too much. Don't leave me now."

"…You get some help, and we'll talk about it. I have to go now."

L. C. did see a counselor for a couple of weeks. Kay, true to her word, supported him during that time. But after only a couple of weeks of counseling, L. C. proclaimed himself to be cured. Kay was skeptical, to say the least, but she continued to see L. C. through the winter of 1992-93. There were brief periods of time when L. C. was decent, even thoughtful. One particular instance was when Kay was making breakfast one morning and her toaster stopped working.

"You can have mine," L. C. said. "I never use it anyway." The next time he came over he brought Kay his toaster. Kay thanked him and set the toaster on her kitchen counter. She had used the toaster for a couple of months or so. Then one especially cold and dark night, as she was getting ready to go to bed, she heard a knock at her door. She unlocked the door and peered out.

It was L. C. He walked inside. Kay had never before seen him look the way he did that night. Normally neat to a fault, on this night he wore jeans, bedroom slippers, and a white sweatshirt with food dribbles down the front.

"What's the matter?" Kay asked immediately.

"I want my toaster," he said.

"*What?*" she asked.

"I came to get my d*mn toaster. Now give it to me!"

Kay walked to the counter, unplugged the toaster and handed it to L. C. He just stood there, holding the toaster like it was made of solid gold.

He stared at Kay… or rather *through* Kay…

"It was his eyes," she told me much later. "It was his eyes that were so strange. You know how his pupils are like so black?" she asked.

"I do," I told her.

"…and how his eyes are brown around his pupils?"

"Yes," I confirmed.

"Well not that night. There was no brown; they were solid black."

"You mean his pupils were dilated?" I asked.

"Yes. I mean there was no brown in his eyes at all. They were just two black buttons. I looked in his eyes, and all I saw was solid black against the whites. It wasn't natural at all, it was… it was… creepy, unnerving."

"*Demonic?*" I asked.

"…Yes," she said at last.

CHAPTER SIX

"Terrors shall make him afraid on every side, and shall drive him to his feet" (Job 18:11)

L. C. Underwood, still employed as a sworn officer by the Salisbury Police Department, was assigned the position of School Resource Officer at Salisbury High School. He and Kay talked about their respective high schools frequently. Kay was still teaching English and Drama at West Rowan High.

On Monday, March 15, 1993, school was cancelled in Rowan County due to an unusual snowfall. Kay and Jason, homebound for the day, decided to replace and rearrange some of Jason's bedroom furniture to accommodate his new waterbed that Kay had ordered him. She had placed the order at the doctor's recommendation to help Jason improve from some sports injuries he had sustained while playing soccer.

As it happened, the waterbed was delivered on that very Monday that school was cancelled, so Jason and Kay were home to set it up. First, though, they had to move his old bed out. Jason's old bed was stationed under the front window of his bedroom where it had sat since the day they moved in. But Jason's new bed was a bit longer than his old one, and the new waterbed had to be set up along another wall in the room. Jason would sleep that night in his new waterbed, against the wall and away from the window where his dresser now sat. Kay and Jason spent most of the day cleaning and rearranging Jason's bedroom. Once the new waterbed frame was in place, the two of them filled the chambers of the mattress with water.

Their snow day had been a productive one. Best of all, Kay had not been bothered by L. C. She was glad L. C. did not know they were moving furniture or else he might have insisted on coming over to help. Kay had not even mentioned to L. C. that she had ordered Jason a new bed for that very reason.

As typical spring snow showers go, however, the only trace left of the brief storm the following morning was the crisp air. School was back in session on Tuesday morning, March 16.

"How did you sleep on the waterbed?" Kay asked Jason as they shared a quick breakfast.

"I slept fine. I think I'm gonna like it pretty well," Jason answered.

"Good," Kay said.

"It's warmer too with that heater in it. I'm glad to be away from that cold window I was sleeping under."

"Yeah. Your bedroom window, being on the front of the house, gets the brunt of the cold north wind," Kay explained, "and speaking of cold, I'm gonna go warm up the car. It's just about time to leave for school."

Kay walked into her dark garage to warm up her car before she drove to work. Not having an electronic garage door opener, she walked directly to the garage door and opened it manually from the inside. Rays of early morning sunlight penetrated the garage and landed on Kay's car.

She turned from the open garage door and stepped toward the driver's door of her Honda. She gasped involuntarily at the sight before her. Spray painted expletives and obnoxious large swirls in red covered the exterior of her car. The side door panels were also dented as if they had been kicked in. Trembling with the sudden release of adrenaline and cortisol into her blood stream, Kay ran back into the kitchen and called the Rowan County Sheriff's Department.

"A deputy has been dispatched to your house, ma'am."

Kay disconnected and after only a moment's hesitation, still trembling, she dialed L. C.'s number. He answered on the first ring.

"Somebody vandalized my car!" she told L. C.

"I'll be right there," he assured her, not sounding in the least surprised that she had called him, nor asking what had specifically been done to her car.

L. C. arrived at Kay's house about the same time that Rowan County Deputy Tommy Ludwig arrived. As Deputy Ludwig photographed her Honda, L. C. stayed close to Kay.

"It looks like the work of juveniles," L. C. told her, in his professional sounding copvoice.

"But why? Why would someone do something like this to me?" she cried.

"Just let me take care of this, Kay. I'll find out who did it," L. C. promised. She leaned into him and rested her head on his shoulder. He pulled her tightly against him.

Deputy Ludwig initially agreed with L. C. "It's almost always kids that spray-paint. It's an act of immaturity, generally. Probably a prank by one of your high school students. They act out in their teen years without thinking about the results of their actions."

"I just don't understand. How could they get in here?" Kay asked.

"Maybe you left the garage door unlocked or unlatched? I'm not sure." Deputy Ludwig admitted. "But I'd contact your insurance company today and let them know what happened. You'll need a new paint job."

"How much is this going to cost me?" Kay asked.

"Several hundred dollars at least, would be my guess," he said. L. C. said nothing.

Kay was so upset she could not go to work. She contacted her insurance agent, and made arrangements to get her car repaired and painted immediately. She was crying with embarrassment at her car. Even the windshield was sprayed in red. It was not just a car, it was the brand-new black Honda Accord that Kay had just purchased for herself, following her divorce.

She was distracted and uneasy, searching her mind for a possible suspect or some logical reason for the vandalism. Kay was unaware that she had an enemy. She walked inside her house from the garage, so distracted that she forgot to close the garage door.

The next morning, Wednesday, March 17, Kay again walked out of her kitchen and into the garage to get into her car. It was then that she realized she had forgotten to close the garage door the night before. She wondered briefly if she was losing her mind. She pulled her car out of the garage, stopped in the driveway, and got out to pull down the garage door from the outside. For the first time, Kay saw the words "Jason is a fag" spray-painted in large red letters on the outside of the garage door. She went back in the house and again called the Sheriff's Department to report vandalism. Deputy Ludwig arrived to take the second report.

"The garage door was open when I arrived yesterday," Deputy Ludwig pointed out, "therefore we can assume the door was painted night before last, the same time they spray-painted your car."

"Yeah, probably so," Kay agreed.

Deputy Ludwig took photos and told Kay he would add them to the investigative file. Kay went on to work but again was unsettled all day long.

On the following day, Thursday, March 18, Kay worked later than usual. She stayed after school to help the drama club with a play rehearsal. She was interrupted during the rehearsal by a phone call from L. C. He told her that he had just received an anonymous phone call from a boy who asked if he knew Jason Weden.

"I told him yes, I know Jason," L. C. said. "Then the boy, uhm, threatened Jason's life. I'm sorry to have to call you at work and upset you like this, Kay, but I thought you needed to know."

"Right. Oh, I don't know what to say, L. C. But I'm glad you told me."

Kay thanked L. C. for the call and asked him to meet her at her house later that night. L. C. agreed, but he did not come that night; neither did he call her. But Kay was so exhausted from worry when she arrived home that she went to bed early, forgetting temporarily about L. C.

Friday, March 19 dawned, and as it did, L. C. called Kay again. He told her that he had just received an anonymous typewritten letter in a plain white envelope, which he said was left on a counter in the office of Salisbury High School.

"Well, what did it say, L. C?" Kay asked anxiously, her throat already tightening.

"It said *Johnny did it*," he told her.

"Johnny did what?" asked Kay, confused.

"He was talking about your car, Kay, and your garage door." L. C. tried to convince Kay that the letter was in reference to the vandalism she had suffered.

"Do you know who left the letter?"

"No. It was just left on the counter in the office."

"Well, why don't you ask the secretary if she saw who left it there? She may very well have seen them."

"Nah, Marilyn wouldn't know," he countered. Kay was frustrated.

A couple of days later, Kay told L. C., "Get me that letter please. I want to see it for myself."

"Well, I don't know where it is now. I can't find it."

As Kay continued to tell me about her conversations with L. C. throughout her time of being terrorized, I listened attentively, trying to minimize my interruptions to her flow of thought except to ask clarification questions. But I stopped her briefly, something nagging at the back of my mind. "Kay, did you tell L. C. about the vandalism to your garage door? Because you didn't find it until he was gone from your house, and you said he didn't come back the next evening like he said he was going to do."

"No," she said, confidently. "No, I didn't tell him. I know I didn't."

During the early morning hours of Saturday, March 20, unbeknownst to either Kay or Jason, a .22 caliber bullet was fired into the outside wall of Jason's bedroom. The bullet penetrated the wall of Kay's house and entered Jason's dresser. Had Kay and Jason not rearranged his bedroom furnishings the previous Monday, Jason might have taken a bullet to the head.

But it wouldn't be found for some time.

Later that morning, Kay discovered that someone had thrown eggs at her house, smashing them on the outside wall of Jason's room, on the living room window, and on her mailbox. For the third time that week, Kay contacted the Rowan County Sheriff's Office. She reported the most recent incidents to Detectives Tommy Swing and Mike Coates. When she told L. C. about the incidents, he did not seem terribly concerned. In fact, L. C. made fun of Detectives Swing and Coates when they came out to investigate, always quick to criticize the work of other officers.

"Those dumb*sses don't know what the hell they're doing," L. C. told Kay. "They couldn't solve a crime if it happened right in front of them."

"Well, L. C., I felt I had to report it," Kay responded.

"I told you I'd handle it, Kay. I know how to investigate a case," he said testily.

The next day was Sunday, the 21st of March, and it was, thankfully, uneventful. On Monday, March 22nd, Kay and Jason agreed that it was a relief to have no vandalism or threats made the past couple of days. Then Kay walked out to the garage for something and observed two long deep scratches down the side of her recently repaired and freshly painted Honda.

This time a different deputy was dispatched to take the police report. Kay was unnerved.

"Why is this happening to me?" she cried to L. C. "Everybody is going to think I'm involved with gangsters or something!"

"Everybody doesn't have to know about it, Kay."

"But the newspaper gets those logs from law enforcement because they publish them every week."

L. C. assured Kay that as a personal favor to her, he would make sure the vandalism incidents were kept out of the newspaper. The incidents were not published in the local paper, and Kay attributed that to L. C. and his "contacts."

The next day Kay received an anonymous and threatening letter in the mail. It was typed on clean white paper.

> We wanted to send you a warning that something is going to happen to Jason soon. And he is going to get hurt real bad. He might think that he is liked by the students at West, but if he does he is crazy. For a long time now, he has treated people real bad, and there is a lot of people mad at him now. He treats people like sh*t and he thinks it is real funny. So let's see how he likes being treated like sh*t. He thinks that he is so much of a stud and all the girls at school are crazy about him, but most people at school think he is a real b**t**d.
>
> The people that are involved in this won't talk either because we all have something against him.
>
> Was he thinking that he could treat people any way he wanted to and get away with it? Some people have been paid to kick his sorry ass, and that are going to do it. Jason won't know when or where. But he can bet that it will be very soon. How did he like the eggs on the house the other week? If we were Jason, we would be watching our

backs. We also hope he likes fire because his house might catch on fire very soon. If we was Jason, he might better stay home to be on the safe side so he can call the fire department. We bet he didn't know that his house was shot at over the weekend, so you might want to look for bullet holes. He can't watch his house all the time. There are more of us than there are of him. If Jason thinks this is a joke, he is very stupid. Ms. Weden, we know when Jason comes and goes so if he thinks he can hide from us all the time he is very wrong. No one can watch him every minute so when we get him he is going to be hurt real bad. It is time that somebody put him in his place. All this has to do with some drugs but that is not all of it. The main reason that he is just a b*stard and he will get his. We know that he has done some things to other people and has f*cked with other people's stuff so we hope he likes things that we have in store for him now.

There are other people at other schools that are after him just to help us out. This ain't over yet, he just won't know when or where. Jason can just kiss our *ss.

Kay's initial reaction was fear. But as she read the letter repeatedly, she realized that nothing in the letter was true. The substance of the letter was inaccurate. Jason was a wildly popular teen both with boys and girls alike, having many friends and always having a girlfriend. Kay's house was the one where everyone wanted to hang out. Kay realized that this letter did not seem to be written by a high school student or students. Although she could not put her finger on it, she knew something was not as it appeared. Moreover, being an English writing teacher, Kay was thoroughly familiar with the writings of high school students, and this writing was not consistent with those.

My first thought upon reading the letter was that it was extremely unlikely that it was written by a high school student. It was far too lengthy and too correctly written, spelling, punctuation and all. Neither was it written by someone demanding just money; it was far too vague. It did not include a payment deadline. It did, however, strike me as having been written by an insecure person, someone jealous of Jason, someone resentful of his popularity, and someone who wanted to tie together the egg throwing, the shot fired into the house, and the drugs aspect. But it also seemed to be written by someone who had a number of issues but without a clear message for Jason. It seemed to be written by someone who had experience setting fires or had ties to a fire department. And if they really wanted money, they certainly had failed to provide instruction on how money could be delivered. They seemed to be more focused on what Jason "thought" and his attitude than money that was owed. Its purpose seemed to be to instill fear more than anything else.

The following night, Tuesday, March 23rd, Kay received an anonymous call at home. She was able to record a portion of the conversation with the recording feature on her answering machine. The male caller angrily stated to Kay, "Tell your f*ggot son I want my $2,000!"

"What for?" Kay asked.

"For drugs!" he replied, then added, "And tell your f*ggot boyfriend cop that we were there, but he just didn't catch us!"

Kay tried unsuccessfully to convince the man that her son was not involved with drugs.

The man ended the conversation by giving her a week to come up with the $2,000, stating, "If you don't pay, it will be $4,000 next week!" Kay was dumbfounded. She did not recognize the gruff voice, except to realize that the caller was an older adult male, much older than a teenager.

That Friday night, April 2nd, L. C. told Kay that a student at Salisbury High School approached him and told him a little rhyme about eggs. That evening, L. C. said he found broken eggs dripping from his own house, but Kay never saw any evidence of any eggs thrown at L. C.'s house. Knowing L. C.'s propensity for neatness, she rationalized that L. C. would have cleaned such a mess immediately upon finding it.

Around midnight that same day, Kay heard Jason's private phone line ring. She heard Jason tell the caller, "I don't owe you anything!" Jason told Kay the unknown male caller asked him how he would like to play soccer with two broken legs. Kay questioned Jason at length about who could possibly be threatening them and why. Jason swore that he had no clue, and Kay believed him.

The next morning Kay told L. C. about the phone call.

He did not seem particularly concerned.

Kay asked him, "So who was the student that made the rhyme?"

"I don't know what the hell you're talking about," he said.

"L. C., you told me a student came up to you yesterday and told you a rhyme about eggs and when you got home you said your house was hit with eggs!"

"Oh right. Well I don't know who the kid was. I'm sure it was just a stupid teenage prank," L. C. said, dismissively.

"Well, don't you know what they looked like? You could surely find them again at the school and they could be questioned," Kay persisted.

"Kay, I see hundreds of kids at that high school every day. They all look the same to me," L. C. said. Kay didn't even know if the student was male or female.

On Saturday evening, April 3rd, L. C. and his friend Bob Ayala, an agent with the North Carolina State Bureau of Investigation, drove to Winston Salem for an evening out. Later that night, L. C. told Kay on the phone that he and Bob had gone out to a bar and that Bob had gotten drunk and vomited in L. C.'s car. L. C. was beyond angry about the vomit in his car; he was livid. He told Kay that he had dropped Bob off and was on his way home. When he did return home, L. C. called Kay again and told her detachedly that someone passing by had fired shots at his house.

"You had a drive-by *shooting* at your house?!" Kay asked, incredulous.

Before L. C. could answer, another call came in on Kay's call-waiting. She put L. C. on hold and answered the second call. It was the anonymous male caller, who announced, "I want my two thousand dollars!"

"Two thousand for what?" Kay demanded again.

"For drugs," the caller answered.

"My son does not do drugs!" Kay shouted.

"You better check him... and tell your boyfriend that the next time shots are fired at his house, they won't be warning shots!" Click.

It took Kay a moment to realize that L. C. was still on hold. She returned to her call with L. C. and told him what had just transpired. L. C. asked her to hold on so he could walk outside to look for the shots that he said had just been fired into his house. He returned to the phone a few moments later and told her it was too dark to see anything; he would check in the morning. Kay does not recall L. C. ever mentioning the alleged shots at his house again.

Sunday passed quietly, but Kay was so consumed by fear that she wondered if she could ever breathe normally again. Then on Monday, the 5th of April, Kay received another anonymous letter in the mail, also typewritten but much briefer.

ROSESARERED
VIOLETSAREBLUE
WEAREGOINGTOF*CKJASON
ANDYOURHOUSETOO

Kay was perceptibly shaken when she told her mother about the recent incidents. Kay hated to worry her mother, but she needed her advice.

"That's it, Kay. Enough is enough. I am hiring a private security firm to keep an eye on your house," Catherine informed her.

Catherine paid $4,000 to a private detective agency in Salisbury to watch Kay's house from April 9 – 18, 1993, during a period when Jason was gone to Virginia to visit his father. Kay told L. C. about it as soon as they were hired. L. C. told her that a private investigator was totally unnecessary because *he* was on the case, but Kay was adamant.

"How's the security going?" L. C. asked Kay a couple days later.

"Fine. They are keeping an eye on my house."

"Where do they park?" L. C. asked Kay a few days later.

"In the driveway of the neighbor's house across the street," she told him.

"What times are they there?" he asked. She told him.

Much to her relief, those nine days passed without incident.

"That was a total waste of money, Kay," L. C. scolded her.

"I don't care," she responded. "Nothing happened to me while he was here, now, did it?" L. C. didn't reply.

"And furthermore, my mother is a widow who lives alone. You know that I just lost my stepdad, and I lost my real dad when I was twenty years old. All these things that have been happening lately are really upsetting her, and if she feels better having security watch my house, then so be it."

Kay found L. C.'s attitude as well as his behavior baffling. At times, he seemed determined to find out who was terrorizing Kay, but then at other times, he minimized it or got defensive when she asked him if he had found anything out yet. He wanted to be her hero, but he had nothing with which to relieve her.

Months later, when I interviewed Kay at length, I asked her, "During all this time, this period of ...terror... did you ever once consider the possibility that L. C. was the culprit?"

"No," she admitted, "I didn't. Not once. I just couldn't imagine it. He was a cop. He told me that he loved me. He had asked me to marry him." None of her reasons precluded L. C. from committing the acts, and she knew better now. I would not berate her for trusting someone who said he loved her. I, on the other hand, had learned to look at the two or three closest people to the victim if the crime or crimes were personal or violent.

"...Plus I thought L. C. was getting victimized too," Kay added. This was true; L. C. had told her that his house and gotten shot into, that his house was egged, and he was also mentioned, albeit indirectly, in the letters.

"But you never saw any evidence of anything having occurred at L. C.'s house," I reminded her.

"That's true," she said.

Kay was so preoccupied with the things that were happening to her and Jason that she hardly noticed that L. C. did not seem interested in her sexually any longer. On the rare occasions they were intimate, L. C. had difficulty performing. But the excuse he gave Kay was that her pleasure was his first priority. When L. C. began to make excuses for not wanting to be intimate with her at all, Kay was too worried about her own problems to dwell on his.

Eventually law enforcement investigators told Kay that based on what they had discovered, L. C. had become the primary suspect in the vandalism and threats against her and Jason. She was bewildered. Although she did not believe he could have had any part in the crimes, she did note that he had withdrawn farther and farther from her.

"Not only that," she told me months later, "but when I was with him, I noticed that all of a sudden, he was perspiring like crazy, for no apparent reason. ...That and his erectile problems were new. When I mentioned this to L. C., he blamed his medication."

"What medication was he taking?" I asked.

"I have no idea. He never told me. ...But he also had this fear, this *obsession*, that he was going to lose his job at Salisbury Police Department... I didn't understand it," Kay added. I did.

Meanwhile, law enforcement investigators found that the evidence against L. C. was mounting. At the very minimum, L. C. Underwood was the only ostensible suspect with a motive, opportunity, ability, and the experience to commit – and get away with – such unimaginable acts.

The growing evidence against L. C. was compelling in spite of his adamant denials of culpability. L. C. had befriended Mrs. Eggers, a special education teacher at Salisbury High, and they often ate lunch together, among others. One day during lunch, L. C. confided to her that Kay had been receiving anonymous threatening letters and phone calls, and moreover that he had been accused of doing it. L. C. maintained his innocence as he shared some of the details with his teacher friend.

"How could I have done it when I was *in bed* with her at the time?" L. C. exclaimed.

These conversations made Mrs. Eggers rather uncomfortable, but he seemed to have a persistent need to vent. Mrs. Eggers had learned one thing from talking with L.C: He never took responsibility for anything bad that happened to him; he always blamed someone else for his troubles.

A few weeks later, L. C. approached Mrs. Eggers again in the cafeteria. "Hey, I know someone at this high school turned me in for typing the threatening letters to Kay, and I think it was Pat Mains [another teacher]..."

Mrs. Eggers did not respond but sat there waiting.

"Well, I'm going to get whoever it was," he said.

L. C.'s comment was the closest thing to a confession he ever made regarding the anonymous threats that Kay received. Mrs. Eggers certainly took L. C.'s comments as a threat and tried to avoid him whenever she could. She did not know that L. C. had borrowed Mrs. Mains' typewriter shortly before Kay received the letters.

Meanwhile, L. C. called Anne Lyles, a teacher at Salisbury High School who was also a personal friend of Kay Weden's.

"Anne, do you know who turned in the typewriter ribbons from Salisbury High to the police?"

"No, L. C., I don't know anything about that," she told him.

"Well, I and Pat Mains had words," he said. "And now that b*tch don't like me... She's a smart*ss."

Anne did not comment.

"Well, will you see what you can find out about who turned in those ribbons to the police?" L. C. asked her.

"I'll see," she told him, tentatively. But Anne did not wish to be involved in that situation, and she silently resolved to stay out of it.

Unfortunately, she soon became part of the investigation because L. C. would not leave Anne alone. Months later, when I requested to speak with her, it was readily apparent that she was dreading the involvement in the case, but she consented out of loyalty to her friend Kay.

Anne confirmed what Kay had already told me, and also that she did recall other statements L. C. made to her at the school.

"What kinds of statements?" I asked.

"Inappropriate ones. Like... He called them "g*dd*mn n*gg*rs." He told me he asked one teacher if she had four or five black students he could use for target practice."

"He didn't!" I said, aghast.

"He most certainly did. And I don't care for that kind of talk. ...But I did get concerned about whoever did turn in those typewriter ribbons to the police. L. C. was determined to find out who it was."

"Anne," I began, "Do you know why L. C. was so obsessive about that typewriter ribbon?"

"Well, I knew that he borrowed the typewriter from Pat Mains," she answered.

"That's right. And analysts from the State Bureau of Investigation Crime Laboratory compared the ribbon from that typewriter with the anonymous letters that Kay received. One in particular was postmarked March 23, 1993."

"And what did they find?" Anne asked, anticipating the answer already.

"They were a positive match. L. C. typed the letters, Anne."

She nodded. "I was afraid of that."

On April 29, 1993, Chief Jacobs of the Salisbury Police Department suspended L. C. Underwood. Chief Jacobs informed L. C. that he was the subject of a criminal investigation involving threatening letters sent to Kay Weden. The letters constituted violations of the law and the Salisbury Police Department's Rules of Conduct. L. C. was informed that an administrative investigation would follow, and that L. C. would be suspended without pay until the investigation was completed or until further notice from the Chief.

Chief Jacobs had received his copy of the crime lab reports.

Shortly after L. C.'s suspension began, L. C. called up his old buddy Bob Ayala with the SBI, a fishing expedition in which he attempted to find out whatever he could about the ongoing investigation. That matter was not the first in which L. C. would attempt to use someone in the law enforcement profession to gain information to which he was not entitled.

L. C. told Bob he had been falsely accused of writing some letters that were sent to his girlfriend Kay. L. C. was crying when he said, "Bobby, I've been asked to take a polygraph test."

Bob advised him, "Well, since you're innocent, you should take the polygraph."

It was not what L. C. wanted to hear. "…Uh man, you know how those polygraphs are. And you know, I've been taking pain medication for my back, and I wouldn't want to get false results or something. I don't know yet what I will do."

Agent Bob Ayala recognized L. C.'s classic excuses for refusing to take a polygraph examination. The most common excuses for refusal are "I'm nervous" or "It will look like I'm lying when I'm not," or "I don't trust machines." Bob had heard them all before. So, have I.

The term *polygraph* literally means "many writings." The name comes from the recording of three physiological activities measured by one instrument. Respiratory activity is measured by the pneumograph, sweat gland activity by the galvanograph, and cardiovascular activity (blood pressure and pulse rate) by the cardiosphygmograph. Lies are detected by physiological changes that take place in the body. More than one type of physiological change usually occurs, such as increase or decrease in blood pressure and heart rate. Sometimes when a subject is being deceptive, the heart will even skip a beat. Changes in blood volume also occur, as well as an increase in sweat gland activity.

The exam consists of a pretest interview, the actual test and collection of charts, and the analysis of the polygraph charts. The typical test lasts from two to three hours. The longest part of the polygraph tests is the pretest interview. During the pretest, the examiner will cover each of the following:

- Detailed instructions for the test
- The subject's legal rights
- The polygraph equipment and how it works
- The crime or situation in question

- All questions to be asked during the actual polygraph test

All questions require a *yes* or *no* response. All questions are determined prior to the actual testing and discussed in detail with the subject. This process serves to clarify the relevant question to eliminate confusion or misunderstanding. In addition to the relevant questions, which specifically address the issue at hand, the examiner will also ask a number of control questions, such as "Is your last name Underwood?"

The actual test is completely painless. The examiner will begin by connecting all the necessary components of the instrument to the subject. This process consists of placing rubber tubes across the upper chest and abdomen of the subject, attaching two metal fingerplates across the ring and index finger of the subject, and wrapping a blood pressure cuff around the upper arm of the subject.

During the actual test, the examiner will ask each question three or four times, and should run a minimum of three to four separate charts before rendering an opinion as to the veracity of the subject tested. After the examiner conducts manual examinations of the charts, he or she may use a polygraph computer program to verify their findings. The computer program should not be used as a sole determination. If there is uncertainty, the examiner should seek the opinion of another certified examiner (Truth or Lie Polygraph Examination Agency, Glendora, California, 1999).

Polygraphs are not infallible. Polygraph errors can occur as a result of the examiner's failure to prepare properly the subject or by misreading the physiological data recorded on the polygraph device. Examiners do, however, use a variety of procedures to ensure an unbiased analysis and to identify those factors that might cause false responses (IQM Polygraph Services, Hurst, Texas, 1999). Assuming the polygraph machine is working properly – and tests are conducted for that purpose each time the instrument is used

– the accuracy of the test depends largely on the expertise and training of the examiner.

As professional as certified polygraph examiners may be, polygraph results are nevertheless inadmissible in court as evidence in North Carolina. The polygraph, however, is often used as an investigatory tool. Polygraphs are often used to eliminate possible suspects. For example, if a business has suffered embezzlement from a limited number of employees with access, investigators may request each employee to submit to a polygraph test for the purpose of elimination.

While the actual results of a polygraph test may not be tendered into evidence, the results can be used to confront a suspect or to prompt a guilty person into confessing. His or her statement can then be admitted into court, provided his or her constitutional rights were not violated in the process. Sometimes even the mere request that a subject take a polygraph test will prompt him or her into disclosing the truth.

L. C. was offered the opportunity on multiple occasions to clear his name and eliminate himself as a suspect in the anonymous letters Kay had received, which now totaled three. As he continued to make excuses for his refusal to his friend, SBI Agent Bob Ayala listened without comment.

L. C. told Bob that he had been dating Kay for a year or so, and that Kay and her son felt like they had full reign of his house just because he had "screwed her a few times."

"I thought you really liked that woman. ...By the way, you never told me whatever happened with your wife?" Bob asked. "Why did ya'll split up?"

"Oh. Well I caught her running around with this doctor. I went to the motel room where they were screwing. That b*stard doctor opened the door, and I had my gun right in his face!" L. C. laughed.

"Oh no!" Bob exclaimed. "What happened then?"

"I made that d*mn doctor leave the motel butt naked!"

"I'm sorry to hear that, L. C."

"Well thanks, but a man's got to get on with his life, ya know?" L. C. said without emotion.

"Yeah...I guess that's true," Bob responded.

"Say, you travel all over the state; do you know of any jobs in the Boone area? Any law enforcement positions I mean?" L. C. asked.

"I'm not aware of any."

"Do you have any contacts in Boone? I'd kind of like a job with Appalachian State University PD, or maybe in Blowing Rock. I'd need to go somewhere I could take a lateral transfer."

"I don't know, L. C.; that'd probably be kind of difficult, I think."

"Yeah, well, if you hear of anything up that way let me know."

"Sure thing," Bob said.

Agent Ayala was curious as to why L. C. was interested in taking a job in the mountains. He also knew it would be difficult for L. C. get a job anywhere in police work if he was not cleared as a suspect in the situation with Kay Weden.

"L. C., you really ought to think about taking that polygraph. What do you have to lose? Prove to 'em that you're not involved with that mess of Kay's."

"I'm taking pain medication for my back, and it could cause me to give a false reading or something. And those clowns are out to get me anyway. I don't even trust them."

"One of our agents could administer the test, one from somewhere else in the state, one that has never even heard of you."

"I don't know, Bobby, but I'll give it some thought," L. C. said, dismissively.

In a criminal matter, polygraphs must be voluntary. However, in an employment situation, for administrative purposes, an employee can be compelled to submit to a polygraph examination. Although the employee still may refuse, the employer is entitled to take action against the employee, including dismissal, for failing to comply with the directive to submit.

Chief Jacobs gave L. C. the directive. He would take the polygraph examination for administrative purposes or face disciplinary action up to and including termination. L. C., valuing his position, status, and authority as a police officer, was scheduled to take the test. He would take it at the Kannapolis Police Department.

Sgt. Joe Andrews of Kannapolis PD, a certified and experienced examiner who had never heard of Officer Underwood, was selected to administer the test. Prior to the examination, Sergeant Andrews was first shown the original anonymous threatening letters, numbered two, three, and four, which were delivered to Kay Weden. Capt. David Belk of the Salisbury Police Department briefed Sergeant Andrews on the investigation to that point.

L. C. Underwood arrived at Kannapolis PD at 9:00 a.m. on the fourth of May, 1993, accompanied by his attorney, who waited outside while Sergeant Andrews conducted the test.

The three relevant questions were:

1. Did you write or type letter number three?
2. Did you write or type, or assist in the writing or typing of letters number two or four?
3. Do you know for sure who wrote the typed letters number two, three or four?

Sergeant Andrews noted that L. C. was rather hostile during the questioning process and stated several times that he did not trust the "machine."

"L. C., have you read the three letters?"

"Yes I have.

"When?"

"When they were in Kay's possession." He added that on the previous Thursday, the SBI investigators had accused him of writing them.

"Did you know the typewriter ribbon from the high school where you work bears the same wording of letter number three?"

"Yes I was told that."

"Are you aware that a person at Salisbury High School is prepared to testify that you are the person who typed the letter?"

"Yes. …If I don't do well on this test, then I'm going to demand an independent test."

"That would be up to you, L. C."

"…and I don't care what your results are because I know I'm innocent. Kay knows it too. She's already trying to get me to come back to her."

L. C. was asked about his use of drugs or medication within the last eight hours. He replied that he had taken medication the day before, that Sergeant Andrews told him it was no problem, and that it was outside the eight-hour time frame.

"Well, I took a Valium and some Benadryl about 6:30 this morning," L. C. stated.

"Okay," Sergeant Andrews said.

The criteria for the numerical evaluation of the charts was plus three or greater indicating no deception, and minus six or greater indicating deception. Sergeant Andrews concluded that L. C. was *deceptive* in his denial of involvement in the writing of the three letters as he scored a *Minus 8*. He flunked the test considerably.

NC SBI Special Agent Mike Culnon was assigned to investigate the allegations against Master Patrolman L. C. Underwood. Agent Culnon is an easygoing guy with a relaxed personality and a reputation for honesty and diligence. He would never attempt to manipulate anyone, but when he told Kay the truth about L. C. and tried to explain the evidence against him, Kay simply could not believe it.

"In addition to the physical evidence, he also failed the polygraph examination," Agent Culnon told her.

"Well he told you he was taking medication, and his nerves have been on edge for some time now. L. C. said the test was inconclusive anyway," Kay said.

"The medication he said he was taking would not have affected the outcome. And ma'am, the test results were not inconclusive; he *failed*."

L. C. accused Agent Culnon of trying to railroad him, setting the test up so unfairly there was no way he could pass it, and that Agent Culnon was attempting to manipulate Kay. Nevertheless, the evidence was sufficient basis for suspending L. C. from Salisbury PD.

Kay exclaimed, "I don't care what you say, Agent Culnon, I know L. C. I know that he would not deliberately do anything to hurt me." L. C. capitalized on Kay's trust and pressured her to get him out of trouble. He played on Kay's uncertainty and her need for someone to keep her safe from whomever was terrorizing her during this awful period of her life.

"Kay, if you don't do something to help me, I'm going to lose the career I've worked for all these years. I will have *nothing*. You know what all I've been through…" L. C. heaped guilt upon Kay at every opportunity. She was emotionally drained; her strength was spent. L. C. hammered Kay in her weakest moments, making her believe that if he lost his career, not only would he be unable to help her in her times of need, it would be *her* fault.

Later Kay told me that not only was L. C. pressuring her to stop the investigation, his attorney David Bingham was also pressuring her to write a letter demanding that the investigation be stopped. Kay had never felt so stressed and overwhelmed in her life, and she relented.

On May 10, 1993, five days after the polygraph examination was conducted, Kay sent the following letter to Salisbury Police Chief Jeff Jacobs. She also mailed copies of the letter to District Attorney Bill Kennerly and to L. C.'s attorney.

Dear Mr. Jacobs,

This letter is submitted to you expressing several concerns that I have regarding your investigation of L. C. Underwood. After reviewing your letter dated April 29, 1993, to Mr. Underwood (notification of suspension), I am very concerned that my name was used, insinuating that I may have been the complainant regarding his suspension. Please let it be known that I did not have any intention of filing a complaint for any reason against Mr. Underwood. Mr. Underwood was then and is now a personal friend of mine, and it is my feeling that Mr. Underwood would never do such a thing to jeopardize his employment with your department or his friendship with me.

It is also my feeling that I was manipulated in my thinking of the entire situation by the SBI agent, Mike Culnon. By this I mean that Mr. Culnon's suggestions and half-truths of certain situations regarding Mr. Underwood caused me to doubt my faith in Mr. Underwood. I am truly embarrassed that I allowed myself to be manipulated in such a way as this.

I have discussed these concerns mentioned above in great detail with Mr. Bill Kennerly in his office last Wednesday.

Furthermore, I will not take part in any court action against Mr. Underwood, and I do not intend to discuss this situation anymore with you or with any of your associates.

Respectfully yours,

Kay Weden

In Kay's defense, she did not have the benefit of 20/20 hindsight. Her loved ones were all alive and well. L. C. was exerting all the pressure he could manage against her. She had relied on him as a confidante, a professional law enforcement resource, and an emotional support throughout the time that she and Jason were being targeted. I understood the difficulty and sense of loss she would have experienced by acknowledging how badly she may have misjudged L. C. It was easier for her to believe he would not do the things of which he had been accused.

While L. C. may have convinced Kay that he was innocent, the internal investigation into L. C.'s culpability continued. The evidence was presented to Chief Jacobs.

On June 7, 1993, Chief Jacobs delivered to L. C. Underwood, pursuant to Personnel Order 93-6, a memorandum describing the disciplinary action ordered against him. L. C. was to receive disciplinary action by being suspended from duty *without pay* for five days. He was to be reassigned to the Operations Division as a patrol officer, no longer assigned as a School Resource Officer to Salisbury High School. He was to undergo a psychological Fitness for Duty Evaluation. Finally, he was to be placed on administrative leave pending the results of the evaluation.

L. C. seethed.

CHAPTER SEVEN

"For, lo, the wicked bend their bow, they make ready their arrow upon the string, that they may privily shoot the upright in heart" (Psalms 11:2)

Despite Kay's defense of L. C., their relationship continued to deteriorate. By late summer, Kay was trying to end it. She still had feelings for L. C., but now they amounted to little more than sympathy. He did not treat Kay like she expected, yet when she talked about breaking up, L. C. would profess his undying love for her. Kay felt sorry for him – especially when he told her his mother Barbara had gotten cancer – but it was not enough to cause her feelings to change toward L. C. She was not getting what she needed out of the relationship.

On the other hand, Kay's mother, Catherine Miller, was able to view their relationship from a clearer perspective. She could see that L. C. was causing Kay unnecessary stress, and she also knew that L. C. was not the type of man her daughter needed as a husband. At seventy-seven years of age and still working full-time, she was well respected in her community and known for her sound values, her humility, and her wisdom. Catherine Miller was assuredly astute enough to realize that L. C. was not the type of husband *any* woman needed.

Catherine said as much to Kay on more than one occasion. Kay did not entirely disagree with her mother, but she could not quite free herself from L. C. either. Catherine ultimately and plainly told Kay she needed to get away from L. C. and stay away from him for good. Unfortunately for Catherine, L. C. knew that she was pressuring Kay to break up with him. This was particularly concerning due to L. C.'s issues with his own mother and his resentment of anyone who interfered with his personal relationships. His resentment toward Catherine mounted.

No matter what Kay said to L. C., he continued to call her. When school started back in August of 1993, Jason was playing on the high school soccer team. On one particular evening, L. C. called Kay and asked her to one of Jason's games, but she refused.

"I already have plans to meet some friends at the game, L. C.," she told him.

"Well d*mn it, Kay" he started. Kay hung up on him.

L. C. continued to call back, but she would not answer.

While she was in her bedroom getting ready for the game, L. C. called again, and when she didn't answer, he started talking to her answering machine. Kay froze when she heard L. C. say, "...Mikkel will not live through the night!" Mikkel, her exchange student, who was spending the school year with her and Jason, would be returning to Denmark in the spring. Kay recalled a comment L. C. had once made that he hated all foreign people, like he hated blacks. When she asked him why, he said that he would explain it to her "someday." He never did.

Kay did not return his call. L. C. continued to call Kay, and she avoided him as much as possible. One night during the fall, Kay came home about 11:30, after picking Jason up after a football game. It was raining and dreary. When she and Jason got home, Kay went directly to bed. The phone rang at 12:45 a.m., waking Kay.

"What time did you get home, Kay?" L. C. demanded.

Kay sighed. "About 11:30, L. C."

"Can I come over?" he asked.

"*Now?* No."

"Why not?" he whined.

"I'm wet, cold, and tired. We can talk tomorrow."

L. C. responded with gritted teeth. "You won't live till tomorrow." Click.

Kay got out of bed and locked all the doors and windows. She waited, afraid that L. C. would come and try to harm her or the boys. She had the phone in her hand, ready to call the police if she saw any sign of him. She sat in the chair at her dining room table holding the phone and her garage door opener until 2:00 a.m. when she finally decided he was not coming and went back to bed. But sleep would not come.

"Kay," I asked her at the Sheriff's Office, "Why did you not report his threats to the police *then*?"

"He *was* the police. I guess I didn't feel like they would take me seriously. It's un-telling what L. C. had told them or would tell them about me. I also didn't believe he would actually hurt me or Jason or Mikkel when it came down to it."

Kay shared with me that L. C.'s Watch Commander was her next-door neighbor. When she spoke with her neighbor about L. C., he simply would not believe the things she was saying.

"That's not the L. C. Underwood I know," he said. He simply refused to believe that L. C. would treat Kay in the manner she had described to him.

I continued to listen as she recounted how L. C. continued to pursue her, proclaiming his undying love for her, while behaving irrationally.

We learned of one of L. C.'s few friends at Salisbury High School, a Spanish teacher by the name of Anthony Atkins. Mr. Atkins – "Tony" – was single at the time, and he and L. C. had met and started chatting, becoming friends. One day Tony found L. C. in the book room at the end of a hall where teachers would go to smoke. He was surprised to find L. C. whimpering in the corner.

"Hey, what's wrong, L. C?" he asked.

L. C. responded, but he was crying so much that Tony could not understand all of what L. C. was saying. He understood enough to know that L. C. was upset about his relationship with Kay Weden. Tony talked to L. C. for several minutes, and after they smoked a couple of cigarettes, L. C. seemed to calm down. They went back to work. Tony never brought the subject up again to L. C., but he knew from L. C.'s comments that he still had his mind on Kay Weden.

Kay received the following letter from L. C., postmarked October 26, 1993.

Kay,

I know that I shouldn't be writing this letter because there is not much hope as the days pass that you have any intention of coming back to me. I told myself that I wouldn't ask or beg you for another chance, but I can't help myself. Kay, please if you ever had any love for me at all, give me one last chance to prove I do love and care about you. Maybe you can turn your love off for me that quickly but I can't stop my love for you. You asked me for a chance once and I gave that chance to you. I will agree to any terms that you say. I can't think of a greater punishment in my life than not having you to love and care for. There is no way I could ever love someone else as I do you. Please don't discard me like a piece of paper. If you would just give me the chance to show you I'll change for the good. We all make mistakes in life and I feel if we don't give this one last chance we are both making a big mistake, not knowing if we could make it in life together.

I want you to know my love for you is still very strong, and I can't help to think you still have some love for me left in your heart. Please try and find that love again for one last try. I would agree to any terms that you say to get back that strong love you had for me. When I say I would do anything I mean it. I honestly don't think you have any idea how true my love is for you. Again I would agree to any terms you want just please give me that chance. I know this all sounds silly to you, but if you ever loved me the way I love you then you will understand, and if you never loved me that strongly then it won't mean anything to you and I will never hear from you again.

Kay, Please at some point before all the love between us is gone let me hold you and touch you again. But if the love you might have had for me at one time in your heart is gone at least tell me in a letter or over the phone or in person that you don't want me and then I know that I have to let you go and try to get back to some kind of normal life.

Sometimes we don't have any control of who we love in our lives and how we feel about a person because you can't always control your heart. If you don't want me anymore at least extend a little kindness and have the courage to tell me in your own words. Not knowing how you feel now is the worst part of all. If you tell me you don't want me then at least I know where you stand. Telling me is the least you can do. I would do the same for you if it was the other way around.

If you could see the hurt in my heart and the pain I'll have to carry for a long time to come you would at least give me the privilege of telling me straight out you no longer want or care for me, then at least I could try and start the healing process and try to get on with my life.

If you never come back then I will have to deal with that, but you can know that for the rest of my life that no matter what happens to me in life I could never give my love and heart to anyone like I have you. Even if I meet someone else I want you to know that you were my first real love and my last.

If you want to make fun of me that's O.K. If you want to think this is silly for me to want you the way I do, that's alright too. If you want to talk about me and say mean things about me go ahead. You can call me stupid and dumb and say bad things about me to your friend. You can even hate me. But there is nothing you can never make me do or take away from me, that is my love for you.

Kay if I was to see you out I would just turn and go the other way. Because it would hurt to [sic] much to see you with someone else, knowing he might be holding you like I used to. The one thing I wish now is that I could make love to you one last time before you walk away for good.

Again, I will ask you to show me some mercy and kindness and grant me the only request I will ever ask of you. If you no longer want me at least have the courage to tell me you no longer love or want me than I will turn and walk away for good. At least I will know that no matter how bad I messed things up I can truly say that I had at one time in my life found a true love, and go on with the good thoughts of the good times we shared once and wish we could share again.

I want you to know that no matter what you decide I will always be there for you if you need me for anything. Even if you don't love me anymore I would be able to show you I still love and care for you. Tell your mother that I am sorry if I caused her any trouble or pain, and that the hate she might have for me now could never be as great as the pain and hurt and heartache that I will carry for the rest of my life. That is more punishment than anyone could ever place on me.

Love you forever,

L. C.

If I don't hear from you in a week or so then I will take that to mean there is no love left in your heart for me and I will try to go on the best I can in life.

Within a day or two of sending the letter, L. C. called a co-worker of his at home, Detective J.D. Barber, a narcotics officer with the Salisbury Police Department. It was about 11:00 p.m.

"J. D." L. C. began. "This is L. C."

"Yeah man, what's up?"

"Are you investigating me and Jason Weden for drugs?"

"Who the h*ll is Jason Weden?"

"I heard you were investigating me and Weden for drugs."

"I don't know what you're talking about, L. C."

Detective Barber thought L. C. sounded very strange. "…L. C., are you okay?"

"Yeah."

"Do you need someone to talk to?"

"No."

"Are you sure?"

"Yes."

"Well, I don't work drug cases anymore." L. C. hung up.

Kay continued to ignore L. C.'s proclamations of love and his pleas to take her back. She felt sorry for him, but she knew the relationship would go nowhere. Her mother,

Catherine, who had always given her sound advice in the past, urged Kay to cut all ties with L. C. and get him out of their lives for good.

L. C. could not accept the thought of losing Kay, however. Almost every day for two weeks in November of 1993, L. C. sat in the break room of the Police Department garage, smoking cigarettes and crying. Capt. David Belk approached him on several occasions to ask him that was wrong.

"My mother is dying of cancer... My brothers don't care about her; they won't even call her..."

L. C. was very angry with his so-called brothers, and even told Captain Belk that his mother had given one of his brothers some money when she really couldn't spare it, and now that she was sick, his brother had cut off all contact with her. Captain Belk tried to get L. C. to seek counseling for his obvious depression. He also encouraged L. C. to go to Ohio and visit his mother. L. C. agreed, but later told Captain Belk that he had to cancel his trip at the last minute because had left a few hundred dollars and his airplane ticket on his bed, and Misty, the dog that Kay gave L. C. for Christmas, had chewed up both the money and the flight ticket, preventing L. C. from being able to go to Ohio and visit his dying mother Barbara Childress. *That's a new version of "The dog ate my homework" excuse*, I thought. I wondered if Captain Belk thought the same.

After that conversation, a few days had passed when Captain Belk saw L. C. in the breakroom at the PD again. L. C. told him that he had been to Ohio the previous weekend and spent $5,000 paying off his mother's medical bills and making her house payments so she would not lose her home. Captain Belk did not know that L. C. was raised in an orphanage or that the woman in Ohio, Barbara Childress, was not L. C.'s mother. He did know that L. C. was experiencing significant emotional problems and needed help, despite the fact that Captain Belk was unaware that the real source of L. C.'s depression was his relationship – or lack thereof – with

Kay Weden. It was November, and Captain Belk worried that the approaching holidays would further depress L. C.

A few more days passed, and Chief Jacobs assigned Captain Belk to conduct an internal investigation into misconduct allegations against L. C. for stalking and threatening Kay Weden.

Trying to put L. C. off her mind, Kay subscribed to a reputable dating service and through that service met a nice man, David Sumner. At six foot three, one hundred and eighty-five pounds, with brown hair, blue eyes, and a neat mustache, Kay was impressed with both his looks and his nice, easygoing personality. When I located him several months later, I could see that Kay's description of David Sumner's appearance and personality was accurate.

Kay met David Sumner initially at a Cracker Barrel restaurant in Charlotte for a brief introductory meeting. They enjoyed some pleasant conversations, and decided to go on a "real" date. So, on Saturday, November 13, 1993, David Sumner drove from his home in Belmont to Kay's house in Westcliffe, arriving promptly at 7:00 p.m. After chatting for thirty minutes or so inside Kay's house, they went to Bogarts Restaurant in Salisbury. Kay offered to drive her car since David Sumner was not as familiar with the town. She parked in front of the restaurant, and they walked inside and were seated. They were enjoying a pleasant dinner when they looked up to see L. C. suddenly standing at their table.

L. C. looked at Kay's date and asked, "Are you –" David could not recall the name that L. C. asked him, but he said, "No."

L. C. then looked at Kay and started talking to her in a low tone of voice that David could not hear.

"At first I thought he was a friend of Kay's who was just saying hello, but Kay kept answering 'no,' 'no,' 'no,' and then she said to him 'Why don't you leave?' That got my attention," David told me.

About that time, L. C. looked straight at David and said, "I'll kill you boy!" David was understandably stunned, and L. C. continued, "See that guy over there?" L. C. pointed to a man standing near the door, leaning on the door post. "We have more friends outside, and we're gonna take you out and stomp your *ss!" L. C. turned back to Kay without waiting for David to respond.

Without warning, L. C. picked up Kay's full glass of iced tea and turned it upside down, dumping it in her lap. He wheeled around then and walked out of the restaurant, behind the man who had been standing by the door. The restaurant manager rushed over and asked Kay if she was all right and what happened. She told him, and he called the police.

Kay, mortified, sat at the table trying unsuccessfully to soak the tea from her pants when she looked up to see L. C.'s friend walk back through the front door.

"Kay, I think you ought to come outside," L. C.'s friend told her.

"No way," she said, "Who are you anyway?"

He said something to her about going to the same high school as she did years ago.

The manager walked back to the table and told the man to leave. The man then took a badge of some kind out of his shirt pocket and flashed it toward the manager. The manager stepped toward the man to get a better look at the badge, but the man quickly put it back in his pocket.

"I've called the police," the manager told him.

Within a few minutes, two Salisbury police officers arrived. Kay and David walked outside to meet them and explain what happened. Then David and Kay got back into her car, and drove out of the parking lot. On the way back to her house Kay told David about L. C. and how he had been stalking her. As they neared her house, Kay saw a car on the shoulder of the road and said, "That's the guy from the restaurant!" She started driving toward him.

"Wait!" David said, "What are you doing? That guy's a cop and he probably has a gun!"

"Okay, okay, I'll keep going," she said, her heart racing.

Kay drove around her neighborhood, but saw that the car was following her. She picked up her mobile phone and called the Sheriff's Department as she was within their jurisdiction then. A deputy came and escorted them to Kay's house. David checked his 1987 Nissan pickup truck still sitting in her driveway to make sure that it had not been vandalized.

"You can go inside now," the deputy said to David. "Everything should be okay now." But David was understandably reluctant. Kay, attempting to save what was left of the date, persuaded him to go inside and meet Jason and some of Jason's friends. He did so, but left after just a few minutes. He never called Kay again. She was disappointed but could not blame him.

Earlier that evening, L. C. had phoned an old friend of his, Danny Hillard. Danny had been in the military for ten years. He met L. C. in the National Guard. Danny, tall and well built, and ruggedly handsome, was somewhat rough and intimidating. Danny's brother Rick was a Salisbury Police Officer.

Occasionally Danny and L. C. would go out for drinks. After L. C. and Marcia divorced, Danny and L. C. hung out more frequently. Danny also was recently divorced. In September 1993, L. C. and Danny began frequenting Twister's Shag Club in Cornelius on the weekends. Danny knew that L. C. had a girlfriend named Kay. L. C. talked to Danny about her a lot, although she never went out with them. L. C. told Danny about checking up on Kay.

"That's stalking, man," Danny said to L. C., but L. C. ignored Danny's admonition. When L. C. and Danny went out together, L. C. made a point to drive by Kay's house.

Danny later told me, "L. C. had a one-track mind, and it was all about Kay Weden… But to be honest, he seemed more upset that she was breaking up with him than that he was hurt because he was losing her. It was more like a matter of his pride than his heart, ya know what I mean?" I did.

Danny also told me about an incident that occurred when he was visiting L. C.

"He was on the phone when I got to his house, talking to Kay. He kept asking her, 'Why are you doing this?'"

L. C. was upset. "He called her all the time," Danny said, "but he'd also have me call her. ...Like he'd call and ask me to call and try to talk to Kay about their relationship, but he would redial my phone to make sure I was really calling her. Then he'd turn right around and call Kay's number to see if her phone was busy. I couldn't believe how he was acting over her."

Danny also recalled Misty, the sweet Shetland Sheepdog that Kay had bought for L. C. Danny was at L. C.'s house on one particular occasion, and L. C. was angry at Kay about something. L. C. walked by the cage where Misty was sleeping inside and kicked the cage hard, frightening Misty.

"I told him that dog hadn't done anything to him, and there wasn't no need for him to be mean to that dog. But L. C. said the dog reminded him of Kay. He was over the top, acting that way. There was no need for him to be taking anything out on that sweet little dog."

Danny said he and L. C. usually went to dinner somewhere before they drove to Twister's. But they could hardly stop anywhere without driving all over Salisbury to look for Kay. "One minute he'd say that he wanted Kay to see him, and the next he'd say he did not want her to see him."

L. C. constantly complained to Danny about Kay. He would cry and ask, "Why does she do that to me? Why does she go out with someone else?" Danny reminded L. C. that they were not married and that Kay was free to do whatever she wanted. Again L. C. completely ignored Danny when he gave him sound advice.

"There were some occasions," Danny continued, "when L. C. and I would drive from Salisbury to Cornelius like usual, and it was nearly an hour's drive, and we'd get there around 9:00, but before 10:00 L. C. would say he wanted to go home. I'd get so frustrated. He would work himself up emotionally so much that he couldn't dance or even talk. He'd say he *had* to talk to Kay. Right then. He'd cry and beat his fists on the steering wheel of the car. Of course, we always had to drive by Kay's house. If she was home, L. C. would relax somewhat. But if she was gone, he'd keep saying 'Why does she do that to me?' He was a broken record. I thought he was about to snap. Maybe he *had* snapped. It wasn't long before I decided I wasn't gonna go out anywhere with L. C. My brother Rick told me he thought it would be good for L. C. if I was a friend to him because he was so sad and all after his divorce, and I agreed, but after I saw how L. C. acted, and how he was over his girlfriend Kay, I told Rick I wasn't gonna hang out with L. C. anymore."

"Did you see him much after Catherine Miller was murdered?" I asked.

"I remember one day, sometime after that Swedish man's body was found in the mountains. I was at my parents' house. Rick was there with L. C., and they were talking to my dad. They were talking about how L. C. was getting questioned about the case and so forth. And L. C. said to my dad, 'Hey I got a dead body in the trunk of my car right now, you wanna come look?' He was laughing, and I just thought that man's cornbread is not done in the middle. He is not right. Something is wrong with him mentally."

"Do you remember exactly when that was?" I asked.

"I just remember that it was after they found that body in the mountains, and it would have been before my dad died. He died of cancer in '95. I'm guessing sometime in the first part of 1994 maybe."

"What else do you remember about L. C. when you were with him?" I asked.

Danny saw other indications that L. C. was mentally unstable. He called L. C. a "neat freak."

"In what ways?" I asked Danny.

"Well, L. C. would stand up and then have to fix the wrinkles in his chair upholstery. He would sit *forever* trying to fix his hair. His car – oh his car was so clean you could eat off the motor."

"Can you tell me what happened on November 13, 1993?" I asked.

"L. C. called and asked me to go get something to eat with him. I drove to L. C.'s house to meet him, like I usually did. We got into L. C.'s Monte Carlo, and L. C. drove to every restaurant in town before he finally saw Kay's car in front of Bogarts."

"Let's eat!" L. C. told Danny suddenly. Danny was relieved L. C. had finally chosen a place. Then before they got inside, L. C. said, "We might not stay and eat after all." L. C. then instructed Danny to stand just inside the door of the restaurant.

Kay was sitting at a table to the left against a wall. She was sitting with a man Danny didn't know. Danny watched as L. C. walked over to Kay, leaned down and said something to her. The guy she was with backed away from the table. Danny said he had no idea what L. C. was saying, but the next thing he knew he heard ice hitting the floor. L. C. wheeled around and walked out of the restaurant. Danny turned to the hostess standing nearby and said, "I think that's my cue to leave."

Danny followed L. C. out to his car. It was about 8:00 p.m. L. C. got into his car and started pounding his fists against the steering wheel, crying and screaming.

"I'm not gonna let that b*tch leave with $1,800 worth of my gold!" L. C. said to Danny. Danny knew that L. C. had bought Kay some gold jewelry. Danny did not know how to get L. C. to calm down.

"L. C., I've got to call and check on my kids. I'll be right back." Then Danny walked to a pay phone outside the restaurant. He called Bogarts and asked them to put Kay on the phone. In a moment, she answered.

"Kay, this is Danny Hillard. Let me come in and talk with you a minute."

Danny walked inside and was met by the manager. Danny realized then that L. C. was going to be in trouble. Danny tried to talk peacefully with Kay, saying things like, "Didn't we go to school together?" but the manager stood there listening and waiting. Then the manager asked Danny for some identification. Danny said he had an ID card in his shirt pocket, and the manager reached for it. Danny said he put it back and walked outside when the manager told him he was calling the police.

"Go ahead," Danny told him. But Danny walked outside and got back into L. C.'s car. "They're calling the police. Let's go home," he told L. C.

"No, I'm gonna wait and deck that boy! I'll bust him into the concrete!" L. C. shouted.

"Don't do that, L. C. You and Kay are not married. You're not even engaged," Danny tried to reason with him.

"She's gonna cause me to lose my job!" L. C. said.

"So, let's go! The police are gonna see your car, man!"

L. C. backed the car out and tried to hide behind some other cars in the parking lot. They watched the Salisbury police officers arrive. The officers escorted Kay and her date to her car. L. C. pulled out and followed Kay and her date to her house. A small pickup truck was backed into Kay's drive.

Danny told me, "L. C. was mad he couldn't see the tag number – he always wanted to run the tag numbers of any vehicle he didn't know that was parked at Kay's house – but then Kay spotted L. C.'s car and drove by her house without stopping."

"Let's go!" L. C. said. He started following Kay and her date.

"L. C., if you don't turn around, I'm going to drive." L. C. turned around and drove back to his house.

Danny told me, "L. C. was absolutely beside himself that she was out with another man. I don't think he'd ever actually seen her with someone else. But all of a sudden, he wanted to be alone, and I was glad to oblige him. I'd had enough of his drama. Then right before I left, L. C. told me if the police ask about the iced tea, just tell 'em it dropped accidentally. I didn't even answer him. I got in my vehicle and drove home."

Danny didn't know that as soon as he left L. C.'s house, L. C. started calling Kay. Not getting a response, L. C. called Anne Lyles, Kay's friend who taught at Salisbury High. He had barely spoken to her since he asked her back in the spring to find out who turned the typewriter ribbons over to the police. Anne was surprised when L. C. called.

"Anne, I've been trying to reach Kay, but I can't get in touch with her."

"Oh?" she said.

"Anne, I really need you to call Kay for me," he begged.

"Why do you want me to call her?" she asked L. C.

L. C. told her what happened at Bogarts and said he was sorry and desperately needed to apologize to Kay. Anne thought he certainly sounded desperate.

"Okay, L. C., I'll try to reach her," she promised.

It took Anne forty-five minutes to get in touch with Kay. During those forty-five minutes L. C. repeatedly called Anne to see if she had gotten through to Kay.

When Kay finally answered her phone, Anne told her she was calling at L. C.'s request. Kay told Anne what happened in detail, and that her date David was still there with her. Kay told Anne she did not want to talk to L. C.

Anne had barely hung up from talking with Kay when L. C. called Anne again.

"I talked to Kay, and I think it's best if you don't talk to her tonight... You really should leave things alone, L. C.," she advised him.

"Was she mad?" L. C. asked.

"She's not very happy about what happened," Anne said, tactfully.

"The iced tea thing was an accident, Anne. I don't know the man Kay was with, and I hope I never see him again. Now how long has she been dating him anyway?"

"...I think this was the first time they went out," she told him.

"No, I don't think so... I've seen his truck at Kay's house before," he lied.

"No, L. C., she told me it was the first time he's been there."

L. C. continued to argue about seeing the man's truck. Finally, he said, "I know who he is, Anne. I know where he lives, and where I could get him if I have to." The desperation Anne heard in his voice along with his actual comments frightened her. *Where he could go get him? Who thinks like that?* Anne asked herself.

"That's ridiculous, L. C.," Anne said. "Kay saw him just this one time... and besides, he has nothing to do with your problems with Kay. That man is just an innocent party."

L. C. made a kind of snorting sound. "No, he's not, Anne. He's been around before." L. C. would not be convinced. "I really love Kay, Anne, and I'm sorry this had to happen. I didn't mean for it to happen..."

Shortly after 8:00 the next morning Kay's mother called Anne. Catherine Miller told Anne that Kay asked her to call and tell Anne that there had been yet another incident with L. C. while Kay was driving to school that morning. Anne became immediately concerned.

"Kay had a run-in with L. C. this morning at the Quality Mart."

Catherine told Anne that Kay had stopped for coffee, and that L. C. pulled into the Quality Mart right behind her. When Kay got out of her car, she saw L. C. But before she could get back into her car, L. C. pushed her car door shut on her, wedging her to the point that she could not get back into her car. Catherine said that L. C. had grabbed and jerked the gold necklace off of Kay's neck and took it. Catherine was understandably upset, and Anne's concern for her friend was rapidly increasing.

"She has to do something about that man before something terrible happens," Catherine said to Anne.

L. C. called Anne several more times the next day. Although he kept venting to Anne about Kay's date, trying to elicit information about him, he never once mentioned the incident at the Quality Mart, and Anne was afraid to mention it. She would get the details from Kay later.

Early that Saturday morning, Kay was on her way to the high school to help with a drama production. As she pulled out of her neighborhood, Kay noticed L. C. parked in his Monte Carlo behind a small store at the intersection. When Kay pulled into the Quality Mart, she walked into the store for batteries and coffee. He followed Kay inside. Kay pulled out her checkbook and planned to write a note to the clerk on the check that said, "Help Me," but L. C. was standing so close behind her at the counter that she could not. She was so nervous she could barely write the check. L. C. watched her write the check; he watched every word she wrote. She paid for her items and walked outside to her car. When she opened the door and started to step inside the car, she was shoved hard. L. C. had pinned her in the open car door. She was not able to get back into her car. L. C. grabbed at her neck, and for a second she thought he was going to choke her to death. But he grabbed at the necklace Kay was wearing, and when he got his fingers around it, he ripped it off with a violent jerk.

"I bought you that necklace!" L. C. yelled at her.

"Oh my God, L. C.! I'm going to call the police!" she threatened.

"You ain't gonna do *sh*t!*" he responded in a high-pitched voice. L. C. then left with the necklace, and trembling, Kay sat down in the driver's seat, locked the door, and then quickly drove to the school. Kay went directly inside and called her mother. She told Catherine very briefly what happened and asked her to call the police for her.

By the time Kay had arrived at the school, the students were all waiting for her, as they were expected at Pfeifer College, half an hour away, for a drama competition. Kay struggled all day to work with the students, as she was required to do, because she was so horrified by what had happened that morning. At the end of the competition, Kay and a few students riding with her, walked back to her car and found a note on her windshield. It was a white envelope with a three-page handwritten letter on yellow legal paper. In the letter, L. C. told her he loved her and could not live without her, and then he ranted on and on. But it was not the letter that troubled Kay so very much; it was the fact that he had followed her to Pfeifer College.

Kay called the Sheriff's Department as soon as she got home. Deputy Tommy Swing arranged to come to Kay's house the following morning, Sunday, to take yet another police report. Around 6:30 that Saturday evening, Kay called Anne. She told her that L. C. had left a note on her car's windshield that day.

"I don't know what to do, Anne. He just won't take no for an answer! Why can't he just leave me alone?!" Kay was quite upset.

"All I know for you to do is get away from him, as far as possible, and *stay* away from him."

"I'm going to the magistrate tomorrow," Kay told her. "Mother is going with me, and I'm going to try to get a warrant or a restraining order – or both – to keep him away from me."

"Okay, Good luck," Anne told her. "Let me know what happens." Anne hung up the phone, but a few minutes later it rang again. She answered it quickly, thinking it was Kay calling back.

"Have you talked to Kay again?" L. C. asked her, urgently.

"…Yes, I have. But she is still very upset over the situation, and she does not want to talk with you right now. She wants the two of you to go your own separate ways, L. C." Anne tried to tell him firmly.

"I, I can't do that, Anne, because I *love* her too much to forget about her or leave her. I'm sorry about what happened. …I just wish Kay would talk to me."

"L. C., I'm really sorry, but I have to go or I'll be late for the concert at the high school." L. C. reluctantly hung up.

He called Anne again about 9:30 p.m., shortly after she returned home from the concert.

"Have you talked to Kay anymore?" L. C. asked her. "I just need to talk to her, Anne."

Anne was trying not to voice her impatience. "L. C., I told you that you would be better off if you did not try to talk to her right now."

Ignoring her advice, L. C. said, "I know she's really mad at me. That is why I want to talk to her. The thing that worries me most is that I'm afraid she's going to try and get my job."

"No, she's not going to do that," Anne tried to assure him.

"I know she *is*," he insisted.

"Look… All Kay wants is to be left alone. She needs some time by herself, L. C."

Again L. C. explained, "I can't do that. I love her so much that when I walked into Bogarts last night and saw her with another man, it, it just upset me…"

Anne finally got off the phone with L. C. Trying to talk to him was mentally exhausting. But he called again at 11:00 p.m. L. C. kept repeating the same things he had said earlier about loving Kay and his fear that she would try to take his job. Anne continued to assure him that Kay was not interested in causing him to lose his job as a police officer and that Kay was not a vindictive person. But he would be neither convinced nor consoled.

"She *lied* to me, Anne," L. C. whined. "She lied to me when she said that she loved me."

"She didn't lie to you," Anne said gently but firmly, "She was very happy, and I believe she *was* in love with you at one point. She did want things to work out."

"No, Anne, the weekend before last when we went to my house, after we went out to dinner, we made love. We made love, Anne, and Kay told me that she loved me. How could she *do* that, Anne? How could she make love to me and tell me she loves me and, and, and then be out with someone else less than a week later?"

"I don't know, L. C.; I can't explain that." Anne was getting tired of trying to explain anything to L. C. He could not be reasoned with.

The next morning Kay called her mother at 11:00 a.m.

"Deputy Swing will be here in a few minutes," Kay told Catherine.

"All right, dear. I'm coming over."

Catherine Miller drove the short distance to her daughter's house. Moments later Deputy Swing arrived. Deputy Swing suggested that Kay call the magistrate and make an appointment to talk with him about L. C. As she always did in times of crisis, Kay talked it over with her mother. Her mother was afraid for Kay, and knew something had to be done about L. C. before something worse happens. Action must be taken and soon.

"It's time to get a restraining order," Catherine told Kay. "You can't go on, living in fear of him like this, with him coming and going, terrorizing you as he pleases, with no repercussions." Kay knew that her mother was afraid for them both.

"He thinks he's above the law, that he *is* the law," Kay replied.

"Well, he may think it, but he isn't. The law applies to everyone," Catherine said firmly.

So, the decision was made. Catherine and Kay drove to the Rowan County Magistrate's Office. But Kay and her mother learned that the law did *not* apply to everyone. She needed protection for which the law did not allow.

Domestic violence was not a new phenomenon. Historically, it even seemed to be condoned. In the sixteenth century, English Common Law allowed husbands to beat their wives for "correctional purposes," and thus early American settlers brought this mindset with them. States, including North Carolina, enacting their own laws mitigated this notion only slightly when they allowed a man to whip his wife with a stick "no bigger than his thumb." My search of Common Law in the reverse yielded nothing; therefore, I am left with the assumption that the stick with which a wife could use to beat her husband senseless had no maximum diameter standard. I could be wrong.

Nevertheless, it took three hundred years later for Mississippi to limit the "right" of a man to administer physical "moderate chastisement only in case of emergencies." I have no doubt as to which gender defined such "emergencies." In 1886, North Carolina courts declared that a criminal battering charge could not be brought against a married man unless the battery is *so* great that permanent injury resulted, life was endangered, or was "malicious beyond all reasonable bounds." 1

As late as the 1970s, while domestic violence was generally accepted as a private problem to be addressed within the home or the family, a greater understanding of the problem and an accompanying solution was sought. Law enforcement officers were asked to transition from the traditional procedures of separating batterer and victim to bringing them together to attempt to mediate. The result of that training on real life calls was "often sporadic, discretionary decisions that were sometimes influenced by frustrating experiences with repetitive calls (at the same residences), dropped charges, and uncooperative victims." 2

Practically speaking, domestic assaults were still not recognized as criminal conduct, which perception undoubtedly contributed to L. C. Underwood's ability to remain in full-time law enforcement and avoid serious consequences for his prior history of domestic violence against women. Throughout this same "ME" decade of 1970s, victims and advocates began to exert public pressure on legislative bodies to recognize domestic violence as the criminal behavior that it is. Further, studies proving the effectiveness of the arrest of the offenders in domestic violence cases were convincingly presented to legislators.

In response to the pressure, North Carolina, along with other states enacting similar laws, introduced legislation and expanded the current legislation pertaining to domestic violence assaults. In 1979 the North Carolina Legislature enacted "Domestic Violence," its own specific law, General Statute 50-B, expanding the authority of law enforcement officers in these cases as well as providing additional protection to victims through civil emergency relief, including restraining orders.

Kay introduced herself and Catherine Miller to the magistrate on duty.

"What can I help you with, ma'am?" he said.

Kay shared with him all that L. C. had put her through, including the most recent incident at the Quality Mart.

"I am sorry to hear that, Ms. Weden," Kay recalled the magistrate's reaction to her statement.

"This is why I need a restraining order," Kay told him.

"Ma'am, were you cohabitating with Officer Underwood?" he asked. "Living together for any period of time?"

"No, I have a teenage son who lives with me in my house. L. C. owns his own home on Lake Drive. But L. C. and I were *engaged,* engaged to be *married.*"

"I'm sorry, Ms. Weden, but that doesn't count. It does not fall under the relief requirements."

"Well, what am I supposed to do?" Kay asked. "He's stalking me! I know he followed me to the Quality Mart, and he just shows up wherever I am!"

"He is making her life miserable!" Catherine interjected.

"Well, since he's a police officer…" Kay recalled that the magistrate pointed out that her taking legal action of any kind against L. C. could possibly provoke him into doing something worse than the things he had done already. Kay recalled that the magistrate kept referring to the fact that L. C. was a police officer, and that having him arrested could really make things more difficult for Kay; it could make him angrier, more violent. Furthermore, he said that if he were to be arrested on an assault warrant, L. C. could lose his job. Kay and Catherine discussed their shared impression that the magistrate did not want to be the one to issue an arrest warrant against a police officer, or maybe it was just L. C. specifically that he feared. Kay and her mother left the magistrate's office with shared feelings of helplessness and frustration.

"I don't know what to do now. But maybe he's right," Kay said to Catherine. "All I want is for L. C. to leave me alone. I'm tired of him stalking me, and I'm tired of being afraid of him! I wish he would just leave me alone!"

Seeing her daughter so upset pained Catherine. "Kay, you just need to go and meet with the Police Chief. Surely, he can do something about L. C. because L. C.'s actions can reflect negatively on the entire police department."

Catherine accompanied Kay to the office of Chief Jacobs at the Salisbury Police Department.

When Kay told me much later, I tried to remain objective as she described how the meeting went. "I told the Salisbury Police Chief everything that L. C. had done to me – the stalking, the assault, everything…"

"And what did he say to all that?" I asked.

"He said – and I quote – 'I'm sorry to hear that,' or 'I hate to hear that.' ...And that was it."

"What do you mean 'That was it'?" I asked. "Did he say what he was going to do about it?"

"He didn't say he was going to do *any*thing about it," Kay told me. "I was stunned."

"He didn't say that he would confront him about it? About any of it? At all?" I asked Kay.

"No, he did not."

"Kay, L. C. should have been criminally charged. Stalking was made a crime in 1990; he was guilty of stalking. He committed an assault against you in the Quality Mart – actually twice – by pinning you in the car door and then by jerking and breaking the necklace off your neck. And incidentally, because the necklace was a gift to you, it did not belong to him. That also makes that a robbery from your person, which is a very serious felony. I could go on," I told her.

"Well nothing was done at that time. I felt victimized again, this time by the system itself. What would you have done as the Chief?" Kay asked me.

"Before or after I fired him?" I responded. "...At the very least, an internal affairs investigation should have been initiated – ideally by an outside agency such as the SBI. L. C. would have been suspended until the investigation was concluded. But he also should have been investigated criminally for the offenses I just mentioned. Incidentally, did Chief Jacobs have you complete a report or provide a signed statement, or in any manner document what you reported to him?"

"No. ...You know, Detective May, people tend to think something is wrong with me that I didn't see all this coming with L. C., and when they do, I try to explain that I *did* see the red flags – maybe not at the very beginning, but certainly as our relationship progressed. I *did* report him. I did try to get help. But no one was interested in protecting me. No one was interested in doing anything about L. C." I saw on her face the depth of her desperation even then.

I shook my head sadly. "Those things should never have happened to you, Kay. L. C. should have had a thorough background investigation completed on him before he was hired by the various agencies, and the background investigators should have found documentation in the files of L. C.'s other problems, his history of violence with his prior wives and girlfriends. He never should have even made it as an officer to Salisbury PD. That is why documentation in the personnel file of an officer is so critical today. Yours is a prime example…"

"Well, I was terrified out of my mind, and L. C.'s behavior was getting worse. I tried to get assistance, but I could not get any."

"So, what did your mother say about the meeting with the magistrate and the police chief?" I asked Kay.

"Oh, she was as frustrated as I was…"

"…You need to be really careful, Kay," Catherine cautioned.

"I know, Mom."

"Since he's a cop, he'll cover his tracks. It could just be your word against his," Catherine added.

"Right. Probably I should at least record his calls," Kay commented.

"That's a good idea," Catherine agreed. "And make sure you call Anne. She was really worried about you when we spoke."

"I will; L. C.'s been calling her."

"Why is he calling Anne?" Catherine asked.

"Trying to get her to talk to me on his behalf."

"My word," Catherine exclaimed, "that man just won't stop."

At 2:00 p.m. that day, L. C. called Kay's friend Anne again. Then he called her again at 6:00 p.m. He continued to repeat everything he had said before and asked Anne the same questions about Kay. He was still worried about Kay taking his job, and he asked Anne to try and talk Kay into not causing him to lose his job.

"I have done so much for her, Anne!" he wailed. "I've given her money and jewelry, and I just don't know why she can't tell me the truth. She told me she loved me, Anne!"

Anne listened but had no idea what to say to get through to L. C.

"And you know what? Her mother has done a lot for Kay too!"

Sighing, Anne said, "L. C., I don't know what else I can do for you." He finally hung up. Anne dialed Kay's number.

Anne told her about all the calls she had received from L. C. and everything he had said. Kay confided to Anne that a couple of weeks earlier, out of sympathy, she had gone to dinner with L. C., and then when they returned to his house, he insensitively pushed her down onto the bed.

"We had very quick and unemotional sex... L. C. kept trying to make me say 'I love you,' but I just couldn't. There was no way I could say that I loved him."

CHAPTER EIGHT

"He sitteth in the lurking places of the villages: in the secret places doth he murder the innocent" (Psalms 10:8)

During the all-too-brief periods when L. C. seemed to keep his distance, Kay enjoyed a quiet life. She enjoyed spending her free time at home with her son, Jason, and their Danish exchange student, Mikkel.

Mikkel did speak English, but Kay wanted to make Mikkel feel as comfortable as possible in her home. One of Kay's girlfriends, Tana Howe, suggested that Kay, Jason, and Mikkel meet a Swedish friend of hers.

"Did you know that Danish, Swedish, and Norwegian people are all really similar, I mean as far as their languages, and that they can generally understand each other? So, my friend and Mikkel should be able to communicate in their own languages."

"Sure, why not?" Kay told her. "I think Mikkel would definitely appreciate that."

So, on Black Friday, November 26, 1993, Tana Howe introduced Kay to a very handsome, charming, and single forty-year-old Viktor Gunnarsson from Sweden. They met at Rascal's, a popular night club in Salisbury. Kay did not think Viktor looked Swedish at all. She had mentally pictured a blond, blue-eyed, pale-skinned man. Tana's friend was just under six feet tall, 190 pounds, muscular, dark-skinned, dark-haired, with the brightest blue eyes Kay had ever seen.

His teeth were very straight and very white, and he was all gentleman. Kay was attracted to Viktor immediately, and the feeling was apparently mutual. Kay felt his warm gaze on her, and the smile that lit up his face seemed only for her.

The two of them quickly became friends; I learned much later that Viktor quickly became friends with many, many people.

Kay was impressed with Viktor. He was intelligent, pleasant, and a very interesting conversationalist. She was understandably reluctant to get involved with a man romantically, but was grateful for the distraction from L. C. and could not deny the natural attraction between Viktor and herself. Kay saw Viktor again on Monday, November 29, when Kay, Jason, Mikkel, Viktor, and Viktor's friend Daniel Johansson went together to Jason's soccer awards assembly. After the awards assembly, the five of them went to Christo's Restaurant in Salisbury for dinner. They laughed together over dinner and thoroughly enjoyed each other's company. Kay avoided L. C.'s calls and pushed all thoughts of L. C. to the back of her mind.

On Wednesday, December 1, Viktor offered to come to Kay's house and cook spaghetti for her, Jason, and Mikkel. Kay quickly accepted. Viktor was an excellent chef. He had brought spaghetti sauce that he had prepared from scratch at his apartment. At that point, Viktor's and Kay's relationship was casual and platonic. But Viktor and Kay spent every evening that first week together, growing closer as the mutual attraction intensified. Kay did not stop to wonder about the fact that L. C. had not called her in four or five days. She had not received any more anonymous letters or phone calls, nor had she experienced any new vandalism. Things were looking up.

On Thursday, December 2, Kay and Mikkel picked Jason up at the Blue Bay Seafood Restaurant where Jason worked part-time. The three of them went to the Blues Café in Salisbury to return an address book to Daniel, which he had left at Kay's house on Monday. Daniel spent many evenings hanging out inside the Blues Café, a popular club located only a mile or so from Viktor's apartment.

When Kay arrived at the Blues Café, she spotted Viktor's car, a large gray Lincoln Town Car, parked outside. Inside the restaurant, she saw Viktor and Daniel sitting at a table with two attractive blond-headed women. Kay did not know the women, but she did notice that one of them seemed to be flirting with Viktor. When Viktor saw Kay, he smiled and pulled up a chair beside him at the table. But when Kay walked over to him, he pulled Kay down on his knee.

She talked with Viktor for a few moments, and then one of the blondes leaned over to Viktor and asked him, "Why haven't I heard from you?"

Feeling the awkward tension, Viktor responded vaguely, "Well, I haven't been home much lately."

Viktor then turned back to Kay and asked, "Would you like to drop by my apartment for a while?"

"Sure," Kay responded, as the two blondes stood up and walked away. Viktor drove to his apartment in his Lincoln, and Kay followed him in her car. It was almost 11:00 p.m.

Inside the plain two-bedroom apartment, Kay sat beside Viktor on the couch relaxing and listening to some pretty, romantic foreign music that Viktor selected. At 11:30, she told Viktor she had to go home and get some sleep because the next day she had to teach, and Viktor had to get up early to drive his friend Daniel Johansson to the airport. Daniel was returning to Sweden after visiting Viktor for the past six weeks. Viktor sweetly kissed Kay goodnight, and she drove home, smiling at the new memory.

Early Friday morning, December 3, 1993, Viktor got out of bed as planned and drove Daniel to the Charlotte-Douglas Airport, about an hour away. Daniel encouraged Viktor to return to Sweden with him to spend the Christmas holidays. But Viktor declined Daniel's invitation, stating that he had decided to stay in the United States.

"It is because of Kay Weden, right?" Daniel asked, grinning.

"Yes," Viktor said. "I plan to get together with her tonight. But I also have to stay because I have a few more things to take care of as far as getting more settled in this country."

So, Daniel returned to Sweden alone. His flight did not depart Charlotte until 9:00 a.m., but Viktor left the airport at 8:20. He drove directly back to his Lakeview apartment in Salisbury.

About 3:30 p.m., Viktor, still in his apartment, called Kay. She had just returned home from teaching school and was taking a nap. Viktor apologized for waking her, and Kay promised to return his call after her nap.

Kay called her mother first, however.

"Hello, Mother."

"Hello, dear."

"How was your day?"

"It was fine. I'm glad it's Friday, though. How was your day?"

"It was good. But the kids are all getting ready for Christmas break, and it's difficult to hold their attention in class."

Catherine laughed. "Well, you can't really blame them."

"I guess not," Kay agreed. "Would you like to go out for dinner tonight?"

"That sounds good. I don't have anything cooked, and I haven't bought groceries this week."

"All right. ...Um, do you mind if I invite Viktor? You know, Tana's friend from Sweden?"

"No, I don't mind. I'd like to meet him as well," her mother said.

"All right, then. I'll give him a call, and you can pick me up about 6:15. Is that okay?"

"Yes. I'll see you then." Catherine was undoubtedly relieved to hear that Kay was interested in a man other than L. C. Underwood.

Kay called Viktor then, and they agreed to meet for dinner at the Blue Bay Seafood Restaurant between 6:15 and 6:30. Catherine picked Kay up in her 1992 burgundy Bonneville. When they arrived at the restaurant, Viktor was already inside. They waited about five or ten minutes before they were seated at a table for four in the smoking section near a window. They enjoyed a nice seafood dinner, iced tea, and pleasant conversation. Kay recalls that Viktor had a large combination seafood dinner with coleslaw and a baked potato. She thought he looked especially nice in his blue jeans, brown leather bomber-style jacket, black sweater, and casual Italian loafers.

Kay recalled that Tana had said Viktor was tight with his money. At the end of the meal when the waitress brought the check, Catherine took out a twenty-dollar bill. The total bill for the three of them amounted to less than twenty dollars. Catherine only intended to pay for her meal and Kay's, but Viktor apparently thought she intended to pay for his meal as well. He did not even offer to pay his share. Instead he took out his wallet, put some money down for the tip, and put his wallet back in his pants pocket. Kay and Catherine glanced at each other, but did not comment.

Between 7:30 and 8:00 p.m., they walked outside the restaurant, which was located in the same shopping center as Bogarts, off Highway 70. As they stood outside, Kay invited Viktor to her house, and Viktor said that he would drive over after he stopped by his apartment to change into more comfortable clothes.

Meanwhile, Kay and her mother walked to Revco Drugs and picked up some photographs that had just been developed. Kay and her mother then drove back to Kay's house. Catherine told Kay that she liked Viktor, that he was handsome and friendly, but that Viktor "talked over her head sometimes." Catherine stayed at Kay's just long enough to look at the photos, and then drove home.

It was almost 8:30 by the time Viktor arrived at Kay's. He was still wearing his brown leather jacket and blue stonewashed jeans, but had changed from a sweater into a rose-colored polo shirt. Kay could not later recall exactly what type of shoes he was wearing, but she did remember his white athletic socks. She also recalled that he wore a gold-colored wristwatch and a gold signet ring. She could not help but notice again that Viktor Gunnarsson was a handsome man.

Viktor asked Kay if she liked to read. Kay assured him that, like most English teachers, she thoroughly enjoyed reading. Viktor was pleased to learn that they both enjoyed reading, and Kay was impressed with Viktor's erudition of literature. Viktor was also interested in government and politics, and he talked at length about the Swedish government.

"I'd like to take you there some day," he told her.

"I'd love to go to Sweden," she said.

"Then someday I will take you and show you the country where I grew up," he promised.

Viktor talked fondly of his family, and Kay learned that his father worked in real estate in Sweden. Viktor shared his dream with Kay that someday he would own a house and about ten acres of land.

"Do you miss your family?" Kay asked Viktor.

"Of course, I miss them. But I love it here in the United States. You see, in Sweden, I was once falsely accused of a crime, and as a result the Swedish government has paid me money for the false charges I was never convicted of. That is why I first came to the United States," he explained.

"To seek political asylum?" Kay asked.

"I guess that is how you would say it, yes."

Kay did not admit it to Viktor, but she had been curious as to how Viktor got money since he was apparently not employed full-time.

"I have also written a book," he told her.

"About your arrest?" she asked.

"Yes. I plan to get it back from the publisher in two weeks."

"I'd really like to read it, Viktor."

"I will give you a personally autographed copy. I will sign it, 'With love to Kay from Viktor.'" Kay's smile broadened, and Viktor leaned closer to Kay and kissed her, sweetly at first, and then again, more passionately.

Kay led Viktor to her bedroom. It was 9:30 p.m. Viktor asked Kay if she had any candles, surprising her. It was three hours after darkness fell, and while Kay did not bother closing the window shades, she did close the bedroom door. Kay lit two candles atop her dresser.

It was just a few minutes past ten, and knowing Jason would be home soon, Kay and Viktor returned to the living room sofa where Kay sat with Viktor's arm around her as they talked. Mikkel was still out with friends when Jason came home. He told Kay that he had invited some friends over and asked Kay if he could build a fire in the firepit beside the house, and she agreed. Viktor was curious about the firepit, so Kay and Viktor went outside to sit around the fire with Jason and his friends.

Kay and Viktor sat in two chairs beside each other. Kay noticed that Viktor's bright-blue eyes shone even brighter in the firelight. She leaned toward him and reached behind his neck to run her fingers through his thick wavy dark hair, and then smoothing it back into place. The gaze they shared and Viktor's knowing smile gave Kay hope for a future she had given up on many months ago.

Holding hands, Kay and Viktor sat close to each other with their backs to the street. Jason sat in a chair across from his mother, facing the street. The tiny sparkle from the small diamond in Viktor's gold signet ring captured Kay's attention. Viktor took off the ring to show it to Kay. She saw that there were three Old English–style initials, which she could not specifically recall afterward. Viktor told Kay the three letters stood for Italian words that meant something like "strength" and "courage." Viktor pronounced the words in Italian, and they all laughed at his phony Italian accent.

As they sat around the fire talking, Kay noticed the lights of a car coming down the street toward the intersection near her house. She watched as it stopped at the intersection. As the car turned left to drive by her house, Jason looked at Kay and simply said, "Monte Carlo." Kay's stomach tightened involuntarily, but she did not comment.

Viktor repeated the words "Moan-tee Cah-lo" in an exaggerated Italian accent, and they laughed again, everyone except Kay, who knew that Jason was discreetly conveying a warning to Kay that the car driving by their house belonged to L. C. Underwood. The time on Viktor's gold-colored watch was 11:00 p.m.

Fifteen minutes or so later, Viktor told Kay that he was tired and needed to go home. He explained that he had stayed up late with Daniel after Kay left his apartment the night before because Daniel was nervous about flying to Sweden alone. Then they had gotten up early to get to the airport. So, Viktor and Kay stood and walked back into her house through the attached garage, and stood just inside the front door. Viktor kissed Kay and said, "I'll call you tomorrow."

Kay opened the front door for Viktor, and watched him walk to his car with his hands in his pockets. It was no later than 11:30 p.m. Kay went to bed and read for a while, not able to fall asleep immediately, thinking of Viktor and the time they had spent together. She finally fell asleep, more content than she had been in a long time.

On Saturday morning, December 4, Kay got out of bed and said "Good morning" to the boys.

"Jason, what time did you come inside last night?" she asked.

"Around midnight, not long after Mikkel got home. Then we came inside and went to bed. What are you gonna do today?"

"I don't have any plans yet, except that I need to clean the house."

"Are you gonna see Viktor again tonight?" Jason teased her.

"I don't know for sure yet," Kay said, smiling.

"He seems pretty cool," Jason assured her. Like Catherine Miller, Jason was glad Kay was moving on.

Kay attempted to occupy her time by doing some housework. As she cleaned, she listened for the phone to ring. She hoped that Viktor would call, even though he was not specific last night about *when* he would call. As the day wore on, Kay toyed with the idea of calling him, but decided against it. She did not want him to think she was pushy, so she decided to wait him out. But Viktor never called.

CHAPTER NINE

"Lover and friend has thou put far from me, and mine acquaintance into darkness" (Psalms 88:18)

Viktor's friend Daniel Johansson arrived in Sweden on Saturday morning, December 4, 1993. He tried to call Viktor as requested to let him know he had arrived safely, but every time he dialed the number, he only heard Viktor's answering machine. Daniel left a message for Viktor, telling him that he had made it home okay, and he asked Viktor call him. But Viktor never returned Daniel's call.

By 5:30 Saturday evening, Kay had grown tired of hanging around the house waiting for the phone to ring. Instead of doing that all evening, she made arrangements to have dinner with her friend Vicky. The two left Kay's house about 7:00 and returned around 11:00. As soon as Kay walked into her house, she immediately checked her answering machine. There were no messages. She sighed in disappointment. Again, she entertained thoughts about calling Viktor, but managed to talk herself out of it. She did not want to appear over-anxious, but she admitted to herself that she had already developed strong feelings for Viktor Gunnarsson. She could only hope that the feeling was mutual.

On Sunday, December 5, Kay decided that she needed a real Christmas tree to bring the Christmas spirit into her home. Arguing to herself that she now had a good reason for calling Viktor, in that she needed help with the tree, she picked up the phone and dialed his number. She glanced at the wall clock and noted that it was 12:30 p.m. As Viktor's phone continued to ring, Kay planned to remind him about a conversation they had earlier in the week when he volunteered to help her with a tree.

Viktor's answering machine interrupted her thoughts. She was disappointed that he was not at home. She paused for a moment and then decided to leave a message.

"…Hi, this is Kay. I'm just calling to see what you're up to. I'll see you later."

Kay had barely hung up when her phone rang. She picked it up anxiously, hoping it was Viktor, but was disappointed when she recognized the voice on the other end.

L. C. told her firmly, "Kay, I am gonna come pick you up at seven o'clock this evening. I'm gonna bring you back over here, and I'm gonna make love to you. We are going to get this relationship back on track – the way it should be."

Kay told L. C., "I can't see you, L. C. I have a lot to do. I want to get a Christmas tree, and I have exams to prepare."

L. C. replied, "We've been apart long enough. You've had your time alone."

"That isn't for you to decide, L. C. You aren't listening to me."

"Now you're just making excuses!"

"This is crunch time, L. C. I've told you that. I have a lot to do."

Not willing to take no for an answer, he said, "I'm coming over there. I'll be there to pick you up at seven."

"I am going to get a Christmas tree, and I will have to call you later." Kay hung up the phone before L. C. could argue again. She made herself some tea. Looking at the clock, she noted that she had less than seven hours to do something about L. C.

Since Viktor still had not phoned, Kay decided to call Tana and see if she would like to go with her to buy a Christmas tree. Tana said that she would, if Kay would go with her to pick up some photographs she was having developed at the Salisbury Mall. Kay agreed.

Tana drove to Kay's house, and then Kay drove herself and Tana in Kay's car.

"Did you see Viktor last night?" Tana asked.

"Yes, we ate seafood. He went with me and my mother to Blue Bay. Then Viktor came over to the house, and we had a nice little visit."

"A *really* nice visit?" Tana asked.

"Really nice," Kay responded, smiling.

"Well good. I'm glad it's working out for the two of you."

"Well, that's just it. I'm not so sure that it is. I kind of thought he'd call by now, but he didn't. I finally called him, but he didn't answer, so I left a message on his machine."

"Hey, do you want to ride by his apartment and see if he's there?" Tana offered.

"Yeah, let's do that," Kay brightened at the thought of seeing Viktor.

When Kay and Tana arrived at Lakewood Apartments, they drove through the multi-building complex to the last building on the right. Kay parked in front of Viktor's building and left the engine running. Viktor's car was parked outside, backed into his usual cockeyed manner of parking. She ran up the stairs to Viktor's apartment while Tana waited in the car. Kay found Viktor's apartment door ajar about an inch.

She stood on the deck and called out, "Hello? Viktor?"

No answer.

She listened for a television or radio, but heard nothing. She pushed the door open and stepped just inside. She was struck by the odor of garlic. His apartment smelled like her own kitchen had after Viktor made spaghetti for her on Wednesday. Viktor used a lot of garlic in his cooking.

Not finding Viktor inside, Kay walked back outside onto the balcony and motioned for Tana to come up. They both stepped into the living room and looked around. They called out again for Viktor, but there was no response. Kay heard something in the bathroom that sounded like running water. She thought he might be in the shower, but when she walked toward the hall, she saw that the bathroom door was open, and it was the toilet that was running. No one was in the shower, and in fact, the shower walls appeared to be dry.

Stepping into the kitchen, Kay saw a couple of onions open on the counter in a green produce tray. An unwashed frying pan sat on an eye of the stove.

Kay followed Tana just inside the doorway to Viktor's bedroom. The bed, or rather just a mattress and box springs, looked like someone had slept in it, but only one side of the bed was turned down. It looked as if Viktor had just gotten into bed and then threw the covers back and got up. Kay wondered to herself if Viktor slept all night without tossing and turning unlike herself. She wondered if he slept so soundly that he did not disturb the bed coverings. She smiled at the recent memory of her own bed in thorough disarray two nights before.

Kay and Tana both noticed Viktor's leather bomber jacket was hanging on the back of the chair in the bedroom.

Tana commented, "He can't be far away because he never goes anywhere without that jacket."

"Then maybe he's just out riding his bike," Kay suggested.

Then Tana noticed Viktor's answering machine and said, "It looks like he has several messages." There was a green light flashing on the machine.

Kay giggled and said, "I feel really weird about being here, Tana. We're acting like a couple of schoolgirls, snooping around some guy's apartment."

"Yeah, we better go," Tana agreed. "I'd hate for him to catch us in here."

Kay and Tana left the apartment and pulled the door back to the position in which they found it, slightly ajar. It was windy, and Kay thought Viktor might not have latched his door securely and the wind could have accidentally caught it and opened it. But just in case he left it ajar for some reason, she decided to leave it just as they had found it.

Kay then drove them to Simpson's where she and Tana selected a Christmas tree. Kay paid for it, and they took the tree back to Kay's house, arriving about 3:30 p.m. Kay, Mikkel, and Jason put the tree in a tree stand and left it in the garage undecorated. Kay was still hopeful that Viktor would call and want to help her decorate it. Tana and Kay then left again, and this time Tana drove. They went to the Salisbury Mall to pick up Tana's photos. After leaving the mall, Tana then drove the short distance back to Viktor's apartment. They wanted to give him copies of some of the photos because a few of them included him and Daniel. Tana knew how sentimental Viktor was and that he would love to have them.

Unfortunately, Viktor was still not home, and his front door was still ajar. His car did not appear to have been moved.

Kay put some of the photos inside an envelope and wrote on the outside, "Pictures for you. Tana and Kay." This time they closed the door to Viktor's apartment and wedged the envelope between the door and the facing. About an hour and a half had passed since they had been at Viktor's apartment earlier. Still, neither Kay nor Tana were really concerned that something might be wrong.

"He probably just took off with a friend who dropped by," Tana suggested.

"Probably so," Kay agreed. She wondered if he could have taken off with a female friend. She hoped that was not the case.

Halfway across the world, Daniel Johansson continued to try to reach Viktor. But then when Daniel tried to call Viktor a short while after Kay and Tana went by Viktor's apartment the second time, Daniel only heard a series of beeps instead of Viktor's phone message. He concluded that Viktor's answering machine was not working properly, and he made a mental note to tell Viktor about it when they spoke again. But Daniel had no way of knowing that at some point on Sunday afternoon, someone had gone into Viktor's apartment and stole the cassette tape of messages from Viktor's answering machine.

Kay and Tana returned to Kay's house just as it was getting dark, around 5:00 or 5:30. Kay dreaded calling L. C., but knew she needed to; otherwise he may show up at her house, and L. C. Underwood was the last person in the world she wanted to see. So, she took a deep breath and dialed his number.

"Hello?" he answered.

"Hello, L. C."

"Hey."

"L. C., I called to tell you that I'm not going to go with you tonight."

"Why not, Kay?" L. C.'s voice was tense. She could tell he was already angry with her.

"I've already explained all that to you, L. C."

Angrily he said, "...I know you're seeing other men."

"L. C., I am not."

"Like the man you had your mother meet at Blue Bay?"

"...Oh, that's Tana's friend." Kay wondered how L. C. knew about Viktor having dinner with them on Friday.

"How did your mother like your new boyfriend?" he asked, his voice dripping with sarcasm. He sounded as if he was struggling to keep his temper in check.

Nonchalantly, Kay answered, "She liked him okay."

"I'll bet. ...especially since your mother hates *me*."

"Oh, L. C. She does not. I have told you before; my mother does note hate *any*body. And if you've really changed like you say you have, then you should just talk to her. Tell her how you feel. She'll probably understand."

"Do you really think so? Do you think I should go talk to her?" he asked, changing his attitude temporarily.

"That's up to you, L. C. ...But listen. You have to stop trying to make decisions for me."

"I am not trying to make decisions for you!" His anger returned.

"Yes, you are."

"How?"

"You can't just announce that you are coming over here and demand I go out with you! You have to stop trying to make decisions for me."

"I'm not."

"Yes, you are."

"I am not!"

Kay glanced up at Tana who was staring at Kay on the phone and shaking her head in disbelief. "L. C., I have to go now."

"Why? Is someone there?" he asked.

"Yes, a friend of mine is here. A *woman* friend."

"I thought you said you had things to do."

"She's helping me."

"Right," L. C. said and slammed down the phone.

Tana stayed for supper. She and Kay ate chili and speculated about where Viktor could have gone. They tried again to call him, but his answering machine was doing bizarre things. It would continue beeping and would not allow a message to be recorded.

"That's strange," Kay said to Tana. "I left Viktor a message on it yesterday."

Tana said, "His answering machine must be messed up. I've tried to call him in the past, and there have been times when his answering machine wasn't working right. ...I don't think it's ever been this messed up, though."

After dinner, while Kay and Tana brought the Christmas tree in from the garage, and while they were decorating L. C. called again. Kay was in the process of untangling the Christmas lights, so Tana answered the phone. She told L. C.

that Kay was busy and would call him back later. Kay never returned his call.

The next day, Monday, December 6, L. C. called Kay again. This time when he called, Kay's friend Vicky was there. Kay told L. C. that she could not talk because she was getting ready to leave.

"You're going out?"

"I'm going to Spencer's tonight with some of my *girl*friends. We're going to celebrate Anne's birthday. I'm running late, and I have to stop by and pick up my mother – she's going too." Vicky later confirmed that Kay told L. C. exactly where they were going.

Vicky and Kay picked up Catherine Miller about 7:00 p.m. and drove to Spencer's Restaurant in Salisbury. They were inside with their friends, eating, talking, and laughing when an unwelcome guest walked in… with a date.

Kay assumed that the pretty woman with the shiny auburn hair accompanying L. C. was "Kim," a woman L. C. had earlier referred to in letters to Kay. L. C. had always flaunted the mysterious "Kim" to her, explaining that Kim was a woman who was strongly interested in a relationship with him. Little did Kay know that there was no "Kim" or that L. C. had bribed this particular woman to accompany him to Spencer's where he could flaunt her in front of Kay.

L. C. and his pretty friend were seated near Kay on a slightly lower level. L. C. did not seem to acknowledge Kay's presence, although he could not help but see Kay. L. C.'s presence certainly disturbed Kay, however, especially after she had just told him on the phone that she was going to Spencer's with her friends. Kay moved a poinsettia and one of Anne's birthday gifts into her line of vision so she could not see L. C. As soon as Kay ate her meal, she told her mother, "I'm going to go wait in the car. Don't hurry. I want to smoke and listen to the radio." Kay then walked out and waited in her car for the others.

When Kay got home, she was frustrated through and through that L. C. had ruined yet another evening for her. She was frustrated with him and also with herself for letting him get to her. Kay changed out of her clothes and into a nightgown. On top of that, Viktor still had not called. Kay set her alarm for 7:00 a.m. instead of the usual 6:00, because she planned to take off work the next day. Jason was about to turn sixteen, and she had promised to take him to get his driver's license. He was looking forward to it so much. She wanted the day to be special for him, but first she needed to rest. She climbed into bed and tried to think about anything other than L. C. Underwood.

At 6:45 a.m. on Tuesday, December 7, Kay woke to the ringing of her phone. Half asleep, she let the answering machine pick up, and then L. C. was talking. "Kay, I put a letter for you in your mailbox. I, I hope you'll read it…" Kay got out of bed, pulled on her robe, and walked outside. She got the letter out of the mailbox and carried it back inside. She went over to the coffee maker and started to make herself a cup of coffee. Before she completed the small task, however, her doorbell rang. She walked to the door.

"L. C.," she said, not entirely surprised.

"Kay, I'd really like to talk to you for a minute."

Too sleepy to argue, she opened the door all the way and said, "Come in." Jason was still asleep in his room.

L. C. followed her into the living area. She offered L. C. some coffee, but he refused. Kay sat down on the couch, and L. C. sat in a chair to her right. He got right to the point.

"I want to talk about us, about our relationship, Kay."

"L. C., I've *told* you. I'm not interested in a relationship right now."

"You said that you loved me."

"I do, but I am not *in love* with you… You push too hard. You should just ease up and …just let it be …normal. I care about you, but I need my freedom and my space. I don't want to be accountable to anyone."

Several times during this conversation, L. C. got out of his chair and walked toward her. Kay told him more than once to sit back down and just listen. Kay could see L. C. was struggling to stay calm.

Kay walked into the kitchen to fill her coffee cup, and L. C. followed her. She hoped he would not stay long.

"Misty died," he announced flatly. Misty was L. C.'s Shetland Sheepdog. Kay knew he loved Misty. She had bought the dog for L. C. as a Christmas gift the year before.

"*What*?" Kay asked him, hoping she had not heard L. C. correctly.

"Misty died."

"How? What happened?"

"She, umm, choked to death."

"*Choked* to death! How?"

"On a quarter. She was in her crate inside the house, and she must have found a quarter inside the crate."

"Oh my God, L. C. I am so sorry!" Kay was genuinely upset.

"I took her to the Salisbury Animal Hospital because they open early. But it was too late; she was already dead and stiff."

"Did you hear Misty during the night? Did you know anything was wrong?"

"No. I couldn't hear her because, uh, the fan in my bedroom was running."

"You must feel awful," Kay said.

"Yeah," he responded, but he showed no visible remorse.

Kay and L. C. sat at the table in her kitchen. L. C. asked, "Did you read the letter I wrote you?"

"I haven't had a chance to, L. C. I just have walked to the mailbox to get it." The letter was still lying on the stove.

L. C. glanced down at the unopened envelope.

Kay said, "I don't want a relationship, L. C. Not with you or with anyone."

L. C. looked at her, pushed back his chair, walked to the door, and as he reached for the knob he said, "You don't need to say anymore."

"It's not just that, L. C.," Kay said, and L. C. let go of the door, turned, and sat back down at the table.

She tried to explain, "I care about you as a person. I'm just not interested in a romantic relationship with you."

L. C. looked around then and asked "Where are Jason and Mikkel?"

"They're here, in bed asleep. Why?"

L. C. did not answer her.

"They'll be getting up in a minute so we can go do the car thing. ...And I really need to go get ready now." She looked at L. C. expectantly, hoping he would get the message and leave.

L. C. started to stay something else but then just looked at her blankly for a few moments, stood up, turned around, and left.

Several hours later Kay decided to open the plain white envelope with L. C.'s return address on a sticker in the upper left corner. She read the five-page handwritten letter that he had composed apparently late the night before, with little sympathy and growing agitation.

> *Kay,*
>
> *It is Tuesday 12:10 a.m. and I am at home, Alone. Yes, Kay, Alone, because I love you. I wish you would open your eyes and see that. There are some things I want to say to you. And all that I ask after you read this letter is talk with me on the telephone or in person. I want it to be face to face. I will not mail this letter, because I intend to bring it to your house later today.*
>
> *First I want to say that if I had seen your car at Spencer's I would never have come in. The entire*

time I was there I wanted to come up to you and tell you that I LOVE YOU. Kay, I know that you have went out with other men since we have been apart, and if that is what you wanted to do, then its O.K. because I couldn't do anything to stop it. It's not that people don't know us in this town and yes people I know have seen you out with other men and couldn't wait to run back to tell me. I am not stupid to think you have been at home all alone. I don't care to know their names and I don't want to know who they were. But let's be honest with each other. I didn't want to go out to eat tonight. But if you knew how each night I eat alone and I get so tired of that I could scream.

I have tried now for almost two months to try to make you understand and something you refuse to do that I had some problems in my life that I had to deal with and yes I had to get help but I'm facing it head-on.

I am the same person you first met. But you refuse to see it. I know you told Rick you didn't want me leaning on you, and I don't want to nor do I intend to. I have tried so long and hard to set things right that I have done wrong. I don't think you understand so I'm saying this all for the final time. Kay Weden, I love you and I want you to love me. My heart is yours and it doesn't belong to anyone else. I want to make a life with you and I told Kim that, and she understands that.

Last night at Spencer's I told her the entire time we were eating that I wanted so much to get up and come over to you and say in front of everyone at your table, Kay I love you and only you, and take you home with me, and hold you all night.

Kim looked at me and she looked over at you and then she said "You both love each other and I can tell you both want your arms around each other, so don't be stupid. You both are so much in love that being apart makes both of you miserable, so why don't both of you give up some of your pride and make this thing work. She understands that I don't love her and she knows how I feel about you, and she is not stupid, to know that I have no intentions of loving her, no matter how she feels about me. I don't want a life with her.

Kay what do I have to do to make you understand my love is yours and yours alone? But darling you can't expect me to wait forever and I can only hold in place for so long. I try each day to have the faith to hold on, but I just can't hold on forever.

Each day that passes without you my heart breaks a little more. I have tried to talk with you several times but each time you either have company or you can't talk or you have to go somewhere, or you say I'll call you back, but you never do. I have waited by this phone long enough and I can't and I won't anymore. I want to make things right with you and make you see I want you, your love your life to be a part of mine, but you never want to give me that choice, and if that is what you want, say so, and I will get on with my life. I don't want to live my life without you but if I have to I will. I can't carry this pain and hurt around with me forever.

It's not fair to me, and I wouldn't do that to you if it was the other way around. Kay you say don't force you into something you don't want to do, well don't force me into something I don't want. I want you, your love and a life of sharing something that we use to talk about so often. I don't want anyone but you and I have tried everything I know to show you that. But I don't know what else to do. I have tried getting you to talk with me but you are always busy.

You told me recently that you didn't want a relationship and if that is what you want I will let go. I have no other choice. I can only keep trying to come back for so long. My life is getting back to normal and I want you in it, not as someone who is better than you but as a person that is an equal partner.

I want you to understand what I am about to say. I love you very much. I want you and only you and no one else. I want to talk with you and say I love you to your face. I want to hold you in my arms and kiss you and make love to you. I want to put this relationship back on track and to show you I care for you, and only you. I have not nor do I intend to make love or hold anyone else, until I can't hold you anymore.

I do not want to force you to do something you don't want to do, but don't force me into something I don't want. I do not intend to be mean by saying these things. My days of being mean and cruel are over forever. I have a heart and soul and I am a decent person even if you don't believe that I know it's true. I've made mistakes in life and I am sure I'll make some more mistakes in the future, But not the cruel kind. I do not want to go through the rest of my life without you, a person I do love, and care for with all my heart. But I will not chase you anymore. I've paid the price for my mistakes but

I will not pay for them for the rest of my life. No one should have to do that, not me, not you, not anyone.

I've told you several times that I would try to spend the rest of my life trying to make up to you for my past mistakes. I love you Kay Weden, and my heart is yours if you want it. I don't want anyone else but I will not allow my heart to hurt anymore, I have to start healing because my health is important. I've lost so much weight my clothes no longer fit. I have worried, hurt and lost enough sleep over this. I have asked you to forgive and try to forget the things I have done to hurt you. I've told you that for the things you have said and done to me I don't need to forgive you, because love is never having to say I'm sorry or I forgive you.

Again I don't want to force you into something you don't want and I didn't say what I did on the phone to make you mad. I ask you but I will not beg for your love anymore. If this relationship ends, it ends now. And if that is what you want then I'll respect that. But if it does end I'll leave knowing I tried to make you understand that this man loves you very much and I wanted to make it work. But I have to put my life back together, for my own health and peace of mind, please understand that. I will ask you once more to take the time if this relationship means everything to you to call me today and talk with me or come to my house tonight even after you get through with your Ace program. I would like for you to invite me to go. Kay please don't throw our love away because of pride, and what has happened in the past, and look only to the future. I am willing to meet you more than halfway. If I don't hear from you tonight I will take it that it's over and I will get on with my life without you. It's not what I want but I can't go on any longer like this. Please don't throw this away. I can do no more than what I've already tried. If you decide not to call or come back to try to make this work I wish you all the best of what life has to offer. I want to go away with you for the weekend if you will go. But if I never hear from you again, I will never say to anyone, no matter what it has cost me that I regret having met you, but most of all, falling in love with you.

Love,

L. C.

Kay got up to wake Jason and Mikkel. It was December 7, and her son was turning sixteen. Kay took Jason to get his driver's license and to purchase a CD player for his car with the birthday money that his grandmother Catherine gave him. Catherine had stopped by Kay's house on her way home from work to wish Jason a happy birthday, but Jason and Mikkel were out in the car. Jason could not wait to drive. Kay wondered briefly if she could ever keep Jason home now that he had his license. He was supposed to have cleaned out the gutters at his grandmother's house over the weekend but had put it off, and now it still wasn't done. Catherine was in good health, but she had no business climbing a tall ladder to clean out her gutters when Jason could do it in no time. He had certainly done so before.

"Well, be sure to tell him I came to see him and personally wish him a happy birthday," Catherine told Kay. Kay told her mother about L. C.'s visit that morning. Catherine frowned and shook her head.

The next morning on Wednesday, December 8, Kay returned to work. It was a busy day, catching up from the day before, and the time passed quickly. When Kay returned home in the afternoon, she found two hang-up calls on her answering machine. Kay used her "call-return" service to discover that the last call to her residence came from L. C.'s home phone. Angry that he was getting around the call block somehow, she dialed the number and L. C. answered.

"This is Kay. Did you call me?"

"I called earlier." L. C. sounded like he had been asleep.

"But why? It's only 3:15 right now. You knew I was at school earlier in the day."

L. C. never really answered her question. "I've been asleep," he said. They hung up, but L. C. called Kay back a few minutes later.

"Do you want to go out and get something to eat with me?" he asked.

"No."

"Why not?" he asked.

She sighed aloud. "…Well, I'm tired of eating out, and besides, I've already defrosted a chicken. I need to cook it for supper."

"You're just making excuses. You've always got an excuse… Well, would you want to go with me Friday to do some Christmas shopping? Maybe at the Hanes Mall in Winston Salem?"

Tired of arguing with him, Kay tried to put him off without angering him again. "I don't know, L. C.," she told him. She was in no mood to fight with him.

"Well, I need to know because if you don't want to go with me, someone else has already asked me to go out of town with them."

"Well… I know I can't go Friday. Maybe Saturday. But I'll have to let you know."

"Okay, but I need to know by tomorrow."

"Okay."

"So, what time will Mikkel and Jason be home?"

"Why do you ask?"

"What's the big deal? I just wondered."

"Well, uhm, Jason has to work, but Mikkel will be here around 5:00."

"Oh," he sounded disappointed.

About 5:30 p.m., L. C. called again. Kay was straightening up her rec room. L. C. was in a bad mood.

He said with voice trembling, "Kay, you are forcing me to make a life with Kim."

"I'm not forcing you to do anything, L. C.," Kay said, matter-of-factly.

"In a sense you are… I don't want that girl; I want you. …I'm just going to have to go on."

"Do it then." Kay hung up.

L. C. called back, and Mikkel answered the phone. Kay told Mikkel she did not want to talk to L. C. Mikkel told L. C. what she said and talked to him for a little while. Then Mikkel told Kay that L. C. said it was important that she talk to him.

Kay yelled out, "I don't care if it's important!" L. C. slammed his phone down.

Less than half an hour later, he called back. Kay had just put the chicken on the stove and was working on the rest of dinner. Two of Jason's friends had stopped by and were in the kitchen talking with her. Kay answered the phone. L. C. asked Kay again what she was doing.

"I'm cooking dinner and watching TV."

"Whatcha watching?" he asked nonchalantly.

"I'm watching *Unsolved Mysteries* on the Lifetime channel," she told him tiredly.

"Oh. So, you're still planning on staying at home?" L. C. tried to sound casual.

"Yes, L. C., I'm staying home."

"Okay. Well, I'll let you go then."

Kay was surprised that L. C. gave up so easily, but she was grateful.

After dinner, Kay called Tana, and they decided to drive by Viktor's apartment one more time. Since Viktor still had not called, Kay was convinced that Viktor was no longer interested in her. But she could not help but think about him and how different he was from L. C.

When Kay and Tana got to Viktor's apartment, they saw that his car was in the same place as if it still had not been moved. Furthermore, the pictures they had left him on Sunday were still stuck in his door. Neither one of them could come up with a rational explanation as to where Viktor could have gone in such a hurry without his car.

"Do you still think he just took off with someone?" Kay asked Tana on the way back to Kay's house.

"I don't know what to think. He must have left in a big hurry because he did not take his jacket or even shut his door all the way. ...But he'll show up. He always does."

"Well, I wish I knew where Viktor was and what he was doing at this very moment," Kay said to Tana, as they pulled into Kay's driveway.

If only Kay had known what unthinkable thing someone else was doing at that very moment just a few blocks away.

CHAPTER TEN

"He shall redeem their soul from deceit and violence: and precious shall their blood be in his sight" (Psalms 72:14)

On Thursday morning, December 9, 1993, Kay went to work at West Rowan High School as usual. About an hour after she arrived, Kay was surprised to see Mr. Paul Brown, her mother's boss, arrive at the school with a lady who was a friend and co-worker of Catherine Miller's. They had come for Kay.

"Wh—what's wrong?" Kay asked shakily.

Paul Brown, touching her gently on the shoulder, said, "Mrs. Weden, your mother was not at work today. If it was anyone else, we wouldn't be concerned. But as you know, your mother never misses work, and she is never late. We were concerned about her, so we called the sheriff's department. We asked them to go by and check on her at her house." That feeling of dread that suddenly solidifies into a rock in the pit of the stomach washed over Kay. She grabbed her purse and got into Paul Brown's car. Jason and Mikkel were in class, and Kay did not want to worry them unnecessarily.

Brown drove them to Catherine's home at 118 Larch Road, at the intersection of Larch Road and Enon Church Road. The house was also part of the Westcliff Development where Kay lived, about four miles west of Salisbury.

When they arrived at the house, Kay saw cars from the Rowan County Sheriff's Office parked in front. Her heart was pounding. She felt like she was going to be sick. She got out of Brown's car and walked quickly toward the house. She was stopped by one of the deputies. "Mrs. Weden, we can't get into the house because we don't have a key." Kay did not understand why they did not force the door open and go inside to check on her mother.

"I have a key," she told them, "but it's at my house just up the street."

The deputy drove Kay quickly to her house where she went inside to get her mother's house key. She picked up a key with one hand, and reached for the phone with the other. For no known reason, Kay dialed L. C.'s house. There was no answer. She left a message on his answering machine, "L. C., something has happened to my mother." She laid the phone down and quickly returned to her mother's house.

Kay walked to the kitchen entrance, which she always used when she visited her mother. The first thing she noticed was that the storm door was not locked. Her mother always kept the storm door locked, and she would never unlock it unless she recognized whoever was at the door. But that was not possible. No one would harm her sweet little mother. Would they?

All of a sudden it dawned on her that if someone had done something to her mother, it had to be someone her mother knew. Not only that, but the face of a specific person flashed through her mind like an electrical shock as soon as she took hold of the storm door handle. It was the face of L. C. Underwood. She recalled his phone calls the evening before. Then she told herself that what she was thinking was just not possible.

Kay pulled open the unlocked storm door, her hand still trembling with the unexpected shock. She needed to unlock the heavier door next that separated her and the deputies from her mother's kitchen. But Kay's key would not fit the lock. She had mistakenly picked up her own extra house key instead of her mother's house key. She nearly collapsed from the stress.

"Please just go on in – just force the door if you have to," Kay told the deputies. Deputy Chad Moose forced open the locked door. Kay wanted to go inside, but the deputies would not allow it. She was made to stand out of the way while two deputies went inside. Rowan County Deputy John Baird, the first to arrive on the scene, followed Deputy Moose to the door and waited behind him. The electronic keypad on the wall indicated that the alarm had been disarmed. Deputy Moose pushed firmly against the kitchen door with his shoulder but was met with some kind of resistance. As he pushed the door open, he saw what – or rather *who* – was causing the resistance. Deputy Moose pushed the door open just enough to get inside and take in the gruesome scene before him.

The atrocities one person can exact upon another human being is, to most folks, unfathomable. But some are not afforded the luxury of blissful ignorance. Some of us are cursed with engrafted images of the unadulterated truth; that no act is so heinous, so outrageous, that it could not possibly be performed on one human being by another... no murder too cruel, no torture too unbearable, no person too invulnerable. We are always aware that safety and security are mere words; the perception of them can be shattered at any given moment in time. Most career law enforcement officers have seen truly terrible things throughout their careers and subsequently have to live with those images the rest of their lives. I certainly had my share of horrific images etched on my mind's canvas, and now Deputy Chad Moose had one to add to his own.

Taking only one step into the kitchen, he was met with the acrid stench of burned beans on the stove and drying blood. He reached down to feel for a pulse but found none. The body was cold to the touch. He backed out of the house carefully, notified his supervisor and called for the Detectives.

Catherine Miller, age seventy-seven, was pronounced dead at the scene. Her plump grandmotherly body was slumped awkwardly against the stark white refrigerator, half-sitting, half-lying, in a scarlet gelatin pool. Two gunshot wounds were immediately apparent on the top of her head, gaping angrily among her thinning white hair.

The blood spatter was an explosion of crimson fireworks that had burst in a circular pattern on the side of the refrigerator, above her head. The narrow rivulets of blood that trickled down from the explosion were fairly dry, but slightly sticky in the heavier areas. Fragments of scalp, hair, and droplets of blood were splattered on the wall behind, and on the ceiling, above Mrs. Miller. Upon closer inspection, a smearing of blood across the floor spread from a point near the kitchen wall forward to the point where Mrs. Miller's left foot slid as she apparently collapsed slowly, sliding down to the floor, coming to a final rest on her buttocks with her legs stretched out into a "V" in front.

She wore a solid-pink dress with long sleeves, accessorized with a strand of gold and white beads. Her eyeglasses had slid down on her nose, nearly having slipped off her face. Her eyes were partially open, and her mouth was moderately open. On her feet were red, yellow, and green flat-soled house shoes over her light-beige hose. Her right arm was resting on her right thigh, and her left arm was on the floor to her side. A white plastic button was on the floor to the left of the body in the center of the floor. The button was determined later to have originated from a kitchen towel that should have been hanging on the handle of the refrigerator door.

From the downward angle and location of the wounds on the top of her head, it appeared that Catherine Miller had been pushed or knocked backward, or that she had stumbled as she was retreating backward, and had fallen or was in the process of falling when she was shot twice in the top of the head. The shooter likely was standing over her when he fired both shots.

Double-tapping, or firing two shots in quick succession to the same general area, is a term frequently employed by law enforcement officers during training drills and thus repeated in real life, deadly force situations. The idea behind the practice is that the two quick shots in one targeted area results in twice the blood loss and twice the damage to a human target, which was claimed to make up for the limitations of full metal jacketed (encased) ammunition.

Still simmering on the kitchen stove was Catherine Miller's simple dinner, a pan of navy beans, which had dried out and scorched over the low heat. She never had the opportunity to partake of the last meal she prepared. On the table was the December 8 edition of the *Salisbury Post*, which was delivered shortly before she arrived home the evening before. The television was set on WSOC, a Charlotte television station, the volume at a low to normal range.

In the living room, there were atypical signs of disarray. While most items were untouched, the magazines on the coffee table had been slung off onto the floor, in what appeared to be a single swiping motion. A plump bank bag plainly lying on a chair was not opened and not moved. A drawer full of silver flatware was pulled open, but no pieces were missing.

In the bedrooms, some drawers had been pulled out of dressers and the contents were sitting on the floor. Oddly enough, the contents were not dumped haphazardly; they were stacked neatly. And again, no items were missing. An extensive quantity of guns, jewelry, and cash was still in the house. In fact, the only thing that seemed to be missing from the entire house was Mrs. Miller's purse.

Several inferences could be made from the crime scene. First of all, robbery was clearly not a motive in this murder, as many items of value were in plain view inside the residence and had not been taken. The items that were disturbed were moved in such a way as to appear "staged." Neither was sexual assault a motive, as the autopsy would later reveal. This motive screamed personal.

Kay had no idea how much time had passed when Jason phoned home. He and Mikkel, feeling helpless and not knowing what else to do after they were informed that Jason's grandmother was dead, had gone driving. With many unanswered questions and not knowing where to go for the answers, Jason told Kay that he and Mikkel had ended up at L. C.'s house.

"What?" Kay asked him.

"We're over at L. C.'s. He told me to ask you if they have dogs there."

"Dogs?" Kay asked, confused.

"Like tracking dogs. L. C. asked if they had tracking dogs at Grandma's house."

"No. Why would they have those?" Kay asked.

"I don't know. L. C. just told me to ask you."

Kay was still struck with the sickening feeling she had experienced when she put her hand on her mother's door handle.

"Jason you need to leave. I don't care where you go. Just leave. Leave now," Kay told him firmly.

"Well okay," he said.

"Just get out of there now, son."

"All right."

When Jason arrived home, Kay asked him why he had gone to L. C.'s house.

"I don't know, Mom; he's a cop. I thought he might know something. I don't know… Why didn't you want me over there? Why did you want me to leave like that?"

"I – I just don't want you over there. I don't want you to go over there again. Do you understand, son?"

"Okay, okay."

"So, what did L. C. say to you and Mikkel?" Kay asked.

"Nothing really. Just what I asked you about the dogs."

"I still don't know why he would ask that. Did he say anything else, when you told him your grandmother had been killed?"

"I, I'm not sure – no, not really. It's just been the most awful day, Mom."

"I know, I know. I'm so sorry Jason... But your grandmother loved you very much. Very much!"

"Mom? L. C. did ask me something," Jason told her. "He asked me if I needed any money. He offered to give me some money."

"He did?" Kay asked, surprised. L. C. had never given Jason money, to her knowledge.

"Yeah. He, he asked me if I needed any cash for anything. I told him I didn't need any." Kay's mind went back to the moment she realized her mother's purse was missing. It had undoubtedly been taken by her killer. It was highly likely that there was some amount of cash in the purse, as was her mother's habit to carry generally. Was it possible that L. C. could have been offering Jason money that was inside his grandmother's stolen purse? The ramifications of this possibility were far too outrageous for a broken, grieving daughter to contemplate on this 9th day of December, unequivocally the worst day of her life thus far, the day her sweet elderly mother was found brutally shot to death.

The autopsy conducted by Dr. Lisa Flagg at the University of North Carolina at Chapel Hill on December 10 confirmed that Catherine Miller had indeed expired as a direct result of two gunshot wounds to the head. Forensic analysis revealed that she had been shot at close range, within approximately twelve inches, by a .38 caliber Colt revolver. One of the specific Colts that could have killed her was a snub-nose .38 caliber Colt Detective Special, just like the one L. C. brought with him from Lincoln County.

A number of latent fingerprints were lifted from inside the Miller residence. Unfortunately, all of the lifts that were able to be identified were made by Catherine Miller. Unaware that we had not found any prints belonging to anyone other than Catherine, L. C. later told several individuals that he expected us to find his fingerprints inside her house, and that it meant nothing because he had been there on several occasions. L. C. also claimed to have taken a shower at Catherine Miller's after completing some yard work for her on one occasion, and that would explain any of his body hair that might be found in her bathtub. He tried to think of everything.

At 6:20 p.m. on December 9, 1993, a Rowan County investigator interviewed an employee of the Salisbury Housing Authority. The Housing Authority employee and his crew were blowing leaves off a sidewalk in front of a public housing apartment building when they found three credit cards, an insurance card, an AARP card, and a blood type card. The cards appeared to have been thrown from a moving car. They all bore the name "Catherine Miller." A few feet away, they also found a flexible band ring-watch later identified as having belonged to Catherine.

A few hours later, another citizen of Salisbury found Catherine Miller's wallet on Horah Street, a few blocks away from where the credit cards were found. But Kay did not know how much, if any, cash was in her mother's wallet. Whoever took Mrs. Miller's wallet and its contents obviously did not intend to keep or use them. Could it be that the cards were discarded in a minority neighborhood known for drug activity to make it appear that drugs or robbery was the motive for the murder?

Analysts in the Latent Evidence Section of the SBI Crime Lab carefully examined each of the recovered items belonging to Catherine Miller. Not even a single fingerprint was found. The cards had all been wiped clean.

CHAPTER ELEVEN

"These ...things doth the Lord hate...
A proud look, a lying tongue,
and hands that shed innocent blood" (Proverbs 6:16-17)

Kay and Jason sat side by side at Catherine Miller's funeral. For each of them in their own way, it was all surreal, like a bad dream from which neither of them could force themselves to wake. The future was as foreign and unknown to Kay as Jupiter and Mars. Yet Kay knew enough that she was frightened. Because she did not know who murdered her mother or why, she did not know if the murderer would come after her or Jason next. So, Kay asked a friend who lived nearby, a retired FBI agent, if he would stay at her house, keeping an eye out while she and the boys went to her mother's funeral service at the Lutheran Church. He agreed, and it was settled.

As she sat in the church pew, Kay pondered the question as to whether she *could* go on or even desired to go on without her mother. Catherine had been a rock for Kay. She had nourished her emotionally as well as physically throughout her life, and had sustained her daughter through some of the most trying times of her life, including her divorce from Matthew Weden and her dysfunctional relationship with L. C. Underwood. Catherine was Kay's sounding board, her confidante, her best friend, her financial and spiritual advisor.

Born on Valentine's Day in 1916 in Cabarrus County, North Carolina, Catherine Louise H. Bentley Miller was a woman who loved steadfastly and deeply. Catherine had, by the grace of God and sheer determination, survived the death of her two husbands, to each of whom she had been lovingly married for more than twenty years. She was active in her church, always ready to serve and care for others. Catherine had worked full-time at the same refrigeration company for forty years, rarely missing a day of work, and was still working eight hours per day up to and including the day of her death.

But now she was gone. The fact that a void, an absence in Kay's heart, could be so physically painful and numbing at the same time was an enigma to her. Yet she knew she had to go on. Her precious son Jason, clearly hurting, confused, and even angry, needed her now more than ever.

As Kay, Jason, and the congregation sat quietly, the minister spoke of Catherine and of her Lord. Suddenly Kay was shocked to see a bright blue bolt of something like lightning, a multi-sided object – no, not an object, but more a source of light, like the hottest part of the flame – that proceeded from her mother's casket and traveled straight and swiftly, like an arrow, directly to Kay's heart. Kay involuntarily lurched in her seat with the impact. Startled, she glanced around, first at Jason and then at the rest of the congregation, but no one else seemed to have seen or felt what Kay experienced. But something had changed. Kay felt a strength filling her on the inside – specifically in her breastbone, as she described it – that was not born of her, but received by her.

Kay was familiar with the scripture, "I can do all things through Christ which strengtheneth me" from the fourth chapter of Philippians. But she had never thought of that strength in terms of an actual, physical experience, but there was no other explanation. Kay remains convinced that God allowed Catherine to give her grieving daughter one last gift, the gift of strength she would rely upon in the trying months and years to come.

It was not my place to doubt Kay or minimize the experience she described to me. What I did see for myself in Kay was a quiet strength, a fortitude that kept her sane and able to function on a daily basis in spite of her internal turmoil. I knew she carried guilt someplace deep inside her for having brought a man like L. C. into the lives of her son, her mother, and herself. Frequently accused of being stupid, anyone who knew Kay knew her to be an intelligent woman and a competent mother and teacher. But she did not have the one thing that her critics had, and that was the benefit of hindsight. In addition, those quick to judge Kay had no earthly idea of just how devious, conniving, and manipulative L. C. Underwood really was. They could not possibly fathom the lengths he would go to control every aspect of Kay's life.

She walked out of her mother's funeral service with a renewed will to live in spite of her broken heart.

Although the next few days passed in a fog, with friends and neighbors coming and going, bringing dishes of food and expressing their condolences, Kay was able to complete the basic tasks required to care for Jason and herself, and to begin to contemplate her options with regard to her mother's estate. Without question, she would never walk through the doors of her mother's home again. She would hire a specialized moving company to pack her mother's things and move them to a storage unit where Kay could sort through them at a much later time. She would contact a real estate agent and get her mother's house on the market as soon as possible. It would never again be a home, a source of comfort to Kay; it was just one more thing that had been maliciously stolen from her. Sadly, however, it was not to be the last.

On Monday, December 13, following her mother's funeral, Kay received an international phone call. It was Daniel, calling from Sweden.

"Kay Weden, this is Daniel... Viktor's friend."

"Well, hello, Daniel. How are you?" Kay said, actually pleased to hear from him.

"I'm fine, I guess." Daniel did not sound fine.

"How was your flight back to Sweden?" Kay asked politely.

"It was very fine as well. However... I am calling you, Kay, because I have not been able to reach Viktor. I was hoping that, ah, do you know where he is?" Daniel sounded concerned.

"Oh. ...No, I'm sorry, Daniel. I haven't heard from Viktor in several days." She realized, in fact, that it had been well over a week since she had seen or heard from Viktor Gunnarsson.

"Oh. Well if you hear from him, will you tell him, please, I have been trying to call him? I am a little worried."

"Sure, Daniel. I will." Kay could not bring herself to tell Daniel that her mother had just been murdered.

"Okay, then, thank you. And tell everyone I said hello."

"Okay, Daniel. Goodbye."

As Kay hung up the phone, she thought of Viktor in earnest for the first time since her mother's senseless murder. So very much had happened in her life during the past week, but at this point she began to consider Viktor in a different light. It occurred to her that he might actually be ...missing. For the first time, Kay considered the possibility that L. C. may be the reason, somehow or in some way, that she had not heard from Viktor since the Friday night they sat by the firepit, and, *oh dear God* – L. C.'s car drove past!

Kay pondered the impossible possibilities until she could no longer bear her own thoughts. She picked up her phone again and dialed the number for the Rowan County Sheriff's Office. She was transferred to Detective Terry Agner, the lead detective investigating her mother's murder, she shared with him her concerns that Viktor may be missing. SBI Agent Don Gale, who was working with Detective Agner in the Miller homicide case, was present at the Sheriff's Office when Kay called.

Both Detective Agner and Agent Gale had been receiving critical information on the Catherine Miller homicide. They also discovered that the Salisbury Police Department had already taken a Missing Persons Report on Viktor Gunnarsson. Viktor was officially reported missing by the assistant manager at Lakewood Apartments, Bonnie Whitley. Following Kay's phone call, Detective Agner and Agent Gale discussed the possibility of L. C. Underwood being a common link between the Gunnarsson and Miller homicides, which had occurred only four days but eighty miles or more apart.

Neither Don Gale nor Terry Agner could deny that a common denominator did exist, and that common denominator was Kay Weden. They knew instinctively that neither Kay nor Jason killed Catherine Miller. But Kay had no idea what they were thinking, or how they were handling the investigation, other than tidbits of information they shared with her sporadically.

"Agent Gale, do you think I killed my mother?" Kay asked him during an interview.

"*Did you* kill your mother?" he responded matter-of-factly.

"No, I didn't kill my mother! I loved her with every fiber of my being!" Kay exclaimed and burst into tears.

But there was only one person Don Gale and Terry Agner knew who would have a motive for eradicating both Catherine Miller and Viktor Gunnarsson from Kay's life.

On the evening of December 9, the day Catherine Miller's body was discovered, Lt. Roy Purvis, Terry Agner's supervisor, went to L. C. Underwood's house. Lieutenant Purvis just wanted to "feel him out" and find out what he had been up to for the past couple of days. L. C. agreed to talk to him, in all likelihood to fish for investigatory information.

L. C. invited Lieutenant Purvis into his home, a dwelling so immaculate that Lieutenant Purvis was silent for a moment, glancing around.

L. C. did not ask why investigators had shown up on his doorstep.

"L. C., how do you feel about Mrs. Miller's death?" Lieutenant Purvis asked him.

"This has just floored me, Roy," he answered.

"…How well did you know her?"

"Well, I hadn't seen her since around June, I guess. It was after my back operation. …You know, I always respected Mrs. Miller. She was a super nice lady. …But Kay and I have butted heads a few times."

"Have you talked to Kay?" Lieutenant Purvis asked L. C.

"I saw Kay when I was in Spencer's a couple of days ago with a young lady named Wanda. We ran into Kay there. She was with her girlfriends. Her mother may have been there, I don't know. Ya know, Roy, I still love Kay, but I don't know what the future holds for us."

"When did you last talk to Kay?" Lieutenant Purvis pressed.

"Kay called me on Monday, the 6th. She got mad and hung up on me. But then she called back and said she still loves me," he added quickly. "I don't know what she means at times. But her mother is a nice lady. She goes to church, and she is a real caring lady. I'm not sure, but I think she's a member of the Moose Lodge. A real nice lady," he repeated.

"So, the last time you talked to Kay was on Monday, December 6?"

"Uh, no, uh, I talked to her twice last night. Once around 7:30 and then around 9:30. I called Wanda last night also around 10:00. Me and Wanda talked about our trip to South Carolina this weekend. We are going to Charleston."

"So, you talked to Kay on the phone last night?"

"My first call to Kay, well, she got pissed off at me. I love her, but she gets so ticked off… Then I always call her back. Well the last time I talked to her, we talked about going to the mall on Saturday."

"Saturday, the 11th?"

"Yeah, this coming Saturday. I didn't tell her I was going out of town this weekend. …Let's see…I don't sleep well because of my back. I watched TV last night until about 3:00 this morning."

"And what did you do today?"

"I had a headlight put in one of my cars at Agner's Amoco Station."

"Ok. L. C., tell me about Kay's son Jason."

"…I came in about 10:00 this morning, and I called Kay. She'd left a message on my machine. Then Jason and Mikkel came over here today. It was about ten after one. Jason wanted me to help him do something to his car; I'd talked to Jason on Tuesday night. Anyway, while Jason was at my house, he told me about them coming after him at school because of his grandmother."

Unsolicited, L. C. launched into a soliloquy about Jason. "Jason is a spoiled brat. His mother and grandmother both cater to him like you wouldn't believe. Jason fights with his mother all of the time. He has *hit* his mother several times." Kay later denied that her son had *ever* struck her in any manner.

L. C. went on. "Kay called me one night and told me that Jason had wrecked the RX7, the gold colored one. Jason only had a driving permit at the time, not a license. I talked with the State Trooper. Kay had lied to him and told him that she was with Jason during the wreck. Jason is selfish, and his mother is the very same way."

L. C. held up the red soft drink can he was drinking. "If this was the only Coke in the house and Jason wanted it, then he would take it. I love Kay and I shouldn't say these things, but they're true! Kay gives into Jason all of the time.

I have been there with Kay and Jason when they had some knockdown, drag-out fights. Kay would get mad at me when I didn't know what was going on. Several nights I was there at Kay's house when her son took phone calls from people he owes for drugs. Jason's mother lets him drink, and I've been there to see it. Always when he wanted something, he wanted it right now. Jason has a drug habit, and his mother knows it. I saw Kay flush some drugs one day. He's nice one minute and a little b*stard the next. Kay and Jason would fight over things, but Jason would still do what *he* wanted to do." When asked, Kay adamantly denied ever having knowledge of any drugs in her home, and she certainly denied ever flushing any drugs. Kay did not drink and did not keep alcohol in her home.

"L. C., can you tell me about any weapons at Kay's house?" Lieutenant Purvis asked.

"Well, I got Jason a shotgun last Christmas. I gave Kay an old .357 of mine, but I got it back some time ago. Kay's mother had an old police special, a .38 caliber. I know Kay had it at her house. That's all the guns I know about."

"Okay. Tell me about Mikkel."

"I've talked to him on the phone a couple of times. I don't know him very well. Kay had an exchange student last year too. But I haven't been around Mikkel that much. Kay and I have been on the outs for a while. I went to Bogarts one night and Kay was there with someone. I said a few words to Kay and then knocked over a drink on her. Kay is quick tempered, and so am I."

"Do you know anyone who might be upset with Catherine Miller?"

"No. I have never heard anyone talk bad about Catherine. I think she got Jason a CD player for his birthday, and Kay told me that she and her mother gave him money also. Catherine was the sweetest lady in the world. She helped Kay make her house payments. Kay and Jason could sure go through some money! Sometimes I even gave Jason money.

But most of his money came from Kay or his grandmother. Jason never seems to want for anything. It really surprised me when Jason got a job."

L. C. continued to disparage Jason, but Lieutenant Purvis finally got a chance to say, "…Well, L. C., we might want to talk with you later, but that's all I need right now."

"By the way, can I call Kay?" L. C. asked.

"I guess that's up to you, L. C."

"You know, Roy, I don't have anything to hide. I sure wouldn't have the guts to kill anybody."

"Okay, L. C., I'll talk to you later. Bye."

"Bye."

Detective Agner paid L. C. a visit himself on December 10, 1993. L. C., somewhat guarded, invited him into his living room.

"We never had a cross word, Catherine and me," L. C. said. "I didn't think that there was a nicer lady anywhere."

"But you and Kay had some problems?" Detective Agner asked knowingly.

"Yeah, everyone is aware of that."

"What did Mrs. Miller think about that? Didn't you see her quite a bit when you were with Kay?"

"Catherine never got into mine and Kay's problems. I think that Kay had her call me back in April when Kay was wanting to come over here and I wouldn't let her… That was before my back operation… But I've been to Catherine's house and been inside it plenty of times. I've ate up there. I've burned trash for her and mowed her yard…" L. C. made a point of stating several times that he had been inside Catherine Miller's residence for various purposes.

"All right, L. C. Can you tell me what you did on Wednesday, December the 8th?"

"Well, I got a headlight put in my Monte Carlo. I wrote a check for that if you wanna see it. Then I came back between 4:30 and 5:30 that evening and talked to Doris on the phone. She works at Days Inn and was helping me with a place for me and Wanda to stay in Charleston. Then I called Kay. Then I made reservations to go to Charleston. Oh – Kay hung up on me when I told her that I was going on a trip with another woman. I talked to Wanda around 8:00, and then I called my mother. ...I called Kay back about 7:00, and I was watching *Unsolved Mysteries*, you know, on the Lifetime channel. I talked about going to the mall. ...I dozed off to sleep and woke up about 3:00 a.m. and watched TV."

"Did you leave your house after you came home from getting your headlight fixed?"

"No."

"Did you go by Kay's?"

"No, I didn't drive by Kay's house at all on Wednesday. The last time I was at Kay's was on Tuesday morning. ... Kay's mother may have been in the group at Spencer's Restaurant on Monday, but I didn't want to look over there. I was uncomfortable, see."

"I see. Wasn't Kay dependent on her mother, financially and otherwise as well?"

"I know that Kay's mother would help her out, but I don't know if Kay depended on her otherwise," L. C. said.

"Where did you get reservations for Charleston?"

"I set those reservations up through Doris at the Days Inn."

"Can you tell me about that trip?"

"Well, we drove to Charleston on Friday night and came back on Sunday. We stayed at the Days Inn in Mount Pleasant."

"Who did you take with you?"

"Wanda Hornbuckle. But keep her out of this." L. C. clearly did not want investigators questioning Wanda nor her relationship with L. C.

"Where does she live?"

"In Concord."

"Had you been dating her?"

"This, uh, this was the first time I have went anywhere with her. I met her at Twister's. There's a bunch of us that meet over at Twister's. ...I've known her for several months, and I just invited her to go with me to Charleston."

"When was it that you decided to go to Charleston?"

"We decided on Monday when we went out to eat at Spencer's. I had thought that I should be here with Kay, but she didn't call me."

"I thought you said your trip to Charleston was the first time you ever went anywhere with Wanda Hornbuckle?"

"Well, we went out to eat Monday night, but we've never gone anywhere out of town together until we went to Charleston."

"Okay. What did you do on Thursday? That was December 9th."

"Let's see... I got up Thursday morning and was going to get a haircut at Walt's Shop. It opens at 8:00, and it was around 8:00. I went to Hardee's first. I went to talk to James Henry at Days Inn about an application. I had a taillight bulb put in the [Dodge]an Diplomat. ...Then I came home... There was a message from Kay. I didn't get it all. It was something about coming by her house... Anne called later and said something had happened to Kay's mother. I asked if she wanted me to come, and she said *not now*. Then Jason and that exchange student showed up here... I asked what happened, and Jason said that his grandmother was dead. I, I asked how it happened, and he said he didn't know, that they weren't letting anyone in the house. ...Jason called Kay and she told him to come home. I called Kay that afternoon, but didn't get an answer. Jason called me back and said that he was waiting on a deputy to come by and pick him up. ...Later I talked to her – to Kay – briefly to find out what was going on. Kay couldn't say a lot about it. That's the last contact that I had with her. The reason that I haven't tried to contact her anymore is because of all these rumors. When I first started hearing rumors, I talked to Doris, and she told me about some then. I told her that there was no use in me going to the funeral home. I wanted to go, but I couldn't... You've got to understand Kay. She will believe anything that you tell her. She wants people to believe that she is all sugar and spice, but she is *not*. Kay wants to be the center of attention no matter what. And her son is a spoiled brat."

"Why do you say that?" Detective Agner asked.

"Well, he had this wreck that I helped him get out of. Kay covered for him. And I know he has done drugs. You know, I have seen that boy so drunk that he couldn't stand up. Catherine gave him anything that he wanted. Jason and Kay are both the same way – if they want something all they do is whine for it. ...And you know, one thing that stood out with me was that Jason didn't appear to be upset the day that he came by here. He sat there and ate two sandwiches. He didn't say much about this grandmother. ...He got up and went to the bathroom and was in there a few minutes, and then he called his mother and left. ...But Jason would blow up over anything. When he wanted something, he wanted it NOW. Kay has made him that way. ...Did you know that Kay is having a court battle right now with her ex-husband?"

"No, I don't think so. Do you know anyone Kay has dated?"

"I have no idea. The only person I saw her with was that deal at Bogarts."

"Do you know Viktor Gunnarsson?"

"No. ...Who is he? I've never heard of him. Is this someone she has dated recently? Does he live here in town? See that is something else, she said she hasn't dated anybody else, that she just goes out with her girlfriends."

"Well, have you ever heard the name Viktor Gunnarsson?"

"No, no, I don't think so. I don't think Kay has ever mentioned it. ...The man that Kay was engaged to before me was Jeff something. Her mother loaned him two or three thousand dollars. They took his motorcycle until he paid it back."

"…I need to ask you about your guns, L. C. How many handguns do *you* have?" Detective Agner asked casually.

"I let Kay borrow a .357 last year. She didn't keep it long, though. That's the only pistol I have. When me and my wife were together, I bought her a .38, a Charter Arms. She took it. I bought it at Frank's. I also bought a .22 at least a year and a half ago." L. C. knew there was a record of the purchase at Frank's Pawn Shop in Salisbury.

"All right. Uh, what time did you say you got home on Wednesday?"

"Around 4:00 or 4:30."

"Okay."

"…Uh, you know, I like this new girl more than I ever liked Kay. I never left the house on Wednesday night. I am not going to sit around and wait on Kay. If she dates someone else, there is nothing that I can do about it."

"Do you know what Kay talked about to her mother?"

"No, I don't know. I don't know what she may have told her about *me*."

Detective Agner made eye contact with L. C. "L. C., have you drove by Kay's house to check on her recently?"

"No. During the past, uh, two to three months I did not check on her. I haven't went [*sic*] by her house at all except the Tuesday morning that I went to see her."

"Okay. L. C., you know, there is something you can do to get the suspicion off you if you didn't have anything to do with Viktor Gunnarsson or Catherine Miller. You can take a polygraph."

"I won't take a police-administered polygraph. I got f*cked on the one in Kannapolis. But I will take one administered by someone I choose."

"Well, we'll talk about it a little later. I appreciate you talking to me, L. C." Detective Agner said.

"Sure. You know I'll cooperate with you guys all I can. I just wish this would all get over with soon."

"Well, I'll talk to ya later."

"Okay. Bye."

After the SBI agents got involved with the murder investigation of Catherine Miller, Special Agents Bill Lane and Vance Farr were assigned to interview L. C. They drove to his house on Friday, December 17, and L. C. invited them into his living room.

L. C. started out by saying, "Now I, I did not have anything to do with the death of Catherine Miller. I have no reason to want to do any harm to her. Mrs. Miller was a very nice lady."

"When did you find out about her murder?" one of them asked L. C.

"When Jason came over to the house that afternoon. Wednesday. Jason was acting real strange that day," L. C. said conspiratorially.

"What do you mean, 'strange'?"

"Well, I thought it was strange that Jason wanted something to eat, and that he wanted to clean up his car. As far as I could tell, he wasn't upset or crying or anything like that over his, uh, grandmother."

"What about your relationship with Kay Weden? Can you tell us about that?"

"I and Kay broke up several months ago. *I* was the one to end it." His comments sounded familiar.

He continued, "Kay was just causing me problems. We had kind of a 'love-hate' sort of thing. Kay was getting too *possessive*, and I felt like I was getting smothered. ...See, Kay had been calling my house, harassing me on the phone. It got so bad that I had her number blocked on my phone." The agents knew that it was Kay that had L. C.'s number blocked, and L. C. that was doing the stalking, but they were not going to confront L. C. with that information at that particular time.

"When did you do that? Block Kay's phone number, I mean."

"Probably better than a week now," L. C. replied. "I haven't called Kay on the phone for several weeks." Again, the agents knew better. L. C. had just told Det. Terry Agner that he had called Kay the night before her mother was found murdered.

"Do you know who Kay has been dating?" one of the agents asked.

"No, I don't know and I don't care. There's no *reason* for me to care who she dates. I mean, *I've* been dating other women."

"Do you know, L. C., or what do you think happened to Catherine Miller?"

"*I* think maybe Jason, her grandson, told somebody about all the things that were in his grandmother's house to settle a drug debt. Jason has a drug problem, and he hangs around with boys I *know* are users, and these boys will do anything. I feel like Jason might do anything to get money for drugs too. ...I don't think that Jason would have killed his grandmother himself, but I think Jason may have set her up for a robbery. Somebody must have gotten inside the house before Mrs. Miller got home and was going through her things when she got home. Then they killed her." His response sounded rehearsed.

"Why do you think that, L. C.?"

"Because whoever did it had to have the code to the alarm system, and they must have gotten it from Jason. I think Jason set the robbery up because of his drug debt."

Agent Lane told L. C., "Evidence from the crime scene indicates that Mrs. Miller was already home when the killer – or killers – entered the house."

"What evidence?" L. C. quickly asked.

"L. C., you know I can't tell you about the specific evidence." He wanted to give L. C. something to chew on. "By the way, do you know anyone from Sweden?"

"No," L. C. said.

"You don't know Viktor Gunnarsson?"

"No." Then he quickly tried to change the subject. "... You know, there have been a lot of rumors told about mine and Kay's relationship, and *some* of those rumors have come from the Rowan County Sheriff's Department. I have already told where I was the day Mrs. Miller was killed, and I'm tired of the Sheriff's Department coming to my house all the time and asking questions as if they thought *I* did the killing. I really don't appreciate how they're treating me."

"L. C., you know they have a job to do, and they're just trying to do it. But that's all we need from you right now. We may be in touch later."

Later that same day, Det. Linda Porter talked with an employee, Mrs. Phyllis Peeler, of the refrigeration company where Catherine Miller had been a faithful employee for forty years. Phyllis Peeler stated that she knew well where Catherine Miller lived, and in fact, she had taken that route and driven by Catherine's home on Wednesday evening.

"Did you see something there?" Detective Porter asked Mrs. Peeler.

"I did indeed. I saw a car there that wasn't Catherine's. It was dark red, or burgundy rather. It was parked in front of her house."

"Mrs. Peeler, are you sure? Are you sure that it was Wednesday, December 8?"

"I am a hundred percent sure."

Detective Porter notified Detective Agner immediately.

The following day, Saturday, December 11, Agent Don Gale interviewed Lucy Spencer, a resident of Salisbury. Mrs. Spencer told him that on Wednesday, December 8th, after making a purchase at Piece Goods Fabric Shop, she was driving in the Westcliff Development, Catherine Miller's neighborhood, when she saw a wine-colored car on the shoulder of the road in front of Catherine Miller's house. She did not, however, see anyone in or near the vehicle.

A few hours later, Agent Don Gale received a phone call from a Salisbury resident, who was driving on Enon Church

Road at 5:30 p.m. on Wednesday, December 8th. The man stated that he noticed a car parked on the side of Enon Church Road. The car was large, dark red, and parked on the shoulder of the road in the grass just before the intersection of Larch Road. There was no one in or near the car. The man told Don that he drives that route regularly but did not recall ever seeing a car like that on Enon Church Road before.

The same evening, Agent Gale received a second phone call from a man who identified himself as the father of the young man Agent Gale had spoken with earlier in the day. He told Agent Gale that he was traveling on Enon Church Road with his son about 5:30 p.m., and he saw a midsize car, late 80s model, burgundy to red in color, American made.

Even later on Saturday, December 11, Agent Gale talked by phone with a female resident of Rowan County. She reported that on Wednesday, December 8, after picking up her husband from work, she was traveling on Enon Church Road and noticed a burgundy car, late 70s model, parked on the side of the road at about 5:15 in the evening.

L. C. Underwood owned and operated a 1979 Chevrolet Monte Carlo, burgundy wine in color.

CHAPTER TWELVE

"Ye are of your father, the devil, and the lusts of your father ye will do. He was a murderer from the beginning, and abode not in the truth, because there is no truth in him. When he speaketh a lie, he speaketh of his own: for he is a liar, and the father of it" (John 8:44)

On January 5, 1994, Agent Don Gale and Det. Terry Agner asked Kay Weden if she would be willing to make a recorded phone call to L. C. in order to gauge his responses to her. In spite of the knots forming her stomach at the very thought of talking to L. C., she agreed. The call was made and recorded from the Rowan County Sheriff's Office.

L. C. answered, "Hello?"

"This is Kay."

Pause. Then, "Yeah, whatcha need?"

"I was just wondering why I hadn't heard from you in so long."

"Kay, I, I don't want to talk, to talk to you right now."

"Why not?"

"Like you don't know why, Kay?" L. C. began to raise his voice.

"No, I don't."

"Yeah, you do know why too."

"No, I don't."

"Yes, you do."

"You know, I just don't know why you never did, you know, even send me a card."

"Kay, all the d*mn rumors that's been going around…"

"Well you know those rumors went around before when that vandalism was going on at my house."

"Yeah, yeah, and the same's going around this time. That wasn't even, I mean, that [stutter] that, soon as, soon as this all happened, you know they started looking at me. They come to talk to me. I've talked to them. I've told them what I knew."

"Why do, why do you think they came to you and looked at you?"

"I'll guarantee you know why, because of that d*mn incident up there at that d*mn restaurant!"

"Because of the incident at Bogarts?"

"Yeah!"

"That had nothing to do with killing my mother!"

"Uh, well, yeah, I mean somebody, ah, the way I acted up there pouring that drink in your lap, don't you think they asked me about that?"

"Well I don't know, but I don't see where the two are related."

"I see where it's a lot related." I bet he did.

"How?" Kay demanded to know.

"Uh, because Kay, they think, they're trying, you know, the rumors and stuff I'm hearing that I've, I had something to do with this to get back at you, and that is total bullsh*t!"

"Well, did you?" she asked quickly.

"Hell no! I ain't never wanted to get back at anybody!"

"Well I don't know, L. C., you know all this vandalism that went on at my house and all this stuff, and they've questioned me. They asked me if I killed my mother! …Did you kill my mother, L. C.?"

"No, I didn't… You know, and I, you know I am sick of this! I'm, I'm sick and tired of it!"

"Well then who would have done it?"

"Kay, how would I know? If I knew I would have told them!"

"I don't know, L. C., you had the perfect motive to do it."

"The, the motive for what? What could have been my motive to do it?"

"I don't know, maybe you wanted to hurt me, you know, like you said I hurt you."

"That is crazy, Kay."

"I don't know, L. C. I just know that my mother is dead."

"I know that too, and I know I didn't have nothing to do with it. And I, I've tried to cooperate with these people."

"Well I had to wait until tonight because nobody's here –"

"Let me tell you something…"

"Mikkel and Jason are at a basketball game."

"I told –"

"I just had to get this off my chest."

"I told them, I, I, I gave them permission to search my house. I gave them my d*mn gun. I, I told them they could do anything they wanted to do."

"Well, you know you were doing an awful lot of stalking on me. You were following me around. I know that."

"Listen. You know, that night that I came out to that restaurant out there, I had no idea you were there."

"L. C., the restaurant has nothing to do with it!"

"All right. What does have something to do with it, Kay?"

"I don't know. I just, I just know that I have been thinking about this for a long, long time."

"Well…"

"You know, and it's crossed my mind that you did it."

"Well, I'm telling you I didn't do it! And I would have had no reason to do that. I never had, had one cross word to say about your mama."

"No, you never had a cross word to say about my mother, but my mother often did have a lot of control over me."

"Listen…"

"And you kept saying stuff. See all this stuff is coming back to my mind now, and you kept saying stuff like 'I bet your mother hates me for all this stuff that's going on,' and I said no, 'My mother doesn't hate anybody.'"

"Let me tell you something. I could tell you now, and I'll tell you a hundred years from now I didn't have nothing to do with that."

"Well, then why didn't you ever come see me? Why didn't you ever come to the funeral home? Why didn't you come to –"

"You, you, you!"

"the funeral?"

"You want me to tell you, why don't you call Doris and ask her why I didn't come to the funeral home?"

"Doris came."

"I know."

"And her daughter came too."

"Why, why don't you call Doris and ask Doris why I didn't come to the funeral home?"

"Well, why don't you tell me why you didn't? Why do I have to call Doris to find out?"

"I think you ought to call Doris 'cause I called Doris and asked her about going to the funeral home."

"Why, I mean, why would you call Doris and ask her if you could go or not?"

"I didn't ask her if I *could* go, Kay."

"…or why you *should* go."

"All these rumors that sprung up. I started hearing rumors that same d*mn day. Gil was hearing rumors, Doris was hearing rumors. You know, if I had come to the funeral home, how in the hell would I have known you wouldn't have went off on me?"

"You know, for somebody who says they love me like you said you loved me, you know, I haven't heard from you for a month."

"Listen…"

"I mean, with all the sh*t that's going on, you know Jason's been accused too. I've been accused!"

"Well, you know, like I told them, you know they could have come looked in my house. The, the, the d*mn, that Thursday or whenever it was after this happened and that detective came over here, I told them to look through my house. Mark Wilhelm came with them. I said anything you wanna look for in my house, you look for it. You know, I gave them free reign. And the g*dd*mn SBI, that g*dd*mn Don Gale, that's the g*dd*mn son of a b*tch that started some of these d*mn rumors!"

"Don Gale didn't start any rumors about you, L. C."

"Bullsh*t! That ain't what I'm hearing!"

"You know, I was scared to death of Don Gale, and I told him so. But you know, he's doing his job because we had a long talk about that, and you know, if I had been lying to him he would have known that."

"Uh, uh, well…"

"I took a lie detector test, L. C."

"Oh, uh, and I told them I would take one."

"Have you taken one?"

"No, they haven't offered it to me."

"They didn't offer you a polygraph?"

"Why I told them I would take a polygraph test if it was administered by somebody other than a police agency 'cause I'm not gonna get f*cked again on a polygraph test."

"Well, I'm gonna tell ya, Don Gale told me that you refused to take a lie detector test."

"He's a lying son of a b*tch!"

"He said that the reason you didn't take one was because you didn't trust him and all that crap about the last time you took it. And something else I found out, you told me back then that they set the perimeter real, real low on you, like minus six and plus three."

"Mmm?"

"That's a lie, 'cause when I sat down in that chair to take that test, Mike Bridgers told me that they set them at minus six and plus three. I knew then you were lying to me."

"Lying about what, now?"

"About those perimeters the last time you took a polygraph. You said they set it real low on you, and they don't. They have to be set the same for everybody."

"Well… That's what my attorney told me."

"Then he told you wrong, because there's a standard they have to set for every test they give."

"Whatever…"

"Jason took a polygraph too, L. C. And Jason passed it, as did I."

"Well…"

"And I talked to Mike Culnon."

"D*mn Mike Culnon," L. C. said.

"And I'm thinking of reopening that vandalism, L. C., because I think you had something to do with it."

"Well, if, if, if that's what you think, you think it. You know, you can think anything you want to think."

"You know, what went on at my house is just a precursor of everything that happened before."

"Say what?"

"I said everything that went on at my house at the very beginning of spring with all that stuff…"

"Uh-huh"

"You know, I, maybe I should have listened to Mike Culnon then, but I was, I was too gullible. I believed what you said too much. But I don't believe it now."

"Well, if you don't believe it, that's fine Kay. You believe anything you want to believe."

And I honestly, L. C., I honestly believe that my mother knew who came in her house because the day I put my hand on her screen door to open the door, I knew right then that she knew – my mother *knew* – who came in her house. She knew exactly what went on and who it was that killed her."

"Well, I can tell ya, I didn't have anything to do with it."

"I don't believe that."

"Well, you believe anything you want to believe, Kay."

"Because, L. C., I believe that if you didn't have anything to do with it, you would have come over here. You would have been with me."

"Because what I was hearing was, you know, that you were trying to accuse me of doing it."

"No! You don't do that. You know, you just don't do that to people you love."

"You're wrong."

"Why?"

"Because what I was hearing was, you know, that you were trying to accuse me of doing it."

"You did. I know you did. I put my hand on Mama's screen door, and I sat in that car and I talked to Terry Agner. And I told him exactly then that whoever killed my mother, *she knew them.* And I know it was you!"

"And you're wrong."

"And I'm *not* wrong!"

"Yes, yes are wrong."

"No, I'm not."

"Yes, you are."

"I am not wrong, and to the day I die, I won't be wrong."

"Well you know, you can think anything you want to think."

"And I think you killed your dog too."

"…Lord, have mercy…"

"You didn't take Misty to Salisbury Animal Hospital like you told me, L. C. –" *Click.*

Kay's comments were interrupted by L. C. hanging up the phone.

Two days later was Friday, January 7, 1994, Kay accepted an offer from a couple of her girlfriends to get her out of the house, to take her out to dinner. Kay returned home afterward to find a message from Tana Howe on her answering machine.

"Kay, a man's body has been found murdered in the woods in the mountains, in Watauga County."

CHAPTER THIRTEEN

"The man, who is the lord of the
land, spake roughly to us,
and took us for spies of the country" (Genesis 42:30)

Shirley Twitty was working at a nursing home in Lexington, North Carolina, where Agent Wilson and I met with her on January 21, 1994. Shirley agreed to meet us on her meal break. She was about to tell us what L. C. was doing on the evening of December 3, 1993, the last night Viktor Gunnarsson was seen alive.

"I met L. C. Underwood at Twister's Club in Cornelius. It was last August, the 28th. We danced and he asked me out. …We dated some. We went to a few North Cabarrus High School football games in Salisbury in the fall. But I told him when he asked that I was not interested in getting serious with anyone."

"How did you feel about L. C. personally?" I asked.

"Well, at first I liked him. But he had a temper. Like he would get really mad when other drivers were speeding. One night when I was with him, he got into a car chase that another police officer was involved in… When it was over L. C. cussed out the cop for something he thought they'd done wrong," she told us. "I was embarrassed for him."

"Were there occasions when he showed his temper?" I prompted.

"Twice I had to cancel my date with him. One of those nights he had made dinner for me, and I had to cancel at the last minute. But I had never told him I could come for certain, anyway. He just kind of insisted I was coming even when I told him I didn't know if I could make it or not. Anyway, he got really mad."

"Were there other instances?" Agent Wilson asked her.

"Yes. One day I was talking on the phone with him, and I happened to mention that I had gone target-shooting with a friend of mine – a male friend. L. C. asked me the man's name, and as soon as I told him, he hung up on me. We stopped dating then. I didn't need that."

"Did he know the man or something?" I asked.

"I have no idea. But then I started getting hang-up calls at home. I tried to trace the calls, but the call-return service I had only said that the calls were being made from a long-distance carrier and couldn't be identified beyond that. I thought the calls were coming from L. C. because his phone was long distance from mine. ...Then one night, I got a message on my answering machine. It was a man speaking with a low voice, and it sounded like L. C. But there was music in the background so I could not hear very clearly. That song "Stand by Me" was playing. But I couldn't be a hundred percent sure it was L. C.'s voice. I gave the recording to the SBI."

"Then that must have been later in the fall, correct?" I asked.

"Yes. Then, he called me on October 17th. He told me that his mother had breast cancer and only had a year to live. He asked me to come over, to his house, so I went. I felt bad for him."

"Did he give you additional details about his mother?"

"L. C. said that they were very close, and that he worshiped the ground that woman walks on. He said he didn't know if he could go on if she died. ... He said that at least once a year he took her and her husband on a cruise."

"Would you say he was visibly upset about his mother when you visited him that night?" I asked.

"He seemed… weird. He was very nervous. He couldn't sit still," she said.

"Did you continue to see him after that?"

"He called me again in early December. He sounded upset. I mentioned that I wanted to see the Robin Williams movie *Mrs. Doubtfire,* and L. C. offered to take me. He said he would check the newspapers to see where it was playing and call me back."

"And did he?"

"He called me back and asked me to meet him at his house on Friday."

"Was that Friday, the third of December?"

"Yes."

While Viktor Gunnarsson was having dinner with Kay Weden and Catherine Miller at the Blue Bay Seafood Restaurant, Shirley drove to L. C.'s house, arriving about 7:30 p.m. L. C. was dressed nicely in slacks and a nice button-up shirt and sweater. But he was pacing in the backyard.

"He was upset, hyper, and just could not be still," Shirley described. "I noticed that he had lost a lot of weight since I had seen him last. I asked him if something was wrong. He said, 'My dog died last night.' I knew he thought a lot of that sheltie. She was his life. He took it every week to the vet, and the vet told L. C. that the dog was perfectly healthy and did not need to come in every week. But L. C. worried and just kept taking him. Anyway, I told him I was sorry to hear about his dog, and I asked him what happened to the dog. He said it died of some virus."

"When had you last seen the dog?" I asked.

"A couple of weeks before that, and it looked fine to me."

"So did you go to the movie?"

"No. L. C. said *Mrs. Doubtfire* wasn't playing around there, so we would just go out to dinner."

Shirley explained that L. C. pulled his Monte Carlo out from his carport so that she could pull her car into the space.

L. C. then drove the two of them into town, but kept running off the road, seeming very preoccupied.

"Do you think he had been drinking?" Agent Wilson asked.

"No, I don't think so," she said. "I didn't smell anything on him."

L. C. drove around several restaurants in Salisbury. He stopped twice to make calls from two different pay phones. L. C. told Shirley he was checking his messages. L. C. then drove Shirley into a residential neighborhood and past a ranch-style brick house. He told her, "I'm thinking about buying that house." Shirley recalls that there was one car parked outside the house at that time.

L. C. drove away from the house then and stopped at a convenience store and filled his car with gasoline. He drove them around some more but finally stopped to eat dinner at Irvin's Restaurant in Salisbury. They arrived about 8:30 p.m. L. C. had a couple of beers. He ordered a chicken dinner but did not each much of it.

"Shirley, I just don't know what I'm going to do," he told her. "I don't want to go back to Ohio."

"Well, L. C., you need to go back and see your mother. She's sick," Shirley told him.

"Didn't I tell you?" he asked.

"Tell me what?"

"My mother died."

"I'm really sorry, L. C. I didn't know," she told him sympathetically.

"She died, and we buried her already. She had just gotten out of the hospital and just lost the will to live. We rushed her back to the hospital, but she died there."

Shirley was shocked that his mother had just been diagnosed with cancer and had died so quickly.

The conversation turned then to L. C. and his personal life. He told Shirley that he had been in a relationship with a woman, but that it was now over.

"Well I figured that you date a lot of people," Shirley told him.

"No, not at all," he said.

After dinner, L. C. drove them back to his house.

"What time did you get there?"

"About 10:00."

Shirley said they walked into the house, and L. C. was still "hyped up."

"Shirley, would you do something for me" he asked.

"What is it?"

"I have a friend whose wife is running around on him. He's trying to get custody of their children. Would you mind driving your car to my friend's house so I can take a look? I'd drive my car, but my car and my tag would be recognized."

"Okay, I guess. But why doesn't your friend hire a private investigator?" she asked L. C.

"He's a police officer. He can run tag numbers and easily get any information he needs."

At 10:15 p.m. Shirley and L. C. left in Shirley's car. L. C. gave her directions as she drove.

"Do you have anything to write on?" L. C. asked.

Shirley reached into the back seat where she kept some medical forms for work. L. C. pointed out the house. It was the same brick house they had driven by earlier, which L. C. said he was thinking about buying. The lights were on inside the house, and the front storm door was closed. Shirley pulled into the driveway. L. C. just about came unglued.

"Back out! Back out!" He shouted at her.

"I can't back out right this second; there are two cars coming!" she argued.

"Back out anyway!" he shouted.

As Shirley backed out, L. C. wrote down the tag number from a large light-colored sedan. There was another car or two there, and L. C. remarked, "Well, I guess that's her kids."

"The kids are old enough to drive and they're fighting for custody?" Shirley asked L. C.

L. C. paused for a moment, shrugged and said, "Well, he's trying anyway."

Shirley realized at that point that the house might belong to L. C.'s girlfriend. Linda Porter, a friend of Shirley's and a detective with the Rowan County Sheriff's Office, had warned Shirley about dating L. C. Linda told Shirley that L. C. had allegedly shot into Kay Weden's house before and that he was not charged only because he persuaded Kay not to press charges against him.

"Back in September, I asked him about shooting into his girlfriend's house. L. C. said it wasn't true, that the SBI was just out to destroy him," she told us.

"What happened next? When you pulled back out of the driveway of that house?" I asked.

"L. C. kept telling me to slow down. He said he wasn't a cop anymore and couldn't help me if I got a speeding ticket. He had already told me that he had retired from the police department."

When they returned to L. C.'s house, Shirley was quiet and thoughtful, wondering what L. C. was really up to. She and L. C. went inside a few minutes before 11:00 p.m. L. C. carried inside the piece of paper he had written the tag number on, and he went to the phone in his bedroom. Shirley walked into L. C.'s bedroom and sat on his bed, listening to L. C.'s side of the phone conversation.

"He called a friend of his, a police officer. I heard L. C. read him the tag number and ask him to run it for him before he hung up. Then about five minutes later, the officer called back and gave the registration information to L. C. The car belonged to some man with a foreign sounding name, like Gunner-son."

"Did L. C. write down the information?" I asked.

"He did. I watched him write it down. Then he hung up. He asked me to spend the night with him, but I declined." I wondered how things might have turned out differently for Viktor Gunnarsson, had Shirley stayed with L. C. that night.

L. C. walked Shirley to her car. He hugged and kissed her goodbye. The temperature was a brisk forty-five degrees in Salisbury. Shirley left L. C.'s house at 11:00. His two vehicles, the burgundy Monte Carlo and the gold Dodge Diplomat, were parked in his driveway under the carport when she left. Shirley drove home to Kannapolis, where she arrived about 11:40. L. C. never called her again. On January 4, 1994, Det. Linda Porter, Det. Terry Agner, and SBI Agent Bobby Bonds drove Shirley Twitty by Lakewood Apartments. Shirley identified a dove gray Lincoln Town Car as the vehicle L. C. got the tag number from on December third. The license plate #DPW-7098 was registered to Viktor Ake Lennart Gunnarsson.

"That's the same tag number L. C. wrote down," Shirley told them.

"Can you remember how to get to the house L. C. showed you on the night of December third?" Det. Linda Porter asked her.

"I believe so," Shirley told them. She directed them to a brick ranch-style house in the Westcliff subdivision. It was Kay Weden's home.

When they returned to the Sheriff's Office, Shirley agreed to make a recorded phone call to L. C. Underwood.

He answered on the second ring.

"L. C."

"Yeah."

"Shirley."

"Hey."

"Hey. How ya doing?"

"Oh, Okay. Just wondering how you are; I haven't heard from you."

"Oh, I'm doing fine, doing fine. Got a cold," he said.

"Have you?"

"Yeah, I've had one for about two or three weeks now."

"Well, listen, do you have a minute? I, ah, I had some police officers come out and ask me some questions."

"Uh-huh"

"– and I was just wondering what's going on. I mean –"

"Nothing that I know of," L. C. said.

"Well they said something about a guy that disappeared and they can't find him."

"Well, I don't know where he's at... I, you know, I wouldn't know where he's at."

"Yeah, but you told me that was your friend's house and that you were checking –"

L. C. stuttered when he tried to answer. "Ah, um, well, the house *we* went to *was*."

"Well, they told me it was your ex-girlfriend's house."

"Nah, that's bullsh*t."

"It wasn't Kay's house?" Shirley asked.

"No. No," L. C. said.

"Well why would they say something like that?" she asked.

"Aw hell! Why would they say anything Shirley?"

"I don't know."

"You know, they tried to screw me one time, and I'm *not* gonna let them screw me again. You know, if this guy, whoever Kay was seeing, if he's missing, he's missing on his own!"

"Well I don't know anything about it. Only thing I know was that you said that was your buddy's ex-wife's house and he was trying to get his kids back."

"You know, that was... You know, I've just, I've just about had it with those d*mn *ssholes! You know, they uh –"

Shirley interrupted him. "I just won't want to get involved in nothing."

"Well, dear, you ain't involved in nothing"

"Well, I am when they come out and question me!" she said.

"Well, hell, tell them what you know!"

"I did!" she said.

"You know, hell, that ain't no big deal. I mean that ain't no big deal at all. You know, ah, uh, I just, you know, I just flat out told them, you know, I told them what I knew about it, what they were asking, and that's all. You know I could tell them, you know, the hell with them! That ain't my problem! That's their d*mn problem!"

"Well…"

"No, you ain't involved in nothing. Don't worry about that. You haven't done a d*mn thing wrong."

"I know I haven't! I mean, I just got a little upset because they come out and asked me questions."

"Well, hell, don't feel bad; they went over and asked my neighbor over here had I ever left anything at his house or asked him to hide anything at his house. And a guy from the Sheriff's Department came here today. I cussed his *ss out! I told him not to never come back to my d*mn house again!"

"Well, I don't know…"

"You know, I told him not to never come back to my d*mn house. You know, I've had it! The, the, they spread rumor and every d*mn thing else and I am not going to tolerate their sh*t anymore! You know, I just told them flat out!"

"They also said you were a suspect in a murder, L. C."

"They said, they said I was a suspect in a murder?"

"Yeah."

"I, I'm, I'm, I'll put a stop to this silly sh*t! I'm gonna put a stop to that. They can kiss my *ss!"

"They didn't question you about that?" Shirley asked him.

"Yeah. You know, I told them what I knew. And, any you know, if that's not good enough for them they can go to hell. You know, I've had it with these d*mn people! And telling you something like that, I'll, I'll talk to my d*mn attorney about this sh*t. I'm gonna put a stop to this d*mn bullsh*t! I mean, them telling you something like that!"

"Yeah."

"That's the d*mn straw that broke the camel's back right there!"

"It really upset me, you know."

"Well, I didn't mean for it to upset you, and I'm sorry you got upset, but you can rest assured my lawyer will take care of this sh*t!"

"But what can your lawyer do?"

"You know, for spreading rumors like that."

"But you *are* a suspect, you know."

"Spreading rumors! This, I mean, this is total bullsh*t! You know, them telling you something like that. I'm not gonna put up with this sh*t anymore! Now they can kiss my *ss!

"Well…"

"Hell, you know me better than that," he said.

"Yeah, I thought I did."

"You know, let me tell you something. I wouldn't have the guts to do something like that. I wouldn't have the d*mn guts to do something like that!"

"You wouldn't?"

"Hell no!"

"I mean, I couldn't see anybody doing that myself, but when somebody comes up and starts asking all these questions…"

"You know, you can rest assured my attorney is going to take care of this sh*t. Now I've had it! I've had it with these b*stards!"

"Uh…"

"You know, I'm sorry, that, you know, you got involved in something like that, but –"

"Well, I am too. But the biggest thing about it, L. C., is you're still saying that was your *friend's* house! …Okay, one of them came to my house and I had to go take them to the house, and they told me whose house it was! And also they told me whose car it was that you got the tag number off of!"

Without answering her question, L. C. continued ranting. "Oh, I tell you, I've had enough of this sh*t!"

"Well I'm just telling you what I had to do."

"And I appreciate your calling and telling me, okay?"

"Well…"

"And I hate, I hate you got involved in anything…"

"Well I hate it too because I believed you. I mean, you seemed so upset over your mother dying…"

"Well, listen…"

"…and your dog dying."

"I hate you got involved in this. They won't bother you anymore. I can guarantee you..."

"Okay…"

"Well, you take care."

"You too."

"Okay. Bye."

"Bye."

L. C. did not hesitate to use his male friends, either. Don and Terry informed Steve and me that it was Deputy Rick Hillard who L. C. called on the night of December third, while he was with Shirley Twitty.

We listened to the tape recording of the phone call from Rick Hillard to the Salisbury Police Department. The call was received by the dispatch center at 2306 hours.

"Salisbury Police. Clark."

"Yo."

"Hey."

"This is Rick Hillard, Special Deputy, and Rowan County Sheriff's Office."

"Hey man."

"I need you to run a 10-28 [license plate registration information] for me."

"Lay it on me."

"Uh, David-Paul-William-seven-zero-nine-eight [DPW-7098]."

"What're ya doing now, boy?"

"Not a d*mn thing."

"Kinda loafing... Hey, this comes back to a 79 Lincoln four-door."

"Uh-huh"

"And ...I'm gonna spell his name."

"Okay."

"First name is "V" as in Victor, I-K-T-O-R. T-O-R."

"Okay."

"And middle name A-K-E-L-E-N-N-A-R-T. The last name is G-U-N-N-A-R-S-S-O-N."

"Good God!"

"And it shows 609 Grove Street. Shows valid, no 29s [not wanted]."

"Hmmm. That's a, a '79 Lincoln?"

"Yeah."

"Hmmm. Okay, thank you, Joe, 'appreciate it...'"

Rick told us he called L. C. immediately and gave him the information. He even spelled it so L. C. could write it down.

"Thanks, buddy," L. C. told him.

Rick was questioned by investigators from the Rowan County Sheriff's Office and the SBI investigators in that district on many occasions. At that time, of course, their primary interest was the Catherine Miller murder. They knew that L. C. had very few friends, but Rick was one of them. In fact, Rick was asked and agreed to take a polygraph examination on January 6, 1994. He passed with ease.

When Rick was first questioned in early December 1993 about the possibility of L. C. having murdered Catherine Miller, Rick was loyal to L. C.

"I just can't see L. C. doing it. It would take a cold b*stard to off an eighty-year-old woman. If it was Kay I would say yeah. If he [L. C.] did it I would turn him in in a heartbeat." Rick had obviously heard enough of L. C.'s garbage to start believing it. At this time, he did not personally know Kay, and I believe he never would have said what he did had it not been for L. C.'s poisonous influence. Rick added "If he was going to do anything, I think that he would do it to Kay, not her mother. Or maybe Jason, because she worships the ground that he walks on."

Rick said that L. C. has been under a lot of mental strain. But he has been seeing a doctor and is even dating another girl now. Rick could not tell investigators what her name was, but Rick also remembered that L. C. made up a girlfriend by the name of Kim, who he created to make Kay jealous. L. C. asked Rick to go along with him about "Kim" if Kay ever asked him.

Rick thinks L. C. feels as if he is being pushed around. Rick told L. C. that the police "have to go fishing" and that he would even start with L. C. considering his stormy past with Kay.

"I told L. C., 'You better leave her alone.' I told him that I knew about the incidents he had done, and he asked how. I told him my brother told me and Kay told me that she went to the magistrate. ...Before the Bogarts incident, L. C. told me he couldn't understand why Kay wasn't there for him and God help her if anything ever happened to her mother like what happened to his mother. This was right after he found out his mother had terminal cancer. He said she only had a couple of months to live. ...Before L. C. left the Police Department he told me that he went up to Ohio and gave his mother his last $8,000. He told me that he made funeral arrangements for her. ...L. C. made reference to the fact that Kay was real close to her mother, but he didn't say he was jealous of her mother."

Rick Hillard stated to investigators that L. C. told him the reason he wanted the license plate registration information ran was because a car had backed up into his driveway, that Kay Weden was in the car, and he did not know the man in the car with her.

The investigators kept going back many times to talk to Rick before Steve and I ever became involved in the investigation. On January 6, 1994, the day before Viktor's body was found, Rick consented to call L. C. and allow investigators to record the conversation. The call was transcribed as follows:

*****

"Hello?"

"L. C."

"Yeah."

"Whatcha doing?"

"Hey, Rick! Watchin' TV."

"Uh, the SBI just left here, man."

"Did they?"

"Yeah."

"What'd ya tell 'em?"

"Well, let me ask you something. You remember that night I ran that tag for ya?"

"Yeah."

"Uh, it come back to Viktor Gunnarsson, or something like that?"

"I don't remember the name."

"Well, you know that night was the last night they ever seen that guy? And that he'd, he had gone out with Kay once or twice?"

"The last time they seen him?" L. C. asked.

"Uh-huh. That's the last, that was the last night anybody seen him."

"Hmmm."

"He's been missing ever since that night."

"He's missing?" L. C. asked.

"Uh-hmm."

"Missing where? I mean, run off, or?"

"They don't know. Nobody can find him."

"Hmmm."

"And that's the same night I called and told you, you know, where he lived and everything."

"Uh-huh"

"Now he's *missing*."

"Where did he live? On Grove Street?" L. C. asked.

"Yeah."

"You know, they asked me about it and I told 'em I never heard of him. I wouldn't know the guy if I saw him," L. C. claimed.

"Yeah. Well, it turned out that, er, it was the guy from that night. Evidently Kay dated once or twice or went out with, and then that night, he turned up missing. And they got, you know, the copy of me calling in to Joe and talking to him, running that tag. And so now, you know, they're wanting to know, you know, what the hell's going on. 'Cause you know, this guy dates Kay, and then he turns up missing."

"Well I mean, you, you say *missing*. Or he's left town?"

"No, he's missing. The – his car's still there, but he's gone."

"Well I wonder where in the hell he could've went," L. C. said.

"Well they don't know. And that's what they're wanting to know. They had it on tape, you know, and I told them, you know, that I'd run the tag for you."

"But I don't, I don't remember the guy's name."

"Yeah. Well I didn't remember his name 'cause Joe with Dispatch spelled it out for me."

"I, I don't, I, they asked me did I know the, know somebody over there. They told me his name, and I, I'd never, ya know, I'd never, I told 'em I'd never heard him 'cause I don't remember. I don't remember his name."

"Well you know, what they're saying is, that it is a funny coincidence that this guy turns up dating Kay, and then that night I run the tag for you and when he turns up missing, the next day nobody's seen him. And haven't seen him since."

"Well, I mean where does he work? I mean, *don't* he work?"

"I don't know. I don't know none of the particulars, where he works or anything like that. But evidently somebody had to miss him to report him missing. But they, they played the tape back for me and like I said, I didn't recognize the name either, and I told them I never heard of the guy. But then they played back the tape of me calling in his tag! I had to tell them, 'Well, yeah, I ran that tag for L. C. that night because somebody pulled up in his driveway.'"

"Well, I remember you running a tag, but I don't remember the guy's name."

"So you know, they're looking at someone for some type of foul play with him. And the way they look at it is that, you know, this could be some type of revenge towards Kay."

"Naw. I don't buy that, Rick. Uh, ya know, they asked me did I know some guy, Vik, or something like that. But I told 'em, you know, I'd never heard of him. And, and I don't remember, ya know, I know I had you run the tag, but I don't remember what the name was."

"Yeah. Uh, you know, Kay told me she went out with some people from Sweden. And uh, this guy evidently was one of them people from Sweden. And…"

"Sweden?"

"Yeah. And see, the thing about it is that he got missing *the same night* I told you where he lived."

"Well, uhm, uh, Vance Furr and Bill Lane [SBI Agents] was out here today. And they told, told me that he lives somewhere out, off 70."

"Nah, well, the address for the tag I gave you was on Grove Street. But he got missing the same night I told you, so you know they're looking at *you* now."

"Oh yeah, I… I understand that. But that's bullsh*t! That is total d*mn bullsh*t!"

"Well you know that, you think about it, it's pretty reasonable. You know, if you're a suspect in her mother's –"

"Well look Rick, I never met the d*mn guy. I wouldn't know him if I saw him."

"Yeah, well I, ya know, I wouldn't either. But like I said, I… they're looking at the fact that I ran the tag for you and then this guy turns up missing that night."

"Well I don't, I don't know him. I wouldn't know him if he —"

"Who, what girl was you with that night that car pulled in there?"

"Huh?"

"What girl was with you over there at your place that night the car pulled in? Remember you was with somebody."

"I think it was that girl from Kannapolis. But you know, other cars pull in here in this driveway all the d*mn time."

"It's mighty peculiar that you call and ask me to run a tag, and they wonder why you didn't call the police department and have them run the tag for yourself."

"I don't work there anymore."

"Well you did *then*, didn't you?"

"No, I was …already… retired."

"Oh. Well, ya know, I want to tell you, they took all my guns!"

"They took all yours?"

"Yeah."

"Why would they take your guns?"

"Well, they think I might have something to do with that guy missing. I ran his tag the night he went missing!"

"Oh sh*t. That is bull sh*t."

"Well, you know, they're just following leads up. Doing what they gotta do."

"Well, you know, when they were out here today, they asked me about Jason and what I knew about him messing in drugs and stuff like that. I told them what I know. There's nothing else I can tell 'em."

"Yeah."

"And you know, there's not a d*mn thing else I can tell 'em. They can do whatever they have to do. But I'm getting sick and tired of these d*mn rumors about me. I'm getting fed up with 'em!"

"Yeah. Well you know, I can see their point because I ran that tag that night, and then the next day this, this guy turns up missing."

"Well, I mean, have they, have they been in his house?"

"I don't know. I didn't ask. But he's missing and evidently there's no *reason* for him to be missing. So you know, given your and Kay's stormy relationship and, ya know, the way ya'll felt about each other, I imagine the way they're looking at it is that possibly you found out that this guy was dating her and got me to run his tag. And then that you went over there and did something to him."

"You know, let me tell you something. I don't know the guy, I've never met the d*mn guy. It don't matter to me one way or the other who Kay goes out with."

"Yeah well, I'm just telling you the way they put it."

"You know I'm getting sick of this sh*t. I have no idea who the son-of-a-b*tch is."

"Yeah"

"And I don't, I don't care to know who she goes with. And hell, I don't know, maybe he went back to Timbuktu or wherever he came from."

"Well, I think the big thing is his car is still there and his belongings are still there, but *he's* not there."

L. C. responded, "Well, then, you know, I hope they find him."

"Yeah. Well I'm sure they *want* to find him. I just hope they don't find him *dead* because, L. C., if they find him dead it's not gonna look good for *you*."

"Well, hell, you know, if they find him they can talk to him. Like I said, I don't know the guy; I've never met the d*mn guy. I've never been around the d*mn guy! How in the hell *could* I know him?" L. C. demanded.

"I don't know. I just thought I'd let you know that they come over here and asked me about it."

"Well, I want to ask you something and I want you to tell me the truth."

"Uh-huh."

"Now you're not using me on this are you?"

"Hell no, Rick, I ain't!"

"I didn't run this tag number for you, and then you went over there and bumped this old boy off, did you?"

"Hell no!"

"*Did* you?"

"No! Rick, d*mn!"

"Well I'm just telling you, L. C...."

"That is, that is crazy!" L. C. insisted.

"Well, you know, I just wanted to get it settled in my own mind. And I don't, you know, I don't think you're capable of doing anything like that."

"I'm leveling with you. If I knew who the d*mn guy was, I would tell you I knew who he was."

"Okay."

"But I don't know the man; I've never seen the man."

"Well, they came over here and raked me over the coals on this thing 'cause I was telling 'em I never heard of the guy, and then they pull this recorder out of their pocket and played it and there's my old sweet voice on the recorder saying, 'Run this tag for me, Joe.' And it turns out to be the guy that's missing who, uh, who it turns out to have been dating Kay."

"Well see, now, that's something else. I had no idea. She told me she wasn't dating nobody. I mean, I would have no idea who she dates."

"Yeah?"

"I mean, 'cause she wasn't about to tell me, and neither were any of her girlfriends. ...But I'm telling you point blank, *I don't know the man*. I've never seen the man. I wouldn't know him if he knocked on my door right now and come in here."

"I just wanted to make sure you ain't playing me for a sucker here."

"Rick, there's no way that I'm playing you for a sucker and you know, if that's what you think, then uh, I don't think we need to talk. But I'm *not*. I don't know the man. I've never heard of the d*mn man."

"Okay. Hey, have they ever asked you about where you was that Wednesday night, the night uh, before they found Kay's mama."

"Yeah, I told 'em everything I done." *No, not everything, L. C.*

"Really?"

"Well, you know, they can, they can think whatever they want to. I don't care. But I'm getting sick of this, all these d*mn accusations!" L. C. said.

"Well, you got to look at it like *they* do."

"I'm looking at it their way, Rick."

"You know how this goes. Considering ya'll's relationship, and then Kay is dating this guy who turns up missing after you got a 10-28 to where he lives at. And then *next* thing you know her *mother* turns up dead."

"Rick... I'm getting sick of them coming and asking me the same d*mn questions day after day. I'm gonna tell 'em to kiss my *ss. ...That's exactly what I'm gonna do. Ya know, Kay Weden, that's all I hear. I'm sick of it. Ya know, hell, if she wants to f*ck n*ggers, I don't give a sh*t. I don't give a d*mn anymore!"

"Yeah. Well I just wanted to call and let you know what's going on."

"Did you tell 'em how crazy the b*tch was?" *The "b*tch?" The only one you will love forever and ever?*

"Yeah... Okey-doke, well, that's what I wanted to talk to you about."

"Well, wait... *Where* did you say the guy was from?"

"Sweden, if that's the same guy that Kay was going out with."

"Well see now, that's the first time I've ever heard her say she was going out with anybody."

"Well, she told me weeks ago, I guess, about the little incident that you and her had at Bogarts. She said her and some friends went out with some people from Sweden and took the guy from Denmark with 'em and they all had a good time. And evidently this guy was one of the guys from Sweden. And uh, I guess the address is on Grove Street, because that's what the address is on his 10-28."

"Yeah, well –"

"And now he's missing. And he got missing that night right after I run that 10-28."

"Well now, if he got missing that night after that, why in the hell didn't somebody look for him before now?"

"I don't know. I'm just saying that, you know, they're saying he's missing. He's been dating Kay, and uh, you know, evidently you're one of the suspects in the murder of Kay's mama."

"Well –"

"And you know, it does look bad for you."

"Yeah maybe it looks bad, Rick, but I don't know the man. I'm just about ready to say 'f*ck it' and put a stop to this sh*t."

"Well, the bad thing about it is they, hell, they might bring you in for questioning, and they ain't much you can do about it."

"Well, you know, they can bring me in all they want to. But unless they got probable cause to believe that I did commit a crime, I ain't going *no*where."

"Well, let me ask you, did they get *all* your guns?"

"Yeah. They come got, they got all my guns. I got, well, I got shotguns I guess. But well yeah, I mean, you know, I let 'em take mine, you know, but I told 'em Marcia had a .38 that, you know, that they could go get it, you know, if they, if they wanted to, wanted to look at it. And I called Marcia and told her, you know, basically told her what was going on, and if they wanted to come get the gun let 'em have the d*mn gun. You know, that's fine. I don't have any problems with that. They can look at anything I got."

"Well, if you had of listened to me six months ago…"

"I, I realize that and I know that. I wish I hadda listened to ya. But I didn't."

"As the old saying goes, a hard head makes for a sore *sshole."

"And about Kay's mama… They want to center in on one d*mn person. One d*mn person. That's bullsh*t."

"Well I guess what they're doing is just eliminating suspects. Right now, you're, you're one of them."

"But you know, I, I had nothing against the old lady. Nothing. Nothing at all against the lady. She was a nice person. I had the b*tch with her daughter."

"Yeah."

"Rick, how long have you known me?"

"Twelve years, I think."

"Do you think for one minute I'm capable of this sh*t?"

"I don't think so. Unless you're doing a good snow job on me."

"Well, I'm not doing a snow job on anybody…"

"Well, listen, I'll uh, I'll talk to you sometime later on this week."

"Okay."

"Oh, hey, when are you going to see your mom?" Rick asked.

"I don't know. Soon hopefully."

"Okey-doke."

"All right. Bye."

The four of us – Don, Terry, Steve, and me – listened to the recording of the phone conversation between Rick and L. C. over and over. It bothered Steve and Terry that the street address for Viktor Gunnarsson that the dispatcher gave Rick and Rick, in turn, provided to L. C. was not his address in December 1993. But it did not concern me or Don in the least.

I explained. "We know for a fact that L. C. had Viktor's correct name, address, *and* phone number right inside the drawer of his phone table in his living room. It was still there in February when we searched. *Furthermore,* I think it is possible that L. C. called Viktor and left him a message on his answering machine before Viktor got home on December third. I think he called him out of anger, and not thinking about evidence at that point. Then after he kidnapped and murdered him and drove back to Salisbury, he would have had to stop and think about what to do next. I think he realized he needed to get that tape out of Viktor's answering machine."

"Or maybe L. C. just wanted to hear any messages Kay left on Viktor's machine. Plus, Viktor's apartment door may not have even been ajar. It may have been closed but not locked. Then L. C. could have gone back in, taken the cassette tape, and then left the door slightly open when he left."

"Exactly," I said. "In any case, there are several possibilities. But the fact remains that all L. C. needed was Viktor's name from his license plate. That, along with the phone book he had right there at his fingertips, was all he needed to find Viktor. Rick Hillard had every reason to jump all over L. C."

Terry added, "L. C. is lucky that all Rick did was confront him on the phone."

"That's a fact," Steve said.

Steve and I did not actually meet Rick until July 1994 because Don and Terry maintained contact with him for the four of us. When we did meet him at the Rowan County Sheriff's Office, I saw that Richard "Rick" Hillard was a tall bulky man, a typical burly cop. I did not think he favored his brother Danny very much at all. But he seemed easy to talk to and seemed to be a good guy. I do believe that he was a little bit nervous talking with us about his involvement with L. C. I think it was embarrassment more than anything else, but he did look a little guilty when we started talking about his running Viktor Gunnarsson's tag number for L. C. But I understood why he might have felt embarrassed that he ran the license plate; after all, L. C. had used that information to locate, kidnap, and murder Viktor.

By the time Steve and I met him, Rick was certain that L. C. had murdered Viktor Gunnarsson "without a doubt." He still was not sure about Catherine Miller's murder, however.

Rick told us that he met L. C. in 1981 through the Salisbury Police Department. Rick worked there for fifteen years until March 1993. Rick was working patrol in 1981, and L. C. came there and was assigned to work on Rick's shift. They worked on the same shift together for two and a half years. As police officers often do, while working on the same shift they became personal friends. They would go out together with a larger group of friends, but never just the two of them alone.

During the time that L. C. worked with Rick, L. C. was married to Marcia. Rick grew up in the same neighborhood as Marcia, and they attended the same schools. Rick did not like the way L. C. treated Marcia.

"In fact, he treated her like sh*t," Rick told us.

L. C. would call her names and curse at her in front of other people.

"After Marcia lost a bunch of weight and then gained it back, L. C. said, 'Why don't you get your ugly fat *ss out of my way!' and then he asked me, 'Ain't that an ugly b*tch?' in front of her!"

Rick does not know of any actual acts of physical violence L. C. committed toward Marcia. They had separated once, however, during their marriage. It was while they were separated that L. C. and another Salisbury Police Officer, Sgt. Dillon Broome, were driving to Charlotte one night to see two girls. L. C. continued to see his girlfriend in Charlotte even after he and Marcia got back together. But Marcia got suspicious one night when L. C. was gone to Charlotte. She parked in a parking lot near the police department. Rick and Sergeant Broome walked over to speak to Marcia, and she was sitting in the car alone, smoking, and visibly upset. She asked them where L. C. was.

Sergeant Broome responded quickly, "He's on a stakeout."

Rick realized that Sergeant Broome was trying to cover for L. C. Rick decided he would help L. C. out as well. Rick told Marcia that L. C. was in his personal vehicle because his marked car would be recognized. He told her that L. C. was staking out an area where several break-ins had occurred. Marcia flipped her cigarette on Rick's arm and said, "In Charlotte?" Marcia then drove off.

Sergeant Broome then called his girlfriend in Charlotte and obtained the phone number for L. C.'s girlfriend. Broome called L. C. and told him about his encounter with Marcia. L. C. left Charlotte and drove quickly back to Salisbury. When he got back to Salisbury, Rick saw that L. C. was drunk.

Rick asked L. C., "What would have happened if you had gotten stopped by a trooper?"

L. C. responded, "They would have had to chase me."

"Man, you're an idiot," Rick told him.

Later Rick asked L. C. what happened when he got home, and L. C. said that Marcia had called L. C.'s girlfriend in Charlotte and that the girl had acted like she did not know anyone by the name of L. C. Underwood.

It was not long, however, until L. C. and Marcia separated permanently.

When Rick saw Marcia recently, Marcia told him that she was afraid of L. C. She served divorce papers on him in March 1994. But L. C. told Rick that he and Marcia had separated because he had caught Marcia in a motel room with some doctor who was naked. L. C. said he took out his gun and made the doctor leave without his clothes. L. C. took the doctor's wallet and threw the contents out while driving down the road. Rick thought this was odd because

Viktor's body was also found nude. I thought it was odd because whoever had killed Catherine Miller threw out the contents of her wallet while driving down the street.

When L. C. and Rick were working, they would be called to bars and would get into fights occasionally. L. C. often lost his temper. He never seemed to have any patience. He usually had good investigative skills, wrote excellent reports, and paid attention to detail. One of the most notable things about L. C. is his extreme neatness.

"I am surprised that L. C. let a dog live inside his house. He is so neat about his person, his vehicle, and his home. He even had a problem with the belts on his car engine squeaking, but the service mechanic told him it was because he kept putting ArmorAll on them. ...I think L. C. is crazy as a loon," Rick told us.

One thing Rick told us that we didn't already know was that L. C. was a heavy smoker.

One night, Rick was acting as patrol sergeant on another shift, and L. C. was working for him. L. C. was in the jail with a prisoner. L. C. had about fifteen arrest warrants in his hand to serve the prisoner with. Rick gave L. C. an additional assignment, and L. C. became angry. He threw all fifteen warrants on the floor and they scattered. L. C. took off his gun belt and handed it to Rick.

"I'm quitting," he told Rick.

Rick was able to persuade L. C. to finish the workday. "You can quit in the morning if you still want to." L. C. agreed, and came back into work as usual the next morning. L. C. then told the captain that he was hooked on Demerol, which he had been taking since his back surgery. Rick believes L. C. got some type of treatment for his addiction. Rick told the lieutenant and the chief at Salisbury Police Department about L. C. threatening to quit that night.

"Why didn't you take his gun and let him quit?" the chief asked him. Rick did not respond.

"Do you remember any other specific incidents when L. C. was having emotional problems?" I asked Rick. "Do you recall a day when Kay could not get L. C. to answer the door?"

"Oh yes," Rick replied. "It was around Thanksgiving in …1992, and I was driving by L. C.'s house. I saw a woman beating on L. C.'s window, so I pulled into the driveway. I hollered at her, I said, 'Lady, what's your problem?' It was Kay, and she said she thought L. C. had done something to himself. I looked in the window and saw that Kay was pointing at a chair with a cover on it. Kay kept saying that L. C. was sitting in the chair and that he wouldn't respond. …I tried to tell Kay that she was just looking at the cover on the chair, that L. C. wasn't there. …I went to the door at his breezeway, on the front, and knocked. L. C. answered the door holding his pants up and said, 'I was in the g*dd*mn sh*thouse.' I apologized and told him that Kay was concerned about his welfare. I asked him if they'd be okay, and he said 'yeah,' and so I left. L. C. told me later that their engagement was off. I didn't even know that they were engaged in the first place. I think that was the first encounter I had with Kay." Rick told us that shortly after the incident at Bogarts Restaurant, he listened to Kay's tape recording of a phone conversation she had with L. C. in which L. C. had faked a gunshot. Rick later asked L. C. about it, but L. C. refused to talk to him concerning the gunshot.

Rick thinks L. C. "snapped" when he got suspended from the Police Department. Danny told me about being out with L. C. and how L. C. would always go around checking up on Kay. Rick knew all about the incident at Bogarts, and Rick knew about the following morning when L. C. ripped the necklace off Kay at the Quality Mart. Rick later told L. C. that was robbery, and he could get in a lot of trouble for that, not to mention losing his law enforcement career. L. C. disagreed with Rick, though, because he said he had given the necklace to Kay and could take it back if he wanted to.

L. C. said she had given the necklace back to him once, and he had given it back to her again under the conditions that she only wear it when she was with him.

Rick found out a couple of days later that L. C. was retiring on some kind of disability for his back. He believed L. C.'s back problem was a legitimate medical problem, but not as serious as L. C. contends. L. C. continued to mow his lawn, painted his house, and danced on the weekends.

We asked Rick in detail again about L. C. calling him on the night of December third and having him run the license plate information on Viktor Gunnarsson's car. Rick told us that initially, L. C. said he was in his kitchen when he saw the car back into his driveway. Being familiar with the layout of L. C.'s house, Rick knew L. C. couldn't get a tag number from a car while standing in his kitchen, so later he asked L. C. again where he was when he saw the car. L. C. told him that time that he was in his bedroom, heard the car, and then walked outside to obtain the tag number. When Rick confronted L. C. about the differences in his story, L. C. simply responded, "Well, maybe we shouldn't talk so much."

But L. C. constantly called Rick, and Rick would listen to him whine and complain, but he did tire of hearing the same old story. Rick estimated that 90 percent of his conversations with L. C. have been by phone. L. C. would cry about Kay and say that he never loved anyone like he loved Kay.

Just prior to Catherine Miller's murder, L. C. told Rick that he and Kay were planning a trip to South Carolina. However, L. C. said that if Kay did not go, he was going to take another woman with him. Rick was surprised that after Catherine Miller was found murdered, L. C. was still planning to go to South Carolina, and he was going with a woman other than Kay. Rick did not know Wanda Hornbuckle. Rick asked L. C. how things were with him and Kay, and suggested that he at least call Kay and see if she needed anything. But L. C. went on his trip with the woman and never contacted Kay.

L. C. denied being responsible for either murder. Rick thought it odd, though, that L. C. never referred to Gunnarsson, a dead victim, as anything respectful. Rather he referred to him as "f*ck face," "*sshole," or "d*ckhead."

L. C. told Rick that people had told him Viktor Gunnarsson was a woman abuser, that he would date women just to use them, and drain them of their money. L. C. speculated that some hitman from Sweden probably came to the United States and killed Viktor. L. C. said he had obtained and read the book about Viktor being accused of assassinating the Prime Minister. Rick asked him if he could borrow it to read, and L. C. said, "I gave it to my attorneys, and ain't no d*mn body gonna get it." What I find hard to believe is not that L. C. knew about the book, but that he could read it. Borje Wingren's book, *Hon Skot Olof Palme* (*He Shot Olof Palme*), is written solely in Swedish (1993).

Rick talked with L. C. once about Gunnarsson's clothing being removed. Rick told him he thought it was an attempt to destroy trace evidence, just as we believed. L. C. told Rick he had never received any training regarding trace evidence. I had to correct him. "Rick, when we searched L. C.'s house, we found a training outline in his own handwriting regarding trace evidence, along with other research materials." Rick was really not surprised.

"Speaking of physical evidence, Rick, has L. C. ever told you what he did with his guns?"

"Yeah. He told me that he gave the .22 and the .38 to his stepbrothers for Christmas one year."

Rick does not believe that, however, because one night he saw L. C.'s .38 Colt Detective Special in the front seat of L. C.'s car when Rick and L. C. were together. L. C. told Rick he got the gun when he worked in Lincoln County. L. C. stopped at a convenience store, and while he was inside the store, Rick emptied the bullets out of the gun and put it back in the holster. He decided to play a joke on L. C. When L. C. got back in the car, Rick took out L. C.'s gun, put it against L. C.'s ribs, and pulled the trigger. L. C. cursed him furiously.

CHAPTER FOURTEEN

"Trust ye not in a friend, put ye not confidence in a guide" (Micah 7:5)

Shirley Twitty was not the only woman L. C. used for his own malicious purposes. Don and Terry had already discovered the identity of the mysterious "Kim" that L. C. brought to Spencer's Restaurant on December 6. I was anxious to interview her. But her name was not *Kim*, for there *was* no Kim.

Don gave me her contact information. I introduced myself to her on the phone and requested to meet with her. She agreed, and we arranged to meet at a restaurant she selected near her home in Charlotte.

"I'm Wanda," she said as she shook my offered hand. "Wanda Hornbuckle."

"Thank you for your willingness to talk with me."

"I don't really want to be involved in all this, but I'll tell you what I know," she said.

I requested a quiet booth in the corner of the restaurant so that we could talk privately.

Her long, shiny auburn hair was striking, and it was no wonder Kay noticed it right away, when the two of them were seated for dinner directly in the line of sight of Kay, Catherine Miller, and their friends.

Whereas Shirley did not comprehend at the time that L. C. was using her and her car to spy on Kay Weden, Wanda

Hornbuckle knew precisely what L. C. wanted from her. He told her as much when he called on Monday, December 6.

"Wanda, I want you to go to dinner with me to make my girlfriend Kay jealous," L. C. told her bluntly.

"Well, what do you have in mind?" Wanda asked.

"She's going to be at this restaurant tonight in Salisbury. I just want to take you there to eat dinner, where she can see you with me, that's all," he explained.

"Umm, Sure. I'll go. It's a free meal," Wanda told him.

"Dress up, okay?" he added.

"I'll do my best," she said, unsure whether to feel flattered or insulted.

Wanda came home from work on Monday evening, December 6, to find L. C. already waiting at her house, nearly an hour early. He seemed nervous. He was dressed in a navy-blue sweater, a white button-up shirt, dark colored dress slacks, and loafers, much like he dressed when he went to Twister's, which is where he met Wanda through a mutual friend.

L. C. was driving the nicer of his two vehicles, a champagne-colored Dodge Diplomat. They left Wanda's home in Charlotte at 7:45 p.m. Wanda noticed right away that the car was immaculate, even the ashtray, which Wanda thought odd considering L. C. was a smoker.

"I really appreciate you going with me to make Kay jealous. She, she told me that I could not get another girlfriend," he said pitifully.

"Awww," Wanda said sympathetically. "Is Kay gonna be on a date with another man at the restaurant?"

"Uh, no. She said she was going for a birthday party for some friend of hers. It's just gonna be women, I think."

"Well, won't she know the only reason that we are there is to make her jealous?"

"Ah, she probably won't even remember telling me she was going there. I'll tell her it's just a coincidence."

Wanda thought L. C. was not giving his girlfriend very much credit, but that was between L. C. and Kay, she decided.

Wanda and L. C. arrived at Spencer's at 8:30 p.m. L. C. drove through the parking lot and pointed out Kay's car, a red Pontiac, which was backed into a parking space. L. C. parked and walked over to Kay's car, looked inside the window in the front and back, and then confirmed to Wanda, "Yeah, this is her car."

Inside the restaurant, they were seated right below Kay and her group of women friends, whom L. C. pointed out discreetly. "This is perfect," he said, pleased. "This is *really* perfect." L. C. was growing more excited by the minute.

L. C. did not speak to Kay, but he talked about her to Wanda almost the entire time they sat there.

"She's a b*tch," he told Wanda. "She's self-centered. She doesn't care anything about me… and she's mean to me."

After about forty-five minutes, L. C. discreetly handed Wanda a hundred-dollar bill, under the table. He told her to pay for their meal with the money if they left at the same time Kay did.

At one point, L. C. told Wanda to reach over and hold his hands, which she did. Wanda laughed as she told me this because she said they were discussing a dog, nothing romantic at all. Shortly after Wanda took L. C.'s hands, Kay got up to leave. Wanda could tell plainly that Kay was upset.

L. C. called the waitress over and, feigning concern, asked her, "Was that blond-headed woman upset when she left?" The waitress said that she was, and that she heard her say she was going outside to wait on the others. L. C. and Wanda stayed in the restaurant for about fifteen minutes longer.

After paying the bill, they walked out of the restaurant holding hands. L. C. opened the passenger door for Wanda, and she climbed in. As L. C. drove, he told her that Kay's best friend had been with her at Spencer's. Wanda did not recall L. C. mentioning Kay's mother. He did say, however, that Kay did not care that his mother had just died of breast cancer.

"That's awful, L. C.," Wanda told him. "I didn't know that happened."

But L. C. did not want to discuss his mother. He continued to complain to Wanda about Kay. He told Wanda that the reason he took an early retirement from the Police Department was because of an incident between himself and one of Kay's dates, when she was out cheating on him. L. C. said he caught her out with another man in a restaurant in Salisbury.

"I punched the man in the face and knocked him out cold," L. C. told her. "Then when he got up, he said that he had never been hit so hard in all his life, and that he wanted to go home."

L. C. told Wanda more about his relationship with Kay than she cared to know. But she just listened.

"She and I would go to ball games together, and you know, she would talk with everybody there but me. ...I loaned her money, which she never paid back or even thanked me for. ...Her son Jason was in a car wreck once, and I got him out of a ticket. But neither one of 'em ever said so much as a 'thank you' for what I did."

L. C. drove them back to his house in Salisbury. They walked inside and sat on the living room sofa.

L. C. got up to make a phone call, and Wanda heard him say, "The plan worked; it was perfect." Wanda glanced around the house, impressed again with L. C.'s neatness.

L. C. poured Wanda a glass of wine, and he had a beer. L. C. showed Wanda photos of his mother and of a cruise they had been on. He showed her other pictures and pointed out some of the items hanging on his walls.

Wanda described to me that "He was kind of bragging about himself. He showed me an article about where he saved a woman's life." I had seen exactly what L. C. had on his walls – things like police mementos, articles mentioning his name, and even "atta-boy" letters citizens had written thanking him for some service he provided – things no one else would display but which he had paid to have professionally mounted, framed, and hung on his walls.

"How long did you stay with him at his house?" I asked Wanda.

"About an hour, until he started complaining about his back hurting. I asked him how he hurt his back, and he said that he had moved some heavy items around in his attic over the weekend." I surmised that the only heavy item L. C. had moved over the weekend was Viktor Gunnarsson's body.

"L. C. told me that he had already been through a couple of surgeries on his back."

L. C. drove Wanda home that night in his Dodge Diplomat. On the way, he stopped at a convenience store. He went inside and bought cigarettes, including a pack of Virginia Slims for Wanda. He made another stop as well. It was about 10:30 p.m., and he turned off the main road and into a large apartment complex.

Wanda asked him, "Is this where Kay lives?"

"No," he answered, "some young officers who like to party live here."

L. C. drove into the complex and looked around without stopping. He drove all the way to the end, to the last building on the right, and slowed down considerably. He focused his gaze on an apartment on the upper-right side of the building at the end of the drive, #910 Lakewood Apartments. Wanda Hornbuckle had no way of knowing that night that the apartment was leased to a man by the name of Viktor Gunnarsson – a man who had been kidnapped from that apartment only three nights prior.

L. C. did not comment further about the apartment, but as he drove away, he told her, "I'll take you by where Kay lives." The neighborhood to which L. C. drove her was not far from the apartment complex. He pointed out Kay's ranch-style house, and Wanda saw that there was a light on inside.

Sometime later, for confirmation, Wanda directed investigators to both Viktor's apartment and to Kay's house, following the exact route L. C. drove that night.

L. C. told Wanda as he drove her home that he was "ready to call it quits with Kay." He became contrite and told her, "I feel guilty about using you to make Kay jealous."

Wanda answered, "Oh, don't worry about it. I don't mind."

"Well, I didn't know that I could date anyone as nice as *you*. ...I'm through with Kay," he said.

Wanda told L. C. that she was dating someone, and that she did not want to get involved with another man until she ended the relationship with her current boyfriend.

L. C. said, "I just need to get out of town for the weekend to get my mind off Kay. ...Why don't we go somewhere for a weekend? We can do some Christmas shopping, relax, and not be pushed."

"Now that sounds like a good idea," she responded.

"What about going to the mountains for the weekend?"

"Sure, that sounds good."

But a few minutes later, L. C. said he had a better idea. "Let's go to Charleston instead. ...How about this coming weekend?"

Wanda again agreed. L. C. said he would take care of the reservations, and that one of his neighbors had been to Charleston and told him about some interesting places to visit in the historic coastal town.

When they arrived at Wanda's house, L. C. walked her inside. Wanda's roommate's son was there. L. C. left about 11:15 p.m.

The next night, Tuesday, December 7, L. C. called Wanda. He said that he had talked to his neighbor, who had recommended a motel in Mount Pleasant for their weekend trip. He said he would call her back soon and confirm the details.

"By the way," he said, "I put call-block on my phone so Kay can't call me." L. C. failed to mention that he had been to Kay's early that very morning begging her to take him back.

L. C. called Wanda on Wednesday evening. She could not recall whether she talked to him directly or whether he just left her a message, but she recalls that she did not get home from work until about 10:00 that Wednesday night. It was the night that Catherine Miller was murdered.

L. C. called Wanda again on Thursday night and they talked for a bit. Then he called her again on Friday while she was at work.

"Did he tell you in any of those conversations that week that Kay's mother Catherine Miller had been murdered in her home?" I asked Wanda.

"No, he never mentioned it at all. We talked about our trip. He said he would pick me up about 5:00 that Friday. About 4:20 I left work and went home and started packing. L. C. showed up at 5:00."

"What was his demeanor when he got to your house?"

"He was chipper as ever."

"Which vehicle was he driving?"

"His Dodge Diplomat."

"Did you need to stop for gas?" I asked.

"He had a full tank when we left my house. He must have gotten gas ahead of time. We drove all the way to Charleston – or Mount Pleasant rather – without stopping."

"How long was the drive?"

"About four and a half hours."

"That's a long way to go without stopping, isn't it?" I asked Wanda.

"Well, he was going on and on about Kay Weden. ... How she was being so mean and cold to him when his mother was sick and dying in Ohio."

"Did L. C. tell you when his mother died?"

"He said she died in late November of 1993."

Wanda shared with me that as they drove to Charleston, she commented at one point that they were driving through a rough looking neighborhood.

"Don't worry; I have a gun in the trunk," L. C. assured her. I asked Wanda if she saw the gun at all, and she said he never showed it to her.

L. C. checked them into one room at the Days Inn in Mount Pleasant. They entered the room and began to unpack and then decided to go to supper. They ate at a place called Jose Joe's. After they had some drinks, they returned to their motel room. L. C. took a shower, and Wanda got into bed. L. C. joined her in bed, and they made love. Wanda described L. C. as "gentle and considerate." L. C. and Wanda fell asleep, not waking until Saturday morning.

When morning came, they got up and Wanda got into the shower. Just as she turned the water off, she heard L. C. knocking on the bathroom door.

"I just called my neighbor Gil. He said Kay's mother has been murdered."

"What?! What happened?"

"Someone went into the house and murdered Kay's mother" he said matter-of-factly.

"Well, if you need to call Kay, I'll leave you alone in the room so you can call."

But L. C. repeatedly refused to call Kay. "I'll just send her some flowers," he said without emotion.

Wanda said that was the only occasion during their weekend trip that L. C. mentioned Catherine Miller or her murder.

L. C. and Wanda then went shopping. They went to the open-air marketd in Charleston and to all the stores in the Omni. They went to bookstores, museums, and to Fort Multry. Wanda bought several Christmas gifts for family and friends. She and L. C. ate lunch and returned to their motel room to take a nap since they planned to go out Saturday night. When they lay down on the bed, Wanda fell asleep quickly. When she woke up, L. C. had gone out to get a soft drink. While he was out, Wanda glanced at L. C.'s luggage and noticed how neatly his things were packed. She saw that he had rubber bands on the tassels of his dress shoes and shoe trees inside each of them.

When L. C. came back in the room, they got dressed to go out. They ate dinner at the Barbados Room in the Mill House Restaurant. They had a couple of drinks and went to Desperados, a nightclub where they drank and danced.

About 1:30 or 2:00 in the morning, they went to the Huddle House Restaurant beside Days Inn and had breakfast. They returned to the room and went to sleep. L. C. did not make any phone calls from their room, nor did they receive any calls.

On Sunday morning, December 12, L. C. and Wanda got up, showered, packed, and ate breakfast at the hotel before heading home. On the way, they stopped in Blythewood and had lunch. Wanda recalled the plaque L. C. bought for himself there that said, "Old policemen never die; they just lose their beat."

L. C. drove Wanda to her house and said he would call her later in the week so they could go out again. He also mentioned taking a seven- to ten-day cruise together in January. She told L. C. she would consider it.

"I still need to get over the relationship I am currently in before I get involved in another one," she reminded him.

The next night, Monday, December 13, L. C. called Wanda.

"Did you call Kay?" she asked him.

"No."

"L. C., you should call her."

"No, I'll just send her some flowers. ...I have a Christmas gift for you," he said, changing the subject.

L. C. called Wanda on Tuesday, December 14, and again on Thursday, December 15. On Friday, December 17, Wanda and her roommate saw L. C. at Twister's in Cornelius. They talked.

Wanda did not hear from L. C. again until he called on Sunday, December 19. She agreed to see him on Monday night. It was then that L. C. gave Wanda a black onyx necklace. He had bought it at a local jewelry store in Salisbury. Wanda felt that she was being pressured into a relationship with L. C., which she was not ready for.

"I have a date with my boyfriend on New Year's Eve. But I'm planning to break up with him after New Year's." L. C. definitely did not like Wanda having a date with anyone other than himself.

"But I want you to be with me on New Year's Eve," L. C. whined to Wanda like a child.

"Well, I'm sorry, L. C., I already have plans." L. C. was not happy.

Although he continued to call Wanda, she declined to go out with him again. She told L. C. she would see him at Twister's, but she did not want to start up another relationship so soon. But then L. C. called Wanda on Tuesday night, December 21. During that conversation Wanda asked L. C. if anyone had been arrested yet for murdering Kay's mother.

"No, but I think Kay's son Jason killed her for drug money," L. C. replied.

"His own grandmother?" Wanda asked, incredulous.

"Oh yeah," L. C. said.

Wanda certainly was not the only person to hear L. C. complain about Jason, the only son of the woman he claimed to love so dearly.

Diane Hayes, a woman who met L. C. at Twister's Club in the latter part of November 1993, was interviewed by Don and Terry. She told them that she and L. C. had spoken by phone several times and often in the club. She recalled that during the latter part of November 1993, L. C. had told her that his mother had just died of cancer.

"Sometimes when we were talking about her, he acted like he was going to start crying, and excused himself to the men's room. I know now, though, that he was lying because his mother didn't even die!" Diane was frustrated with herself for believing L. C., and how she had comforted him at length, telling him how she had a close friend who had died, and that she knew how he felt.

Don asked Diane, "Do you know when exactly he told you that his mother had died?"

"Not the exact date, but it was right after Thanksgiving. He didn't come in the club that whole weekend. Later when he told me she had died, he suddenly left Twister's. Then another friend told me L. C. had mentioned committing suicide, and I tried to call him all night, but I never could get him."

Diane told Don and Terry that that L. C. loved to dance, and he especially loved to dance to Elvis Presley songs.

"And he always requested 'Grand Tour' by Aaron Neville," she added.

"Did he ever complain about any back problems he had?" Terry asked her.

"Not that I recall. He sure liked to dance, though."

"Diane, did you talk with L. C. during the first week of December of 1993?" Don asked her.

"On Monday, December 6, I called him at home." According to Diane's phone records it was 9:26 p.m. "I remembered L. C. saying he had just walked in his house after being out somewhere. I had tried to call him and our friend Doreen earlier because I thought Doreen was going out with him to make his ex-girlfriend jealous. Then I found out later that Doreen couldn't go with him, so he got someone else to do it."

"Was that the last time you spoke with L. C.?"

"Yes, I believe it was."

CHAPTER FIFTEEN

"For there is nothing covered, that shall not be revealed; neither hid, that shall not be known" (Luke 12:2)

On January 31, 1994, I appeared before Superior Court Judge Robert Burroughs who was holding court in Watauga County. Peering over the top of his glasses at me, he took the search warrant affidavit I reached to him, and he began reading. I stood by silently as he read every sentence on every page.

He looked up at me again. "Well, Detective Sergeant, you have certainly put a lot of work into this. ...I'd like to know what you find during the search." He signed the document, and I assured him I would let him know what, if anything, we found. The most sought-after items would be the .22 and the .38, both of which we knew L. C. had in his possession at one time. Having the forensic firearms experts analyze those two weapons in relation to the bullets that took the lives of Viktor and Catherine would be very telling. But I also knew it was highly improbable L. C. would be careless enough to leave either of those guns anywhere on his property where we might locate and seize them. There were, however, countless other possible items of evidentiary value that could be beneficial as well.

The next day, Tuesday, February 1, 1994, at 11:15 a.m., we gathered at L. C.'s residence at 405 Lake Drive in Salisbury. Present to assist in the search were: Special Agents Don Gale, Bobby Bonds, Steve Wilson, and John Bendure of the

North Carolina State Bureau of Investigation, Detectives Terry Agner and Tommy Swing, Deputy Chad Moose of the Rowan County Sheriff's Office, Sheriff Red Lyons, and Lt. Allen Stout and myself of the Watauga County Sheriff's Office. Within minutes, reporters from the *Salisbury Post* were there as well. L. C., however, was not.

Terry and Don notified L. C.'s newly retained attorney, David Bingham, who arrived shortly thereafter that we were about to execute the search warrant. Mr. Bingham then contacted L. C.'s friend Rick Hillard, who brought over a key to L. C.'s house.

"L. C. has gone to Ohio to visit his mother Barbara," Rick Hillard explained.

"Oh, has she been resurrected from the dead?" I asked.

He shrugged but said nothing.

L. C.'s house, which sits slightly above the street on a sloped embankment, is a one-story, gray asbestos-sided house with white trim, red shutters, and a red-brick foundation, with a dark-gray shingled roof. An open-sided double carport and redwood deck is located at the rear of the house. L. C.'s Dodge Diplomat and his Monte Carlo, both immaculate, were parked on the carport, and all the car doors were locked. The black asphalt driveway to the right of the house connects to Lake Drive, a two-lane highway in a middle- to upper-class residential neighborhood. His lawn in front and back of the house was well manicured.

The house itself has two entrances and one back entrance. The left front entrance leads into a foyer. The right front entrance leads into a breezeway, which connects a utility room and the kitchen. Before we entered, Agent Bobby Bonds, a crime scene technician, photographed and videotaped the entire residence, inside and out.

Meanwhile, I walked around the exterior of the house. Directly behind the house was a metal outbuilding containing only yard tools and a couple of lawn mowers. On a concrete patio were a gas grill, folding chair, and a stereo boom box, which had a cassette player. I could see a cassette inside. I hit the play button.

"It's 12:45 a.m. on January the 28th 1994..." It was L. C.'s voice. "...This tape I'm making at this time... I want anyone who listens to this to know that I'm not intoxicated, on no medication. I know exactly what I'm saying, and I'm doing this of my own free will.

...I'll be talking mostly to my attorney, Mr. David Bingham, to whom this tape will be delivered. I want Mr. Bingham to know that I had nothing to do at all – at ALL – with these things that happened... But I just don't see any other way out for me. I don't trust anybody anymore. I don't want to be around people anymore. You know I want Kay Weden to know that I had nothing to do with what happened to her mother, and that's the God's-honest truth. At this time, point in my life, I have no reason to lie... I won't be alive that much longer anyway. I just can't run the risk of being implicated in something that I didn't do, standing the chance of going to jail. That's something I can't stand the thought of being caged up ...like some kind of a wild caged animal. And before that happens, I'll end it myself. Mr. Bingham, I – there are several things I'm gonna ask that you do for me. Number one: I want you to handle my affairs after I'm gone. My retirement and everything else money-wise and all, I've left to my ex-wife. Her name is Marcia. Mr. Bingham, I want you to tell her – and her phone number is 637-0983 – that the, probably the stupidest thing I ever done in my life was losing her. She's a good decent honest person. And I, I really regret that it just never worked out for us. And I take most of the blame for that. I don't, I can't blame her. I wouldn't try to blame her for my mistakes.

...As far as Kay Weden goes, I hope she has a good decent life. I really tried to give her one with me, but apparently, she didn't want that. She, she did, and she didn't. She wanted her cake and be able to eat it too. Kay is a very selfish, self-centered, egotistical b*tch. I'm not saying that out of meanness, I'm saying that for the way that I feel. Every man that she's ever come in contact with she's destroyed, or tried to make a mirror-image of her.

...I've been alone most of my life. And I'm not afraid to die. ...Also, Mr. Bingham, when the time comes, I want you to contact the following people for me: Rick Hillard, Mark Wilhelm, and Kenny Lane. I want all three of them to know that I appreciate them being my friend and having faith in me. Seems like they're the only three that did. Don Gale, he – he's hounded me. He's ruined my name. He's – he's said bad things about me and has even resorted to telling lies. ...I never thought that I could ever say that the SBI had lied. But I know they did. And deep down, Don Gale knows that he did. I've never killed anybody in my life ... and never would. I just don't believe that. Mr. Bingham, I also appreciate, you know, you trying to help me out the way you have, and for having faith in me. Yes, I, I admit right now, yeah, I'm scared. I'm nervous and I'm upset... 'cause I've had a lot of pressure put on me for something I didn't do..."

I may never know if L. C. was actually toying with the idea of suicide, or if it was just more attempt at manipulation, a ploy for sympathy. In any case, he never attempted suicide.

I turned at the sound of two of the SBI agents coming out of the home's crawl space where they had entered to search for L. C.'s guns. Nothing of interest was under the house. It was time to go inside.

Upon entering through the front door, into the breezeway and then the kitchen of L. C.'s house, I was struck immediately by the sheer neatness of... everything in his house. Even the magnets on the front of the refrigerator were situated at perfect right angles.

"Remember that movie, *Sleeping with the Enemy?*"

"The one where Julia Roberts is married to that abusive man with severe OCD?" Terry answered.

"That's it," I responded. "Welcome to *their* house."

Inside L. C.'s kitchen cabinets were typical canned food items, but each product was turned in the same direction with the labels facing forward, and each item was categorized into groups of the same type.

Every cabinet was organized in the same fashion, as well as his refrigerator. The table, the chairs, each piece of furniture was perfectly square with the room, and the place mats on top of the table were the same.

I could not find a piece of lint or dust on anything. Even the trash-can liners were clean.

"He has serious control issues," Don said.

On the wall hung a beige telephone with an extra-long cord. Beneath the phone was a small wooden table where he neatly kept a 1993 phone directory, pencils, pens, note paper, and an answering machine. We listened to the messages on the tape, which were from Rick Hillard and another officer at Salisbury Police Department. Neither message was unusual. I flipped through L. C.'s 1993 telephone book. I turned to the G's, in case he had marked Viktor's phone listing. Although there were no markings by the listing, I noted that Viktor's name and address, 910 Lakewood Apartments, was plainly and accurately listed in the published directory.

On the small table under the phone directory was a red spiral-bound composition notebook. Inside the notebook was a list of items L. C. owned including model numbers, serial numbers, and some purchase dates. The list was several pages long, and each item was numbered. The pages making up that list had never been removed from the wire bound notebook. As I looked through the list, which contained items such as power tools, televisions, stereos, microwave ovens, and guns, I noticed something peculiar. The first page of the notebook began the list with item #11, an RCA VCR. The next five pages followed suit, ending with item #39, a Marlin 30-30 rifle. On the sixth page, however, the first item listed was item #1, an RCA twenty-seveninch color television. I could only reach one conclusion as to why the items would be numbered out of chronological order.

"Take a look at this." I showed Don and Terry the notebook. "At one time, most likely when he first decided to make this list of his personal property, there had been a page beginning with item #1 at the beginning of that notebook. On that page, he must have listed the .38 caliber Colt Detective Special revolver, which he brought with him from Lincoln County. After he used that weapon to murder Catherine Miller, he had to get rid of not only the revolver, but all records pertaining to that revolver, right? So, I think he had to have torn out that first page, leaving the new first page to begin with item #11. At the end of his list, he had to go back to the first clean piece of paper after item #39, and beginning with item #1, list again the items that were originally on the first page."

"Omitting the revolver," Don surmised.

"Exactly."

"It's possible," Terry said.

The notebook was eventually submitted to the Questioned Documents section of the SBI lab for examination of indented writings. Indented writings are impressions made on a piece of paper, which have resulted from writing directly onto another piece of paper on top. Sometimes indented writings can be discovered by coloring lightly over the visible scratches or impressions with a pencil. The lab analysts were able to determine that on the first page in the notebook, the page beginning with item #11, were indented writings referencing a ".38 revolver." Unfortunately, there was no other indication specifying the .38 as the specific Colt Detective Special we were looking for. This was just another piece of nonspecific circumstantial evidence.

L. C. had written other guns on the list as well. We were particularly interested in the gun he had listed as item #18, a Ruger .22 caliber rifle, and item #21, a .22 caliber Dan Wesson revolver. Both guns were purchased at Frank's Pawn

Shop in Salisbury, the rifle being purchased by L. C. on July 14, 1989, and the revolver on October 30, 1990. The four of us concurred that Viktor was most likely shot with the Dan Wesson .22 caliber revolver. The SBI Crime Lab analysts confirmed that out of a small number of weapons that could have fired the .22 bullets into Viktor, a Dan Wesson .22 revolver just like the one L. C. owned could indeed have been the murder weapon. Unfortunately, they could not say conclusively that it was L. C.'s Dan Wesson, because we did not have L. C.'s gun for them to compare with the bullets.

To the left of the kitchen was the living room. The walls were painted white without a single smudge that I could spot. The beige carpet was unspotted and free of debris. In the living room was a maroon plaid couch and chair, a blue recliner, a television, an end table, and a wood-and-glass gun cabinet. Inside the gun cabinet was a 12 gauge shotgun, a 9mm rifle, a 30/30 rifle, and a Daisy Red Ryder BB gun. In the bottom of the gun cabinet were two .22 caliber gun cleaning kits, but alas, no .22 caliber gun. There were boxes of 9mm ammunition, 30/30 ammunition, and 12 gauge shotgun shells, as well as a box of BBs and an empty shoulder holster. There was no .38 caliber gun nor a .22 caliber gun.

In the drawer of an end table beside L. C.'s couch was a North Carolina state map.

"Why would L. C. need a map of North Carolina?" Steve asked.

"Maybe it has something to do with the fact that he has circled the town of Boone," I informed them.

"No, he didn't," Steve said.

"Look for yourself," I said, and I showed him.

In the same end table drawer was an address book. We seized it and planned to examine it thoroughly at a later time.

Passing through the living room, I walked into another hallway, large enough for furniture, sort of a small foyer. The most notable thing about this room was a wooden bookcase containing volume after volume of crime scene and criminal investigation texts. L. C. had denied having any professional knowledge of trace evidence, yet the following notes in L. C.'s handwriting were in his home as well:

> "Every contact leaves its trace... Every criminal brings evidence to the scene and leaves evidence at the scene. The Courts rely ever-increasingly on scientific evidence. The tools of science are eminently suited to the solution of forensic problems, and newer and more powerful applications of the scientist's arsenal are being made daily. ...The famous Edmond Locard... removed particles of a substance from the fingernails of a suspect charged with the murder of his girlfriend. The substance turned out to be face powder of the same kind as that used by the victim... Searching for evidence, a crime scene technician happened to examine the earwax of a murder suspect under a microscope. He found tiny seeds, invisible to the naked eye. It turned out that the seeds were a rare type of pollen found at the scene of the crime."

There is no question in my mind that Viktor's clothing was removed on December 3, 1993, for the sole purpose of removing any trace evidence the clothing may have collected from L. C. or his vehicle. Before we all began our diligent searching, SBI Analyst John Bendure walked through the house collecting fiber samples from carpet, clothing, and other items. We hoped for some type of fiber match that would link L. C. to one of the crime scenes. I was impressed with how thorough the SBI lab analysts were; it was a tedious job.

As I walked through the house, I noticed that the fringe on every rug was pressed neatly and straight. They did not stay that way, though, with a dozen or so people trampling over them. When we left, we made a special effort to put things back just like we found them, but that was asking a lot in this house.

On nearly every wall inside the house, L. C. had professionally framed portraits of himself, his marked patrol car, his uniform patches, and even what we refer to as "atta-boys," which are letters of appreciation from various individuals to his supervisors over the course of his employment. I can understand why someone would keep a copy of these types of letters, but to have them professionally mounted and framed and on display on every wall of the house to me was ridiculous. *Narcissistic* was an understatement.

The master bedroom, situated at the rear of the house, appeared to be where L. C. spent most of his time at home. His queen-size oak bed, neatly made, sat in the center of the room, with a nightstand situated on each side of the bed. The comforter set was neither feminine nor particularly masculine. A dresser was located on the opposite wall of the bed, complete with an oversized mirror for L. C.'s self-inspection. A stereo system was in the far-left corner of the room. In the near-left corner was a chest of drawers and a full-length freestanding mirror. In the far-right corner, were two recliners in front of an entertainment center with a television and a VCR. The entertainment cabinet was filled with a variety of popular movies.

The blinds were closed on both windows, so that no single ray of light could enter from outside.

To the immediate right of the door was a closet. Its contents were immaculate. Rows of dress shirts hung on one end of the closet rod, perfectly starched and all facing the same direction, equal distance apart, and on the other end of the closet rod hung dark-colored dress slacks, more neatly than a dry-cleaning service would hang them. On the floor of the closet were ten pairs of dress shoes. Each pair, either black or brown, was nearly identical. The tassels on each shoe were secured with rubber bands to prevent fraying, and wooden shoe trees had been placed inside each single shoe to preserve its shape. I saw no tennis shoes, no boots, and no house slippers. Was it possible that he wore *only* dress shoes?

In the nightstand to the immediate right of his bed, I found the book *Co-Dependent No More* by Melody Beattie (HarperCollins Publishers, 1987). *The first step is admitting you have a problem*, I thought.

The subtitle on the cover read "How to Stop Controlling Others and Start Caring for Yourself." L. C. had actually highlighted parts of the text, particularly on the chapter that discusses codependent relationships. L. C. had apparently highlighted the author's definition of a codependent person: "…one who has let another person's behavior affect him or her, and who is obsessed with controlling that person's behavior" (p. 31).

In the bottom drawer of that same nightstand was a typing-paper box with half-written letters addressed to Kay. They read as follows:

> *Kay,*
>
> *I really don't know how to start this letter but I will do the best I can. It is with great sorrow that I must say goodbye. I did want this relationship to work out but I know that it never will no matter how hard I try.*
>
> *When we first met I would have* (end)
>
> *Kay,*
>
> *No matter what happens now in my life I do want you to know that I do still love you very much and always will. I know that I really messed things up, and I harbor no ill will against you for the break-up of this relationship. I think in everyone's life there is one person that you love more than anything in*

the world. Even if you don't have any feelings for me (and I don't know if you do) my love for you is still very real and strong. I might not have always told you or showed you by my actions, but I want you to know my love for you was there and still is. I know I pushed too hard now, when I should have let up on you. But as they say "Hindsight is 20-20." I was trying so hard to hold onto you and Jason but I just didn't know how. Mistakes, I did make and there were many. But still I never let up, and I don't know why, and that is being very honest. I don't want you to feel bad about yourself because I know you are a good person and you deserve the very best. Once in my lifetime the persons that were the most important people in my life are gone. I want you and your mother and Jason to know that no matter what happens I will always love the three of you very much and that is something no one can ever take away from me. (end)

I wondered if he wrote this just before or after he murdered her mother. And I did not realize that "spoiled brat" and "f*ggot" were terms of endearment for Jason, either. I considered the possibility that he may have written these – especially the references to Jason Weden and Catherine Miller – for our benefit. In any case, he had not finished these letters. He kept starting over, apparently trying to say just the right thing.

>Kay,
>
>I really don't know how to start this letter but I will do the best I can. It is with great sorrow that I must say goodbye. I really did want this relationship to work but I know that it never will, no matter how much space and time goes by. You

just don't (know) how much sorrow and pain that I have inside me.

When we first met I would have given you the moon and the stars if you had only asked. More than anything in the world, I want a family with you and Jason. I wanted to show you love ??? understanding and wanted you to love me the way that I loved you. There was so many good times that we had, after we first met. And I never wanted to see them end. I miss sharing wine with you in bed, our weekend trip to the mountains. We were so much in love and I felt as if I was on top of the world. But all those times are gone forever, and they will never come back. Kay I really do think you have lost a lot of love for me, but I just keeping loving you more and more until I made a mess of things. Until now I didn't know what a broken heart was and the empty feeling I have inside makes me now very sad. I pray to God that you would come back to me and open your heart and allow me to come back but I doubt you will or have any desire to. During the past several weeks I really wanted to give your ring back to you but I guess you wouldn't have taken it. That ring was a token of my love that I have for you. Without you wearing that ring, it means nothing. So since you won't take the ring and wear it the only thing left for me to do is take the ring back. If I was to keep the ring it would only serve as a reminder of how good things use to be between us.

Kay, I really have tried to do things your way in allowing you to come back to me in your own way. But that will never be. Even if you don't want to *admit it now, or ten years from now, in your heart you already know that you won't come back.*

I really don't want to lose you but I just can't go on living a lie. Within me all the love that I have for you is still there. But I have to get over you the (end)

Kay,

I really don't know where to start this letter, but I will do the best I can do. I don't write very well but there ?? just things I need to say and this is the only way I know how, since we don't talk on the telephone. First I wanted to say is that whatever you think of me as a person (end)

In the stereo system in the corner of his bedroom, an unlabeled cassette was found inside the tape deck, ready to be played. I pushed "play" and nearly jumped out of my skin as the volume blared.

"My boyfriend's back and there's gonna be trouble…Hey nah, hey nah, my boyfriend's back…"

"Can you all believe this?" I said to Don, Steve, and Terry, "He has a theme song!"

"That's sick," Terry said.

L. C. had other unusual musical recordings as well. One cassette tape in the stereo rack bore the handwritten title "N*gger Songs." The main lyric of the first song was "If I had a gun I'd pull the trigger… because she ran off with a n*gger."

"That's beyond offensive," I said to Don.

"That's about what I would expect from L. C." Don said, matter-of-factly.

"Paula, look at this," Terry said. I looked up from searching and Terry was holding a small velvet jewelry box. Inside was the engagement ring Kay had apparently returned to L. C.

"Aren't you going to get down on one knee first" I asked Terry.

L. C.'s bathroom was immaculate. In the combination shower/tub unit, there was not one hair, one speck of dust, one water spot. The towels hanging on the rack could not have hung more neatly if they had been folded, ironed, and stitched down. The medicine cabinet was a work of art. Again, the items all faced forward, none without their lids or caps, and spaced equal distance apart. The man had more hair care products than I had. He had skin care products, vitamins, herbs, and grooming utensils for almost every part of his body. Each one was on display in its own place.

"It would serve him right to leave his house like he – or someone – left Catherine Miller's," Steve remarked.

The bathroom was situated between L. C.'s master bedroom and the spare bedroom. In the closet of the spare bedroom, L. C. had several Salisbury Police Department uniforms, which he had never turned back in. Specifically, there were five short-sleeved shirts, seven long-sleeved shirts, and seventeen pairs of uniform pants.

"I can't believe he kept this many. I wonder how many he actually turn back in?" I commented.

"Why are you surprised? After all, he didn't even bother to turn in his service revolver to Lincoln County," Don said. Touché.

We seized the uniforms thinking that he may have worn one of them to kidnap Viktor. We also seized from that closet two black patent leather uniform belts with equipment attached, a stun gun, a mini-Maglite, and his uniform shirt brass. We did *not* find a badge or ID case or a pair of handcuffs, which struck me as rather unusual for a police officer of nearly twenty years.

In the same closet, we found a scrapbook of L. C.'s law enforcement career. The first article I saw was a Lincoln County newspaper article about a murder where the victim was shot twice in the head and left in the woods. The rest of the scrapbook was made up of various articles in which L. C.'s name was mentioned, miscellaneous photographs, and a few atta-boy letters.

Other members of the search team had covered the dining room by this point, which was tastefully decorated and not at all like I would picture a bachelor cop decorating. From drawers and cabinets in the dining room, they seized bank statements, cancelled checks, telephone bills, medical bills, and other miscellaneous documents, which we would have to go through with a fine-tooth comb at the first opportunity.

Two members of the search team climbed into the attic. One of them discovered a box with the words "Ruger Model 10/22 Carbine Rifle" on the outside. Unfortunately, the box was empty, but the instruction manual was still inside. He also found a box for a Smith & Wesson Model 36 .38 caliber revolver. This box was for a gun that L. C. had already released to the Rowan County Sheriff's Office when they first visited him in December 1993. Inside that .38 box were two spent Speer .38 caliber cartridge casings. The lab later confirmed that these cases had been fired from the Smith & Wesson. Two rounds to Viktor Gunnarsson, two rounds to Catherine Miller, and two rounds to… Misty the Shetland Sheepdog. Unless and until the dog's remains were found, we would never know for certain what happened to her.

Agent John Bendure, who took the carpet fiber samples from every room in the house, also had the unpleasant task of seizing and sifting through the bags of L. C.'s vacuum cleaner. John Bendure's expertise as an analyst was in Trace and Fiber Evidence.

The final room to be searched was a utility room just off the foyer on the right end of the house. A utility sink, and washer and dryer occupied most of the room. L. C. had a toolbox sitting open in the room as well. Immediately catching my eye was a roll of black electrical tape. I hoped for a match of L. C.'s tape to the tape used to bind Viktor, which Sheriff Lyons uncovered at the scene off the Blue

Ridge Parkway. L. C. also had some pieces of rope, which we seized along with an extension cord, and a second roll of black electrical tape. While the agents were collecting the evidence, I looked around trying to make sure nothing had been overlooked. I happened to notice that black electrical tape had been wrapped around the wire on the back of the clothes dryer.

"John?" I waited for Agent Bendure to finish sealing the plastic baggie he held in his hand to answer me.

"Yeah?" he answered.

"Do you think we ought to seize the tape off the back of that dryer?" I asked.

"What tape?" He leaned over the dryer to see what I was talking about.

"See it? Down there at the very bottom, wrapped around that wire?"

"Oh yeah. Yes, we can seize it. Who knows – it may have come from a different source than the two rolls we found." It took him a while to unwrap and remove the tape without damaging it, but he marked it and took it with him.

Throughout L. C.'s house, Civil War memorabilia was on display. His obvious interest in United States history was evident by the numerous books and models in nearly every room. Most of the items in his collection represented some battle fought during the Civil War. His obvious interest intrigued me for a couple of reasons. First of all, he had actually spent only a few months active time in the military, despite his interest in history and the military, and his apparent need for intensive structure in his life.

Secondly, and perhaps most intriguing, was something I recalled about the crime scene in Watauga County. On Highway 421 at the entrance to the Blue Ridge Parkway, a hundred yards or so from the site where Viktor Gunnarsson's body was discovered, there was a gray metal sign, the only such sign in all of Watauga County. Coincidentally, such signs were prominent throughout Rowan County. The sign was erected as a Civil War memorial, marking the location of General George Stoneman's raid in the spring of 1865. Perhaps the connection was sheer coincidence; perhaps the monument was an easily recognizable marker should L. C. ever need to return to the scene. Perhaps L. C. in his own twisted way of thinking, took pleasure in bringing his enemy to die at the historical site of a bloody Civil War battle. As I looked around his home one last time, I thought that, above all others, L. C. was at war with himself.

It was 8:20 p.m. by the time we finished our search and locked up the house. One of the SBI agents again videotaped the interior and exterior of the house before we left. We had damaged nothing and made special efforts to leave everything just as we found it, though L. C. was unlikely to acknowledge that fact.

At 8:45 p.m., SBI Agent Bobby Bonds put his video camera equipment away and we waited for the two roll-back trucks to arrive to tow L. C.'s two cars to a secure garage with an indoor facility where we could search both vehicles thoroughly. We were all hungry and exhausted but kept working. In all likelihood this would be our one shot to search L. C.'s house and cars.

We followed the tow trucks to the garage, where L. C.'s cars were unloaded at 9:25 p.m. Again, Agent Bonds videotaped and photographed the interiors and exteriors of both the Dodge Diplomat and the Chevrolet Monte Carlo.

Not surprisingly, both vehicles were immaculate. A coat of vinyl protectant had been applied to the door panels, dash, and even the floor mats. The engines appeared to be polished as well. The ashtrays were empty, which is not unusual except when the only person occupying the car smokes. In the glove compartment of the Diplomat were two toothbrushes, a tube of Colgate toothpaste, a tube of Crest toothpaste, two pocket calendars, a Charlotte street map, L. C.'s separation agreement, a menthol inhaler, a tube of lip balm, miscellaneous papers pertaining to the vehicle, and sixty-seven cents.

In the trunk were a Motorola cellular telephone, a magnetic antenna, a fire extinguisher, a roll of paper towels, a portable vacuum cleaner, a first aid kit, a windshield cover, a road atlas, a wrench, and a set of jumper cables.

The most riveting item found in the Diplomat was an unfired .22 caliber Super X bullet lying in the front driver's side floorboard in the groove beside the seat belt mount bracket and the door sill. The location where the bullet was found would make it extremely easy to overlook.

Agent John Bendure processed both cars for hairs and fibers with alcohol soluble tape. Agent Bobby Bonds then processed the interiors and exteriors of both vehicles for latent fingerprints. No fingerprints were developed because every inch of L. C.'s car had been wiped clean.

In the glove compartment of the Monte Carlo were a map of Salisbury; a Salisbury Police Department pay stub dated October 1, 1993; a ballpoint pen; and miscellaneous papers relating to the vehicle. In the console between the seats was a pair of sunglasses. The trunk was completely empty except for the black carpet mat lying on the floor of the trunk.

Agent Bendure seized and packaged the carpet mats out of the trunk of each of the two cars for further examination.

I looked around for a place to sit because the concrete was killing my feet. I had nothing to do but wait until Agents Bendure and Bonds finished processing the cars. I daydreamed about going to bed and falling asleep.

"Hey guys, come over and take a look at this," Bendure said. I got up off the stack of tires on which I was sitting and walked to the back of the Monte Carlo.

"What do you make of this?" John asked, pointing to a dusty impression on the underside of the trunk lid.

"Is that what I think it is?" Terry asked.

"It looks like a shoeprint to me," John said.

I was convinced it was a man's shoeprint the instant I saw it. The position of the print on the underside of the trunk lid had to have been made, in my estimation, by a man thrust into the trunk headfirst, on his belly, with knees bent and feet up in the air, kicking the trunk lid as it was shut.

The problem was that since the killer had apparently removed Viktor's clothing and shoes, we were unlikely to ever find the right shoe to compare with the impression. John Bendure photographed and lifted the print anyway.

"Now take a look at this," John said.

On the left wall of the Monte Carlo trunk was a series of random scratches. The marks were defined by shiny silver metal showing through the flat-black paint. The scratches were confined to about an eight-inch-square general area. They appeared to have been made with a sharp metal object such as a screwdriver, pocketknife, or nail file. I imagined Viktor Gunnarsson bound inside that trunk desperately trying anything and everything to escape.

My thoughts were interrupted by a shooting pain to my back. Standing on the cold concrete, hard-soled shoes were not helping matters. Had the muscles in my legs not been achy and fatigued, I could have fallen asleep standing up. There was not a single chair in the entire garage except in the tiny office, which was locked. It was 1:40 a.m. The lab agents were just getting ready to test both cars for the presence of blood with luminol.

There were no indications of blood in either car, but we had not really expected any. We were all of the same opinion that Viktor had been marched into the woods and shot there. The luminol testing was completed at 2:30 a.m.

At 2:45 a.m., we finally called it a night. Steve documented the date and time and indicated that the search conducted pursuant to the search warrant in the matter of Lamont Claxton Underwood was complete.

A few short hours later with very little sleep, on Wednesday, February 2, 1994, Steve and I met SBI Agent

Wayne Bridges at Lakewood Apartments. Agent Bridges had arranged for us to have access to Viktor Gunnarsson's apartment. We climbed the exterior flight of stairs to the first apartment on the second level. When I stepped inside the door, I was met by an unpleasant odor of mustiness and garlic.

The apartment itself was a typical one, with a living area, combination kitchen and dining area, two bedrooms, and a bathroom. The front door led directly into the living area. The walls were painted white, and the floor was covered with beige carpet. The window curtains were closed so that no one could see in or out without moving them. The furniture consisted of a floral-print couch, a small round dining table, an entertainment center housing a television and stereo, a coffee table, a brown tweed recliner, a wooden dining chair, and a black vinyl beanbag chair. A large U.S. flag was hung by all four corners on the left wall and made for a central focal piece. Junk mail, magazines, and miscellaneous papers were lying in piles in nearly every available surface.

In the kitchen I saw that a counter, stove, sink, and a large refrigerator were on the left wall of the room. Dirty dishes, and pots and pans were in the sink. A frying pan containing hardened grease and a pot with popcorn kernels sat on the surface of the stove. An open package of onions from Food Lion was lying on the counter, bearing a package date of November 29, 1993. Above the counter were countless snapshots and postcards from people all over the world, mostly women, taped to a piece of poster board.

On the right side of the room was a smaller refrigerator. Viktor's apartment manager explained that the large refrigerator was ruined during Viktor's last visit to Sweden because he forgot to clean it out before he left. I imagined maggots. Even though the presence of insect life in decaying human or animal material, known scientifically as forensic entomology, could aid in determining the time of death of a person, I still could not stand the sight of maggots.

"Last summer, Viktor Gunnarsson went to Sweden and forgot about the ground beef in the refrigerator, and the whole refrigerator was full of maggots when I came in to inspect the apartment. He was supposed to clean it out, but he bought this small one in here and still hasn't cleaned out the larger one."

"Paula, why don't you check the larger refrigerator since you really like maggots," Steve suggested.

"No problem," I retorted. "Next to riding for hours in a car full of cigarette smoke, maggots are my second favorite thing."

"Good one," he said.

I opened the smaller refrigerator door. Inside were two plastic gallon milk jugs. The first jug, nearly empty, had a sale date of December 4, 1993. The second jug, which had not been opened, had a sale date of December 17, 1993. I learned, after a thorough research study on dairy production and sales, that milk can be sold for up to seventeen days. Therefore, the milk bearing the December 17 date could not have been purchased prior to December 1, and the milk bearing the December 4 date could not have been purchased after January 3, 1994. Both jugs of milk were sour and curdled. But we learned even more.

This particular brand of milk was sold only to one convenience store in Salisbury, conveniently located within a couple miles of Lakewood Apartments. Also, because those milk deliveries are only made on Fridays, Viktor had to have purchased the unopened gallon of milk on Friday, December 3, 1993. We knew he was missing already by the following Friday, which was December 10. Mostly likely Viktor stopped at the store on his way home on Friday, December 3, when he returned from taking Daniel to the Charlotte airport.

Next to the small refrigerator was another small round dining table. On top of the table were stacks of mail, a cordless telephone, and the keys to Viktor's car, which was still sitting in the parking lot in his customary space.

There was a rear door in the kitchen leading onto a small balcony. Neither of the doors showed any signs of forced entry. On the balcony was Viktor's bicycle, a broom, a mop, and a bucket.

I walked out of the kitchen and back into the living room. I saw a small end table to my immediate left. On the back of that table in black magic marker were the letters "L. C." We all just about had a fit when we saw that. It did not take us long to learn, though, that the letters did not stand for Lamont Claxton, but rather for Livingstone College, a nearby private college where Viktor had obtained the surplus table.

I walked into Viktor's bedroom next. Viktor's bedroom was on the left of a small hallway, and the bedroom door was all the way open. Viktor's bed was actually only a full-size mattress and box springs, which sat directly on the beige carpet, without a bed frame. The head of the bed was against the wall.

On top of the bed was a leather bomber jacket, a rose-colored short-sleeve golf-type shirt, a pair of faded blue denim jeans, and bed coverings. The blankets and quilt were turned down, and appeared to have been slept under, at least briefly. I noticed some random pink stains on the sheets, but I could not readily determine where they may have originated from. They seemed to be scattered all over the fitted sheet, so they did not appear to be the result of a spill of some kind.

On the floor to the right of the bed was a combination telephone/answering machine. The green light on the machine was on, but the cassette tape holder for the voice messages was empty.

Beside the phone on the floor was a hairbrush. At the foot of the bed were two dining room chairs faced together and touching, forming a substitute table. Clothes, shaving items, and two Italian language audio tapes were lying on the seats of the chairs. An attaché case, pieces of junk mail, books, a pair of men's brown leather loafers, and a pair of men's black Cuga tennis shoes were lying at the base of the chairs. The window was closed in the bedroom. The curtains were closed as well. Beside the window hung a large poster of John Wayne in his Western attire.

In the small bathroom between the two bedrooms, a constant drip ran in the sink. The commode and shower were about as clean as a bachelor's would be. One hairbrush lay on the back of the commode, and another hairbrush lay on the rim of the sink. Tan-and-white vinyl tiles covered the floor, and the walls were painted white just like the rest of the apartment.

The second bedroom was rather bare. Viktor's friend from Sweden, Daniel Johansson, apparently slept in the small unmade bed in the corner when he visited Viktor. The only other items visible in the room were a bicycle and vacuum cleaner.

The apartment overall was cluttered, but mostly with photographs, books, magazines, letters, postcards, and an overwhelming amount of junk mail. Viktor must have been on every mailing list imaginable. He had saved junk mail dated as early as 1990. He kept sweepstakes entries, chain letters, product advertisements, newspaper classified advertisements, credit card applications, catalogs, and even mailings addressed "Dear Occupant."

We found no information concerning the Swedish Prime Minister, his assassination, or any extremist groups.

Agent Bobby Bonds had previously interviewed Bonnie Whitley, the assistant manager of Lakewood Apartments. However, at that time they had only discussed her observations on December 13 and 15, 1993, when she reported Viktor Gunnarsson missing to the Salisbury Police Department. Bonnie told Agent Bonds that on December 13, Viktor's friend Tana called her and said she thought Viktor was missing. Bonnie Whitley and Bucky Straub, the apartment maintenance supervisor, went to his apartment.

Bucky told her that he had already been by there once, and that he had closed and locked the door himself when he did not find Viktor at home.

When Bonnie and Bucky went into the apartment together on Monday, December 13, Bonnie walked into Viktor's bedroom and saw that the telephone answering machine was on, and that there was a blinking red light. She also noticed that a cassette tape was visible in the machine. Bonnie recalled that a pair of jeans, a rose-colored golf shirt, and a bomber jacket had been neatly laid across a chair. Viktor's car keys were in the pocket of the jacket. Bonnie also recalled that a lamp was on in the living room, and food was sitting out in the kitchen.

On Wednesday, December 15, 1993, Bonnie went back to Viktor's apartment with four officers from the Salisbury Police Department and the Rowan County Sheriff's Department. When they walked inside, Bonnie noticed immediately that the lid on the answering machine was up and the tape was missing. Later in the day, the police had the locks changed on the apartment. Bonnie provided as much information as she could to the police so they could fill out a missing person's report.

When Steve and I approached Bonnie Whitley in the office of Lakewood Apartments, she seemed genuinely interested in helping us solve the case. She had gathered quite a collection of newspaper articles and personal notes on Viktor and his personal life, including names and descriptions of people who had come to his apartment since she learned he was missing. She seemed very eager to help us.

Bonnie was thin, had long wavy sandy-colored hair, and was dressed in business casual. Her wire-rimmed glasses gave her a professional appearance, and she wore them down low on her nose. She exuded a lot of energy as she reacted to each question.

Steve asked her if she saw any unusual cars at his apartment since Viktor had been missing.

"Oh, dear God!" she said, "Do you think the murderers might come back here?!"

I stepped in to help her relax a bit. "No, we don't have any reason to believe that, but we just wanted to make sure you hadn't seen anyone who did not belong here around his apartment after he disappeared."

"No, I don't think so… Is it true that criminals really come back and revisit the scene of the crime?" Steve looked at me to answer.

"Not if they're smart," I answered.

"Oh," she said, considering my response.

"When did you last see Viktor?" I asked her.

"At the Salisbury Mall. He and Daniel were getting ready to go to Florida. Viktor always came in and told me when he was leaving and when he would be returning, except this last time. His friend Tana Howe was the first one to realize he was missing. She contacted me and told me."

Steve and I left the office and drove on into the apartment complex to the building where Viktor lived. We found and interviewed Reginald Wright, Viktor's next-door neighbor. Mr. Wright told us that he remembered walking his dog as usual around 11:00 a.m. on Saturday, December 4, when he noticed Viktor's apartment door was slightly ajar. He did not see Viktor, but looked to the parking lot where Viktor usually parked his car; the car was there. The next day, December 5, when walking his dog, Mr. Wright saw that the apartment door was closed, and that Viktor's car was still in the parking lot where it had been parked the day before. However, he still had not seen Viktor around.

Steve and I walked down to the apartment directly under Viktor's, on the first floor of the building. The apartment belonged to the maintenance supervisor. Steve knocked on the door. When the man answered his door, I took a small step backward. The small short man standing half in and half out of the door was dressed in camouflage clothing and stood somewhat defensively. He looked at us intently for a second, and then his eyes darted around and beyond us before stepping toward us. Steve met him halfway.

"Are you Mr. Straub? We are looking for the maintenance supervisor Mr. Bucky Straub."

Steve introduced ourselves to him and we showed him our identifications, which the young man looked at carefully.

"Yeah, that's me. Come on in," he said quickly, glancing around again and then hurriedly shutting the door behind us. "Have a seat," he said. We sat.

"You can call me Bucky," he said. "You two are investigating the murder of Viktor Gunnarsson, aren't you?"

"We are," Steve told him, "and we just wanted to speak with you since you lived below Viktor."

"Oh yes, oh yes," Bucky said. He seemed uncomfortable.

"Did you know Viktor very well?" I asked him and smiled, trying to put him at ease.

He turned his attention from Steve to me and sort of smiled back. Then he opened up.

"Gunnarsson was always in and out of his apartment. He had a lot of visitors."

"Oh really?" I said. "Were you around in early December when Viktor disappeared?"

"Yeah."

"Did you know any of Viktor's other friends?" I asked him.

"There was a guy Daniel from Sweden who visited with Gunnarsson for a while. He kept calling me in December to see if I had heard from Gunnarsson. Other people came here looking for him too. His friend Tana – I don't know her last name but Whitley will – but Tana came... Bonnie told me she kept a log of the visitors and other details about Gunnarsson's disappearance." Don, Terry, Steve, and I had reviewed Bonnie Whitley's records already.

"Do you remember seeing anything out of the ordinary in Viktor's apartment after he went missing?" Steve asked.

"I went in with Whitley not long after Gunnarsson was reported missing. I remember the red light on the answering machine blinking like crazy, like he had a bunch of messages. Then a few days later when I went back in to change the locks on the door for the police, Gunnarsson's phone rang. I went to answer it, and I saw then that a green light was on this time. But I decided not to answer the phone, and whoever was calling didn't try to leave a message."

"Mr. Straub, are you saying that there was a tape or at least recorded messages on Viktor's answering machine when you first went into the apartment, and then when you went back the next time, the light was green and there were no messages?"

"That's right. And I told you to, call me Bucky. There was a tape in the machine the first time I went in with Whitley, but the second time when I went in – with the police – it was gone."

"Were you at home on the night of December third?"

"Yes, but I'm pretty sure I was in bed asleep. I go to bed early and get up by sunrise in the morning."

"So, you don't remember seeing or hearing anything strange that night?"

"No, not that I can recall."

"If you heard people going up and down the steps, say to and from Viktor's apartment, would you have heard that?"

"No. A lot of people come and go here all the time. But if I were sleeping, I sleep so soundly that I probably wouldn't even have heard a gun go off."

I thought of L. C. Underwood and his leather-soled dress shoes or his rubber-soled police-issue shoes, and of Viktor and his rubber-soled casual shoes. I doubted that Underwood would do or say anything to draw unnecessary attention to himself.

Underwood returned to his home on Lake Drive in Salisbury on Saturday, February 5. Concerned that our search may prompt L. C. to do something drastic, we established a rotating team to conduct surveillance on L. C. It was possible that he might lead us to the murder weapons in an attempt to destroy them or change their locations, or he could meet an accomplice of whom we were not yet aware. But for the entire week that followed, L. C. rarely left his house.

CHAPTER SIXTEEN

"So we laboured in the work: and half of them held the spears from the rising of the morning till the stars appeared" (Nehemiah 4:21)

Fact: Viktor Gunnarsson was murdered with two .22 caliber bullets in December 1993.

Fact: Kay Weden's house was shot into by a .22 caliber bullet during the spring of 1993.

We had the two spent rounds compared with each other. The Firearms Section of the SBI Crime Laboratory reported the following:

The .22 caliber bullet that was fired by a .22 caliber gun into Kay Weden's residence was determined to have firing characteristics of six lands and grooves with a right-hand twist. Confirming our suspicions, the two .22 caliber bullets fired into the body of Viktor Gunnarsson by a .22 caliber weapon were determined to have firing characteristics of six lands and grooves with a right-hand twist.

Therefore, all three bullets could have been fired from a single gun or guns made by one of six different manufacturers. One of the possibilities was Dan Wesson, and of those Dan Wesson guns, the murder weapon could have certainly been a revolver. On November 11, 1990, L. C. Underwood purchased a .22 caliber Dan Wesson revolver at Frank's Pawn Shop in Salisbury.

Fact: A .22 caliber unfired bullet was seized from L. C.'s Dodge Diplomat during the execution of the search warrant on February 1, 1994.

Fact: Kay Weden found a .22 caliber unfired bullet under her kitchen table on December 7, 1993, the very morning L. C. had showed up at her house and sat at that table trying to talk to her.

The Crime Lab compared the .22 caliber bullet fired into Kay's house with the above two .22 caliber unfired bullets. All three were .22 caliber rounds with copper coating.

If only we could get our hands on the guns we knew that L. C. had in his possession prior to the murders of Viktor Gunnarsson and Catherine Miller, we could compare them with all the fired bullets in the case. But despite our repeated requests to L. C. and his attorneys, no guns were forthcoming.

By April, my hope of finding L. C.'s .38 and .22 caliber handguns was beginning to fade. But I did not want to give up until we had exhausted all the possibilities. So, Steve and I decided to drive to Ohio and talk with the people L. C. referred to as his family: his "stepbrothers," his "stepdad" Burl Childress, and his "mom" Barbara Childress, all of whom were alive and well. L. C. had told several people that he had given his stepbrothers the guns he had for Christmas a few years earlier, and I wanted to confirm or disprove his claims.

After contacting and arranging to meet with agents from the Ohio Bureau of Criminal Investigation (BCI), Steve and I drove the eight hours from Boone, North Carolina, to Columbus in mid-April 1994. I believed that L. C. had gotten rid of both guns immediately after the homicides of Viktor and Catherine. I did not expect anyone in Columbus, Ohio, to have any information concerning L. C.'s guns, and I certainly did not expect one to be handed over, but still we had to give it a shot.

At the time, with a population of over 1.8 million, the Columbus Metro area was America's fifteenth largest city. Columbus, named after the explorer, was planned as a hub for political purposes, and during the Civil War it became a staging area for Union forces. After the war, Columbus's population grew rapidly. Situated at the junction of the Oletangy and Scioto Rivers, Columbus was an ideal location for industry, and it boomed. Columbus became one of the country's largest manufacturers of horse-drawn vehicles, and other companies were drawn to the area, encouraged by rapid development along the Scioto River in the early twentieth century. By 1940, Columbus experienced unprecedented industrial growth, which attracted many struggling southerners northward, doubling the population in the next fifty years. Adding to the population, and following her divorce from John, Barbara married Burl Childress and moved to Columbus. Also residing in the area were son Burl Junior, and three other sons.

At the Columbus Bureau building, we briefed the agents who were assigned to assist us. The agents drove us to the various locations we had researched to find and interview all of the sons except for Burl Junior, who would not be available until later in the evening. None of three claimed to know L. C. hardly at all, other than to speak to him if and when they ever saw him. Each of them denied ever having received any guns from L. C. Underwood at any time. None of them seemed to want to defend L. C. or have an opinion either way as to his culpability, but each of them denied any type of brotherly relationship with him at all. They were all cooperative with us.

The BCI agents then drove us to the home of Burl and Barbara Childress, an address that turned out to be in a well-established neighborhood. This contact would be touchy. The Ohio agents waited in their car and watched while Steve and I walked to the front door of the neat middle-class home. Steve knocked on the door, holding his identification at the ready. I stood aside, listening for movement inside the house. We were not expecting a very warm welcome, and I was confident they had already been made aware that we were in the area.

Burl Childress answered the door.

"Mr. Childress? Burl Childress? My name is Steve Wilson. I am an agent with the North Carolina State Bureau of Investigation. This is Detective Sgt. Paula May with the Watauga County Sheriff's Office. We would like to –"

"I know who you are. We know all about you, and we don't have anything to say to you," Burl said firmly.

"Mr. Childress, I do understand your reluctance to talk to us. But we have some information *we* would like to share with *you*. Please understand that we have nothing personal against L. C. or anything personal in this case. We are merely investigating the facts of a homicide."

"Well, you have your facts all wrong. We don't know anything about your case, and I don't understand why you'd think we do."

"Well sir, if we could just have a minute of your time. If we could just speak with you and your wife for just a few minutes, maybe we could explain why we're here." Barbara, who was standing behind her husband, walked toward us, standing in the doorway only a few feet away. She appeared exceptionally vibrant – a picture of good health – for a person who had allegedly died a few short months earlier.

"Why are you doing this to L.C?" she began. "Why can't you all leave him alone? He did not have anything to do with those murders, and you all are ruining his reputation! You already have ruined his reputation in Salisbury!"

"Ma'am, I understand your concern, but we don't believe you have all of the facts," Steve told her.

While Barbara Childress did not invite us inside her home, she did stand at her front door and talk with us for over half an hour. During that conversation, she made several comments about her relationship with L. C. As expected, the overwhelming majority of the things she had heard about the case came solely from L. C. I could only imagine the picture L. C. had painted of us to these people. I held no animosity toward Mr. and Mrs. Childress for the hostility they held toward Steve and me. In fact, I admired their willingness to take foster children into their home and raise them as their own. Barbara Childress, in particular, clearly had a heart for children.

"I'll tell you right now that I don't like that Don Gale!" Barbara volunteered. "Don Gale has been spreading lies about L. C., and he's trying to frame L. C. for those murders." It was not a mystery from who she had heard that.

I gave Steve a reprieve and patiently addressed the hostile Mrs. Childress. "Ma'am, I can assure you that no one is trying to frame anyone for these murders. But we have to follow up on the leads we have. And unfortunately, a lot of things point to L. C. and he has refused to cooperate with us to offer any explanations."

Barbara spoke a little more calmly. "L. C. is doing just what his attorney has told him to do. I personally believe, though, that L. C. needs a new attorney. I don't think David Bingham is representing him very well. In fact, I told L. C. on the phone recently that I didn't want to hear anymore of his sh*t until he got a new attorney."

"I understand that you've known L. C. for a number of years," I told her. "I believe you cared for him when he had *no* one else to care about him."

"Yes, he refers to me as his mother. We never actually adopted L. C. because his parents were alive and could not be located. But I consider him my son, and he considers me to be his mother."

"Right. ...Ma'am, have you read the search warrant that was published in the *Salisbury Post*?"

"Yes, I have. And Burl asked L. C. about running that Gunnarsson's license plate. But L. C. said that was a mistake. Burl told him everyone does things they aren't supposed to do when they have access to certain information, but that didn't make L. C. no murderer. It's not that unusual for police officers to run tag numbers for personal reasons."

"You're right about that. But that is not the whole story. There were several other problems besides the fact that he ran the guy's tag number that same night he was kidnapped and murdered."

"We know L. C. had women problems, but he wouldn't *kill* somebody because of it."

"People are killed every day for those very reasons, ma'am," Steve informed her.

"*Every* day," I stressed.

"But when you all searched L. C.'s house in February, L. C. said the officers damaged his paint on the upstairs, tore up his cars, and that certain parts on the cars could not be replaced."

I answered her with practiced patience. "Ma'am, that simply is not true. But you know what? You don't even have to take our word for it. We videotaped the entire house, lawn, and vehicles before we did anything else. And then when we finished, we videotaped it all again. We were extremely careful not to cause any damage to anything L. C. had. It's standard procedure."

"Well, L. C. was pretty mad about it. I don't think he'd just make that up."

"You have a right to believe L. C. if you want to, ma'am. We're not here to argue with you."

"Then why *are* you here?" she asked.

Steve chose to answer that question. "We came here because L. C. has told several people that he gave his guns to his brothers here in Columbus. If that's true, then all we need to do to eliminate L. C. as a suspect is to compare those guns with the bullets used in the murders. Again, we wouldn't have to be here if L. C. would just cooperate and get the guns for us."

"I can't tell you about any of L. C.'s guns, but ... well, Burl and I did swing back and forth on our opinions about whether L. C. had committed these murders, but that was all before L. C. came to Ohio. When he came up here and we talked with him face to face about it, we are convinced that he could not have done those murders. I really believe that the Swedes killed that Gunnarsson man. ...I just can't believe L. C. would hurt a kitty." I wondered if she knew about L. C. as a young boy slinging a "kitty" into the barn by its tail until he killed it. I judged it best not to ask.

I tried to prolong the conversation with Barbara before she had a chance to ask us to leave, hoping that we might learn something new. "Mrs. Childress, did L. C. actually ever live with you when he was at The Children's Home?"

"No, he lived in the cottages, not with us. But he visited us regularly. After he graduated from high school, he'd still visit me and my ex-husband John – well he was my husband then – on weekends and holidays. He worked on the farm. ...L. C. went to The Children's Home when he was six or seven years old. His sister, Margo, was only three. Neither of them were ever any trouble. Then when L. C. went to community college, he had a grade point average of 4.0. ... He wanted to work as a police officer. Once after he started work, someone shot at him six times and missed him. It was a miracle that L. C. was not killed! L. C.'s natural father read about it in the newspaper and contacted him. But L. C. told his father he didn't want to talk to him again, that his biological father and mother were not his real parents, and that he considered *me* to be his real mother. ...L. C.'s natural mother lived in California."

I knew L. C. would say to her whatever he needed to benefit himself. But if it made Barbara feel better to believe L. C., then that was her prerogative. I strongly suspected he was taking advantage of their good nature.

"May I ask *you* something?" Barbara asked us.

"Sure, you may," I answered.

"Why was that search warrant signed in Watauga County rather than in Salisbury?"

I explained that Viktor Gunnarsson's body was found – and we contend that he was murdered in the same place, within the jurisdiction of Watauga County, and that was why it was being investigated by myself and the Watauga County Sheriff's Office. I further explained that a Superior Court Judge had signed the search warrant, which made it valid for service anywhere in North Carolina.

"I told L. C. that he should call the investigators in Watauga County and provide information to you rather than to his attorney in Salisbury. There are things going on in Salisbury that you all need to know about."

"I appreciate that, Mrs. Childress, but L. C. has refused to cooperate with *any* investigators."

Barbara replied, "When he called me the other day, L. C. was crying on the phone. He was upset because of these investigations."

"Again, though, Mrs. Childress, all he has to do to eliminate himself is let us take a look at those guns he has," Steve reminded her. "We only need them long enough to compare them with the bullets used in the murders."

"That's all you need to eliminate him?" she asked.

"Well that would certainly go a long way towards eliminating him. If the guns don't match the bullets, there wouldn't be much of a case against him. But the problem is, the bullets were fired from the same types of guns L. C. had, and now those guns have disappeared, and L. C. won't even try to account for them. Surely you can understand why that's very suspicious to us."

"Yes, I do," she admitted, "and I told L. C. he should give you the guns if you need them to eliminate him as a suspect. But L. C. said he has not had those guns in years. *I* certainly don't have them. I don't believe in having guns. Now what did you say L. C. said about the guns?"

Steve told her, "L. C. has told people that he gave them to his brothers in Ohio as Christmas gifts."

Barbara told him, "You don't believe that do you? I just don't think L. C. ever made that comment."

I asked both Mr. and Mrs. Childress, "Do either of you have any personal knowledge about L. C.'s guns?"

Mr. Childress answered, "We've seen a gun cabinet in L. C.'s house when we visited him in Salisbury, but I don't remember specifically what kinds of guns he had in it."

"Has L. C. ever, at any time, given you a gun or guns for safekeeping or as a gift or for any reason at all?" I asked.

"Certainly not."

"How often do you talk to L.C?"

"He calls me every week. He has never missed a week."

"And how many times has he visited you here?"

"Oh, three or four times, I guess."

"Have you been ill recently, Mrs. Childress?" I asked her.

"I had some minor surgery a while back."

"I don't mean to pry, but have you ever had cancer of any kind?"

"No, not hardly. Why would you ask that?" She seemed genuinely taken aback.

"Because L. C. has told several people that you did. In fact, he told them that you had died." She did not quite know how to respond to that.

I could not help but add, "He also said that he had spent all his money to pay your medical bills and funeral expenses."

"That's ridiculous," she said.

"But that's what he has told a number of people. His friends, at that."

"I find that hard to believe," she said.

"Again, you have a right to believe anything you want. But we are not making these things up, Mrs. Childress," Steve said.

"Do you work outside the home?" I asked her.

"Yes. Burl and I care for AIDS patients. Burl also works in a job settling union disputes."

"And how many children do you have?"

"Burl and I have eight sons between us. We haven't had any trouble with any of our other sons. Burl has four sons, and I have four, counting L. C."

"Okay, well, we will go now, but in case you ever want to talk with us again, I'm going to leave you our cards with our phone numbers."

"All right, bye."

"Goodbye." I hated to see people taken advantage of, as L. C. Underwood had obviously done to these people, but it was not my job to convince them. I hoped they realized the truth before they got in any deeper.

We had one more interview to attempt in Columbus. We drove directly to Burl Childress Jr.'s residence in an upper-middle-class neighborhood. The BCI agents again waited inside the vehicle, while Steve and I walked to the front door. I knocked. Burl Jr. answered the door, and pleasantly agreed to talk with Steve and me. He invited us inside. At thirty-three years of age, Burl Jr. had a good job with a major corporation and seemed to be doing well for himself. He volunteered that he manufactured one of only two man-made diamonds in the world. After some small talk about diamonds, Burl Jr. told us that he knew very little about L. C. Underwood and our homicide investigation.

He said, "To be honest with you, my father called me this evening and told me to expect some investigators to contact me. He also told me I didn't have to tell you anything. But I told my father that I didn't have anything to hide, and that I saw no reason not to answer your questions."

"Well, we certainly appreciate that, Mr. Childress," Steve told him. "So how long have you known L.C?"

"L. C. is my dad's wife's adopted son. I know he wasn't legally adopted, but Barbara considers him to be her son."

"Do you know L. C. very well?"

"No, I'm afraid I don't know him well at all."

"Has L. C. contacted you about any guns? Or has he given you any guns?"

"No, and I haven't talked to L. C. about this case at all. But no, he hasn't ever given me any guns or to anyone else that I know of."

"When was the last time you talked with L.C?"

"L. C. came to Ohio for a weekend, and I saw him only briefly, maybe five minutes. That was after the investigation in North Carolina had already started, but L. C. didn't mention it. I remember I asked L. C. what it was like to be a cop. L. C. said something about cops starting out on one thing and ending up working on something totally different. I can't remember exactly what he was saying. But we were sitting down, and L. C. was drinking a cup of coffee at the time. ...The longest I have ever spent with L. C. was when I went with him, Mom, and Dad out to dinner. They talked about a cruise that the three of them went on in November 1992."

"How long have Burl and Barbara been married?"

"They got married about seven or eight years ago, but they lived together about five years before that."

"Do you think any of your brothers would know more about L. C. than you do?"

"I doubt it. All my brothers just speak to L. C. to say hello, and that's about it. L. C. is probably closer to Barbara and my father than anyone else."

We thanked him for his cooperation, and we left.

We returned to North Carolina without any of L. C.'s guns.

CHAPTER SEVENTEEN

*"Thou shalt love thy neighbour as thyself.
There is none other commandment greater" (Mark 12:31)*

Back in my office the following week, after much research, I decided to direct my attention toward Viktor's acquaintances. I located a phone number for one William "Bill" Rambo who was residing in the state of Florida. He answered on the second ring, and said he would be happy to answer any questions I had. He had already heard that Viktor had been found murdered.

Mr. Rambo told me that he met Viktor Gunnarsson in 1985 at the Royal Viking Hotel in Copenhagen. Viktor was "vacationing" with Mr. Rambo's daughter at the time. Then in 1989, Viktor came to the United States.

"He called me from Charlotte and invited himself to Florida. I did not invite him. He showed up on my doorstep and stayed a couple of months. He said he was between jobs, and he never offered to pay any rent."

"I believe he was known for doing that," I told him.

"Yes, that's what I hear. I found out later that Viktor had used my address to get an ID.

"Viktor Gunnarsson had a friend in Germany, I know who he was, and the two of them had some kind of plan to ship Mercedes cars into the United States or something like that, but it never got off the ground. I think Viktor went as far as to have business cards made, and that's about it. Viktor didn't have any income, but he took a lot of leisure trips. He just sponged off people, I think. He went to Brazil and stayed two or three weeks one time."

"Are you saying that you were suspicious of Viktor's activities?"

"Not really. I know Viktor didn't like drugs. But he loved to travel. He went to Puerto Rico, the Virgin Islands, and Brazil for at least three weeks, just traveling around the countries."

"What were you doing when Viktor came to visit you in Florida?"

"I was married then. My daughter didn't like Viktor then, and my wife didn't want him around either. I guess he finally took the hint and left. ...The last I heard from him was in 1990. I lived in Salisbury for twenty years, and then I got divorced in '86, and that's when I moved down here."

"All right. What else can you tell me about Viktor Gunnarsson?" I asked.

"I understand he had his pick of the ladies in Sweden. But I haven't seen or heard from Viktor since he left Florida that time. He never came back."

"You said you had a daughter that Viktor was vacationing with in Copenhagen. Did she maintain contact with him?"

"That's my daughter. She's in college, and living in Salisbury now. My ex-wife still lives in Salisbury. When I talked to my ex-wife, she told me that Viktor had not called to talk to her in a long time."

"...Mr. Rambo, do the initials R.M.R. mean anything to you?"

"Yes. I had a corporation named R.M.R. I owned a laundry in Salisbury, and we called it R.M.R. The two R's stood for me and my brother, but for the life of me I can't remember what the M was for. I had seventeen different corporations, see. You know, I owned the largest nursing home chain to ever go bankrupt. My employees embezzled one and a half million dollars from me. Thank God they're in jail now – that was five years ago. But why do you ask about R.M.R?"

"When Viktor's body was found on January 7th in Watauga County, he was wearing a signet ring with the initials 'R.M.R.' We don't know where he got it."

"I have no idea because I never gave him a ring; I never had one like that."

"Okay then. Perhaps it's just a coincidence."

"Now, let me see… What else do I know about Viktor? I know he would get on this kick about the Lord, but I don't know if his religion was genuine or not. I know he did go to church a lot. In fact, he started attending a Christian school, the same school my daughter attended. He seemed nice, but he kind of rubbed me the wrong way."

"How did you find out he had been murdered?" I asked him.

"My daughter in Salisbury told me …either my daughter or my ex-wife."

"Do you know other friends of Viktor's?"

"Mostly he talked about women. He spoke several languages and had women from all over the world it seemed. Viktor said he had four attorneys, one in each of the Scandinavian countries. I told him he would need them as many women as he had. He just laughed. While he stayed at my house, he made a bunch of long-distance calls, talking to women. He paid for them a week at a time, and it was $80 or $90 a week. I think his dad helped him out financially, and he got some settlement from the Swedish government or something. And then he got a lot of mail, mostly from women. …But you know, he got away from them quickly. He'd never actually fight for any woman. So, I'd be really surprised to hear his girlfriend got him shot and killed. Viktor Gunnarsson would always back off if he got in trouble."

Perhaps if he knew it was coming, I thought.

I did not learn much more about Viktor than I already knew from talking to Rambo. I was disappointed that we had not yet solved the mystery of the signet ring and the initials "R.M.R." None of his family in Sweden knew, and none of his friends that we had talked to knew either.

"We'll probably never know what R.M.R. stands for," Steve said, coughing. "He could have just found it on the street. Who knows?"

"True. I'll just bet it's the initials of some woman who bought him the ring."

"You're probably right," he agreed.

CHAPTER EIGHTEEN

"A man that hath friends must shew himself friendly" (Proverbs 18:24)

In spite of many other interviews we had with Viktor Gunnarsson's acquaintances, nothing we learned seemed to be significantly relevant to his disappearance. I mulled over the last day we knew Viktor was alive, the evening of Friday, December 3, 1993. Viktor left Kay's house after telling her he needed to get back to his apartment so he could get some sleep. In all likelihood, having no reason to be deceptive, Viktor probably did just that. But we could not be certain that Viktor did not talk to anyone else either by phone or in person between the time he left Kay's and the time he was kidnapped. Again, we went through all the statements Don, Terry, Steve, and I had obtained from people who knew Viktor Gunnarsson. We included those whose names were found in Viktor's personal address book, which we had removed from his apartment. The overwhelming majority were women, with addresses all over the world, and we talked to so many of them that I eventually lost count. The story was basically the same with each one, however.

They would meet Viktor for the first time in some public place; he would approach them in his friendly and outgoing manner and introduce himself. They would begin having some light conversation, and within a short period, Viktor had made such an impression that a brief but passionate relationship would ensue. None of Viktor's friends had anything negative to say about him; not one. In fact, Viktor was held in the highest esteem by his friends, even women with whom he was no longer involved. I understood that Viktor had quite the reputation as a lover, a friend, and just someone that people loved to be around. No instances of violence involving Viktor Gunnarsson were ever disclosed to Don, Terry, Steve, or me.

As I learned more about Viktor, I had a few more questions to ask of a few of his closest friends in Salisbury. The first was Keith, a quiet young man in his early twenties who lived at home with his mother. Steve and I drove to an address in a mobile home park and were welcomed into the small but tidy living room.

Keith, a bit nervous at first, said he was anxious to help in any way he could because Viktor was such a good friend of his. Keith asked if it was okay if his mother remained in the room while we talked.

"Sure, it's your home; you're more than welcome to say," Steve told Keith's mother.

"Do you work, Keith?" I asked him.

"Yeah, I do odd jobs."

"How did you know Viktor Gunnarsson?"

"I met Viktor, let's see, in the spring of 1991, just before he was returning to Sweden from the United States. ...I can't believe he's gone," Keith said. "I admired that man so much."

"So, you and Viktor were rather close?" I asked him.

"Oh yes. Weren't we, Mother?" Mother nodded.

Keith explained, "When he left for Sweden in May of last year, I took care of his apartment at Lakewood. Viktor gave me a key. I cleaned the apartment some because Viktor never had time to do any cleaning. I picked up his mail for him too. ...Viktor told me I could stay at the apartment some while he was gone. I stayed a couple of nights, but then Viktor's apartment manager, Bonnie, told me that Viktor's lease wouldn't allow me to stay."

I asked, "Keith, what did you get out of cleaning Viktor's apartment and taking care of things for him?"

"Oh nothing," he said, "I just did it... as a friend. I knew I could count on Viktor if I ever needed anything. Isn't that right, Mother?" Mother nodded.

"How often did you see Viktor when he was in Salisbury?"

"Oh, we saw each other two or three times a week. We *always* kept in touch. We ate together a few times at Christos Restaurant in Salisbury."

"Did Viktor have a lot of other friends?"

"He had a bunch of girlfriends and a lot of other acquaintances too."

"Did he ever mention the name Kay Weden to you?"

"No, Vik never mentioned her. We have a mutual friend by the name of Glen Faris. You might ask him. Glen works at the Quality Mart on Highway 70. ...Me, Viktor, and Glen went shopping together at the Hanes Mall in Winston Salem a couple of times. The three of us were real close..."

"Do you know what Viktor was doing or who he was hanging around with between Thanksgiving and the time he disappeared?" Steve asked.

"On the Friday after Thanksgiving, Viktor helped me and Mother move in here. He invited us to a spaghetti supper he was having that night, but Mother and I were too tired from moving."

"Do you know Viktor's Swedish friend Daniel Johansson?"

"Yes, I met him a couple of times with Viktor at the Blues Cafe. The three of us went to some clubs together a few times too. Viktor enjoyed meeting people. But he didn't drink. Well, he drank wine with his meals on occasion, but he never drank to get drunk. He was very religious and did not believe in getting drunk. He was so happy and fun-loving..."

"Did Viktor ever complain to you about anything? Was he having any problems that you're aware of?"

"The only thing I ever heard him complain about was losing money when he returned from Sweden and exchanged it, due to the value of a dollar."

"How did Viktor earn a living, Keith?"

"He made money by tutoring language students. Vik spoke nine different languages. He charged fifty dollars an hour. Viktor had students calling him all the time. I heard him talking to them on the phone. …You know, Vik even offered to tutor my sister who was in the ninth grade at the time, and he said he'd only charge her half price. But she never followed through."

"You said Viktor was religious. Did he attend a particular church regularly?"

"He went to church in Sweden. He was a youth director there. …I think it was a Baptist church. Vik wanted to be some kind of missionary in America. He went with me and Mother to our church in Salisbury a couple of times. … Viktor never would fight or argue. One time Viktor, Glen Faris, and I were in Shoney's, and Glen almost got in trouble. He liked this girl, and her boyfriend came in running his mouth. Viktor took up for Glen. They didn't fight, but Vik talked to the guy and helped resolve the problem. …Vik was very open and just a great person to be around. One time he bought me a battery for my car and wouldn't even take any money for it, would he, Mother?" Mother shook her head.

Steve apparently could not resist asking him the next question. "Did any of Viktor's friends seem unusual to you at all?"

"No, why?" Keith asked.

"I was just wondering," Steve answered and looked intently down at his notes.

"Vik never did meet a stranger," Keith said proudly. "I really miss him," he added, and I noticed his eyes were glistening with unshed tears.

"He sure was fond of Viktor," Steve pointed out when we got back into the car.

"Fond enough to clean his apartment for him," I agreed. "...and take him shopping, and pick up his mail..."

"I wonder if Viktor just took advantage of the boy," Steve said.

"I don't know. Viktor was apparently a very charming man."

"But he couldn't charm himself out of getting kidnapped and murdered," Steve pointed out.

"No, he sure couldn't."

As we drove back through Salisbury on Highway 70, we decided to stop at the Quality Mart. As it happened, Glen Faris was on duty, and business at the QM was slow. Glen, a thin thirty-seven-year-old white male, had curly brown hair with a receding hairline, and wore small wire-rimmed glasses. He was soft-spoken but pleasant, and readily agreed to talk with us.

"I was very good friends with both Viktor and Keith," he said. "I can't believe this has happened. I really admired Viktor. I don't know anybody who didn't like him."

"Well someone did not like him," Steve told him.

"Obviously," Glen said.

"So, you went out with him, or hung out with him fairly often then?" Steve asked.

"Yeah, fairly often, I'd say. He was a good friend."

"When was the last time you talked with him?"

"December third. Friday."

"Are you sure about the date?"

"Absolutely."

"Did you talk to him in person on the phone?"

"On the phone. I was at his apartment with him on Monday or Tuesday of that week. Daniel was there too. We all went to Los Palmas and then to the Blues Café. Viktor and Daniel were supposed to meet Tana at Blues, but she didn't show up. Daniel and I stayed for a while, but Viktor left in his car."

"Do you know of Viktor having any problems with anyone?" Steve asked.

"No, not at all. Everyone really liked Viktor as far as I knew."

"About what time did you talk to Viktor on Friday the third?" I asked him.

"It was sometime between 6:00 and 6:45 p.m. I had called and left a message for Viktor, and he returned my call. We planned to get together the next day, which was Saturday the fourth. We were gonna go to Rock Hill and eat at Max's Mexican Eatery. We had been there together before."

"Were you supposed to meet Viktor the next day at a specific time and place on Saturday, or were you supposed to speak by phone first?"

"Well I tried to call him all day Saturday. I left him several messages. I got tired of waiting and finally went over there late in the evening, like at dusk. Viktor's door was open a little bit, the door to his apartment. Viktor always kept his door closed and locked. Even when we'd leave to go somewhere together, he would double-check it."

"Did you go inside his apartment on that Saturday evening?"

"No. I went back to my car and waited for ten or fifteen minutes, but he never showed up. I gave up and decided to try and find him the next day."

"Did you see his car parked in front of his apartment when you were there?"

"Yeah, it was parked in his usual spot. He always backed it in at an angle."

"Did you go back on Sunday?"

"Yeah. I tried to call him all day Sunday. After I got off work around dark, I went back to his apartment. The door was still ajar, just like it was on Saturday. That time I decided to go in and look for him, but I didn't want to go in by myself, so I took the maintenance man from downstairs with me. Bucky is his name. We went in and walked through each room, but of course Viktor wasn't there. When we left, we closed and locked the door."

"You're sure?"

"Positive."

"Were the lights on inside the apartment?"

"Hmm, I'm not sure. I think Viktor's bed was unmade. I know the TV and the radio were not on. ...Anyway, I called back every day after that. But his answering machine was messed up... I even drove through the parking lot about once a day, but I never found anything different. I called the police department after a week, but I think the apartment manager had already reported him missing."

"Did you know Viktor very well?"

"He was open in some ways. He told me he was arrested for killing the Prime Minister of Sweden. He told me that, when we first met. Viktor made friends with everyone. He was always easygoing, never aggressive or hostile. He hated drugs and crime and stuff like that. He never drank much at all, and he never got intoxicated. Viktor was very artistic, a gentle type. And you know, Vik was fairly trusting, never really suspicious of anyone."

Other friends of Viktor had described Viktor as trusting but cautious, always using the peephole and using the chain lock on his apartment door. Polly Edwards was another one of Viktor's friends who described him the same way. Steve and I interviewed her at her mobile home where she cohabitated with her boyfriend, who was also present and sat quietly during our visit.

Polly, in her early twenties, was pleasant and friendly, significantly obese but with a bright, sweet smile.

"I visited Viktor at his apartment real often," she told us. "We even had our picture made together one time, with some of our friends." She pointed to a frame portrait on the wall. It was an eight-by-ten-inch Olan Mills portrait of five people, a duplicate of the same portrait I had seen on the wall in Viktor's apartment.

"This is my boyfriend," she said, pointing to a wiry young man in the photo, "and this is me, Viktor, Keith, and Glen Faris." It would have looked like a family portrait, except that no two in the picture looked remotely alike.

"How did it come about that you all decided to have your portrait done?" Steve asked her. "Was it just because you were all such good friends?"

"Well, that was the first time my boyfriend and Viktor met," Polly said.

"You mean the day you had the portrait taken?" I asked to be sure I understood correctly. "…That was the first day some of you met, and you all had your portrait taken together?"

"Uh-huh," she said affirmatively, like nothing at all was unusual about that. "Glen wanted to have his picture made with all his friends, so we met around Christmas of '92 and went to Olan Mills."

"I see," I said. I did not see exactly.

"When was the last time you saw Viktor, Polly?" Steve asked, as I continued to stare at the portrait.

"Uh… went to his apartment on that weekend that started with Friday, December third, but I didn't find Viktor."

"When precisely did you go?"

"I went all weekend. My boyfriend didn't go with me, though. I had to do a report on Sweden for a class and I was gonna get Viktor to help me. It was due on Monday, the sixth of December. I was desperate and went to his apartment almost every hour. His car was there the whole time, but Viktor weren't. One day I saw he had some pictures in an envelope stuck in his door, and I did look at 'em. But then I put 'em back. Glen told me the door was open when he went there, but when I saw it, it was shut."

"Do you know of anyone who Viktor may have been having problems with?"

"No, Viktor was wonderful. I don't know of anybody who didn't like Viktor. …I heard about what happened, but one time, Viktor told me that no one should ever get in a car with a man who had a gun. Viktor said it was better to get shot there than somewhere else."

"Was Viktor talking about anything or anyone in particular or just safety in general?

"Just in general," she said. "Viktor didn't believe in violence. He just believed in love."

"Do you know of other friends Viktor had?" Steve asked her.

"He was friends with that Tana girl, but I don't like her. She's two-faced. That's really the only one I know besides us and that Kay Weden girl I read about in the paper," she said as she bristled slightly.

"Polly, did you and Viktor ever have a romantic relationship or were you just friends?" Steve asked tactfully. I gave Steve a look. I did not expect Polly to answer truthfully with her boyfriend present.

She hesitated, glanced briefly in her boyfriend's direction and answered, "Huh-unh," negatively.

A short while later, her boyfriend got up and walked down the hall of the mobile home.

"Uh, I need to tell ya'll something," Polly whispered. I leaned closer to her. "Me and Viktor, we did sort of have a thing, just for a while."

"Pardon?" Steve asked.

"Me and Viktor. You asked if we had a relationship."

"Oh," Steve said. "Was your relationship of an intimate nature?" he asked.

"Uh-huh," she said, affirmatively and turned to me. "But that was before my boyfriend, though," she added quickly. "…'cause I wouldn't cheat. But still he doesn't know. I didn't want it to cause him not to like Viktor. …One thing's for sure and for certain though; Viktor was a very romantic man."

"Was he?" I asked.

"Yeah. This one time, we were on his bed, and Viktor wanted to put rose petals on the sheets, so we did. Then we did it on top of the rose petals 'cause they was real soft. And we had some massage oil, too, that smelled like roses. ...It got dark pink stains on the covers, though." And that explained the pink spots I saw on Viktor's mattress. I wondered how long it had been, if ever, since Viktor changed his sheets and bed covering. Steve and I thanked Polly for her help and returned to Watauga County.

A few days later, I confirmed that Viktor's estate was handled by two executrixes, Bonnie Smith and Barbara Sills. Barbara agreed to meet Steve and me in Charlotte in the lobby of the Adam's Mark Hotel, one of Charlotte's most luxurious. Although Barbara easily consented to an interview, like others she felt more comfortable meeting us in a public place.

Barbara wore a bright, colorful long and full-flowing skirt that matched her pink-tinted hair and bright-coral lipstick. She was open and friendly, and I liked her immediately.

"Bonnie Smith and I are co-executrixes of Viktor Gunnarsson's estate in Rowan County," she confirmed.

"How did that come about?" Steve asked her.

"Well, I'm not sure, exactly," she said, smiling. "But Bonnie Smith and I met at Viktor's memorial service, and his family in Sweden requested that we handle his estate together since we were friends of his. Viktor's family members weren't able to travel so far."

"How did you meet Viktor?" I asked.

"Well, I had a little car accident in January of '93, when I hit a deer. Would you believe one little deer totaled my car?" I would.

"Anyway, I had to buy a new one. So, I was at the Honda Dealership in Salisbury where one my friend works. She was talking to Viktor who had come by, and she introduced us. Then to my surprise, Viktor started calling *me*."

"Did you and Viktor date?" Steve asked.

"We went out for a couple of times, but only as friends. I was only interested in Viktor's mind because he was brilliant. He spoke eight languages fluently. And he knew the origin of any word. He was a true scholar. We spent several hours just talking about intellectual things. Viktor and I were both interested in studying psychology, also. But I was never interested in him sexually." I was not convinced.

"How often did you talk to Viktor?"

"When I first met him in the spring, we talked about once a week. But in the fall just before he disappeared, I heard from him more often. He'd call me up and invite me to go places with him and Daniel, but I didn't go. He asked me to go with them to Florida in November, but I couldn't. They ended up staying for about ten days in Tampa, and later Viktor told me that he had slept in his car. I told him it was dangerous to sleep in his car, but he said he didn't mind."

"So, you were friends with Daniel as well?"

"Yes, he was a nice young man. I know some other friends of his as well."

"Like who?"

"I met several at the memorial service we had for Viktor. I know that Viktor knew a lot of women. When we looked through his things in his apartment, trying to settle his estate, I saw letters from all kinds of women. I'm glad we didn't have some kind of romantic relationship. I found a recent letter from Tana Howe. I believe she was in love with Viktor, but Viktor wasn't in love with her."

"When did you last see Viktor?"

"On Tuesday, November 30th or Wednesday, the first day of December, Daniel was planning to go back to Sweden for the upcoming weekend. I met Daniel and Viktor at the Cracker Barrel in Charlotte. I was a little late, and when I got there, they were already seated at a table. Viktor was happy and upbeat. ...It was so odd, but for no apparent reason Viktor told me not to worry about him, that he could take care of himself. I don't know why he said that; I didn't tell him I was worrying about him or anything."

"Did you ask him why he said that?" I asked.

"No, I just said okay, and he said he just wanted me never to worry about him. He told me that while we were looking around the gift shop in the Cracker Barrel. Oh, and Viktor said he carried a knife in his car and that he knew karate or tae kwon do or something like that. While we were eating, Daniel told me that Viktor had a new girlfriend, a teacher. I'm not sure if they mentioned her name... Anyway, Viktor said he met her the Friday night before."

"Did you talk with Viktor any on December 3rd?"

"No, on that Friday, a friend and I took a trip to Waynesville, North Carolina. We returned to Charlotte the next day. Then I was in New Orleans between December 14th and 20th. When I got back, I had a message on my answering machine from Captain Stutts with the Rowan County Sheriff's Department."

Captain Stutts actually worked for Salisbury PD.

She continued. "Captain Stutts said Viktor was missing. He told me that Viktor's car was parked outside his apartment and all his things were inside. Captain Stutts thought maybe Viktor was with me in New Orleans. I told him he wasn't with me. I knew it was not like Viktor to leave without telling somebody where he was going to be, and I got worried."

"How did Captain Stutts know to get in touch with you?"

I think he got it from Viktor's personal phone book, or maybe from Daniel Johansson. He was careful about what he told me. I just couldn't believe Viktor was missing. My first thought was that someone from Sweden came and abducted him because of that Prime Minister thing."

"When did you go in Viktor's apartment?"

"Not until March 14th, when some friends of Viktor's and I began cleaning out the apartment, after you all released it."

"Can you think of anything at all that might be of help to us?"

"No, I've tried to think if there's anything I heard him say, but I don't know anything except that Viktor was a wonderful man. He never seemed to care about money or nice clothes. He hated drugs and he talked at length about how they corrupted the youth. Viktor didn't drink hardly at all or smoke cigarettes. He loved his apartment and his car. He loved to feed the ducks in the pond. His commode was broken the entire time he lived at Lakewood, but he told me he didn't want to complain about it because he didn't want to bother anyone. I can't imagine why anyone would want to harm Viktor."

"You don't know of him ever being violent?" I asked.

"No, not Viktor. You know, one of Viktor's friends, Bonnie, went to see a psychic after Viktor died. The psychic, whose name was Beverly, was just a normal person until she died on the operating table and was brought back to life. From then on, she had some kind of supernatural powers. After Viktor disappeared, Bonnie Simms went to see her. Beverly told Bonnie that Viktor was dead, and that his body was nowhere near Salisbury. And she said Viktor was a person of many faces or identities, for whatever that's worth. ...I wish I had something to offer to help you all out, but I just don't. If there's anything I can ever do to help, though, please let me know." Her genuine and brilliant smile shone right through her bright-coral lipstick, and then she breezed out of the hotel lobby.

We decided to visit Bonnie Simms next. Steve and I went to her house in Salisbury, which when we arrived, we also realized was the County Humane Society. We were greeted by energetic dogs, cats, and other four-footed furry friends. I did not know if I should fear getting bit or licked to death.

"I'm the cruelty investigator for the Humane Society," she said as she met us in the front yard and walked us inside. I entered behind Steve, trying to watch where I stepped.

Bonnie invited us in to sit in a living area, which was full of large cardboard boxes. She moved several items so that Steve and I could each sit on opposite ends of a long sofa while she pulled up a couple of chairs for herself and another lady across from us.

"This is Lena Gustavsdotter," Bonnie introduced. "She is from Sweden and was a good friend of Viktor's as well. She is helping us handle Viktor's estate."

Lena was a tall middle-aged blonde, quite attractive, neatly dressed and well-mannered. Bonnie, in contrast, had a wild hair thing going on, was casually dressed, a little heavier, and seemed quite at home among all the animals and the clutter in her house. Bonnie was extroverted and very energetic. Lena seemed a bit more reserved but pleasant.

Lena had been living with Bonnie for several months. She hoped to move to the United States permanently.

"How do you know Viktor? I asked Bonnie.

She looked at Lena and they shared a laugh. "That's kind of a funny story."

"Oh good," I replied. "Do tell."

"I met Viktor during the summer of '89. I was working at a movie rental store in Salisbury. Viktor came in to rent movies on a regular basis, but he didn't have a membership card, so he always used Bill Rambo's. But then, one day Bill Rambo came in to rent some videos using his own name, but I thought Viktor was Bill Rambo. Then Rambo showed me his driver's license… Anyway, when Viktor came back in the store, I told him I knew he had lied about his name. Then Viktor told me who he really was and showed me his international driver's license and told me he was from Sweden. I didn't know he wasn't American because he didn't have any kind of obvious accent. So, I issued him a rental card in his own name, and we started talking. He came back in on New Year's Eve, 1989, and then he came back a few hours later to rent another one. I asked him if he didn't have anything better to do, and he said no. I told him I didn't either, so Viktor met me after I got off work that night.

We went out for coffee, and I took him home with me that night."

"Where was Viktor living at that time?"

"Viktor was dating this girl in Archdale and had been living with her. Viktor and the girl had just broken up and he didn't have a place to stay, so I told Viktor I had a spare bedroom he could stay in for a while if he wanted to. So, he stayed here for about a week."

"Did you have a personal relationship with Viktor?" I asked.

She answered, "You mean intimately? Yes, for a while. Then after about a week, Viktor went back to his girlfriend's in Archdale and tried to patch things up. Viktor and I remained friends, though. When things didn't work out between Viktor and the Archdale girl, he came back here. I helped him get the apartment at Lakewood."

"Do you know when he moved in at Lakewood Apartments?"

"January 12th."

"1990?"

"Yes. But he still came over here and watched TV until he got his cable hooked up. We went out a lot to eat. ...I did two photo sessions with Viktor. Photography is my hobby."

"You are a photographer too?" Steve asked politely.

"Yes, and I also work part-time hanging wallpaper and painting. I was restoring a building for the Humane Office in mid-January of '90, and I worked there for six months straight. Viktor would often drop by and watch me work. He liked to watch people work, you see. He often told me how to do things, but he never actually seemed to do them, or work much himself. He was full of ideas and suggestions, but he didn't like to work. He was a dreamer, a free spirit, not so much a doer. But he did bring me food while I worked."

"What were Viktor's interests?"

"He often talked about the government in some other country, which was something I didn't know a lot about. ...

And, of course, he was very interested in women. He'd bring new girls to meet me – he went through women fast..." Bonnie started laughing at herself, glanced at Lena, and then continued, "You know, it's really kind of comical, but after the memorial service, Lena, and Barbara and I were here and we were sitting at the table talking about our memories of Viktor, and Barbara said something about Viktor being a passionate lover, and Lena and I both said, 'Oh no! You too?' and come to find out, Viktor had slept with every one of us. But that was just the way Viktor was; he just loved women. I remember one girl named Mona from Sweden, and another girl named Carmen. Both of those girls seemed to be very religious. Viktor and I often argued about religion because I believe in reincarnation, but Viktor did not. ...I hope he has been reincarnated."

"So, what you are saying is that all three of you were friends who had slept with Viktor and didn't realize it until you were talking about him?" I said.

"That's right," Bonnie said, "and if the truth were known, he had probably slept with all the other women who came to his memorial service that day." I was glad that she saw the humor in it because if I had been in her place, I may not have taken it all so good naturedly.

"When did you last see Viktor?" Steve asked Bonnie.

"The day he and Daniel came back from Sweden. It was sometime in October of '93. Viktor called me from Sweden the day before he left. I had been starting his car to keep the battery charged while he was in Sweden. When Viktor came back, he introduced me to Daniel."

"Lena, when did you meet Viktor?" I asked.

She answered with a lovely Swedish accent, "I met him two summers ago in 1992 in Rodeby, Sweden. I was getting off a bus and I stumbled, about to fall down, when Viktor, this strong, beautiful man, caught me. It was like some romantic comedy! He then wanted to go inside the building where I worked, but the building was closed and no one was there. I let him inside the building. We exchanged names and telephone numbers. He called me a few days later and we began to date."

"How long did you date?"

"We dated during the entire summer of 1992, until the time that he left Sweden to come to the United States. When he was in Sweden, he would come to visit me, staying for three or four days and then go back to his parents' house for a few days. But our love story faded during the summer of 1993. Still Viktor and I remained friends. You see Viktor was this way with all his women; he would date them for a while and then they would be just good friends."

"And when did you last talk with Viktor?"

"It was about a week before he left Sweden for the United States, in mid-October of 1993."

"Do you know Viktor's family?"

"Somewhat. I know that Viktor's father is seventy-two years old and has been in the business of real estate for several years. Viktor's mother is sixty-nine years old and helps out in the business also. Viktor was very much interested in politics, and his parents as well but not so much as Viktor. Viktor was much worse. He worked for about one month in the state church during the summer of 1993. His job was to greet tourists at the church. Viktor spoke many languages and was a good communicator with all the peoples. ...Viktor seemed to know everyone. He was always talking about people. I remember that Viktor would talk about Barbara Sills and Bonnie Smith while we were in Sweden."

"Do you know much about the assassination of the Prime Minister in 1986?"

"Yes, it was very big news all over Sweden. I know that Viktor was arrested and detained for that murder. But he was soon released. By 1988 or 1989, Viktor was no longer in the media in Sweden. They were just not interested in him any longer. I wrote letters to the media on behalf of Viktor's defense, but no one was interested in them. I will never believe Viktor could do such a violent thing. He was a talker, not a fighter. ...In January of 1990, Viktor made a radio interview with a reporter in Sweden. I have translated that interview on an audio tape if you both would like to hear it."

"I'd like to hear it," I said, eagerly.

"Please," Steve told her. We waited while Lena and Bonnie searched among the boxes for the cassette. I was surprised they were able to locate it in a matter of minutes.

The following is a portion of the transcription of that tape made on January 1, 1990, based on Lena Gustavsdotter's translation.

> *Question posed by reporter to Viktor: How do you feel today about four years after the killing of the Swedish Prime Minister?*
>
> *Response: Well, today, I'm feeling much better because I'm living here (in the United States). And here in this country, I think, I feel that I can breathe much more freely than I can back home. And even if you know that you're innocent of a crime, it's not very pleasant to have people's eyes upon you. You see, I'm not the sort of person that wants to be famous and popular. ...All right, I like to be popular, and I very much like to be loved. But not in that way.*
>
> *Question: This is a queer situation... Do you still feel that you are a sort of suspect?*
>
> *Response: Well, there are always a few good people, and who have uh, problems sorting things out. I think, well, this is a question of politics. It is what it has been all the time, and uh, this is what makes the whole thing more complicated than it should be. You see, this murder was considering to most people to mean a political murder, and*

uh whoever did it, did it out of hatred against the president or the prime minister. And as soon as there was a suspect, people's hatred focused on this person. And I think that it could take a very long time before people realize. The majority of people – they know, but there is always a little bunch of people, but it is enough that there is one crazy person, one lunatic.

Question: Does that mean that you are afraid of being or living in Sweden?

Response: Yes, actually I am afraid of being in Sweden.

Question: Are you going to stay in the U.S.A.?

Response: Well, I'm not sure I'm going to stay in the U.S.A. and there are other alternatives. I have thought a little about Brazil, which is a country which I like very much. But I know I will not return to Sweden to live there permanently.

Question: Do you feel more insecure now that they have let this other suspect out of prison and started all over again from the beginning now?

Response: No I don't. I don't feel more unsafe or more insecure, no. I can't say that.

Question: Have you had any problems getting a job in Sweden?

Response: Well I don't think it's impossible for me to get a job in Sweden, but the problem is as soon as people know who I am, the problem starts...

Question: Do you mean that you left Sweden for political reasons?

Response: Yeah, where I was, they sort of hanged me out for people to look at. I mean, the press did. And uh, afterwards, they have been totally unwilling to try and repair the damage they did to me.

Question: You are planning to sue the Swedish government?

Response: Yes we did that a few months ago... My lawyer and myself sued the Swedish government for two million crowns.

Question: Let's go back in time... What happened when they took (arrested) you?

Response: ...What happened was that I was in bed in my apartment, and it was early in the morning. And these police officers they knocked on my door, and they really knocked very hard, and they shouted, "This is the police! Open the door!" I have no idea about what they wanted. And I was totally shocked when they started to talk about things I really didn't understand, and it took me a few hours to realize what it was all about. ...The worst thing was that I had this feeling that among all those people accusing me, there was at least one person who knew that I had nothing to do with the thing, that I was totally innocent. There was something in the atmosphere that made me feel that they just wanted to, to put me in jail. To put someone, anyone in jail. And that was the most awful dream of all. I had the feeling that something evil, something really devilish in all this, if you can *understand what I mean, was happening. There was sort of nothing human in this. It was evil.*

Question: Why did they get you?

Response: Well, I have always spoken freely, and I have always thought that I had the freedom to express my opinion totally freely. But apparently you cannot always do this. You often make enemies with persons who have a different opinion. When something like this happens, people get very upset and almost hysterical. And I can understand that. If your prime minister is killed, people get upset about it, and then there is a nervous feeling about it, and uh, people don't always know what they do. I can understand that, but what I can't understand is this nonsense investigation which the police force made about me. I have no understanding of that. I realized then when it happened that they needed someone, anyone to blame quickly, and they chose me, and then that's what I still think about it. And I was hurt when this happened, and I still am, because this is something that is still in people's minds and memory. It's such a grave event, or was, that it will stay there for decades. I know I'm innocent, and it's good for a man to know he is innocent. And I know that I have never ever been close to a crime like this and I never will be...

If only Viktor knew how wrong he was. If only he had known he was not safe in the United States. If only he had known when he uttered those words that someone would again knock on his door in the middle of the night, again perhaps claiming to be the police and take him away, never to return again. If only he had known of a man named Lamont Claxton Underwood.

CHAPTER NINETEEN

"He shall not fail nor be discouraged,
till he have set judgment in the earth" (Isaiah 42:4)

While we continued to investigate both murders, Kay Weden was doing her best to resume a normal life. By the time spring had sprung in 1994, Kay had settled her mother's estate, sold her house in the Westcliff development, and purchased a larger nicer home in an upper-class development. As she had planned, she hired crews to clean her mother's house, and to pack and move all the contents to a storage unit so she could sell the house. Kay could not bear to go back inside it after her mother was murdered. I could certainly understand that, although I was not so sure I would trust people I did not know to pack up and move all of my mother's things. Probably, though, it was the best decision for her at the time. Kay needed to try to find a way to get back to a semblance of normalcy, if not for her own sake, then for Jason's.

After a while, Kay began to go out occasionally with her friends. In turn, they encouraged her to date again and try to get her mind off all the horrible things that had happened to her. On her friends' recommendations, Kay agreed to go out with a forty-two-year-old businessman by the name of Wayne Eller. During this time, Wayne Eller was a candidate for sheriff of Rowan County but lost the election to incumbent Robert Martin in November. Kay and Wayne began a dating relationship. Kay told me later that Wayne was particularly interested in her mother's murder case.

On April 29, 1994, Mr. Eller came to the Rowan County Sheriff's Office to meet with Don and Terry.

"I don't know if you all are aware of it or not, but I've been dating Kay Weden for a couple months now."

"Kay did mention that, I believe," Terry told him.

"Well, Kay is the only person I have dated in a long time, and some things have happened, which are causing me a little concern."

"What's that?" Don asked him, already alarmed.

"Well, about two or three weeks ago, probably the week before Kay moved to her new house, which I think was April 15th or 16th, I got a call at my house. An anonymous call."

"So that would have been about the first or second week in April?"

"Yeah, something like that. It was a man's voice, and when I answered, he said, 'You don't mess with another monkey's monkey.' He also said I shouldn't hang around City Park because people who hang around City Park might get run over or hurt by a motorcycle. He said I wouldn't see the motorcycle until it was too late, and that the motorcycle was …inside or something like that." Wayne Eller knew that L. C. lived directly in front of City Park.

"Did you recognize the voice at all?"

"No. And when I hung up, I tried to trace the call, but I got a recording that told me it couldn't be traced."

"Is that the only call you have received?"

"Yeah, the only call, but then a few days later, when I was in my new barn, I heard a car pull up to the back door of the house."

"How many days later?"

"Within seven or eight at the most. It was about 5:00 or 5:30 in the evening. I walked to the edge of the barn loft and looked out. I saw a car leaving my driveway. It was a grayish-colored car."

"Which way did it go?"

"It turned left on Liberty out of my driveway. It was a mid- to full-size car."

"Could you tell how many people were in it?"

"No. And I wouldn't have thought much of it if I hadn't gotten that call a few days before. Then Kay told me that L. C. had been keeping somebody's motorcycle in his house, and recently when one of L. C.'s neighbors was working on their roof, they saw the motorcycle drive into L. C.'s house."

"Well, you can't be too careful when you're dating L. C.'s ex-girlfriend," Don told him.

"But that's not all... Yesterday about 11:00 in the morning, I was in the back of my barn and heard a car pull in the driveway again. My dogs were barking. I walked to the front of the barn and saw a car, pulled up to the back door of my house. I started walking towards the house and got about fifty feet of it. It was a Dodge or Plymouth full-size gray car, late '70s or early '80s model. The driver must have seen me in the mirror because all of a sudden, it backed up and sped out of the driveway. I had to move out of the way when the car backed up."

"Did you get a look at the driver?"

"Yeah. The driver was a white guy with light-brown hair in a long ponytail. And he had a black girl in there with him. But I couldn't get the tag number."

"Was it the same car you saw at your house before?"

"I think so, but I can't say for sure."

"And you don't have any idea why anyone would come to your house like that?"

"No, none."

"Okay, well, you did the right thing by letting us know. Be careful and keep us posted about anything else that happens out of the way."

"Sure will. Thanks."

I feared that if we did not find enough evidence to charge L. C. soon, someone else would fall victim at his hand. Don, Terry, and Steve were equally concerned. We had gone to extensive lengths searching L. C.'s credit card statements, bank records, and all of his financial resources in hopes that he had purchased gasoline or food or any item during the night of December 3 and the early morning of December 4, 1993, while on the way from Salisbury to Watauga County. We knew, however, that L. C. had filled his gasoline tank in the Monte Carlo while he was out with Shirley Twitty. We checked local and state law enforcement records with every agency between Salisbury and Boone to see if either of L. C.'s vehicles had been stopped, logged, or if his driver's license number had been checked during those times. We tried to follow up on every remote possibility, but our efforts had not yet paid off. We continued to have brainstorming sessions.

Sometimes, while working a major criminal case, investigators have to throw out a group of darts in all directions, in hopes of hitting something. By early summer, we had come to realize that the traditional methods of interviewing people and searching for physical evidence were not turning up much in the way of proof beyond a reasonable doubt. The time had come to look into some nontraditional approaches and expand our investigation. We felt like there was something or someone out there who knew more than we did, so we set out to find them.

We had interviewed a significant number of people, but we still had only a mediocre case against L. C. at best. I simply could not understand how a human being could kill two people in cold blood and never breathe a word about it to anyone. After talking it over, we decided to look a little deeper for a possible associate of L. C.'s whom L. C. may have made incriminating statements to. One way we figured to do that was to install a pen register and trap and trace device on L. C.'s telephone line.

After obtaining the necessary court order in May of 1994, a pen register and trap and trace device was placed on L. C.'s telephone line at Southern Bell Telephone Company.

By using the necessary computer, software, and modem, we were able to download a list of all phone numbers calling to and from L. C.'s residence. While we could not listen to the actual conversations, we were quickly able to identify the phone service subscribers with which L. C. spoke most frequently. We checked his calls daily for a period of ten months, in an attempt to discover a possible associate of L. C.'s, or at least someone he was close enough to who might elicit pertinent information from him. While we were gathering data from L. C.'s phone service, we continued to throw investigative darts in other directions.

In July of 1994, we obtained a court order for a mail cover on L. C.'s mail. A mail cover consists of post office personnel making and sending to us photocopies of the outside envelope or packaging of each piece of mail addressed to the subject under investigation. The mail is not opened or tampered with in any way, and is delivered on time to the subject as soon as copies are made. The mail cover was activated on August 8, 1994, and remained in effect through September 1994. We monitored L. C.'s mail closely, but discovered no personal letters, no unusual correspondence.

Also in July, we learned about something called satellite imaging.

According to a pamphlet printed by the Psytep Corporation in Corpus Christi, Texas, satellite imaging is:

> "*the remotely controlled photographic reproduction of the earth's surface as seen from above. Satellite imaging provides a new dimension to current law enforcement investigation techniques. ...A photograph is taken six (6) times per minute, providing an image of 60 square kilometers of the earth's surface. Technicians at the individual satellite's control point program the satellite on a daily basis to accomplish a variety of missions...*"

We hoped to find that a photographic satellite had covered the Gunnarsson and Miller crime scenes in early December of 1993. The possibility of an actual photograph of the suspect at either scene at the right time seemed too good to be true. I read the pamphlet repeatedly.

"What use can be made of this technology by law enforcement...?

1. Capture historical photographic data of a crime scene.

2. Assist in locating missing homicide victims who have been dumped or buried, given certain limited parameters.

3. Locate illegal crops of drugs, being grown in this country or on the NorthPlease fix.American continent.

4. Locate sources... of chemical or other forms of pollution and hazardous chemical spills, to assist in environmental investigations."

The basic concept is that photographs can be obtained and enlarged from satellites that orbit the earth and photograph as they travel. If one of the satellites should happen to pass over a particular crime scene during a certain block of time, it may be possible that a suspect would be caught on film during the criminal act.

Weather could be a factor in determining whether we could obtain clear photographs of our crime scenes. A records search by the National Oceanic and Atmospheric Administration of the National Climatic Data Center in Asheville revealed the weather as it was recorded on December 3 and 4 in Salisbury and Deep Gap, and December 8 and 9 in Rowan County. On December 3 in Salisbury, the high temperature was 64 degrees, the low 34, and .05 inches of precipitation. The next day, the temperature ranged from

34 to 65, with no precipitation. In Watauga County, the temperature ranged from 24 to a high of 48 during the day on December 3. In the early morning hours of December 4, the temperature was a brisk 24 degrees, with heavy cloud cover and snow flurries. I wondered if L. C. was prepared for the wintry weather in the mountains when he left Salisbury late at night. On the evening of December 8, Salisbury was comparably warmer at a range of 30 to 60 degrees, with no cloud cover and no precipitation.

We learned from the satellite companies that all that was needed for a search of satellite photographs is the date the crime occurred or a block of time in which it occurred, the coordinates of the crime scene, and as we were soon to learn, a great deal of money.

We had no problem determining the blocks of time in question: December 3-4 and the evening of December 8, 1993. We used a Global Positioning System (GPS) device to determine the latitudinal and longitudinal coordinates of both the Gunnarsson and Miller crime scenes. The final requirement was funding.

Several satellite companies offered this service across the country, but all were quite expensive. After some discussion though, we arranged to share the cost between the State Bureau of Investigation, the Rowan County Sheriff's Office, and the Watauga County Sheriff's Office. We were excited at the prospect of such technology, and were told at one point that the satellites could capture such a quality image that we would be able to count the dimples on a golf ball.

Much to our dismay, however, the image samples we saw were so blurred that it was extremely difficult to tell the difference between a vehicle and a house. There was no way anything as small as a person could be identified, much less a golf ball. The resolution of these types of satellites were not nearly high enough for what was needed in criminal cases. Furthermore, after we started researching the reputations of the satellite companies, we were aware of, we learned that several fraudulent claims had been made in the past. Other agencies we spoke with who had attempted to use satellite imaging had nothing positive to say about their experiences, and furthermore advised us not to throw money in that direction.

Based on what we learned, the department heads ruled out satellite imaging as an investigative option. However, we made our efforts public through the media as a tactic that would hopefully cause the murderer and any accomplices worry that they had been captured on film during the commission of the crimes. Unfortunately, nothing we did prompted anyone into making a confession, but my expectations were never so grandiose.

We decided to throw out yet another dart. In August, we petitioned the governor of North Carolina to issue a reward in the two homicides. On October 10, 1994, Governor James B. Hunt Jr. issued the following proclamation:

> *"As Governor of North Carolina it has been made to appear to me upon satisfactory information furnished to me, as follows:*
>
> *On January 7, 1994, the body of Viktor Ake Lennart Gunnarsson was found in a wooded area just off the Blue Ridge Parkway in Watauga County, North Carolina. Mr. Gunnarsson had been shot.*
>
> *To preserve law and order the person or persons who committed such an infamous crime must be brought to justice.*
>
> *NOW, THEREFORE,*
>
> *I, James B. Hunt Jr., Governor of the State of North Carolina, under and by virtue of the authority contained in N.C.G.S. 15-53.1, do hereby offer a reward of up to $50,000 for information*

leading to the arrest and conviction of the person or persons responsible for the murder of Viktor Ake Lennart Gunnarsson.

The payment of this reward or any portion thereof is conditional upon the information being furnished as a direct result of the issuance of this proclamation. The total reward paid to all persons in this case shall not exceed $50,000.

The reward offered herein does not extend to any law enforcement officer of the State or any political subdivision thereof.

Anyone having information about this case should contact the Watauga County Sheriff's Department or the State bureau of Investigation.

This the 10th day of October, 1994. Signed by Governor Hunt.

An identical reward was issued for information leading to the arrest and conviction of persons committing the murder of Catherine Miller.

On October 24, 1994, we made a news release announcing the rewards on local and statewide television stations, radio stations, and newspapers. At that time, we also made a public request for assistance in locating L. C.'s .22 caliber and .38 caliber guns. Again, our efforts seemed futile. No one called with any information concerning the guns or either murder.

Just when we were about to despair, Steve received a page from John Bendure, the SBI lab analyst in the Trace Evidence Section who had assisted us with executing the search warrant on L. C.'s residence and vehicles. At the time, Steve and I were sitting in Pizza Hut in Salisbury trying to have a bite of dinner between interviews.

Steve looked at his pager and then at me.

"Can't you let it wait till we eat?" I asked him. "We haven't stopped for a minute all day and I'm starving. I know you have to be too."

"It's from the Lab; I'd better call before they close up for the day. If the food comes out before I get back, just go ahead and eat."

Steve walked to the pay phone just inside the restaurant's entrance. I could see from where I sat that Steve was deeply engrossed in conversation and taking notes on the PalmPilot he carried with him everywhere. He talked and talked and talked. After our food arrived, I waited until the pizza got cold. Steve was still on the phone, but I was tired of waiting on him. I ate a couple of slices of the pizza and pushed my plate away. Finally, Steve came back to the booth and sat down.

"Do you want to guess who was on the phone?" Steve asked me.

"The Lab," I said flatly.

"But who, at the Lab?"

"Dr. Jekyll?"

"No. John Bendure."

"From Trace Evidence?"

"Yes."

"And…?"

"*And* he just matched the electrical tape left at Viktor's crime scene with a piece of electric tape seized from L. C.'s house."

"Get out."

"It's true."

"A conclusive match?"

"As conclusive as a tape match can be. He couldn't match the ends up perfectly, but he says both pieces in all likelihood came from the same roll of tape. What took me so long on the phone was that he explained twenty-some different ways in which the two pieces were alike. The width, the thickness, the polymer, the color composition, the adhesive composition, the lot design, and other things I didn't grasp."

"Wow," I said. "So where did the electrical tape come from in L. C.'s house? Was it one of the rolls in L. C.'s toolbox?"

"No… John said it was the one you found on the back of the dryer."

"Are you serious?"

"Is a bullfrog waterproof?" he said, grinning.

"I knew it. I knew there had to be something in L. C.'s house that would tie him to Viktor," I said.

"They've finished with the hair and the blood analysis on the length of tape found from the Watauga crime scene. John said there were sixty human hairs on the tape from the scene, and all of them were consistent with Viktor's."

"That's no surprise. And the blood?"

"Insufficient quantity for analysis."

"We have to call Don and Terry about the tape."

Steve asked for a carryout box for his pizza. We paid the bill and headed out to find Don and Terry.

They were equally pleased. They were also ready to arrest L. C. right away. I could not wait to tell Sheriff Lyons. As soon as I did so the next morning, Sheriff Lyons and I walked across the street and into the District Attorney's Office. Tom Rusher was the elected District Attorney. Tom's administrative assistant Jason was at the front desk.

"Gotta see Tom right away," I told him.

"Oh my, my," he said, "you must have big news. May I come too?"

"Come on," Sheriff Lyons told him.

We breezed into Tom's office and he looked up from his desk, surprised to see us both. Sheriff Lyons motioned for me to give Tom the news from Agent Bendure. When I did, Tom was not quite as excited as I anticipated.

DA Tom Rusher explained, "It's good circumstantial evidence, Paula, but it's only a small piece. Go find out who put that tape on L. C.'s clothes dryer. If he hired an electrician to work on it, we stand to lose some ground. If he admits to putting the tape on himself, it would help."

"Tom, you know L. C.'s isn't going to tell us anything, and if he did, he would just lie."

"That's probably true, and I'm not so sure that we ought to let them know so soon what we have. Give me a few days to think about it, okay?"

"Okay, Tom. I really want to do this right."

"I know you do, Paula. Just keep plugging along…"

Three days later, Tom called Sheriff Lyons, Steve Wilson, and me over to his office. He informed us that he had given a lot of thought to the electrical tape, but he did not believe it was enough to get a jury to convict L. C. The short of it was that he was not going to prosecute L. C. for murdering Viktor Gunnarsson until we had more evidence.

In mid-October of 1994, Steve called me to let me know he had located an old acquaintance of L. C.'s in Winston Salem.

"Who would that be?" I asked.

"George McFadden. Not the guy on *Back to the Future*," Steve remarked.

"It was George McFly, the character on *Back to the Future*," I said.

"Anyway, George McFadden was an instructor at a local college. He taught L. C. Crime Scene Processing and Criminalistics."

"Okay…"

"Well, he ran into L. C. somewhere, and L. C. told him to stop by and see him sometime."

"Okay…"

"So I talked with George McFly on the phone just now –"

"McFadden."

"George Mc*Fadden*. And he said he would wear a wire and go ask L. C. some questions about the case."

"So when will he do it?" I asked.

"Next Friday. October 21st ."

Don, Terry, Steve, and I met George McFadden at the Rowan County Sheriff's Office on Friday, October 21, 1994. Don placed the recording device on George's left ankle and tested the unit. George drove to L. C.'s house, arriving seven minutes later.

L. C. was cutting his grass when George pulled into the driveway and got out of his car. George explained that he was in Salisbury to visit his father, and thought he would drop in and pay L. C. a visit.

"I didn't recognize you there for a minute," L. C. told him.

"Well, I'm getting old and fat," George answered.

"I am too. What have you been up to?"

"Nothing."

"I was thinking about you the other day, wondering how you were doing." L. C. went on to complain about his leaf blower getting stolen along with his brand-new weed eater. George let him ramble on about that for a while, and then L. C. told George in detail about his back surgeries.

George interjected, "I had two surgeries this year."

"Really? What happened to you?" L. C. asked, not too sympathetically.

"I was climbing up on the storage building and tore the bicep tendon off this arm. They had to go in there and hook it, bore a hole in the bone and reattach it."

L. C. laughed inappropriately. "D*MN," he said. Then L. C. launched into a detailed conversation about his roses. I guess he was not interested in anyone's ailments other than his own. They walked to L. C.'s back patio, and L. C. offered George a drink. George said he would like some water.

L. C. told him, "I'll get you some… That's good water. That's straight from the sewers of Salisbury." How colorful.

"Uh, how long were you with Salisbury? You retired, didn't you?" George asked.

"Yeah, eleven years."

"Okay."

L. C. did not need any more prompting than that. "Yeah, I got accused of some sh*t I didn't do. I got, I got a royal f*cking. But sh*t, you know, what happens, happens and I mean, there's nothing I can do about it..."

"What? ...So you took disability retirement?"

"Yes. It works the same as your regular retirement. Based on your four highest years of income." They continued with an in-depth discussion of retirement benefits and health problems.

L. C. added, "Well, I think when I get seventy, I'm gonna get myself a couple of twenty-year olds."

George laughed.

"I got a joke for you," L. C. said, and proceeded to tell him a very inappropriate, sexually explicit joke.

"L. C., you ain't changed a bit."

L. C. went right back to the original subject. "...Ya know, George, I got a royal f*cking here. Yeah, and I don't know why. Just can't believe they'd f*ck me like they did. You know, hell, I may be a lot of d*mn things, but what they were accusing me of, I'm not. You know, I'm sure you read that sh*t in the Winston paper."

"What was written in the Winston paper, I did read."

"You know, there's a lot of things they didn't, they didn't tell. Number one, you know, two months before they come and searched my house, I gave them two opportunities to search it."

"Did you?"

"I didn't have anything. There wasn't nothing here. I didn't do anything wrong. And I was dating this old gal. And her son, he's a d*mn drug addict. He's only sixteen. And the last two years, he's torn up two d*mn cars. I got him out of the first one. Well, I just read in the paper the other day where he just totaled another one up here at Innes and Jackson Street. And, uh, the stuff that they put in that search warrant, George, was nothing but a bunch of theory and what they *wanted* to happen. Some of the people they went to talk to have called me and have already went to talk to my attorney, saying what the investigators put down was not what they said. ...Uh, when all this sh*t first happened, they started trying to tie it in with, with this girl I was seeing, and that's not, that's not true. I don't know this son of a b*tch. The one they found in the mountains –"

"Hmm..."

"I didn't know him! Never met the d*mn guy. The only time, the way I got that son of a b*tch's tag number, when me and this girl broke up, was that, you see, she would come over to my house and she'd pull up the driveway to see if there was anybody here with me."

"Yeah?"

"Well she never could back down this driveway without getting on my grass. So I told her, I said, 'Look, back up the d*mn driveway, and just pull out forward.' I finally got her to backing into my driveway rather than backing out into the road. She could back *up* the driveway, ya know?"

"Yeah," George understood.

"Well, I had a girl over here that night. And I was just coming in the house. The house was dark. So a car pulled in and went by, and then backed back up and back to that light pole [pointing] out in the front yard...

"I said, 'Who in the hell was that?' Well, I saw a blond-headed girl in the front, and I, I just felt that was her, the girl I'd been seeing. Well, when I started down the driveway and got his tag number, he cut his lights out and took off. ... Well I didn't think no more about it. And I said, 'The hell with it.' Well, and then they found this girl's mother dead. You know, I hate to say it, but the F-, this SBI agent here we got, he lies. They served the first court order on me to get fingerprints and hair samples. Now there's no evidence whatsoever to link me to these crimes... 'Cause I didn't *do* the d*mn crimes."

"Yeah," George replied.

"My attorneys found out that, you know, this old boy, he was uh, arrested for killing the Swedish Prime Minister at one time."

"Uh-huh."

"He's even told people that he did that," L. C. added.

"You're kidding," George said.

"No. ...And so, you know, not thinking, you know, when they found this girl's mother dead, you know, and uh, and they wanted to talk to me, I was trying to do the right thing by talking to them. And everything I told them they've turned and twisted it around..."

"What did they say?" George asked.

"They said that a car like this one [L. C. indicated his Monte Carlo] was seen in the area prior to this woman getting killed. ...That d*mn car wasn't even running for two weeks before that murder and two weeks after – 'cause I had the carburetor off of it. It was sitting right there where it sits now. Well, they, when they came to talk to me the first night, well now I told them they could come in, and I'd talk to them. Well, they come in the house, and you know, I sat and talked to them and told them what I knew about it, the kid, and the girl. ...See, the girl was always needing money. And since her mother's died, she's run through it, she's bought a new car, and she bought a brand-new house with a swimming pool. The woman *gained* from that murder. I didn't gain anything from it. She gained something from it, not me. And so I told them that night, and Mark Wilhelm, the lieutenant with the police department, I asked him to come with them 'cause I didn't trust them. I've never trusted the Sheriff's Department, and not – and now I know you're an ex-SBI agent – but I sure in the *hell* don't trust Don Gale either. He's a transplanted Yankee."

"Is he?" George laughed. "...I don't know him, 'cause I've been gone from the Bureau so many years."

"Yeah. ...And the f*cking *Salisbury Post* – the newspaper here – they have *never* printed an affidavit for a search warrant in the newspaper. But they printed that one word for word."

"I saw that. A buddy of mine who lives in Salisbury –"

"Uh-huh?"

"– You arrested him – for driving drunk. He saved me the affidavit, and I read it."

"That wasn't no probable cause to get a search warrant. …Well, do *you* think it was?"

"I don't know. I'd have to go back, and read it. It's been so long since I read it, I'd have to read it again."

"Oh. …But you know, they literally destroyed me here in this town."

"Yeah," George said sympathetically.

"Number one, *physically* I would have been unable to do what they're saying I did. 'Cause from what I understand, this was a pretty big old boy. And my attorneys found out that what got him bumped off was that sh*t that happened in Sweden. See they even arrested him. And then they arrested his friend. Okay, well, they turned him loose, but well, the friend got tried and convicted. Of killing the Prime Minister!"

"I didn't know that."

"…Yeah. Well, they turned him loose. Then, right after this happened – this old boy that was found in the mountains – fled Sweden and hid. He didn't work, he's got no visible means of support. He was a teacher here at one time, and they told him he was unsuitable to be a teacher. But that's all they ever said; they never elaborated on it."

"Where did he teach?" George asked.

"Oh, uhm, at one of the schools here. And they said he wasn't suited to be a teacher. Well, number one, there was no crystal-clear evidence to link me to these crimes… Oh and they sat and watched my house for a week. Right across here from me. They didn't even try to act like they were hiding. …To show you how smart they were, I came out my back door, went through my neighbor's yard, and met a friend of mine up here at the parking lot. We went to Charlotte and had dinner, and come back and they were still sitting here."

They laughed.

L. C. continued, "I'd come out and get in my car and drive down the driveway and they'd all run get in their cars. Then I'd back up again."

"Well, that serves 'em right."

"They're trying to say that I am so smart that I could have pulled off this stuff and never left a trace." L. C. paused in the midst of his wishful thinking to contrive more lies. "... You know a week and a half before they found this girl's mother, this guy that they found up in the mountains who was dating this girl, he beat her *ss over at her house, *and* busted out all the windows in her car. But the Sheriff's Department didn't want us to find *that* out. And I tell you something else. Did you know that the cops here never told the cops in the mountains that I'd offered to let them search my house twice?"

"Hmm. That's strange," George commented.

"You know, I've weathered the d*mn storm. ... You know, it's like my attorney told 'em. ... They want to come by his office once or twice a week, and say, 'We'd like to talk to your client,' and he says, 'Well, he didn't talk to you last week, what makes you think he'll talk to you this week?'"

George laughed again. "Who's your attorney?"

"Uh, it's David Bingham. One of the best here in town."

L. C. and George talked about some of the well-known citizens of Salisbury, but L. C. would not let the subject of the murders drop.

George was looking at L. C.'s Monte Carlo., which L. C. had falsely claimed was not running in December of 1993.

"I'm surprised you still have that old Monte Carlo," George told him.

"Oh, I restored that thing. I still drive it. That's a good car."

"Well, you never did bring me the clock to rebuild for you."

"No I sure didn't."

"I only offered to do that five years ago." George laughed.

"You know, George, I want to tell you something. Can you imagine how all this has embarrassed me here?"

"Yeah, I can imagine the embarrassment and the stress."

"You know, I'll never forgive those sons of a b*tches for what they did. *Never*! Now, now they're trying to say because I was a policeman, I was a detective, and all that sh*t, that I could do this and get by with it. That's bullsh*t! But you always, well what have you always said in your classroom? You know, you always take something to a crime scene, and you always leave something if you're the perpetrator."

"That's true," George agreed.

"Well they didn't find *one strand of hair*. They didn't find nothing!"

George shook his head.

L. C. continued. "…You've lived in an apartment before, George. You tell me how a person that's disabled, *like me,* is going to be able to get somebody out of their apartment and get 'em all the way up to the mountains to dump 'em off. Bullsh*t. My attorneys found out there was *four* people that came to his house that night. And one of 'em was a *girl*. And he had no idea what was going to happen to him."

"Oh yeah?" George asked.

"What got him bumped off was that stuff that happened in Sweden."

"Well, it makes sense."

"…And this one SBI agent here, his name's Don Gale, I hate to say it, but I do. He told my attorney, he said, 'I'm gonna nail your client,' and he said, 'Good luck!' And I'm still here. If all that sh*t in that paper, that search warrant was the truth, why ain't I in *jail*? I mean, I know the d*mn law. If I had something here to hide, and I give – and I give them permission to search my house, and you had no probable cause to get a warrant to search it, wouldn't you have took me up on it and searched the house?"

"Absolutely," George said.

"Well I offered twice and they didn't want to search… They came here. Vance – I always considered Vance Furr a friend of mine. He wanted to know if he could come in and talk to me. I said yes, come right on. Well, I had a model of an old handgun sitting on top of my gun cabinet. 'I'd like to see that,' Vance said. So I go over, and I turn on the lights. But he wasn't looking at that model; he was looking in that d*mn gun case! And I told him, I stood there a minute, and I – I got kind of tickled at him. Then I said, 'Vance, open that g**d*mn gun case and get all the looks in there you want. Then get your f*cking *ss out of my house!' I said, 'Do you think I'm stupid enough to think that I don't know what you're doing?' I said, 'You come here wanting to be my friend and the whole time you're wanting to cut my d*mn throat!'"

L. C. and George's conversation was interrupted by a phone call L. C. received from a Salisbury police officer. After L. C. hung up, he explained to George, "That was one of the guys I trained. He's a good old boy. He's, uh, he was married to one of our dispatchers. A good-looking gal. Well he came over here one day when I was out in the front yard working. He sat down and said, 'Well, me and Shana broke up.' And then I said, 'Well, g*dd*mn, boy, if you're looking for advice from me…'"

George and L. C. were both laughing.

"…I said, 'Hell, what you ought to do is just shoot the b*tch and take her to the mountains!'" L. C. exclaimed.

"You crazy fool," George laughed.

"You just don't know how embarrassing this has been for me. …Did you know that they put something in the paper about me pulling a gun on my girlfriend's kid one day?"

"Yeah, I think I recall that."

"Well, one day I was in bed asleep." Then he amended, "You know, I had the flu. And Dr. Perry, the doctor that told me that joke I told you a while ago, he called me in a prescription. And they delivered it from the Salisbury Pharmacy. Meanwhile I'm in bed asleep. Now I heard a thump and I woke, you know, I woke up. And all I could see was somebody standing at my dresser drawers, going through the drawer. I jumped out of bed and grabbed a gun. And then I realized who it was, that it was her son. I didn't even know the b*tch had a key to my house! ...And I run 'em *both* off. I said, 'You're d*mn lucky I didn't shoot your f*cking *ss!' But that boy is nothing but a drug dealer. I mean, they say he's the biggest drug dealer at West [Rowan High School]. And he, and a couple of guys he used to run around with, ran a drug deal together. Well, the deal went bad. And my girlfriend's kid kept the money. And they were after his *ss *big* time. I mean, this girl was having all kind of sh*t done to her d*mn house, uh, somebody was blowing up her mailbox and sh*t. They even wanted to try to accuse *me* of that. Hell, I was there all the time that happened!"

"You're kidding."

"I was in her d*mn house! Now how could I have been at her f*cking house and done this?" L. C. stressed.

"That's true."

"You wouldn't believe the d*mn lies and sh*t that were told about me here. ...And I hate to say it, I mean, maybe I shouldn't say what I'm gonna say, but if I ever *did* find out anything, I wouldn't tell 'em. Not now I wouldn't. I wouldn't tell 'em *sh*t!*"

Maybe we had wasted another dart; maybe we hadn't. But L. C. Underwood's ability to contrive lie after lie seemed to have no bounds. Neither did his contempt for the investigators, especially Agent Don Gale.

CHAPTER TWENTY

*"Be not hasty in thy spirit to be angry:
for anger resteth in the bosom of fools" (Ecclesiastes 7:9)*

In the late fall of 1994, Don had an idea for shooting another dart. In light of the upcoming one-year anniversary of Catherine Miller's murder, and no new leads to follow up on at present, he suggested that we call a press conference.

"Not just a press conference about the case and a reminder of the Governor's Reward," he said, "but I think we should also play the tape recording of the anonymous threatening calls that Kay received." Don, Steve, and I quickly agreed, in hopes that a citizen might recognize the voice of the caller and identify him.

We knew that because L. C. was either physically present with Kay or on a phone call with her when she received the calls back in the spring, L. C. could not have made the calls directly. Furthermore, she would have recognized L. C.'s voice, had he made the calls himself.

So, on December 8, 1994, the one-year anniversary of Catherine Miller's murder, a press conference was held in Salisbury. On December 9, the following day, Steve called me with news.

"I have some good news," he said. "It's a Christmas miracle."

"Am I getting a blender for Christmas?" I asked.

"Even better. Don's plan worked," he said.

"I'm listening."

"A man – actually a federal probation officer – called in, after listening to the voice on the recording. He identified Kay's caller."

"How certain is he?"

"A hundred percent. He says it's a man he has on federal probation, Rex A. Keller."

"Well, jingle my bells."

Rex A. Keller had just served a nine-month sentence in federal prison. He was ordered upon release to report regularly to his probation officer. Don, Terry, Steve, and I planned to be at his next appointment and attempt to interview him about the threatening calls and hopefully find out his motivation for terrorizing Kay Weden.

Until then, we worked overtime to gather as much information about Keller as we could.

A few days later when the four of us met in Salisbury, Don said, "I think we ought to go to the federal prison."

"Why is that, Don?" I asked. "Were you wanting to take treat bags or just have a sing-along?"

"You're killing me, O.J.," he responded. "I think we should go and listen to Keller's phone conversations. All inmate calls are recorded."

"Sweet," Steve said.

"Do you really think he'd say anything incriminating on a phone line he knew was being recorded?" Terry asked.

"You'd be surprised," Don and I answered simultaneously. I had worked at a county jail long enough to know that.

Steve added, "There are so many calls, so many inmates, and they are there for such a long period of time that they get careless."

"Besides that," Don said, "if there are any calls at all between L. C. and Keller, we can prove an association."

"Let's do it," Terry said.

As it happened, Keller actually spent his seven months in two separate federal prisons, beginning on March 30, 1994, at Seymour Johnson Air Force Base in Goldsboro,

North Carolina, and then he was transferred during the early summer to the federal prison in Petersburg, Virginia, where he stayed until his release on November 29, 1994. Since Steve and I were closer to Virginia, we elected to go listen to the recordings in Petersburg, while Don and Terry went to Seymour Johnson.

In Petersburg, Steve and I met the prison warden at 8:00 in the morning. He led us to a tiny room where we spent three days monitoring hour after hour of RexKeller's recorded phone conversations on individual headsets. The vast majority of conversation was between Keller and his girlfriend Cher, which had to be one of the most dysfunctional relationships I had ever heard.

Keller and L. C. were chips off the same obsessively jealous block. In the earlier conversations, which occurred shortly after Keller's incarceration, Cher seemed a little more sincere in her proclamations of devotion to Keller. But as time passed, the conversations seemed to turn a bit one-sided.

"Do ya miss me?" Keller would ask.

"Yeah," Cher would answer blandly.

"Do you love me?" he'd ask.

She would sigh before she answered, "Yeah."

"Are ya gonna marry me?" he would ask.

Another sigh. "I told you already," she would say.

"I want to hear you say it. Tell me you want to marry me," he would whine.

Another sigh. "I wanna marry you," she would say with absolutely no conviction.

"Did ya go out today?" he always asked.

"Uh, for a little while," she would answer.

"Did ya see anybody?"

"Nah."

"Are ya sure?"

"I'm sure, Rex."

"Where'd ya go?"

"Just walkin'."
"By yourself?"
"No, with Jocelyn."
"Where to?"
"To the park."
"What'd ya have on?"
"Huh?"
"Ya didn't wear shorts, did ya?"
"No. I had on sweatpants."
"Tight ones?"
"Rex…"
"I just don't want nobody lookin' at ya, baby. You're my woman, ain't ya? I don't want nobody eyeing' that nice round *ss you got."
"Ain't nobody eyein' my *ss, Rex."
"You swear?"
"I swear."
"Okay. I love ya, baby."
No response.
"Ya love me?" he would have to ask.
"Yes," she'd answer.
"Yes what?"
"Yes, I love you," she would say unconvincingly.

Every conversation was essentially the same between Keller and Cher. He kept trying to force her to say that she missed him and loved him, and she grew more and more weary of it. He continued to interrogate her about what she did every minute of the day and to whom she spoke. She ultimately started avoiding his calls, and in turn, his insecurity and his jealousy intensified. By the end of the first day we spent listening to the calls, I knew what he was going to say before he said it. By the end of the third day, I was ready to pull my hair out. Keller was an insanely jealous man, obsessive, and controlling to no end, in spite of the fact that he was incarcerated at the time. It was almost funny except it wasn't.

"I've smoked nearly a whole carton of cigarettes in three days," Steve said.

"Listening to all that makes *me* want to smoke a pack," I said.

"Really?" Steve asked, coughing.

"No way," I said.

"Right," he said.

Unfortunately, we found no calls recorded between Keller and L. C. Underwood. But Keller *had* dialed L. C.'s number in the late fall of 1994, but had not gotten an answer. Don and Terry, on the other hand, had better luck at the federal prison in Goldsboro, where Keller was first incarcerated. There were two recorded phone conversations between L. C. and Keller, and both occurred shortly after Keller first went to prison. Nothing in the conversation was particularly incriminating, however, but made reference to things mentioned in letters between the two of them, letters that we never saw.

I wondered how in the world Keller, a convicted federal felon, came to be associated with a police officer by the name of L. C. Underwood. Furthermore, I wondered if their relationship – whatever the nature of it – had picked up where they left off when Keller was released from prison November 9, 1994. I did not have to wonder long.

On Thursday, January 5, 1995, Terry Agner interviewed the wife of the federal probation officer who identified Keller's voice as Kay's anonymous caller. She had called the Rowan County Sheriff's Office and asked to meet specifically with Detective Agner.

"On the eighth of December," she began telling Terry, "somebody called our house in the evening. The caller was angry. He said, 'Who is this?' and I said 'Who would you like to speak with?' Then he said, 'What is your name? Where do you live?' and then he slammed the phone down. I wouldn't be concerned about it necessarily, except that this call came right after my husband identified that voice on the tape. We've received several hang-up calls since then too."

"Are you sure about the date?" Terry clarified. "Are you sure it was the eighth?"

"Yes, I'm sure. It was right after he called the Sheriff's Department and the SBI ...But that's not all."

"Okay, what else?" Terry asked.

"Yesterday, which was Wednesday, the ...fourth, I got home from work a few minutes after five, and I went outside to pick up the newspaper. That was probably, oh, 5:15 or 5:30. As I was picking up the paper, a burgundy-colored car pulled up on the street in front of me with the driver's window rolled down. The driver, a man, yelled at me, 'You tell your husband he'd better watch it, b*tch!' He caught me off-guard so bad that I couldn't even say anything, and then he took off."

"How close were you to the car when it pulled up?"

"Well, the newspaper was at the curb of the street in front of my house, and I was within fifteen feet or so of the car as it passed by."

"What's the name of your street?" Terry asked her.

"Lance Avenue, and the car left toward Robin Road."

"Can you describe the car?"

"Like I said, it was burgundy, and kind of large. I think it was a two-door car, maybe a Chevrolet. It was shiny, and clean, not dirty at all. I can't remember the wheels or anything like that, but the headlights were on."

"Can you describe the driver?"

"He was white, probably middle-aged, with a medium build, maybe kind of muscular. He had short black hair parted and swept to one side. He was wearing a dark-green shirt and a dark jacket."

"Anything else at all that you can remember?"

"I think that's all, but if I think of something else, I'll call you."

"And please call if you have any other phone calls or any other visitors, okay?"

"I most certainly will. Thank you."

Terry hung up and turning to Don, said "It sounds like L. C. might be up to his same old tricks."

We all were somewhat on edge, knowing that L. C. was feeling the pressure from us, from the media, and even from his friends. We did not know what to expect from him next. Steve and I thought it was time that we introduced ourselves to L. C.'s next-door neighbor. Optimistically, I thought maybe he could shed some light on L. C.'s present frame of mind, or at least his general habits.

In reviewing the phone calls identified on L. C.'s pen register and trap and trace, we discovered that a number of calls were made to and from L. C.'s next-door neighbor, who lived alone. This was the neighbor Gil we had heard mentioned before. Ordinarily, there was nothing unusual about phone calls to a neighbor, but these calls lasted for hours on end at times, and the lengthy ones took place in the wee hours of the morning, anywhere from 1:00 a.m. to 4:00 a.m. Such a relationship between next-door neighbors seemed unusual.

Don and Terry had interviewed Gil in December of 1993 to find out if he had witnessed any unusual activity around the time Catherine Miller was murdered, but he told them he had not observed anything out of the ordinary, nor did he claim to know of L. C.'s comings or goings. But after learning of the extensive late-night phone conversations, we all believed he knew more about L. C. It seemed a good idea for Don to sit this one out.

So Terry, Steve, and I walked up the drive to the beautifully landscaped house and rang the doorbell. After several minutes, a man opened the door. I estimated him to be in his mid-sixties, but pale and thin, he did not look altogether healthy. I wondered if he slept during the day since he apparently spent many of his nights talking on the telephone.

After we identified ourselves, L. C.'s neighbor Gil let us know in no uncertain terms that he knew well who we were and did not wish to speak with us. In a high-pitched voice with one hand on his hip, and his other hand shaking and pointing a bony finger in our direction, "Why don't you people all just leave that poor boy alone?"

Steve calmly attempted to rationalize with the man, but he simply refused to calm down.

"And what does all this have to do with me?" Gil clamored. "I've told you people everything I know. I have no idea when L. C. comes and goes, and I've already told you what I knew when you interrogated me right after the murders. I surely don't remember anything more now!"

"That isn't why we're here, sir," I interjected.

His vision passed from Steve to me in a single cutting glare.

"Then why *are* you here, young lady?" he asked me, not very pleasantly.

"We're here to ask you the nature of your late-night phone conversations with L. C." Not the most tactful approach, but definitely to the point. The blood drained from his face.

"I don't know what you're talking about, *Detective!*" he said sarcastically.

I pulled out my handy-dandy phone log and gave him a few specific examples.

He got the wrong impression, and he was outraged. "Why, you all can't listen in on my phone conversations! That's illegal!"

I explained briefly how the pen register and the trap and trace work, and the fact that we did not monitor the actual conversations, but he was not listening.

"You have to get a court order to do that!" he exclaimed.

"You're absolutely correct, sir. And we did. But not for your calls, for L. C.'s. That's how we discovered your lengthy conversations with him."

"My conversations with that boy are none of your business! Now you all must leave this instant!"

"Okay," I told him calmly, "if you don't want to cooperate, then I guess we have no choice. Let's go," I said to Steve and Terry. We turned to leave.

But Gil was still ranting, "I did cooperate! You can't say I didn't cooperate! I have nothing more to say to any of you! You all have ruined that boy's life, I say! You ought to be ashamed! And you better be careful about the illegal things you're doing!" He slammed the door in a snit.

"You're the one who should be careful," I said to the closed door, "You're the one living next door to a murder suspect."

CHAPTER TWENTY-ONE

"He that covereth a transgression seeketh love; but he that repeateth a matter separateth very friends" (Proverbs 17:9)

By this time Kay had settled into a routine in her new home. Ready to relax after one particularly long day at the high school, she turned into her driveway and stopped to check her mailbox. Her heart started racing instantly when she saw the side of her mailbox. In the same color of red spray paint she had found on her black Honda roughly a year ago was the word "HO," written in the same type of capital block letters. She drove into her garage as quickly as she could and then she sat there trying to catch her breath and slow her racing pulse. Surely the vandalism, the stalking, and the threats were not about to start all over again.

L. C. had recently learned that Kay was dating Wayne Eller. Kay's emotional wounds, which had just begun to heal, were ripped back open with a single incident. She could not feel safe even in a new home in a new neighborhood as long as L. C. Underwood was a free man. Kay reported the vandalism and took additional security measures at her home.

Finally satisfied that we had done our best to locate an associate of L. C.'s, we stopped the call tracing process. In February of 1995, after analyzing all the call data we had collected, I could hardly believe the number of calls L. C. made in the middle of the night. Also, on a number of occasions, L. C. would pick up his phone, start to dial a few digits, hang up, and then do the same thing again a few minutes later. It seemed as if he wanted to communicate with someone but could not bring himself to make the call. He apparently was sleeping very little. L. C. still lived alone. We could find no obvious explanation for L. C.'s telephone behavior.

We quickly identified the phone numbers L. C. made calls to or received calls from most often. We also identified the calls where there were long periods of conversation time. This process was relatively easy using a database program I set up to enter data including phone numbers called to and from, dates, times, and subscriber addresses. Once the data was entered, we could then sort the data in multiple ways such as by phone numbers, by dates and times, and by length of conversation. The program also enabled us to search for any particular phone number called to or from on any given day.

Once we printed a list of the phone numbers L. C. was connected with most frequently, we had the numbers identified through the telephone service covering that particular calling zone. Some of the phone numbers were large businesses, and we were unable to determine if L. C. was making personal calls to an employee of the business. The majority of the calls, however, were made to and from residential addresses. Many of the residential calls were made from L. C.'s house to female occupants.

For the next several weeks, we tallied the calls, identified the subscribers of the phone numbers, and prioritized a list of people to interview.

In late July 1995, Steve and I headed to Salisbury to spend a week with Don and Terry, interviewing the persons on our list. At the last minute, though, Terry had to testify in a murder trial, so Don arranged for Special Agent D. T. Castillo, a young Italian nicknamed "Vinnie," to help us conduct the interviews.

Don and Vinnie took the first name on the list, and Steve and I took the second. Both were females. Steve and I drove to an apartment complex in Charlotte, where a Miss Joni Barnes resided. We arrived at her apartment at noon on Thursday, July 27. Joni was a friendly, attractive forty-seven-year-old brunette divorcee who lived with her grown son, who happened to be a stand-up comic. Miss Barnes welcomed us into her home, and after learning who we were and why we were there, she began to talk freely about herself and her social life.

"Just call me Joni," she said with a friendly smile.

Joni Barnes met L. C. at Boppers Dance Club in Charlotte in late 1994. She discovered that L. C. was a good dancer, and the two of them danced together often. They began talking by phone on a regular basis, but according to Joni, they were never romantically involved. One night, however, L. C. did spend the night with her when they left Boppers at 2:00 a.m. On another occasion, she went out to dinner with him.

"He was a strange one, though," she told us.

"What do you mean exactly?" I asked her.

"Like, I asked him how he got to be such a good dancer, and he told me it was because he practiced with a rope tied to his bed. I guess he practiced with the rope or whatever... Now, he constantly complained about his back, which surprised me because of the way he danced," she said, "But then I always thought he was a hypochondriac, always complaining about something."

"So I've heard," I said.

"L. C. acted like he needed a mother but I didn't want to fill that role for him. And I didn't want to get involved in a relationship with him because I kinda felt like he was just using me for something," she stated. *Imagine that.*

"Did L. C. ever tell you about being in trouble with the police or being a suspect in a murder case?" Steve asked her.

"No, he sure didn't. He did say he was a former police officer, but he told me that was because he retired on disability due to his back problems."

"Well, he did retire on disability," I told her, "but he also is a suspect in two homicide cases."

"He didn't say a word to me about that."

"Did L. C. introduce you to other friends he had?"

"Well, there was this woman that L. C. said was his ex-wife. She came into Boppers a lot."

"What did she look like?"

"She was very slim, petite, and had long shiny hair that was sometimes dyed red and sometimes brown." I looked at Steve, and we both concluded this woman must be Wanda Hornbuckle, who was never married to L. C.

Miss Barnes went on, "L. C. told me that he had caught his ex-wife and the doctor she was having an affair with. L. C. said the doctor was white-haired. He didn't say a whole lot about his ex-wife, though, and it was a while before he ever pointed her out to me. But anyway, L. C. said he caught the doctor and his wife in a motel in Concord, I think. He followed them there. Then he went in and took the man's clothes or keys or wallet or credit cards and threw them out along Interstate 85. But that's all he said about that incident, I believe. Is that not true?"

"Well, that certainly does not fit the description of any of his ex-wives, and as far as we can tell, there was no doctor who had an affair with one of them."

"You mean he was married more than once?"

"He was. What else did the two of you talk about?"

"I discussed my own marriage with him. See, I caught my husband and another woman in bed together in my own house," she said.

"I'm sorry," I said to her. "Did L. C. tell you a lot about his background?"

"Well, he told me once that his mother was sick. L. C. said he went to visit her."

"Did he ever tell you that she had died?" I asked.

"No, I don't think so. But I remember it was over Thanksgiving when he went to visit her in Ohio, because I had invited him over for Thanksgiving dinner."

"Do you know of other women L. C. dated?"

"No, but one time, L. C. made a cake for this girl who went to Boppers a lot. Her name is Gina Graham. But I haven't seen or talked to L. C. in a long time. In fact, the last time I talked with him was when he picked up his cake plate from me. You know, he seemed very concerned about that cake plate he left at my house. I thought that was really weird. It wasn't any kind of special plate or anything, but it must have meant something to him because he never would hush about it until he came and got it... So how did you all know that I knew L. C.?"

"His phone records showed several calls between the two of you."

"Oh. Yeah," she said. "I talked to him a lot on the phone. And practically every conversation was about L. C. But he never did tell me about the murder cases, for obvious reasons, I guess. But I got so tired of hearing him talk about his problems. He just depressed me. He tried to get my sympathy, I guess, but I really didn't want to hear all about someone else's problems. I had enough of my own. But he did talk about the O. J. Simpson case. He was talking about some technical things about the crime scene, how the detectives didn't do some things correctly, and I kind of tuned him out."

"Did he ever tell you about his last serious relationship with a woman, besides his wife, I mean?" I asked her.

"He mentioned dating some girl whose son was on drugs. L. C. said her son cost L. C. a lot of money getting him out of trouble. L. C. said he took up for the kid to try and help him out because he felt sorry for him. L. C. gave me the impression that he broke up with her on account of her son."

"So you haven't heard from him in a long time?"

"That's right. He quit coming to Boppers, but I don't know why. He asked me once to go with him to the Holiday Inn on Woodlawn where they always play beach music, but I didn't go."

"Joni, have you ever seen L. C. angry?" I asked.

"Well, I've never really had a reason to see him angry. He did seem to be quick-tempered though, and I thought it odd that he was in law enforcement. I don't think he's really suited for that kind of work. He seemed to be the type to act before he thought. But he took a lot of pride in his police work. I got the impression that he missed being a cop."

Meanwhile, Vinnie and Don were attempting to interview Elizabeth Richardson, who also lived in a large apartment complex in Charlotte. At 6:45 p.m., Don and Vinnie located apartment #3223 and knocked on the front door. Miss Richardson answered, and both Don and Vinnie presented their identifications. Miss Richardson became instantly hostile and refused to allow them inside. She closed the front door behind her as she stepped out onto her small deck.

She quickly informed them, "Oh I know all about the homicide investigation involving L. C. Underwood. I know about you, Don Gale, and I know all I need to know."

"I'm sure you have been told a number of things," Don told her in his usual calm, professional manner.

"How do you know about me? How did you know L. C. and I were dating? And how did you find me?" Her cheeks were flushed, but her eyes were sharp and cutting.

"Through L. C.'s telephone records," Don told her candidly.

"You have my phone tapped!" she accused Don.

"No, we don't have your telephone tapped," he assured her, and then went on in an attempt to explain the pen register and trap and trace.

"Well, why do you want to talk to me?" she asked, breathing hard.

"We want to inquire as to whether L. C. has told you anything about this case or about his prior relationships with other women. We're also interested in any violence he may have shown toward you."

"Well, he has not, and I don't have anything to say to you." She reached for her door handle.

"Ma'am, can I just leave you my card in case you change your mind and want to talk with us later?"

She hesitated, and then reached out and took the card. Then she turned and walked back inside her apartment without saying goodbye.

Don and Vinnie left then, and Don paged Steve. The four of us decided to meet and brief each other over dinner.

We met at a Chili's Restaurant in Charlotte. It was approaching 9:00 p.m. and none of us had gotten lunch or dinner. We ate chips and salsa as Don filled us in on L. C.'s latest girlfriend. But Don paused when his pager went off. Don looked at the display, and then in his typical halcyon manner, he said, "Well that's a familiar phone number. L. C.'s paging me."

I looked up. "What did you say?" I asked.

"It's L. C. He's paged me to call him at his house." I could not believe after months of avoiding us, L. C. now was initiating contact.

"That didn't take long," Vinnie stated.

"I bet you really made his day, Don," Steve said, coughing.

"He's going to be furious," I added. "…So are you going to call him nor not?"

"Yeah, I'll call him," Don answered. "But not from here. I'll call him from the District Office so we can record it."

Having lost interest in dinner, we quickly paid our bills and drove to the SBI District Office in Kannapolis. At 10:30 p.m., Don connected the recording device to the telephone. After conducting a test call to make sure the recorder was working, Don dialed L. C.'s home phone number, which we all knew by heart. Steve, Vinnie, and I watched and listened intently. L. C. picked up one the first ring.

"L. C.?" said Don.

"Yeah."

"This is Don Gale."

Without pausing for a breath, L. C. began to rant and rave in the most hostile voice I have ever heard on the telephone. "I'm going to tell you something, Don Gale! My girlfriend and I are gonna, we're going to see any attorney, uh, tomorrow. You're going to stay away from her, you're going to quit spreading these d*mn lies and rumors that you've been spreading around about me! I'm going to guarantee you that! I'm tired of it and I ain't taking your sh*t no more, Don! You, you've tried…"

"But –"

"Shut up! You've tried to ruin me in this d*mn town! You're not going to do it anymore! Now, g*dd*mmit, I'm tired of it and I'm going to put a f*cking stop to it, and you can bet your sweet *ss if you ever go within one g*dd*mn mile of my d*mn girlfriend again she's going to take your *ss to court! You understand me, you son of a b*tch?! Do you understand that?"

"I hear what you're saying." Don said, cool as the other side of a pillow.

"You d*mn right you'd better hear what I'm saying! 'Cause she ain't taking your d*mn sh*t, and I ain't taking it no more either! Now g*dd*mmit…"

"Well, you know –"

"I guarantee you're going to hear from her lawyer by Monday!"

"L. C?"

"L. C. Hell!"

"Listen to me for a second."

"I ain't got a d*mn thing to say to you, you son of a b*tch! You, you've tried to ruin me, you've spread lies about me!

You can kiss my d*mn *ss, you son of a b*tch! You ain't – you can hear *that!"*

"Yeah, I hear that."

"Now you want a g*dd*mn f*cking fight, uh, we can go to court and we'll fight this g*d, g*dd*mn thing out in civil court you son of a b*tch! I've had it! I ain't taking your g*dd*mn sh*t no more you mother f*cker! You g*dd*mn back-stabbing son of a b*tch!"

Then Don said calmly, "Well, you know, all you have to do is turn over those two guns." There was a split-second pause.

"…You go to hell, you mother f*cker! I ain't got nothing else to say to you! You better stay g*dd*mn away from my f*cking girlfriend or you are going to find your f*cking self right in the middle of a g*dd*mn civil suit! Now you understand that! Now mother f*cker, you want a f*cking fight, come get it!"

"All you've gotta do is turn over that –"

"F*CK you, you mother f*cker! I ain't got sh*t to say to you! I don't have nothing to say to you about nothing!"

"Well give us that Colt Detective Special and that Dan Wesson .22," Don said.

"*F*CK you!*" Click. The conversation, such as it was, ended at 10:47 p.m.

I watched Don as he turned off the tape recorder.

"Well, that was a perfect carnival of fun," he said.

CHAPTER TWENTY-TWO

*"Faithful are the wounds of a friend;
but the kisses of an enemy are deceitful" (Proverbs 27:4)*

"She's gonna call," I told Don.

"I don't think so. She drank the Kool-Aid. She believes every word L. C. told her," Don responded.

"That's only because she had nothing to compare it against, no reason not to believe him. She does now."

"What makes you so sure, Paula?" Vinnie asked.

"I'm just trying to put myself in her shoes. If it were *me*, even if I wanted to believe L. C., there would still be something in the back of my mind asking, *Are you sure? Are you a hundred percent sure he's not a killer?* Would I base my whole future and ultimately risk my life on what some guy says? Some guy I've been dating just a few weeks or months? I don't think so."

"But –"

"...AND knowing L. C., I'd say he has done or said things that just didn't sit quite right with her, things that will come to her mind, and soon she will start questioning everything he's ever said and done. L. C. cannot hide his true colors for long."

"Well –"

"...AND, at the very least, I think curiosity will get the best of her, and she will at least want to hear what you have to say, Don."

"Maybe. But that could take days or weeks or even longer. You didn't see how upset she was when Vinnie and I showed up on her doorstep," Don pointed out.

"She was furious," Vinnie added.

"It's weighing on her mind even as we speak. I'd guarantee it," I said. "And it won't take weeks. A few days tops. She's gonna call."

She paged Don the following week. Elizabeth "Beth" Richardson had decided to meet with investigators and hear what we had to say, but requested that the meeting take place at her parents' residence in Matthews, so that her mother and father would also be present. After talking it over between the four of us, Don and I decided to do the interview together. We arranged to meet her on Saturday, August 19, 1995.

On that Saturday afternoon, I met Don in Kannapolis and we drove together to Matthews, where we located the address of Beth's parents. The house was very upper-middle class in an older prestigious neighborhood. We were greeted at the door by Beth's father, who invited us into the living room. Present were Beth, her parents, her brother, Josh; and sister, Mandy. It was obvious Beth had good family support, and they were very protective of her. I was thankful that was the case, for Beth's sake.

Don introduced both of us to the entire family.

"Miss Richardson," he began.

"I go by Beth," she said.

"Okay. Beth, I just need some basic identifying information from you…"

Beth Richardson and her eleven-year-old daughter, Gail, live in her apartment in Charlotte. When I thought of L. C. spending time around an eleven-year-old girl, it nearly made me nauseous. Beth was working for her father, an insurance adjuster. I gathered that Beth leaned on her father for support. Blond, middle-aged, and slightly heavyset, but well-manicured and rather attractive, Beth reminded me a great deal of Kay, who had been rather dependent on her mother. I thought of all the other women in L. C.'s past who looked to their own fathers to take care of them, particularly when L. C. would not leave them alone. I thought it best not to share the comparisons with Beth, at least at that time.

Beth told us that she had been divorced since her daughter was two years old. She had not been in a serious dating relationship with anyone until she met L. C. They began dating in October of 1994, longer than we had expected. They met at the Embassy Hotel ballroom in Charlotte. Beth was quite impressed with L. C.'s dancing ability. She simply could not understand, though, how he could dance like he does with an injured back. Neither could we.

L. C. and Beth usually went dancing on Friday nights to a club in Charlotte called Boppers. L. C. had some other friends who frequented there, a couple of guys and a couple of girls, but for some reason unbeknownst to her, L. C. would never introduce Beth to them.

L. C. did not share much about his childhood with Beth except to say that he had been raised by some couple, and that his mother now lived in Ohio. But he painted quite an ugly picture for her of the homicide investigations, and how the police were trying to frame him for it. I felt compelled to convince Beth that we were not trying to frame L. C., and that we had no personal stake in the investigation at all.

"Beth, we are not personally out to get L. C., and we certainly are not out to harass you or interfere with your relationship or your life. In fact, it doesn't matter to us if you become his fourth wife..." Don threw that last comment out there, strongly suspecting that she had no idea how many times L. C. had been married.

"Wife number four?!" she exclaimed, "What do you mean?! L. C. has been married only *one* time! He told me he had only been married once!" She covered her face with her hands, and at that moment, I knew she was ready to listen to what we had to say.

"Two divorces and one annulment, to be accurate," I added.

"OK so now I wonder what else he lied to me about," she said and looked at her father.

"Well, you certainly are not the only person L. C. has ever manipulated," I said in a weak attempt to make her feel better. "...What did he tell you about his having been married?"

"He uh, he said that he had gotten married at the age of thirty, and he had remained married for ten years. He said they parted on very amicable terms."

"Well, his third marriage ended just two years ago," I told her. We have the legal documentation if you don't believe us."

"No, that's not necessary," she said and sighed.

Don then began to ask questions about her relationship with L. C. I strongly suspected that as she verbally expressed to us things that had happened during their relationship, she began to view her relationship with L. C. in a different light. Beth described L. C. as "meticulous and extremely neat" in his house and his vehicles. He even puts ArmorAll on his engine and has cleaned her cars the same way. Beth considers herself neat, but not to the extent that L. C. is. His cabinets are all neat and the items inside are in a particular order.

"He even organized my pantry for me," Beth shared with us. "He turns all the labels the same way, and he categorizes the items. ...But what is strange is that he is not neat in my house like he is at his. He leaves dirty ashtrays sitting around, and throws his clothes around at my place. He would *never* do that at his own house."

We asked Beth about any close friends or associates L. C. may have. Beth informed us that L. C. is very close to his neighbor Gil.

"What do you know about L. C.'s neighbor?" I asked Beth.

"Well, L. C. painted his bathroom for him, and the exterior of his house. L. C. told me that he helps Gil out because he is deaf. Oh and L. C. told me his neighbor is homosexual. I have no way of knowing if that is true, of course, and it's his business anyway."

"Beth, did you say L. C. told you Gil was *deaf*?" I glanced at Don with raised eyebrows.

"Yes, that's what L. C.'s said. He said that's why he helped him out because he is totally deaf. Is he not deaf?" she asked.

"Well, I don't know if he is hearing impaired or not, but we did not have any trouble communicating with him a few weeks ago," I told her. She just shook her head in disbelief.

"You know what's odd?" she asked. "L. C. can't stand homosexuals. L. C. has a cousin who occasionally comes to visit him, and his cousin is homosexual. L. C. fed his cousin's family on paper plates when they visited him, and then he scrubbed his bathroom when they left. L. C. told Beth afterward, "I can't stand those g*dd*mn faggots.'"

Beth told us that when L. C. visited Beth overnight, they did not sleep together. L. C. thought it was best since Beth's daughter was present. But Beth was not the first woman to whom L. C. had made excuses for not sleeping together. "I wondered sometimes if L. C. had any homosexual or bisexual tendencies, but then I would think about how bad he hated homosexuals. Of course, he hates a lot of things. Like driving in Charlotte, for instance."

Beth explained that L. C. cannot drive well in the city. Beth usually drives when they go out in Charlotte, and she often visits L. C. in Salisbury. But when she visits him at his home, L. C. always parks her car for her, facing forward. He told her he was afraid she would drive on his grass if she backed out of the drive rather than simply pulling forward. L. C. keeps a chain on his driveway to prevent people who are visiting the park in front of his house from turning in his driveway and getting on his grass.

"What other oddities have you noticed about L. C.?"

When Beth was visiting on one occasion in L. C.'s house, he showed her a photograph of two U.S. soldiers and a Vietnamese man, who was on his knees. L. C. told Beth that he was one of the men in the photograph, and that he had been in the military and had served in Vietnam.

According to Beth, when he showed her the photo, L. C. told her, "You know, after that picture was taken, my commanding officer told me to shoot and kill the Vietnamese man, and I did. ...Do you think it ever bothered me that I killed him?"

Beth said, "I hope so."

"No," L. C. told her, "it didn't bother me at all."

At times during their relationship, L. C. told Beth that there was something he needed to tell her. Finally, while at his house one night around Thanksgiving 1994, L. C. told Beth that he had been accused of murdering Viktor Gunnarsson and Catherine Miller.

L. C. explained to Beth, "I got stuck with this crazy b*tch Kay Weden. *All* of Salisbury knows that Kay is crazy. Everybody tried to tell me not to see her, but I wouldn't listen." L. C. went on to explain that Kay's son, Jason, was a drug dealer and owed a lot of money for drugs. He said that Kay's mother, Catherine Miller, and this other Gunnarsson guy was killed, and Kay Weden had told the police that L. C. killed them both.

Beth told us that L. C. said that the guy who was killed was found in the woods in Watauga County. L. C. explained to Beth on three or four different occasions that he had never been to Watauga County and would not even know how to get there.

L. C. also told Beth that Viktor Gunnarsson had been accused of assassinating the Prime Minister of Sweden. L. C. concluded that some people in Sweden must have had Viktor assassinated here. L. C. told her that Viktor had been led out of his apartment with no signs of a struggle. He was led into the mountains where he was shot and killed. Viktor was found naked, but his clothes were found in his apartment. L. C. explained that he could not possibly make a man leave his own apartment because he was 50 percent disabled.

L. C. had told Beth at one point that he hated foreign people, especially Vietnamese, because he said he fought in the Vietnam War.

L. C. further explained to Beth that Catherine Miller had come home and was later murdered there. L. C. thought Jason set it up to look like a breaking and entering job. L. C. argued that Jason owed drug money to some guys, so he gave them the alarm code to Catherine's house and told them to "clean the place out." This would have cleared Jason's drug debt. However, Catherine must have come home unexpectedly and got herself killed. L. C. told Beth that Kay had been receiving anonymous threatening calls about Jason dealing drugs and owing drug money. L. C. explained that he could not possibly have made those calls because he was inside Kay's house with her when some of the calls came in.

Beth believed everything L. C. told her. She never asked him where he was when the murders occurred. Beth has not read any of the articles published about the murders, and so she had no reason to question anything L. C. told her. L. C. told her that because of the way the investigators had harassed and ruined him, he refused to cooperate with them.

L. C. said, "I wouldn't give them any information now if I had any."

Shortly after L. C. told Beth about the murder investigations, a newspaper article was published along with something on TV news about a recording of someone's voice. L. C. advised Beth that she had better tell her parents about the murder investigations before they found out from someone else. L. C. later told Beth that he could not see her anymore because he loved her and her family, and that they did not need L. C.'s problems and reputation to hurt them. Yet L. C. continued to pursue Beth and their relationship.

The truth was that Beth's parents did not even like L. C. Thankfully, Beth had the foresight not to tell L. C.

"That was the very thing that got Catherine Miller killed," I told her and her parents.

She shivered involuntarily. I did not want to be cruel, but for her own good I felt it was important that Beth realize what kind of man she has been dating.

Not long into their relationship, Beth discovered that L. C. was quite the jealous lover. He did not like Beth going out with her friends at all. L. C. told her he did not like her hanging around with those "wh*res," and that she should just spend her time with him.

"L. C., it's just too bad if you don't like me seeing my friends, because I'm not going to stop going out with them."

L. C. despised one friend of Beth's in particular. Beth's friend Kayla is a mother of two children and is, in Beth's opinion, an excellent parent. L. C. threatened Beth that if she ever broke up with him, he was going to call the Department of Social Services and report Kayla to them as an unfit parent. L. C. said Kayla was the "biggest wh*re of all." This manipulation tactic was just so typically L. C.

Shortly after this conversation, L. C. called her and said that he had just received two anonymous phone calls at his house. He said that the caller told him that Beth was out "wh*ring around" in Charlotte. L. C. told her that he was very upset at having received those calls.

Beth replied, "Well, L. C., you have enough to deal with already. You shouldn't see me anymore because I don't want to cause you problems and upset you."

Immediately L. C.'s attitude changed. "Well," he said, "the calls didn't upset me *that* much." For once, L. C.'s little manipulative game didn't work. But I knew L. C. was not likely to give up easily.

Sometime in January 1995, Beth and L. C. were arguing in his home. L. C. told her that he had bought her an engagement ring, and that he had planned to propose to her. However, he had since changed his mind. Beth could not believe that he was going to propose to her after they had dated for only about three months, but L. C. walked into his bedroom and came back into the living room with a ring box. He told her that he had purchased the ring just that week from a local jeweler he knew. However, L. C. did not give the ring to Beth.

When L. C. was not looking, Beth opened the box to sneak a look at the ring. She was shocked that he was actually telling the truth. The ring was a beautiful diamond surrounded by rubies. When Beth described the ring, I was not that surprised. It was the same engagement ring L. C. had given to *Kay*. It was the epitome of tacky, in my book.

A few days ago, L. C. was visiting Beth in her apartment. While he was in the living room watching a movie, she had walked to her bedroom to change clothes. L. C. yelled for her to come back in the living room. She ran back and L. C. told her, "I just saw a man looking in your window, Beth!"

L. C. went outside to check it out, and a few minutes later he yelled for Beth. Beth walked outside, and L. C. pointed out two footprints by her window where the prowler had been.

She said, "L. C., I need to call the police!"

"Go ahead," he told her calmly.

Beth did call the police, who came and took the report and told her that was all that could be done at that time. They looked around but could not find a prowler.

L. C. told Beth that he had just recently made a report to the Salisbury Police Department. L. C. reported that one Saturday evening his house was broken into and a gun was stolen. He told Beth that whoever broke into his house entered by jimmying the lock between his kitchen and breezeway. L. C. concluded that it was Jason Weden because the suspect must have picked up the key to his gun case, which he kept hidden and Jason knew where. The suspect unlocked L. C.'s gun case and stole a gun.

"Is that another lie he told me?" Beth asked.

"Yes, it is," Don and I answered simultaneously.

"I just can't believe it," she said, "I can't believe he told me so many lies, and I believed him."

"Well, he betrayed your trust," I told her, "It's not your fault. You only believed what he told you."

"But I can't believe how naive I've been."

What could we say? She was telling the truth. She *had* been naive. But L. C. took advantage of her trusting nature as he had done to so many others.

At one point, Beth did confront L. C. "I told him he was verbally abusing me," she said. "He denied it, but he said he would try to do better."

Then during the summer of 1995, Beth and some other adults in her apartment complex had a pool party for the kids who lived there. After it was over and the kids were gone, Beth drank one beer at the pool while she talked with the other adults. L. C. came over about 4:30 p.m. and said, "You've been drinking. Look at your eyes!" L. C. said she was "nothing but a crazy b*tch and a drunk." Beth asked L. C. to leave, and he stormed out. He could not stand for Beth to have any kind of social life that did not include him. In fact, he wanted to know every single person Beth ever talked to, and why.

Beth told us that immediately after Don left Beth's apartment in his first attempted interview with her on July 26, she called L. C. to tell him. He was extremely upset that Don Gale had gone to Beth's apartment. L. C. told Beth that he absolutely hates both Don and me.

"Don Gale is just an *sshole who is out to get me, and that Paula May is a conniving little b*tch in cahoots with Don Gale."

L. C. persuaded Beth to go see her attorney to complain that the investigators were harassing her, although Don and Vinnie had only showed up on that one occasion. Nevertheless, On July 31, L. C. accompanied her to see her attorney in Charlotte. Beth's attorney told them that basically there was nothing he could do because the investigators had not acted inappropriately. L. C. paid for the attorney consultation, but was not happy with what he had to say.

L. C. asked Beth, "If we were no longer dating, would you talk with the police about me?"

"No, L. C., I wouldn't," Beth assured him, giving him the answer she knew he wanted to hear.

L. C. has demonstrated his anger before to Beth in fits of rage. During the past weekend, for example, L. C. lost his hairbrush. He quickly became frustrated and went into a rage because he could not find it. Beth finally located the hairbrush and told him to calm down.

On New Year's Eve, L. C. came to Beth's apartment. He was going to paint the interior for her. First, they went to Kmart and Beth bought the paint while L. C. bought a new answering machine. L. C. paid with a credit card. Then they walked out to the parking and got into the car. About three minutes later, L. C. became extremely upset and told Beth that he had lost his wallet. He told her he had $500 in cash and several credit cards and his driver's license in that wallet. He was so angry that he frightened Beth.

"He was just totally out of control and irrational," she told us.

They went back inside the Kmart and searched the whole store, as well as outside in the parking lot. He told her he could not spend New Year's Eve with her because he would have to drive back to his house in Salisbury to get the information to report his credit cards stolen. Beth went back to Kmart the next day and searched everywhere, but did not locate L. C.'s wallet.

Sometime later, L. C. told Beth that he had gotten a letter from the State, informing him that his driver's license was about to be suspended because he had gotten a traffic ticket in some town where he had never been. L. C. figured whoever took his wallet must have used his driver's license.

The four of us were curious about this little story of L. C.'s. Don was so curious, in fact, that he contacted the Division of Motor Vehicles in Raleigh. Not surprisingly, they were unable to find any record of any correspondence to L. C. in any of the one hundred counties in North Carolina. Furthermore, they could find no record of any deletion they had made to L. C.'s driving record, and nothing whatsoever to substantiate a claim that L. C. had received a citation as a result of his driver's license being lost or stolen in 1994 or 1995.

Beth eventually tried to break up with L. C. He was very persistent, though, and would not leave her alone. L. C. claimed to love both Beth and her daughter, Gail.

L. C. told Beth once that he wanted to take Gail to Tweetsie Railroad, a Western-style train-centered amusement park located in Blowing Rock, in Watauga County. L. C. talked about the chairlift at Tweetsie, and gave Beth the distinct impression that he had been there before. Funny that he told her he would not even know how to get to Watauga County.

On Tuesday, August 15, 1995, Don had left a message on Beth's voicemail asking that she return his call. On Wednesday, August 16, Beth contacted her attorney, who again advised her not to talk to the SBI. She also told L. C. that Don was trying to reach her. L. C. told her that if she did talk with Don, that Don would twist the truth into lies about him. But Beth was not fully persuaded that she should not at least hear what Don had to say. Finally, her family members convinced her to at least listen to the investigators. But Beth was not about to tell L. C. of her plans.

On Thursday night, August 17, L. C. called Beth. He told her that he had learned from some people in Salisbury, although he would not state their names that Beth had been talking with the police. L. C. then hung up on her.

L. C. repeatedly called Beth over the next few days. He left a number of messages on her voicemail. She had also received a number of hang-up calls. When she activated her "Call Return" service, she found that the calls had been made at L. C.'s residence. She was relieved to know that L. C. was at his home in Salisbury, and not driving around Charlotte stalking her.

5:31 a.m.: *Beth, I don't know why you haven't gotten in touch with me going on two days now. Uh, but if you leave what few things I have left at your house out on your, uh, porch there, call me and let me know and I'll come by and pick 'em up, and ya know, we'll just end it there. I – I don't know what I've done that you won't, won't call me back. I guess that's, you know, up to you, you know, so there's nothing I can do about it.*

The next message he left less than twenty-four hours later.

3:24 a.m.: *Beth, I love you. How could you stay out all night and hurt me like this? How can you... Why do you try to destroy a person that loves you? You hurt me for the last time, Beth! I would've done anyth- I'd give you the shirt off my back if you wanted it! And you treat me like I'm a pile of sh*t!*

Because she was frightened of L. C., Beth decided to spend the night with a girlfriend. The following call was later the same day.

7:22 p.m.: *Uh, Beth, I called and left word over two hours ago for you to call me! Ah, I left it with your friend Allison. I see that you didn't call me. I've always said those d*mn f*cking wh*res you run with are more important than I am! So you want 'em, you got 'em! Do whatever the h*** you want to do!*

And some two hours later...

9:44 p.m.: *Beth, I've tried all day to get you to talk to me. And you won't do it. So I'm gonna be a man for once, Beth. You know, if this relationship don't mean no more than that to you, I guess you got what you wanted all along. It – I don't think it ever was me. So I hope you're happy, and, and you enjoy the rest of your life.*

The same evening…

11:30 p.m.: *Beth, if you'll call me when you come in... I – I'm asking you to do that, and ... But if you don't call me, when you come in tonight, then I'm not, I'm not trying to bully or push you around... don't call me at all.*

The next day, yelling…

9:07 p.m.: *The least you could've done was call me back and let me know what the h*** was going on!*

On Thursday, August 24, 1995, one week to the day after he interviewed her at her parents' home, Beth called Don. She was shaken, and so was Don after he heard what Beth had to say.

"I got home from work as usual about ten minutes after six. My usual habit – which L. C. well knew – was to unlock the kitchen door, walk in and light a cigarette."

"Is that what you did today?" Don asked her.

"No, thank the Lord. I don't know why, but I didn't immediately light up a cigarette. I, I saw that the gas burner on my kitchen stove was on! My apartment was full of gas!"

"Had you left the gas on?" Don asked.

"No! I hadn't even used the stove in two days!" Beth realized that someone had entered her apartment – with a key – and turned on the gas. She had a pretty good idea of who it was, as did we.

Don was particularly concerned about Beth's safety. So, he suggested that we ought to provide around-the-clock surveillance at her residence. He believed that we would catch L. C. trespassing or attempting something even worse. So, beginning Friday evening, August 25, we took turns staying inside the residence with Beth and patrolling her neighborhood.

On Sunday, August 27, Beth received a call from L. C. at 12:55 a.m. At 2:35 a.m., SBI Agent Wayne Bridges, assisting in the surveillance, reported that a burgundy-colored Monte Carlo turned directly behind him and drove into Beth's apartment complex, and passed directly by Beth's apartment. Steve Wilson, in a separate vehicle, watched the Monte Carlo continue through the neighborhood. Steve recognized L. C. About ten minutes after Steve lost sight of L. C., Beth received a hang-up telephone call. Don instructed Beth to answer the phone, but the caller hung up as soon as she answered. At 4:30 a.m., another officer confirmed that L. C. was back at home, with both of his vehicles parked in the driveway.

Surveillance ended with no other activity occurring on August 28, 1995. Beth decided to move back in with her parents until she was certain L. C. would leave her alone. Don kept in touch with Beth, who continued to receive calls from L. C.

Fortunately, however, the next time Beth saw L. C.'s face was on the evening television news.

CHAPTER TWENTY-THREE

"Wrath is cruel, and anger is outrageous; but who is able to stand before envy?" (Proverbs 27:4)

The time and effort it took to enter and analyze all the call data from the trap and trace and the pen register on L. C.'s telephone was well worth it. It had led us to Beth Richardson, and others; and it was still producing critical information for us.

Twelve calls were made from L. C.'s house to a residence listed to Cherylette Passion Martin, 525 South Caldwell Street in Salisbury. Martin's phone number was non-published at the time. The calls were placed between June 2 and October 27, 1994, during which time we were actively monitoring L. C.'s calls. An additional call was placed from Martin's residence to L. C.'s.

I showed the calls to Sheriff Lyons and Lieutenant Stout as I was updating them on the case. "Who is the Martin girl? Is she another one of L. C.'s women?" Sheriff Lyons asked.

"I don't think so, Sheriff. I just learned that she is the girlfriend of Rex A. Keller."

We did not want to risk overwhelming or frightening her. Terry and I were nominated to approach her.

The day after Beth Richardson moved in with her parents, August 28, 1995, Terry and I drove to the residence of Cherylette Passion Martin in Salisbury. As we drove through the old part of town toward her house, I was reading the street signs. Just before we turned on to Martin's street, we traveled down Horah Street.

I said to Terry, "Horah Street... Why does that name ring a bell with me?"

"I don't know, but it's a crack neighborhood," he said, "and there's a lot of government housing in this area. ...Oh wait – I bet I know why you remember Horah Street."

"Why?"

"That's where Catherine Miller's wallet and credit cards were found!"

"You're right. That's exactly where I heard that street name from."

Martin lived on South Caldwell Street, which intersected with Horah Street.

"And here we are..." Terry said. He pulled into a driveway in front of a small white wood-frame house that looked very similar to every other house on the same street, which was not an accolade. It looked like a neighborhood where illegal drugs flowed like sewage and violence was apt to erupt at any given moment.

Cherylette Martin answered the door after about the tenth knock. She was a twenty-eight-year-old black female, heavyset, and she had apparently been asleep. Terry and I introduced ourselves.

"Are you Cherylette Martin?" I asked.

"I go by 'Cher,'" she said. She looked around the neighborhood, clearly uncomfortable that we were there. I explained as nonchalantly as possible that we would like for her to accompany us to the Rowan County Sheriff's Office to answer some questions. She was visibly reluctant, but finally agreed after she realized that we were there only for her help. She followed us in her own vehicle.

At the beginning of our interview with Cher, she seemed hesitant to provide detailed answers to our questions. She seemed nervous and afraid but without an apparent reason. As the interview progressed, however, she did relax somewhat.

Cher told us that she dated Rex A. Keller for about three years. They were engaged but never married. They lived together most of that time, although Rex had his own apartment in Salisbury. Cher met Rex when her sister Jacqueline was working for him at his convenience store. Rex expressed an interest in Cher to Jacqueline, and when Jacqueline quit working for him, Cher began working in her place. Cher and Rex started talking and began to date.

L. C. Underwood, a good friend of Rex's, visited him often at the store. Cher described L. C. as a cop working for Salisbury Police Department. Cher did not understand why a cop would be friends with a convict like Rex, who had been convicted in federal court of Food Stamp Fraud.

Cher stated, "Rex went to prison in March of '94, and he got out in November. I broke up with him kind of gradually while he was in prison."

"Did you write to each other while he was in prison?"

"Yes, we did."

"Do you still have the letters Rex wrote to you?"

"I might have. Somewhere. I'd have to look."

"Did Rex try to contact you again when he got out?"

"Yeah, he came to my school, where I was taking cosmetology classes. He come to see me twice I think, but I told him I didn't want to see him. He called constantly, wanting to get back together. He'd cry and beg me to get back together with him. Once he even came to my house. I had his stuff boxed up and sitting on the table where he could get them quickly and leave. My sister was there at the time. Rex asked her to leave so we could talk, but I told him I had nothing to say to him, and I told my sister not to leave. Finally, Rex got his things and left."

"What about when you *were* with him, what type of vehicle did he drive?"

"He had a small beige Toyota or Nissan pickup. I really don't feel good about talking with ya'll about Rex."

"I know it must be uncomfortable, but we really need your help."

"I don't know how I can help you. Rex isn't in my life no more, and I don't want him to be ever again."

"Cher, the reason these things are important is because other lives could be at stake. We have a lot of information already. But we really need to get to the bottom of a few things, and you are someone we thought might have been through enough pain and trouble yourself to understand how some other people might be feeling, and that you would care enough to want to help, hopefully to prevent other tragedies, that you would be willing to at least answer a few questions," I prodded gently.

She sat thoughtfully a few moments and then asked, "Like what questions?"

"Like about Rex's guns."

"What about them?"

"What guns did he have?" Terry asked.

"…He always had a gun at his store maybe a .380, I think, and some others, but the cops took his guns when I called them because Rex was beating me."

"Do you know if he ever got any guns from L. C. Underwood?" Terry asked her.

"I don't know. Rex always had a gun with him. He was never without one. But I don't know where he got them from."

"Cher, did you know about the murder of Catherine Miller?"

"Yeah, sure. Rex read it out loud to me from the newspaper. He told me that the cops thought Underwood killed her."

"Rex Keller told you the cops suspected Underwood of murdering Catherine Miller?" I clarified.

"Yes."

"How well did you get to know L. C. Underwood?"

"Not real well. He was more Rex's friend than mine."

Cher went on to say that she had been to L. C.'s residence on Lake Drive in Salisbury once, maybe twice. On one occasion, she went there with Rex about two years ago, when L. C. invited him over. Cher could not recall anything other than that the three of them had sat and watched television. Cher was not volunteering any information not asked.

"So, you and Rex are not together now, as a couple, I mean?" Terry asked.

"No, we're not. I told you, I don't want anything to do with him. I haven't talked to Rex since May of '95. He called me when my Dylan died – my son was handicapped and died when he was young. Rex called and wanted to get back together. I thought he had a lot of nerve calling me to say he was sorry about Dylan when he'd treated us both so badly when my little boy was alive." Cher told Terry and me about Rex physically abusing her and her son, which she had reported to law enforcement at the time.

"Rex was just *so* jealous, and for no reason. I never cheated on him. But he'd hit me and hurt me bad. He drank a lot, and he would start hitting my son too. But he couldn't defend himself because he was so handicapped. He was in a wheelchair and could barely communicate at all."

"So did the police ever arrest Rex for the way he treated the two of you?"

"Yeah, I've pressed charges against him before. Once he pulled a knife on my little boy and told him that he'd kill him and me too. I think Rex got a kick out of terrorizing both of us. But I don't want to dredge all that up again…" I could see the sadness in Cher's eyes, remembering some of the things she and especially her son had to endure.

"Have ya'll talked to Rex yet?" she asked.

"Not yet, but we plan to soon," I told her, "and we are going to ask him all the same questions and give him an opportunity to tell us what he knows. ...He's over a barrel, so I think he will tell us what we need to know."

"Okay."

"Okay then. Going back to December of '93, Cher, what all did you learn about Underwood during that time?"

"Well I know he was dating some girl who was a teacher. I think her name was Kay. Underwood said he was in love with her. But sometime around the end of the year, or late in 1993, he saw her with some other guy that he thinks was this Swedish guy that he saw later in a restaurant in Salisbury. Underwood is jealous just like Rex. And he was *extremely* jealous over this girl. When they broke up, Underwood said she was dating some other guy. I know he watched Kay's house and saw a strange car there once."

"Do you know when that was or who the car belonged to?"

"No, but about 11:00 one night he asked to borrow my car to ride by her house. Rex and I were about to go to bed, and Underwood came in. He was upset and nervous and asked to borrow my car."

"How did he get to your house?"

"He drove his own car to my house, but he didn't want to drive his car by Kay's because he thought she'd recognize him. So, he asked to borrow mine. I didn't want to let him borrow it, but Rex told him he could. I didn't like to argue with Rex, because he was usually mad or upset about something all the time. Rex drank a lot, and he smoked rock too. And Underwood said he'd bring my car right back, but it was about an hour and a half before he brought it back. I was in bed when he came back, so he gave the keys to Rex."

"Did Rex have his truck at that time?"

"Yes."

"Well, why didn't Underwood ask to use Rex's truck?"

"I asked him that, but Rex said everyone knew his truck and they didn't know my car."

"Is there any way that you could remember exactly what night that was?"

"No, but I know the weather was cold. It was one night after the night Underwood caught Kay with a guy in the restaurant, but it was before the old woman was murdered."

"What kind of car do you have?"

"It was a 1988 Ford Tempo, beige, and it was a four-door. But I traded it at Brooks Auto at the end of the year in '94."

"Have you personally seen Underwood really upset?"

"Oh yeah. He was upset at the store one time. He was in uniform and sitting in a chair not speaking to anyone. It wasn't like him to sit there and not talk, but I never did know what he was upset about, though."

"Did you ever hear him say anything about Kay's son or her mother?"

"Underwood did say that he didn't like the old woman, Kay's mother. But that was before she was killed. I think the two of them had some kind of falling out over Kay. And he didn't like Kay's son either. Underwood always called him names. He usually just referred to him as 'f*gg*t.' He said the boy – Jason, I think his name was – used drugs and that he always had to get him out of trouble. Then Underwood talked about Kay having some foreign exchange student living with her too. And he said the guy Kay was seeing was a foreigner too, a Swedish guy."

"Do you know if Underwood saw the Swedish guy that night he borrowed your car? Is that possible?"

"I don't know. It's really been too long for me to remember all the details."

"Do you know about Kay's house being shot into?"

"No, I didn't know about that. ...But ...I did see Underwood really upset one night at my house."

"Oh really? What do you mean, upset?"

"Let's see... He drove one of his two cars – I don't remember which one – and he parked behind my house. Rex and I were there when he came in. He was extremely upset, shaking, and sh*t. I never saw him like that before. I looked at Rex and asked him what the hell was going on because I was scared. Rex said he didn't know. Underwood was so upset that he couldn't even think. I asked him what was wrong, and he said he was all right and said, 'Just give me some coffee.' Rex made him some coffee and he drank cup after cup of coffee and smoked one cigarette right after another. I finally told him I was going to bed. I was really scared because of the way he was acting. Underwood said okay, but to let him stay a while and talk. He did not want to leave. He acted like Rex was his only friend."

"Would you describe him as angry? Frightened? What?"

"He was wild as a cat and out of control."

"Do you know what night this was?"

"I really believe it was the night the cops thought the old lady had been murdered. You know, she was found the next morning, but she must've been murdered the night before. I think it was that night. I think Underwood got Rex to go somewhere with him that night after he came to the house and I went to bed."

"Do you know that?"

"No, I don't know for sure."

"What was Underwood wearing that night? Can you remember?"

"I think he had on shorts – or sweat pants with the legs pulled up – and a baseball cap. I even tried to look at Underwood to see if I saw any blood on him or anything."

"And did you?"

"I tried to look without being obvious, but I didn't see any."

"Do you remember if he ever went to use your bathroom? To wash his hands or anything?"

"I …don't remember."

"Can you be certain about which night it was?"

"Not for certain, but I think it was the next day when Rex read the article to me about the old lady being found murdered. Rex said, 'Cher, that old woman that L. C. hated... she died.' I asked him if Underwood killed her. He said he didn't know. But I was convinced that he did kill her after the way he acted that night at my house, so wild and all. I kept saying to Rex, 'He killed that woman! Underwood killed that woman!' Rex told me to shut up, that I didn't know what I was talking about. I told Rex I didn't want Underwood coming to my house anymore. I don't know if he told him what I said or not, per se, but after that, Underwood pretty much quit coming over."

"Cher, are you saying that you believe L. C. Underwood was at your house in such an upset state because he had just murdered Catherine Miller?"

"I don't know for sure, but it's possible. It sure seemed that way."

"Do you think Rex Keller had anything to do with it?"

"He couldn't have. He was with me at my house until Underwood came over."

"Well, do you recall other times when Underwood and Rex went out places together?"

"Several times Rex would come home later after he'd been out drinking. I don't know where he'd been, and I never asked. Sometimes he'd tell me he had been at a bar or shooting pool. On weekends, Rex wouldn't close the store until about 2:00 in the morning."

"Did you and Rex discuss on other occasions your suspicions about Underwood?"

"Yeah. After that Swedish guy was found murdered, I told Rex that Underwood had probably killed him too. Rex told me the Mafia could have killed both of them – the Miller lady and the Swedish guy – and were just trying to frame Underwood. When he mentioned Mafia, I got scared and told Rex he needed to stay away from Underwood."

"Did Underwood see Rex a lot?"

"He called a lot asking for him."

"So when was it that you went to Underwood's house?"

"Well, it was just before Rex went to prison. I remember now... Underwood had agreed to store Rex's motorcycle at his house while Rex was in prison. He didn't want to leave it at my house cuz I live in a bad neighborhood, and I didn't want it there anyway. I was afraid something would happen to it at my house. I sure didn't want Rex ticked off at me."

"Cher, this is very important, and we need you to be completely honest with us. You are not in any trouble, but we really need to know if you know *for sure* whether Underwood killed those two people or not?"

"I can't say for sure cuz I wasn't there. But, well, I remember that Underwood did not like that old woman, not at *all*."

"If you suspected that he might have killed her, why did you not contact the police?"

Cher did not hesitate to answer, "You don't live in a neighborhood like mine and call the cops for anything. I was afraid. I was afraid of both of them – Underwood and Rex."

"...Did you see Underwood any while Rex was in prison?"

"No, but he called a few times. He wanted to know why Rex wouldn't return his letters. I told him I didn't know."

"Do you think Rex would talk to us if we tried to ask him some questions?"

"No, he won't say a word. Even if he has to go back to prison, he'll never admit to anything."

Terry took out a microcassette tape and laid it on the table. "Cher. I'd like for you to listen to a tape recording of an anonymous call placed to Kay Weden in the spring of '93. We just want to know whether you recognize the voice or not."

"Okay."

Terry played the tape, and after only a few short words, Cher said, "That's Rex. That's Rex. No doubt about it, that's his voice."

"Do you know about that call, Cher?"

"Yeah. I know that Underwood had Rex to make that call."

"How and what do you know about it?"

"Just what Rex told me about it. He said Underwood offered him money to call Kay. I asked him what he said to her, and he said he was just saying some stuff and didn't tell me the details."

"Do you know where Rex made the call from?"

"Yeah. Inside his store on the pay phone. I told him he'd get in trouble for it, but he said he wouldn't."

"Are you sure you don't know anything about Kay's house getting shot into?"

"No. I'm sure."

"What about her garage being spray-painted?"

"No, I didn't know about that either. What was painted on her garage?"

"It said, 'Jason is a f*gg*t.'"

Cher laughed. "Ha! That's what Underwood always called that boy," she said.

"Do you know if Rex ever went to Kay's house with Underwood?"

"Yes, he did. It was around the time he made the phone call. He rode with Underwood to her house."

"What did Rex and Underwood talk about when they were together?"

"Mostly about Underwood's girlfriend Kay. He griped about her *all* the time. Me and Rex both got tired of hearing Underwood talk about her."

"Did you hear them talk much about the Swedish guy?"

"Some. After he was found murdered, I overheard them talking. I heard the words "Blue Ridge" and "Lakewood," but I don't remember which one of them said it. It was one night when they were at my house. It could have even been that night Underwood was so upset, or the night he borrowed my car. It probably was the night he borrowed my car."

"You said Rex often stayed out late. Was he staying out late during this time? When the murders occurred?"

"Well, two or three times he stayed out until 6:00 in the morning."

"Did Rex use your car often?"

"Yeah, some. He drove it several times without even asking me, or without my even knowing where he was going."

"Cher, do you believe it's possible that Underwood and Rex used your car in the murder of Viktor Gunnarsson?"

"I guess it's possible. Would I be in trouble if they did?"

"Not if you weren't involved in the murder and you weren't helping them."

"Cher, do you know where the guns, the murder weapons, are?"

"No. I overheard Rex talking to Underwood on the phone one day, and they were discussing ways to get rid of guns. I know the word 'thirty-eight' was mentioned, and maybe even 'twenty-two.' But I don't know where they are."

"Cher, do you remember when that conversation took place?" I asked.

"I think it was after the Miller woman was found murdered."

"Rex ever pull a gun on you?"

"He put a handgun to my temple on more than one occasion and cocked it. He also told me that he'd kill himself in front of me."

"Was he violent very often?" Terry asked.

"Once, he beat my head against the bathtub, like multiple times. He hit me once with a cue ball as hard as he could. He'd often close down his store in order to come to my house, kick the door down, and beat me. One time I knew when he was coming, because I found out he closed his store down, and I called the cops. They came out and hid in the house and waited for him. Rex forced his way in the house and charged at me. The cops grabbed him and asked him what he was planning to do. Rex told them he just wanted to talk to me."

"Do you know where Rex is living now?"

"With some white girl in Salisbury. I don't remember her name…"

Cher expressed her concern over and over that Rex Keller would find out that she had talked with us. I could certainly understand her point, and it was not until much later when he agreed to cooperate with us, that he learned that she had given us a statement. We told Cher we would be in touch, and she left the Sheriff's Office.

A spark of hope ignited inside me that someday we would find L. C.'s guns. In the meantime, though, we had a vehicle to check out, Cher's 1988 Ford Tempo, which she allowed L. C. to borrow. If Cher allowed L. C. to borrow her car, he could possibly have kidnapped Viktor Gunnarsson in it. Perhaps there were fibers in the car that could be matched to fibers on the tape found at the crime scene in Watauga County. Perhaps fibers from Catherine Miller's house or her clothing the night she was murdered could be found inside the car.

After a bit of effort, Steve and I were able to track the car from Brooks Auto dealership to a couple in Greenwood, South Carolina. They agreed to let us search the car. On a hot September morning, we left Boone and drove directly to the residence in Greenwood. We searched the car thoroughly and found it to be neat as a pin.

"Looks like the owners cleaned it up before we came," I told him.

"Wouldn't you clean yours if a couple of strangers said they were driving from another state to come look at it?"

"Yeah, I guess I would."

"And anyway, all we need are fiber samples."

Hair and fiber analyst John Bendure had found a single beige carpet fiber on the tape with which Viktor Gunnarsson was bound. We were excited to see that the interior of the

Ford Tempo was beige. We collected upholstery fiber samples from the seats, the ceiling, and the walls, and carpet fiber samples from the front, rear, and trunk of the car, marking each location on the exterior of the plastic baggie. Interestingly enough, there was no carpet mat in the trunk of the Tempo.

We drove to Charlotte, where we met John Bendure and hand-delivered the fiber samples to him for comparison with the single beige fiber he had found on the tape. It was well after dark when we returned to Watauga County. I hoped it was not a wasted trip.

It was a wasted trip. None of the fiber samples matched the single beige fiber found on the back of the tape from the crime scene.

"It was a long shot anyway," Agent Bendure told us. "That fiber on the back of the tape could have come from anywhere. It may not even be related to the suspect or the victim. It could have come from something that was just blowing in the wind. It was a rather small fiber.

"But I would be happy just to have one single fiber, or one single hair, or any piece of physical evidence linking L. C. to the victim or the crime scene," I said.

"I know, Paula, and I hate to disappoint you. But you hang in there, okay?"

"Okay. And thanks for all your work, Agent Bendure."

"You're welcome. I just wish I could have given you some good news…"

I was quiet on the drive back to Boone.

Steve said, "You know, there's no guarantee L. C. will ever go to trial, Paula."

"I understand that. But there is a God in Heaven who witnessed both murders, and His ways are not ours. Neither is His timing."

"That's true enough. Maybe something will break soon."

CHAPTER TWENTY-FOUR

*"Boast not thyself of tomorrow;
for thou knowest not what a day may
bring forth" (Proverbs 27:1)*

While the four of us were strategizing in the early fall of 1995, another interesting piece of information fell upon Terry Agner. On September 11, 1995, Terry spoke with Kenneth Miller, manager of Sam's Car Wash in Salisbury.

Sam's Car Wash is a professional car cleaning business in Salisbury. They have a full-time staff on duty every day to clean the interiors and exteriors of all types of vehicles. Shortly after the murders of Viktor Gunnarsson and Catherine Miller, L. C. Underwood showed up at Sam's with his Monte Carlo.

Kenneth Miller told Terry that he recognized L. C. Underwood both as a Salisbury Police Officer and as a regular customer at Sam's. "He normally comes for a car-cleaning about once a month," Mr. Miller explained. "Only a few days after one particular visit, though, L. C. came back in. It was sometime in December of 1993, definitely before Christmas."

Mr. Miller knew that Underwood was very particular about his cars, and would typically inspect his vehicles after they had been washed, pointing out anything he thought had been missed.

On that occasion, however, L. C.'s behaved unusually. He approached Mr. Miller, looked at him for a few moments, and then asked, "Do you know who I am?"

Mr. Miller answered, "Yes I do."

L. C. said nothing for a moment, and then he proceeded to order everything he could – the super wash, vinyl dressing, shampooed carpet, and trunk cleaning. After the car ran though the wash and came to the area where the crew was wiping it down, L. C. walked out to the car as well, rather than waiting as usual in the waiting area. L. C. pointed out very specifically what he wanted done to his burgundy 1979 Chevrolet Monte Carlo.

L. C. ordered the area where the back of the rear seat meets the bottom of the seat pulled apart, vacuumed, and wiped. He directed the employees to remove the carpeted mat from the trunk and *shampoo* it. The trunk carpet was cleaned by using a cold-water brushless extraction method, whereby water is sprayed into the carpet and vacuumed out. L. C. demanded that every crack and crevice of the car be thoroughly cleaned. The employees sprayed and wiped the trunk walls and every other obvious surface in the trunk at L. C.'s request, with one exception. They did not touch the underside of the trunk lid. The remainder of the entire vehicle was cleaned as thoroughly as possible.

During the entire cleaning process, Kenneth Miller noticed that L. C. seemed terribly nervous. Mr. Miller told Terry that he almost asked him if anything was wrong, but decided not to pry. When the employees finished cleaning the Monte Carlo, however, L. C. seemed to "loosen up." He told them that since they did such a good job on the Monte Carlo, he was going to bring in his Dodge Diplomat and have it washed. He did so the very same day, but without the extensive worry he displayed over the Monte Carlo. L. C. spent forty-one dollars and fifty cents on each vehicle that day for the cleaning, a total of eighty-three dollars.

Mr. Miller found L. C.'s behavior particularly suspicious since he had read in the newspaper that Underwood was a murder suspect. Mr. Miller planned to call the police earlier about L. C.'s unusual cleaning request, but had never gotten around to it until recent newspaper articles reminded him that we were still actively investigating the murders. If we had received Mr. Miller's information earlier, perhaps we could have pinned down the exact date L. C. brought his cars in to Sam's. We learned enough, though, to realize that L. C. thought he had thoroughly destroyed any physical evidence that may have been left in his vehicle.

By October of 1995, the investigation had slowed again. The four of us had run out of fresh ideas, and the prospect of charging L. C. with either murder looked grim. We had talked by phone with analysts from the SBI lab, our last hope, who sounded as if they too had exhausted every possibility of physically connecting L. C. to the murders. They were prepared to package up all the evidence we had collected and return it to us. It seemed as if the good guys were not going to win this one after all, and our morale as a team of investigators was at an all-time low.

"Where's your faith now, Paula?" Steve asked me.

"I'm afraid it's a little weak," I answered. I have learned, though, that when we have done all we humanly can, that seems to be right about the time that the Lord steps in.

On October 11, 1997, SBI Agent John Bendure, Analyst from the Trace Evidence Unit of the SBI Crime Lab in Raleigh, gave me a call.

I still remember standing in the doorway of my office leaning against the door frame, looking at Lieutenant Stout, who I motioned to listen, at least to my side of the conversation.

John said, "Paula, I have something to say that you're not going to believe."

"You have my undivided attention, Agent Bendure," I said.

Then he told me an amazing story. John, who had been carefully examining all the things we had seized from Underwood's residence for nearly two years, had resolved himself to the fact that he had no physical evidence to link L. C. to either murder. In fact, he had completed his analysis and was in the process of packaging the final items when something caught his eye.

Now John had conducted numerous tests and completed various processes in order to uncover any trace evidence – fibers, hair, minute particles of any substance – particles that might be present on any of the items we submitted to him. He spent hours upon hours looking under microscopes and various lighting sources in an attempt to find trace evidence on the trunk mats from both of L. C.'s vehicles, without success. So, what happened next was nothing short of miraculous.

I John 1:5 reminds us, "This then is the message which we have heard of him, and declare unto you, that *God is light*, and in him is no darkness at all." What John Bendure could not see with his professional lighting equipment, God showed him with His light.

As John held up the trunk mat from L. C.'s Monte Carlo one final time and began to fold it for packaging, he saw in the daylight at a particular angle what he had been unable to see before… hair. Seventeen human head hairs to be exact. Moreover, they did *not* belong to L. C. Underwood.

John said, "Paula, I've compared the hairs I found to the known head hair of Viktor Gunnarsson, and microscopically, they are a perfect match." I found it difficult to believe; I kept asking John to make sure. I think he was about as pleased at his finding as I was. I said a silent prayer of thanksgiving to God for his divine intervention in this case. "…in the name of my Savior and Your Son Jesus Christ, Amen."

The next question was who to contact first. I paged Steve, then Don, and then Terry, one right after the other. I may have waited an entire fifteen seconds for one of them to call me back. Then Lieutenant Stout said, "Let's go tell Sheriff Lyons." We walked quickly down the hall to Sheriff Lyons' office.

"Sheriff, you're not gonna believe this, but John Bendure just called from the Lab. He found seventeen hairs matching Viktor Gunnarsson's head hairs on L. C.'s trunk mat!" He was almost as excited as I was.

"Have you told Tom yet?" he asked, referring to Tom Rusher, the elected District Attorney.

"Not yet," I said.

"Let's go tell him," he said.

Together we barged into the District Attorney's Office and straight on into Tom Rusher's inner office without knocking. I told him about the hair evidence.

The first words out of Tom's mouth were, "Well, Paula, why haven't you arrested L. C. Underwood yet?!"

By the time I got back to my office, my pager had gone off several times. Steve had already talked by phone with John Bendure, and Don and Terry were both trying to reach me. When we were all relatively calm, we arranged a conference call with Agent Bendure.

John Bendure explained that most of the hairs he found were telogen hairs.

"Telogen is one of three stages of hair growth. The first stage, anagen, is the growth stage. The next stage is catagen, described as the transition stage between anagen and telogen. Hairs in the catagen stage are still firmly rooted in the scalp, but have basically completed the growth stage. Telogen hairs are in the resting stage, and are those which are loosened from the scalp and ready to fall out naturally."

"So am I correct in understanding that the hair from Viktor's head fell out naturally as he squirmed around in L. C.'s trunk?" I asked.

"That's right. It's not the kind of hair that would have been pulled out intentionally," John explained.

"Would you say that is another indication that Viktor was conscious and moving about when he was in the trunk of that car?"

"That's my opinion, Paula, yes."

Steve clarified "And you looked at the hairs extensively through a comparison microscope? To compare it with Viktor Gunnarsson's known head hair?"

"Yes. There are a number of characteristics we look at in hair comparisons… For instance, if you compare a hair shaft to a pencil, you can imagine that the paint of the pencil would equate to the scales of a hair. The wooden part of the pencil would be the cortex of the hair, where the pigments are found, and also known as the "meat" of the hair. Finally, the graphite of the pencil, the hair's core, is known as the medulla."

"And are those all characteristics you observe through a comparison microscope?" Don asked.

"Yes. But we also examine the entire hair itself, not just the individual components. We look at the entire length of the hair, from the roots to the tip, and the characteristics that progress at varying stages of growth on the hair."

"And the color?"

"The color as well. For instance, red hair has mostly red pigments in the hair's cortex. Brown hair has mostly brown pigments in the cortex…"

"John, I have to ask you one more time. In looking at all those characteristics, are you convinced that they all match Viktor Gunnarsson's hair?" I asked.

"They do."

"You have just become my new best friend."

"Believe me, Paula, I'm as happy about this as you are."

"I doubt it," I said, smiling.

"What we need now is a DNA match so that we can exclude the hairs as being from anyone else."

"Right. What do you need to do a DNA analysis?"

"First we need enough of a hair sample to extract DNA from."

"You said there were seventeen hairs on the trunk mat. Isn't that enough?" Don asked.

"The number of hairs is not as important as the amount of DNA we can find in the root of any one single hair. If we're able to extract enough DNA from the root of one of the hairs, then we'll need a blood sample from your suspect to compare it with, for eliminations purposes, since the hair came from his vehicle. Of course, we already have the victim's blood sample. I'll let you know as soon as possible when we have enough DNA."

A chorus of thank you's followed for John Bendure.

"My pleasure. I'll talk to you soon..."

We called a formal meeting with the District Attorney for the next morning in order to plan L. C.'s arrest. We had more than probable cause; we felt like now we had enough evidence to convict beyond a reasonable doubt. Tom Rusher was finally satisfied. I slept more soundly that night than I had in the many months since Viktor Gunnarsson's body was found. I hoped we could finally bring some peace to Kay and to Viktor's family and friends as well. But most comforting to me was the thought that L. C. Underwood would be locked up soon, and others could dwell in safety, at least from him.

The atmosphere was charged with excitement in the meeting on Wednesday, October 11, 1995. It was time to reap what we had sown, and it was time for L. C. Underwood to do the same. After some discussion and a great deal of input from District Attorney Rusher and Assistant District Attorney Gerald Wilson, the decision was made to appear before the Grand Jury of Watauga County, which was conveniently scheduled for that week, and request an Indictment. This way we would not have to bother with an arrest warrant from a magistrate, and we would not have to go through a Probable Cause hearing in District Court. As soon as the Grand Jury returned a True Bill of Indictment and issued an Order for Arrest, we could arrest L. C. I could not wait to arrest Lamont Claxton Underwood for Murdering Viktor Gunnarsson in the early morning hours of December 4, 1993, in Watauga County.

The four of us – Don, Terry, Steve, and I – held another meeting of our own to determine the best and safest means of taking L. C. into custody. Weighing our various concerns and the safety of other officers, ourselves, and even to L. C., we ultimately decided the best method was to form an arrest team and arrest L. C. at his residence. But if for some reason he left his house in a vehicle, we would have local officers in place to conduct a felony vehicle stop and detain him until we could take custody of him. The last thing we wanted was to create a situation where L. C. could take a hostage or commit suicide.

The Grand Jury of Watauga County found True Bills of Indictment and Superior Court Judge Beverly Beal signed the Orders for Arrest for Lamont Claxton Underwood for one count of First Degree Kidnapping and one count of First Degree Murder. As soon as I had the Orders in hand, I hustled back across the street to the Sheriff's Office and met Steve, Lieutenant Stout, and Sheriff Lyons. We left immediately after the dispatcher entered the Orders into the computer system and returned them to me.

Sheriff Lyons drove Steve and me from Boone to Salisbury. We arranged to meet Don, Terry, and the other members of the arrest team at 2:00 p.m. But as we drove through Wilkesboro, our pagers all started going off at once. I knew in that instant that I would not be the first to take L. C. into custody. Steve immediately called Don and learned that they had him in custody already. L. C. had left his house, in his car, at 12:45 p.m., and deputies from the Rowan County Sheriff's Office stopped and arrested him as soon as he turned onto the street from his driveway. L. C. was arrested without incident. I was really disappointed that

I had missed the big event. I wanted to see his expression – if indeed he had one – when he was finally told that he was under arrest. But we continued on.

As arranged by phone, we met the officers transporting L. C. about halfway, in a town called Harmony about 1:50 p.m. SBI Agents Wayne Bridges and Daniel T "Vinnie" Castillo had transported L. C. from Salisbury. At L. C.'s request, Agent Bridges called L. C.'s attorney and notified him of L. C.'s arrest.

I walked to the vehicle where L. C. was handcuffed and seat belted in the front seat. I saw that he was dressed casually but neatly in a white-and-kelly–green striped golf shirt, blue jeans, and tennis shoes. A mixture of cigarette smoke and some musky cologne emanated from him. It was hard to believe that after all this time, we had him in our custody. He sat in the car looking straight ahead, like he was deep in thought, but instinct told me that he was taking in every minute detail around him. I knew he must be panicking inside, but except for the random beads of perspiration appearing on his temples and forehead, he was holding himself together rather well.

Both Underwood and I had undoubtedly spent many sleepless nights. Not doubting for an instant that he knew who I was, I nevertheless introduced myself to L. C. and served him with the two Orders for Arrest I still held in my hand. As I placed the copies of the Orders for Arrest in his cuffed hands, I could not help but notice his slight trembling. I was deliberately polite to L. C., and he seemed to respond in like manner to me, superficial though it was. But he refused even to make eye contact with Don or Steve.

"L. C., I know you've already been informed, but you're being charged with Watauga County Grand Jury Indictments for one count of First Degree Murder and one count of First Degree Kidnapping of Viktor Gunnarsson." He gave me no response except to look away.

I continued to talk to him directly. "Mr. Underwood, I need you to come with me now, and Sheriff Lyons is going to drive us back to Watauga County." L. C. looked around, probably contemplating his options, and then looked straight ahead and nodded. I leaned across him and released his seatbelt. When I stepped back, he got out of the car. I held onto his upper arm for the dual purpose of preventing the fall of a restrained man and in anticipation of an attempted escape. I felt the involuntary response of his bicep stiffen when I took hold of him. Undoubtedly, he did not care for his role reversal in this scenario.

After a few moments, L. C. finally chose to speak. He spoke quietly to me, "I just don't want to be around any SBI agents, please." I did not tell him Agent Wilson was going with us too.

I patted him down for weapons for my own peace of mind, although I knew he had been searched already. Sheriff Lyons shackled L. C.'s feet and placed him beside me in the rear passenger seat, directly behind Sheriff Lyons. I reached across L. C. and fastened his seat belt. Steve sat beside the Sheriff in the front seat, directly in front of me. The Sheriff notified our dispatcher by radio that we were on our way back to Watauga County with our prisoner. It was 2:10 p.m.

I was alone in the backseat with L. C. Underwood, and he was in cuffs and shackles. I was keenly aware of every move he made.

After a few minutes, things became almost comical. L. C. was not the obnoxious mouthy prisoner I expected. Rather he was humble, like a chastened child. I would have thought he was almost relieved to be arrested finally, except for the telltale sign of his pulse beating wildly, which I noticed was visible outside his carotid artery.

After we had been travelling for seven minutes, and while we had witnesses and privacy, I took out my preprinted Miranda Rights card. I read the rights aloud to L. C. from the card, though I knew them well by heart. He stated, "I have already talked briefly with my attorney, and on his advice, I'm not going to answer any questions at this time, ma'am."

"Okay," I said, and put the card back in my wallet.

"Can I call my attorney?" L. C. asked.

Sheriff Lyons answered him. "You can call him when we get back to the jail."

L. C. rode in silence most of the time, but at one point he turned to me and asked, "Ma'am, will you ask him if he can turn down the air some. It's cold in here."

Sheriff Lyons reached up and adjusted the air conditioner after glancing at me in his rearview mirror. I shrugged in response as if to say I must have missed something because I did not know why L. C. was only speaking to me.

In a few moments, L. C. asked me, "Ma'am, will you ask the sheriff if he minds if I smoke?"

"I'm sorry, but there's no smoking in our cars. We'll let you smoke before you go back in the jail, though," I responded.

Steve made eye contact with me, and I raised my eyebrow at him slightly. L. C.'s behavior was... interesting.

"Ma'am, do you have a mint or some gum please?" he asked me.

"I'm sorry; I don't," I told him. "But would you like some water?"

"No thank you," he said.

As we crossed the Wilkes County line into Watauga County, I saw that L. C. had begun to fidget. He started tapping his fingers, but stopped when he caught me watching them. Then he put his head down and closed his eyes. But when we passed the intersection of Highway 421 and the Blue Ridge Parkway near the scene where Viktor's body was discovered, he could not help himself. L. C. turned his head in the smallest of movements toward the woods where Viktor had lain. He flinched, almost imperceptibly.

But it was so slight that if I had blinked, I would perhaps have missed it. L. C. did not dare look in my direction, but immediately closed his eyes again and kept them closed until we were well out of Deep Gap.

We arrived at the jail at 3:18 p.m. L. C. kept his head down to avoid having his picture taken by a couple of reporters who had already gotten word from Salisbury and were standing by.

Sheriff Lyons, Steve Wilson, and I led L. C. directly to the processing room where I prepared to fingerprint him.

"Ma'am, Does the SBI have to be here too?" L. C. asked me, without looking at anyone.

Steve did not give me the chance to respond. "Let me tell you something right now, L. C. You do not make the decisions here. Do you understand? You need to do as you're told, and there won't be any problems. Do you hear me?" I rarely saw Steve lose his temper, but he was livid.

"Yes. I'm sorry, I was just asking," L. C. answered.

"Well, the answer to your question is that I will be wherever I need to be to do my job," Steve said plainly.

"Okay. I didn't mean anything by it."

"Yes, you did mean something by it, L. C., and I don't appreciate your attitude towards the Bureau and towards me. You do not even know me."

As we walked down the hall toward my office from the jail, I picked at Steve. "It's nice to know that trying to quit smoking hasn't affected your mood at all."

He looked at me sternly for a moment and then laughed.

"Maybe," he said.

"Are you still using those patches?" I asked.

"No," he responded. "They're too hard to light."

At 3:35 p.m., the sheriff and I walked L. C. across the street and into the courtroom, where L. C. appeared before Judge Beverly Beal for a bond hearing. Judge Beal determined that L. C. should not have a bond set because he was too much of a flight risk and a potential danger to the State's witnesses. When asked about counsel, L. C. told Judge Beal that he had two attorneys already on retainer, and he did not need court-appointed attorneys until his money ran out.

We took L. C. to the jail and released him to the Detention Officer on duty, making sure he was securely locked behind bars, and then sat down in the Officers' Room to watch the five o'clock evening news.

CHAPTER TWENTY-FIVE

"Lay hands suddenly on no man, neither be partaker of other men's sins: keep thyself pure" (I Timothy 5:22)

On October 13, the day following L. C.'s arrest, I met Steve, Don, and Terry at the U.S. Probation Office in Salisbury. At 10:30 a.m., the four of us were introduced to Rex A. Keller by his federal probation officer. Keller was a large muscular guy with tough tanned skin, super dark brown eyes, thick black hair and mustache, a tight worn-out T-shirt, black jeans, black motorcycle boots, and tattoos up and down both arms. He agreed to meet with us, and we all walked to a private conference room together.

"Mr. Keller, you're familiar with L. C. Underwood…" Steve began, without waiting for a response, which Keller did not give initially.

"Did you know that L. C. was arrested for murder yesterday?"

"I had no idea," he said. "– that he was arrested, I mean. I knew he was a suspect in both those murders."

"Both murders?" Steve asked.

"Gunnarsson and that Miller woman," he acknowledged.

"He called her 'The B*tch.'"

"Who?" I asked.

He looked over at me then. "That Miller woman. Kay's mama. L. C. called her 'The B*tch.'"

"Well, let's back up and start with when you first met L. C. Can you tell us about that?"

"Yeah. Me and my wife at that time, Mattie, we bought this convenience store. It was the Village Variety over on Hopkin. It was in a rough neighborhood, but we didn't know that when we bought it. Anyway, one Sunday night not long after we opened, somebody busted a window out in the store. L. C. was on duty that night with the police department, and he was the one they sent out to answer the alarm. When I got there, I met L. C. I remember it sure was cold that night..."

Keller told us that a lot of cops hung out at his store. L. C. started hanging out there also to talk. L. C. was still married to Marcia at the time. Then one day, L. C. told Keller that he and his wife separated. L. C. was upset, but Keller thought he was more worried that she would try to take everything they owned. Keller simply responded, "Sh*t happens."

Despite Keller's less than sensitive nature, L. C. continued to complain about his personal problems to Keller. Not long after L. C. and Marcia split up, L. C. started dating Kay Weden.

In 1993, Keller and Mattie separated, and Keller moved to an apartment at Holly Leaf. Keller met a young black girl by the name of Cher Martin, who he had met at his store. He moved in with her at her house on South Caldwell Street, "right in the heart of a crack neighborhood." That much was true.

Keller told us that L. C. visited Keller and Cher in their house on South Caldwell Street two or three times. Keller visited L. C.'s house on three or four occasions as well. Keller was sentenced to serve a prison term beginning in March of 1994, and he left his motorcycle at L. C.'s house while he was in prison.

"Why did you do that?" I asked.

"I didn't want to leave it at my mama's house because I got this brother, and he's handicapped, see, and I didn't want him to get on it and get hurt. And then I couldn't leave it at Cher's because of the rough people who lived in the neighborhood. I *knew* it would get stole there. So… I left it at L. C.'s place."

"So how well do you know L. C?" Steve asked.

"Well, I know that he, uh, he's not rational. I know that he had some problems when he was dating that Kay Weden. …L. C.'s a weird guy. He's crazy jealous and real, uh, real possessive-like."

"Uh-huh," I said. "What kind of problems did L. C. and Kay have?"

"Well, the first I know of it was when L. C. told me he'd caught her in a restaurant with some other guy. L. C. was real upset. He said he had a cop friend with him and just happened to be in that same restaurant when he caught her. He told me he just walked up to 'em and poured tea in Kay's lap. L. C. got thrown out of the restaurant and suspended from his job. L. C. said it was Kay's fault he got suspended because she went to the Chief."

"What else did he tell you about their relationship?"

"Well, after he told me about that night at the restaurant, he started talking about a lot of other sh*t. L. C. said he had let Kay borrow a bunch of money, and she wouldn't pay it back."

"How much money?" Steve asked.

"He didn't say. But he said he loaned her the money for her sick mother, but L. C. thought Kay really used the money to get her teenage son out of drug trouble. …L. C. said that Kay's son, uh, Jason, that Jason stole Kay's car and wrecked it. Kay took the blame for Jason and said she was driving it. …But I never did know what to say to L. C. about his problems, so I just listened. I did get tired of hearing about it after a while, though. But L. C. couldn't talk about his problems with any of the other cops he worked with because he had got suspended. …But I was having plenty of problems of my own at the time. My thirteen-year-old son was having problems at school. We had that new business, and we had to take a second mortgage on the house to get it, and I, I was just under a lot of pressure then. I didn't really want to hear his whining, but he just kept on."

"What else did L. C. complain about?"

"He talked about some back problem he had. But over and over he kept talking about the tea incident, the money he loaned Kay, and Kay's son. I kinda sympathized with L. C. because I've got a jealous streak m'self." I thought of all those hours of phone calls between Keller and Cher we had listened to at the prison.

"So, when did L. C. refer to Catherine Miller as 'The B*tch'?"

"Well I didn't know what her name was till after I saw it in the paper about her murder. Then L. C. told me that Catherine didn't like him. L. C. claimed that she was part of the reason he and Kay couldn't get along."

"Why did he think that?"

"Well I took it to mean that Kay's mama ran her life. She thought L. C. was too possessive over Kay. But I didn't question L. C. in detail about Kay's mama 'cause I was sick of hearing about their problems. ...But L. C. kept right on talking about it. He said Kay's mama gave her money all the time. He said her son was messing in drugs. L. C. said him and Kay found a bag of pot in Kay's house that was Jason's. Kay wouldn't do nothing about it, and he flushed the pot down the toilet. I told L. C. not to worry about it, 'cause if the boy's mama wouldn't do nothing about it, then he sure as hell couldn't."

Keller told us that when he was running his store, he worked usually sixteen to twenty hours per day, usually from 7:00 in the morning until 2:00 or 2:30 the following morning. He normally closed at 2:00 a.m. when they had to stop selling beer. Then Keller would clean the store, restock, and do paperwork and inventory, and other tasks before finally going home around 3:00 a.m.

Keller continued, "You know, after L. C. had his back surgery, they made him a school officer. Then L. C. started telling me about some threatening letters he was accused of sending to Kay. The letters was supposed to have been typed at the school where L. C. was working. L. C. said the case was dropped against him, but he said he got in trouble over it because the cops had the ribbon cartridge from the typewriter. But L. C. and Kay worked things out between 'em and Kay went to the District Attorney and withdrew her complaint. But L. C. still never admitted to me that he had wrote the letters."

"Did you ever see those letters?" Steve asked.

"No, but I figure L. C. wrote 'em. He was just plain crazy when it come to that woman. L. C. would rant and rave about Kay sneaking around on him, and he'd say he was gonna kill himself. After a while, I got so tired of hearing the same thing all the time that I quit taking his phone calls. Even when I'd talk to him and then hang up, L. C.'d call right back a few minutes later. I reckon I was his sounding board."

During the interview, we had to stop several times and remind Keller that he needed to be completely candid with us. He would talk plenty about L. C., but did not incriminate himself at all. Finally, we confronted him with the anonymous telephone calls to Kay.

"Mr. Keller, one of the reasons we are here today is to ask you specifically about some phone calls that were made to Kay Weden. Now you said you would be completely honest with us, and we expect you to honor that," I said.

Keller looked down at his lap and then slowly started nodding his head.

"Yeah, I know what you're talking about. ...L. C. asked me to make some calls to Kay, and I did."

"How many calls?"

"I guess four or five."

"How was it that he asked you to do that? What did he say?" Don asked.

"Like I said, he would call me at the store all the d*mn time. He started asking me to call the b*tch, referring to Kay, and scare her."

"Did L. C. tell you what to say to Kay?"

"Yeah, basically. And he would always call when I was tired and wanted to go home. I made the calls just to get him off my back so I could leave. …But L. C. wanted to make it look like he wasn't involved in them calls. He knew Kay would call him as soon as she got one of those calls. Sometimes I would tell L. C. that I had called Kay when I really hadn't. I just wanted him to get off my back."

"Do you remember the first time L. C. ever asked you to call Kay?"

"Yeah, he said, 'The b*tch owes me money. Call her and scare her.'"

Keller went on to say that L. C. told him to demand an amount of money somewhere between $2,000 and $5,000 when he made the anonymous call. L. C. wanted Keller to make it sound like Jason was on drugs.

"Every time he wanted me to call, it was the same thing. He would say that he was sick of the b*tch doing him this way, the b*tch owed him money, etc., so that's what I said when I called her. I told her Jason owed money for dope and he needed to pay up."

"Did he ever ask you to do anything else to Kay?" Don asked.

"…Yeah. Not long before that woman was murdered, L. C. came to our house. He said he wanted me to bushwhack Kay and her son. He always referred to her son as 'The Little F*gg**t.'"

"L. C. wanted you to do *what* to Kay and Jason?" I asked.

"Bushwhack 'em. You know, hide, and then jump 'em and beat 'em up. But I flat out told him no. But then he told me he'd give me $500 in cash and this gun he had, a .38."

"So you agreed?"

"Yeah, I told him I would, but I never did."

"Did he give you the money and the gun?"

"Yeah, he gave them to me the day he came over and asked me to bushwhack 'em."

By this point in the investigation, we had thoroughly reviewed L. C.'s bank records. I recalled a cash withdrawal of $600 that L. C. had made from his account at his bank in Salisbury in early December of 1993. I wondered if L. C. had given Keller his $500 out of that withdrawal. Those bank records would help to corroborate Keller's statement once we went to trial.

I asked, "Mr. Keller, how long did you keep the .38?"

"A few days. He came back to get the gun a few days later, but I never did pay him back the five hundred."

"What kind of gun was it?"

"It was a Colt .38, a shiny nickel-plated revolver, with a small frame. He said he got it from when he used to work at the Lincoln County Sheriff's Department. …He had it real clean. He carried it wrapped up in a rag. L. C. claimed that nobody knew he had it."

"Do you mean L. C. indicated to you that he stole the gun from Lincoln County?"

"Yeah, that's the impression I got."

"Did he give you any bullets for the gun?"

"Yeah. A box. But I had some .38 bullets too."

"What did you do with the money?"

"Me and Cher spent it on the kids for Christmas. But I only had the gun for about a week. Then L. C. came back and got it. L. C. was pissed that I hadn't bushwhacked Kay and her boy. He said, 'I ought to just go kill the b*tch myself.'"

"And when was that?"

"A few days or maybe about a week before that Miller woman's murder came out in the papers."

"*Before* she was murdered?" I clarified.

CHAPTER TWENTY-SIX

"They speak vanity... with flattering lips and with a double heart do they speak" (Psalms 12:2)

On Saturday night, October 14, 1995, Kathy Johnson, a dispatcher at Watauga County Sheriff's Office, notified me that L. C. wanted to speak with me. I could not believe it. I called the Detention Officer on duty, who told me that L. C. had indeed asked to speak with me, and me alone. The Detention Officer told me that L. C.'s two attorneys had been to see him earlier in the day, but now he wanted to talk to me by himself. I called Steve before driving to the jail.

"He wants to talk," I told him.

"No he doesn't," Steve said.

"I'm serious. He told the jailer he wanted to talk to me. Alone."

"Paula, he's not going to tell you anything."

"I know that, but I have to go see what he wants."

"I'll give Don and Terry a call to let them know what's going on, and then I'll meet you at the jail."

It was 9:00 p.m. Steve waited outside the small conference room inside the jail, out of sight, while I entered the room where L. C. was already seated across a small table from me. I told the jailer I'd be fine, and he stood and walked out of the room, leaving the door cracked.

Only a telephone sat on the small table. I sat my notebook down, and then I pulled up the only other chair in the room. L. C. did not strike me as a broken man who was about to confess, but I had not expected him to. His body language was closed and he even seemed a bit arrogant, maybe proud of himself for getting me to come to the jail on a Saturday night. He sat up in the chair and pasted an artificial smile on his face. He acted like he was there to interview me, not vice versa. *Let the games begin*, I thought.

I took out my preprinted Miranda Rights form. This form lists the rights of a person who is in custody and is about to be questioned about a crime. It starts, "You have the right to remain silent…" Both L. C. and I knew that he had to waive his rights before I could question him about either murder. But L. C. interrupted me as soon as I brought out the Miranda Rights form, which I know he recognized immediately. I also knew at that moment that he would never waive his rights. He had his own agenda for calling me in.

L. C. explained his reason for not waiving his rights. "I met with my attorneys earlier in the day. They advised me not to discuss the case with you *right now*." I wanted to ask him why he bothered to call me in if he did not want to talk about the case, but I decided to play it out and see what he was up to.

He must have thought me the most naive of all the investigators. "L. C., you know I can't talk to you if you don't waive your rights," I told him.

"I don't want to answer questions now about the case, but I do have some things I want to say to you. I want you to know, though, that if I ever decide to talk about the case with anybody, and I'm not sure if I will or not, but if I do, I will only talk with *you*." I was neither fooled nor flattered.

And there was more. "I appreciate how nice you've been to me, and how you've treated me."

"L. C., I believe in treating everyone fairly. And I will be as good to you as I can be. You're doing okay, then?"

"I'm actually doing pretty good. I haven't smoked, of course, since I've been in here, and I really don't even miss it."

"That's good," I told him, "it would be a good time to quit, because they say the first twenty-four hours are the hardest."

"Yeah, I'm surprised I haven't even missed it like I thought I would." I was surprised that he had not asked me for a cigarette. I felt sitting there with him that there was some other kind of struggle going on, but at that point I could not put a finger on what it was precisely.

As we talked, L. C. and I made eye contact with each other, but it was as if L. C.'s body was a physical barrier between me and someone or something else. If eyes are the mirror of a person's soul, then L. C. was soulless. The dark brown eyes looking back at me were more like miniature stones rolled in front of whatever the tomb held behind them, keeping his inner self closed off to anyone on the outside. When he spoke, he looked at me as if he knew something I did not, and he seemed to find it vaguely amusing, although he never cracked a genuine smile.

I shivered involuntarily at the sudden coldness in the room, but L. C. did not seem to notice as he went on with his prepared speech.

"Ma'am, I hope you're not going to let others – like those d*mn SBI agents – excuse me, ma'am, I'm sorry for swearing, but I hope you're not going to let them dictate what you do in your investigation. I understand you're the lead detective, not them."

"I am. L. C., I've gotten to know a lot about you in the past several months. But I can assure you that whatever action I take has been and will continue to be done legally and properly. And by the way, I don't have any personal problems with you." *Except that you are a mean cold-blooded killer.* I was careful to make no facial expression.

I said, "Regardless, I always aim to treat every *offender* with fairness and decency." That much was true.

"Well, I sure appreciate the way you've treated me so far. No matter what happens as a result of this investigation, I will not hate you because I know you're only doing your job. And you've treated me very fairly."

"Okay, I appreciate your saying that, L. C." I hoped we were finished appreciating each other and could get on with it. My rubbish filter was filling up fast.

"But I don't fully trust that Steve Wilson either," he said, "but that's because I have a personal problem with the SBI. I didn't mean to offend him when ya'll were processing me Thursday afternoon, you know, when I asked if the SBI agents had to be present. If I have the opportunity, I'll apologize to Wilson for having offended him. I didn't mean anything personal by what I said." I was not going to argue with L. C.

"Now, do you think I'll be sent to Central Prison for safekeeping?" L. C. asked me, as if he were controlling the interview. "I am not suicidal. I haven't caused any problems whatsoever for any of the jailers or the arresting officers, and I don't intend to do so. You know, I've already been given sheets and a blanket and I haven't attempted to hang myself." *Hats off to you, L. C.*

"I don't know. That's not my call," I told him.

"I really don't want to go to Central Prison. There's no need for it. Do you think you could tell them that for me?" He met my eyes, and for a moment he looked like a scared little boy. It was fleeting, however.

"I'll tell them what you said, but at this point, I don't know what will happen. I can't make any promises." I was always careful not to make such promises.

"Why were some people told that they should be afraid of me?"

"L. C., if you want to discuss the case with me, I'll be glad to do that. But you know you have to waive your rights first."

"Okay, I'm sorry. Well tell me this," he said. "If everybody thought I was such a great officer, if I was so great and so smart in law enforcement, why wasn't I ever a Chief of Police?"

"I don't know. I frankly haven't heard anybody say you were a great officer." I admit it was a bit of a dig. I saw a flash of something hot light his eyes, but he recovered quickly. "Actually, just the fact that you have been in law enforcement so long makes you generally knowledgeable about certain things we all learn about, such as physical evidence," I added.

"Well, all the cases I worked as a detective were gimmies. The SBI lab did all the technical stuff. And everybody knows that law enforcement doesn't require anything more than common sense." I think he was trying to insult me now, an eye for an eye.

"Really?" I asked.

"…Ya know what I've been thinking about since I've been in here?" he continued.

"I do not," I answered. But I could just about imagine.

"I've been thinking about calling my sister. Do you think she would talk to me?"

"I don't know. Maybe she would like to hear from you after all these years. I think I would want to hear from my brother if we had been estranged for years."

"When I was little, I did not have parents that loved me and cared about me, but when I went to The Children's Home, one woman did. That's my mother in Ohio. I'm not a bit ashamed to call her my mother."

"I am familiar with your background, your childhood. I know it was not ideal and that you and Margo suffered things that no child should have to suffer. I am truly sorry about that. In fact, I know a great deal about you, L. C., how you grew up, the things you did as an adult and so forth. But do not misunderstand that my treating you fairly is an indication that I doubt your guilt. I do not doubt your guilt. In fact, since you brought it up, understand this: I know that you killed Viktor Gunnarsson, and I know that you killed Catherine Miller."

"Well..." He did not finish whatever sentence he had started. I predicted that his "well" was as close to a confession as I may ever get from him.

I continued with my response. "I know you killed them both. And yes, I am still sitting here talking to you like somebody. Perhaps you should realize that not many people would do even that much. But regardless of what you did, you are still a human being, a soul, and it's not the end of the world. We are all sinners. God is willing to forgive sin, and no doubt He will help you deal with anything, including whatever you have done in the past. None of us are perfect, but He is. And God loves us no matter what we do. In fact, it was when we are at our worst that God loved us so much that He gave His only son to die on the cross to pay for our sins. He loves all of us, L. C., including you." I looked pointedly at him.

"I know that," he said, jerking his head away and changing the subject so quickly he could not get his next words out fast enough. "So how long do you think it will take before the case goes to trial? I figure it'll take a couple of years."

I did not answer him immediately.

"I don't have any way of knowing how long it will take, L. C., but I think it will probably be a matter of months, not years."

"So why is there a no-smoking policy in the jail? ... You know, I've surprised myself. I haven't craved a single cigarette since I've been in jail."

"That's good. Now is a good time to quit then, don't you think?"

"You know, I know that nothing I've said can be used against me."

I did not respond.

"But I do want you to know how much I appreciate you. And I hope that *you* have control over what happens to me and not someone else who's vindictive towards me."

"I told you that I cannot promise that you won't go to Safekeeping at Central. That's the Sheriff's decision to make. I can assure you, though, that Sheriff Lyons is not vindictive. That is not how he makes decisions. Whether or not you go to Safekeeping will be greatly impacted by your behavior. If you cause problems in this jail you will significantly increase your chances of being sent to Safekeeping. ...Now, L. C., again, since you won't waive your rights, we really should stop talking now."

For a moment, he went stone cold. Then, for just a few seconds more, I saw his eyes. They had gone black. No brown around the pupils, just ...two black buttons. I remembered what Kay had told me all those months ago when he came to retrieve his toaster. I had angered him. But how? I wondered.

"Officer Yates, he's ready to go back to his cell," I called out. Then I realized L. C. was angry because I was leaving.

L. C. recovered then, and spoke quickly, before the jailer took hold of him. "Thanks, ma'am. Thank you for being so good to me," he said. His tone was not sarcastic, but neither was he believable, though he had tried hard to sound sincere.

There was no sincerity to be found in L. C. Underwood. There was, however, a great void where a conscience should have been. Maybe, though, that void was not unoccupied at all. Maybe it was occupied by something... demonic.

The jailer, Danny Yates, led him back to his cell. I hoped L. C. would not give him any trouble. Danny was a goodhearted guy and a friend of mine. At least for the time being, L. C. was endeavoring to portray a model prisoner.

On the following Monday, October 17, 1995, Sheriff Lyons and I transported L. C. from the Watauga County Jail to the Madison County Court House in Marshall, North Carolina, for a pretrial bond hearing. Madison County is about an hour-and-a-half drive from Watauga County, but this was the only county in our judicial district where a Superior Court Judge was presiding. We could not have made the trip on a lovelier day. The sky was clear and the mountains were vibrant with the brightly colored leaves of autumn. L. C. seemed to be in a rather chipper mood himself, I thought, considering his circumstances.

Neither Sheriff Lyons nor I attempted to elicit any statements from L. C., but he chatted away during the entire trip. L. C. was shackled and handcuffed, and I put him in the front passenger seat and fastened his seat belt. The sheriff drove, and I sat in the rear passenger seat opposite L. C. I discreetly took notes each time he made a comment, regardless of the content. By the end of the trip, I had written several pages.

L. C. asked about our department's patrol cars. He asked about some of the towns we drove through. He commented on the changing color of the leaves and on the weather. He observed that there were many Fords and Toyotas on the highway. He observed that the houses were a good distance away from each other. He complimented the sheriff on his ability to drive on the curvy roads. He told us about his back injury and his subsequent surgeries. He talked about the Rowan County High School football teams.

L. C. noticed some music cassette tapes that the sheriff had lying on the seat.

"Why, both of you are on here!" L. C. said, looking at the photography on the front of the gospel music cassette case.

"Yeah, we sing with my family in a gospel music quartet. We just sing at churches around here. We're nothing special," the sheriff explained. "This lady [gesturing to me] plays the bass guitar for us."

"Can you play it? I'd really like to hear it." L. C.'s interested tone was sickeningly superficial.

Sheriff Lyons put the cassette in the player, and I watched L. C. He started swaying back and forth to the music in a childlike manner. His dramatics were a bit much. The sheriff glanced at me briefly in the rearview mirror, and I shook my head subtly.

"This is really good. You all should go professional," L. C. commented.

Then he turned to me and said spontaneously, "You know, when Vance Furr came to talk to me at my house, I know he wanted to look at or look for something. But I didn't know what. The gun was in my gun cabinet at the time."

I did not comment, but assumed that he meant the .22 caliber gun.

L. C. further added, "You know, that gun was in my house when ya'll searched it."

I could not question, but I continued to listen.

He went on, "There were a lot of statements from other people in that search warrant that SBI agents haven't told the truth about. I know because those people who gave statements to the agents called me and told me that what was printed in the search warrant was not what they said."

I told him, "You know, L. C., that's what a trial is for. You can present your own evidence and cross-examine witnesses. But you know, we can't discuss the case with you unless you waive your rights."

"Do you have a mint or a piece of chewing gum, ma'am?"

I found a stick of gum and a wrapped piece of peppermint candy in my purse. I handed him both.

"Oh – thank you, ma'am."

"You're welcome."

We arrived at the Madison County Court House about 2:00 p.m., just as court was beginning to reconvene after lunch. I saw L. C. glancing around skeptically. The Courthouse stood in the center of the Mayberry-like town at one of only two stoplights. Directly in front of the courthouse and parallel to the street is the French-Broad River. The old courthouse was a rock-and wood-front two-story building, which had stood for nearly a century.

We led L. C. up the wooden staircase, as there were no elevators, to the courtroom on the second floor. The Madison County Courthouse was the stateliest in all of the 24th Judicial District, with its super tall windows, heavy blue draperies, elegant chandelier, hardwood floors, and the balcony above the audience. The grand courtroom commanded respect.

At the hearing, Judge James U. Downs appointed Attorneys Chester Whittle and Bruce Kaplan to represent L. C. because he claimed he could not afford to hire his own. He was disappointed, though, that the Judge would not appoint his own attorneys in Salisbury to represent him, and he did not know Mr. Kaplan or Mr. Whittle. I knew them both well.

"L. C., they're both good attorneys. You're in good, competent hands," Sheriff Lyons assured him.

He asked, "Have they ever tried a capital case before?"

Sheriff Lyons answered, "Chester Whittle has. The case of Daniel Bryan Lee who was charged with First Degree Kidnapping, First Degree Rape, and First Degree Murder."

"What happened in that case?" L. C. asked.

The sheriff allowed me to answer that one. I tried to be nonchalant. "He was sentenced to Death."

L. C. did not respond. Sheriff Lyons glanced at me again in the rearview mirror.

A few days later, I walked out of the Sheriff's Office and met Chester Whittle in the parking lot.

"Congratulations, Chester. Are you pleased with your new client?" I asked.

He laughed. "Well if it isn't Watauga County's ace detective."

I looked behind me to see who he was talking about. "Where?" I asked, teasing him.

"You sure have put a lot of time into making a case on Underwood," he observed.

I wondered what he was trying to get at. "Just spare me the sob story about how he couldn't possibly be guilty."

"Oh, he's guilty as hell." His comment caught me by surprise.

"What?" I asked, surprised that he would make such a comment off the cuff.

"I don't chew my cabbage twice; you heard me. I said L. C.'s guilty as hell. But that still doesn't prevent him from the right to legal representation."

"How can you do it, Chester? How can you work so hard for him knowing that he's a cold-blooded murderer? How can you sleep at night?"

"I do it because I believe every citizen deserves the right to equal treatment under the law. It's my job to make sure he gets a fair trial and that his rights aren't violated."

"And to do your best to get him off scot-free," I added.

"I will if you don't do your job right," he said grinning.

"And yet there's no one realistically to keep defense attorneys in check. You can go into court and accuse the police of lying, of planting evidence, etc., etc., and it all falls under the noble umbrella of legal representation. That just doesn't hardly seem fair."

"You're confusing me with Johnny Cochran," he said.

"No, your complexion is a little lighter," I replied. "But I do realize that 99 percent of lawyers give the rest of you a bad name."

Chester almost nodded in agreement and caught himself.

Personally, I liked Chester Whittle. He was always friendly and easy to talk to. As a lawyer, he was certainly competent and well-versed. His co-counsel, Bruce Kaplan, was equally competent and sharp as a tack. Bruce would never remotely suggest that his client was guilty, in or out of the courtroom, but he had an otherwise pleasant personality. But until the trial was over, both Chester Whittle and Bruce Kaplan were the adversaries. The enemies, so to speak. I concur with Edmund Burke who defined an enemy as "one who strengthens our nerves and sharpens our skill." Bruce and Chester aimed to do just that.

On October 19, 1995, the sheriff and I took L. C. to the courtroom where he was scheduled to have a bond hearing. Although it was just across the street, we transported him in the Sheriff's car because news reporters and photographers were hovering around like vultures over a field of dying cattle.

L. C.'s attorneys were requesting that the Judge set an amount of bond for L. C. so that he would not have to spend his time awaiting trial behind jail bars.

"Do you think the Judge will set a bond I can make?" L. C. asked Sheriff Lyons and me.

"It's hard to say what the Judge will do," the sheriff answered him, "I really have no idea."

I did not comment, but I doubted that the Judge should allow L. C. to bond out of jail before his trial. Not only did I fear that L. C. would flee; I feared for the safety of many of our witnesses.

The District Attorney called me as the first witness to testify for the State. L. C. was actually smiling at me when I sat down on the witness stand. I pulled the microphone toward me and started answering the District Attorney's questions. Before long, L. C.'s smile began to fade.

"...Detective Sergeant, are you the lead investigator of this case for Watauga County?"

"Yes sir," I answered.

"Based on the results of your investigation, do you have reason to believe that the defendant, Lamont Claxton Underwood, should not have a bond set for his release pending trial?"

"Yes sir."

"And what is the basis for your conclusion?"

"It is my opinion that the defendant's release would endanger the safety of several of the State's potential witnesses."

"And could you explain further to the Court, Detective Sergeant?"

"There are a number of female witnesses who have been involved in personal relationships with the defendant in the past. They have all expressed fears of the defendant."

"Have any of those witnesses described incidents of violence by the defendant in the past?"

"Yes sir. They have described incidents of physical violence and threats, including three who independently stated that they were held down by the defendant, who placed a gun to their head and told them he was going to kill them."

"Are you talking about three different incidents?"

"Yes sir. These events occurred at various times during the defendant's relationships with these women." L. C. was squirming in his chair and whispering frantically to his attorneys.

At the onset of cross-examination, L. C.'s attorney Bruce Kaplan pounced.

"Detective Sergeant May, just who *are* all these fearful women?" he asked superciliously.

I paused to give the State an opportunity to object, but there was none. Jerry Wilson was rummaging through some papers in a file.

I was not about to give the defense any names. "They have requested that their names remain confidential."

Mr. Kaplan sighed dramatically and paused for emphasis. "Sergeant May, I will ask you *again*. What are the names of those witnesses?"

I turned to the Judge and said, "Your honor, I prefer not to divulge their names at this time – for the reason I gave. I am not going to give them that information." At the risk of being held in contempt of court, I had made up my mind.

Judge Ferrell looked down through his bifocals with piercing eyes toward the defense table. He spoke quietly but firmly. "Mr. Kaplan and Mr. Whittle… I am *not* going to compel this witness to give you the names of witnesses whom she believes would be placed in danger."

I looked at Bruce and raised my eyebrows in anticipation of his next question. L. C. continued to whispering to him frantically. They were obviously trying to decide what to do, since the Judge had not made me give them the names of those potential witnesses whose safety would be endangered, should L. C. be released on bond. They were in a bit of a pickle not knowing what exactly they were arguing against.

Attorney Kaplan continued with other questions, and I stressed different reasons why we were opposed to L. C. being released on any bond before trial. On the stand, Agent Don Gale explained not only that L. C. was a flight risk because he had no job and no real family in North Carolina, he also was a threat to himself and others he thought might testify in trial against him. Finally, in an attempt to drive the points home, Don played the recording of the phone call where L. C. paged him and then cursed him thoroughly for attempting to interview Beth Richardson. The sounds of L. C. ranting and raving echoing through the old courtroom drove the points home.

"There will be no release bond set for the defendant," Judge Ferrell ordered.

When Sheriff Lyons and I put L. C. back in the car, he was completely silent. I could tell by the way he held himself that he was furious. We walked him down the hall of the Sheriff's Office and back into the jail. L. C. still had not said one word. Then, in order for the jailer to pat him down before taking him to his cell, the jailer told him to stand up against the door. Steve Wilson and I were watching without comment about two yards away, just to make sure the jailer got him inside safely. Then L. C. broke the silence.

"Hurry up and get me out of here, away from these g*dd*mn sons-o-b*tches!" he said, obviously referring to Steve and me.

"L. C., that's enough," I said calmly. He did not comment further but avoided looking at me as he was led through the door and down the hall to his cell.

"So much for your newfound friendship with L. C.," Steve said to me.

"Yes, that's unfortunate," I said, "and just when we were beginning to bond. Do you think he'll cross me off his Christmas card list?"

"I don't think you'll be getting a new blender this year."

L. C. never spoke to me after that day. He did, however, say several things *about* me.

But L. C. was not getting along with anyone really. The entire time L. C. was in our jail awaiting trial, he complained. He griped about the food, about the no-smoking policy, about his lack of exercise, so on and so forth. He complained so much about his back (I guess his condition was aggravated by the fact that he only had time to rest as opposed to shag dancing) that the jailer on duty made him a doctor's appointment.

A uniformed deputy drove him to the doctor's office. When he returned, he told me that L. C. criticized everything he did, including the way he put the handcuffs on, the way he fastened his seatbelt, the way he drove. L. C. apparently presumed himself to be the more knowledgeable and seasoned police officer. The deputy listened to L. C. politely and told me everything he could remember when he got back to the Sheriff's Office.

"So how did Paula May get her job?" L. C. asked him.

"What do you mean?" the deputy said.

"Well, she made it up the ladder awful quick. Whose *ss did she kiss? The Sheriff's?"

"Actually, she's been here a lot longer than I have. I think she's worked hard to get where she is."

"I hate that b*tch," L. C. said.

So, in spite of L. C.'s initial promises to me that he would be a model prisoner if we would not send him to Central Prison for safekeeping, he failed to keep his word. One day not long after L. C.'s bond hearing, one of the jailers approached me.

"I just wondered if you know who the woman is that keeps sending L. C. packages?" he said.

I assumed it was his pseudo-mom Barbara Childress. "Is it from Ohio?" I asked.

"No, these are coming from Salisbury. But there's a reason why I'm asking."

"Okay," I said, "What is it?"

"She's smuggling him contraband. Cigarettes and matches in magazines."

"What?" I asked.

"Come to the back with me and I'll show you."

I walked back into the jail to see the package that had just arrived. The jailer had already opened the package to inspect it, which is procedure. The jailer took out a magazine and flipped through the pages. I did not see anything out of the ordinary. But then he held the magazine up and shook it over the desk. Loose tobacco and matches fell onto the surface of the desk."

"Unbelievable," I said.

"This is not the first time she's done this. She's also sending him letters. Do you know who she is?"

"No, but I'm gonna find out," I said.

I looked at the packaging. The return label did not have a name listed, but indicated that the package was mailed from a particular post office box in Spencer, North Carolina, a small community just outside the city limits of Salisbury.

I notified Don and Terry with the hopes that we may have found another associate who could have some personal information about L. C. So, they drove to the Spencer Post Office and discovered that the return address from the packages was a post office box rented by a female. It did not take long for Don and Terry to discover that the woman who had been sending L. C. contraband in the jail was a civilian employee of the Salisbury Police Department.

"Well, well," I said. "What is she to L.C? A girlfriend?" I asked.

"We'll have to find out," Don said.

"I think Sheriff Lyons and I should talk to Chief Jacobs about his employees sending contraband to our jail."

"Whatever you think you need to do."

"Let me talk with the Sheriff and see what he wants me to do."

"Okay, just let us know."

"In any case, I'll probably be down tomorrow," I said.

"I figured so. We'll check her schedule to see when she's working."

"Okay, see you guys tomorrow."

Steve and I left about midmorning the next day, January 5, 1996. We met Don and Terry at the Sheriff's Office, then Steve and I left to locate the woman's house.

We knocked on the door, and Dee, a medium-build, middle-aged brunette answered the door. She looked very tired. Steve identified himself to her and asked if we could come in and talk with her. She told us that she was willing to talk to us, but she was getting ready to leave to pick her daughter up at school. She asked if we would come back about 2:30, when it was more convenient for her. We agreed.

I suggested that we meet back up with Don and Terry for lunch. So, we ate that day at Spencer's, the same restaurant where L. C. had taken Wanda Hornbuckle on December 6, 1993, to make Kay jealous. They served what came to become one of my all-time favorite salads, their "cheese-steak salad," and it was made with various types of lettuce and other greens, tomatoes, cucumbers, croutons, and all the normal salad ingredients, but it was topped with the most tender shaved steak and melted American, Swiss, and cheddar cheese. On top of that was a layer of crispy fried onions. Spencer's extra-sweet homemade honey mustard dressing topped it off perfectly. I preferred it over the barbecue pork offered at diners on seemingly every corner in Salisbury, which we had eaten at or picked up food from for the past two years.

While we ate lunch, Steve's pager went off. He got up and went to the pay phone in the lobby. After a few minutes, he came back to the table and said to all of us in general, "You guys won't believe this."

"What?" we asked.

"Guess who just ran my tag number?"

"Not Dee."

"She *did*. She called the agency where she works and had someone run my tag as soon as we left her house."

"I guess she wasn't in such a big hurry to go pick up her daughters after all."

"Guess not," he said. I knew that when an SBI agent's license plate is run, an immediate notification is made to the SBI district office. The person running the license plate, however, has no idea because the plates are registered confidentially.

"Maybe she has more in common with L. C. than we thought," Terry said. "Neither one of 'em will hesitate to run a tag for personal reasons."

"Apparently not," Steve agreed.

After lunch, Steve and I returned to Dee's residence. It was 2:30 p.m. She again answered the door and invited us inside. Her three teenage daughters were present inside the house at the time. She led Steve and me through the living area to a dimly lit den. Although her Christmas tree was still up and decorated, the house looked rather dismal.

"I prefer to have my daughters with me if you don't mind," she said.

"Really? Well, that's totally up to you, ma'am," Steve told her.

Steve confronted her then with copies of the magazine packages mailed to L. C., and photos of the tobacco and matches smuggled inside them. She was immediately defensive and denied sending the contraband, in spite of the fact that the handwriting was very similar to the letters she had also mailed him and acknowledged.

Steve questioned her matter-of-factly, "Ma'am, do you agree that the handwriting on the one you said you mailed is remarkably similar to the handwriting on the packaging you say you did not mail?"

She squirmed a little and said, "Yes, they do look similar."

"But yet you're saying that you didn't send those as well?"

"No, I did not."

"Well, ma'am do you also deny sending the package with the typewritten label?" he asked her.

"I did not send that one either," Dee said, and I noticed that her complexion had suddenly become very pink.

Steve spoke to her as if he was speaking to a child who had been caught with her hand inside the cookie jar. "Ma'am, it's obvious that you at least addressed the packages which contained the tobacco. Ma'am, we spoke with the postal employee who handled one of those packages, and he was able to identify you."

"Well, I'm sorry, but you've gotten some wrong information," she said. Steve looked at me, and I shrugged. She continued to deny sending L. C. anything other than the first package she acknowledged.

It was my turn to try. "Ma'am, if you didn't send those packages, then there's no reason we should find your fingerprints on any of the materials inside. Is that what you're saying?"

"That's right," she said.

I let the matter drop for a moment and then asked her, "How long have you known L. C?"

"Oh, for a long time. I know he was a good person, and I know he's innocent of the crime he's charged with."

"How is that you know L. C?" I asked.

"I worked with him temporarily one time. I considered him a friend, and I still do. I know he's not capable of doing anything violent towards another person."

"Ma'am, I assume he didn't tell you about the times he's threatened and assaulted women in his past relationships?"

"No, and I don't believe he's ever done anything like that."

"Well, you are certainly entitled to believe anything you want. But it never hurts to keep an open mind and be extra careful. Would he really be worth losing your job over? And what if he IS guilty? Have you considered your daughters' safety, not to mention your own?"

"Is this a *criminal* violation?" Dee asked, somewhat changing the subject, "I mean, sending cigarettes to the jail?"

"No, it isn't," I told her honestly. "It's simply a policy violation, but we are here to find the truth and see that it does not happen again."

"Well, I'm not going to change my statement," she said. *I predict you will.*

"Okay then. We'll leave you alone. But there is one more thing. Just out of curiosity, why did you run my tag number when we came by earlier?" Steve asked her.

Her blush deepened. "…Oh, I just wanted to make sure you were who you said you were."

"Okay, then," Steve said, "I guess I can understand that."

She did not even ask how we knew she had run it. I took a business card out of my wallet and handed it to her. "Here is my business card with my pager and office phone numbers on it. Agent Wilson will give you his as well. If you decide you want to talk with us later, just give us a call."

"All right," she said.

We left her house and drove directly to her place of employment.

On the way, I told Steve, "I just can't believe she would lie like that. She knows we know she did it."

"I know."

"And she lied to us right in front of her own kids. They can probably tell she's lying too. What kind of message does that send?"

Steve shook his head sadly.

"So do you think we're doing the right thing by going to talk to the Chief?"

"It's all we can do," Steve said. "It might have been different if she'd admitted to it and promised not to do it again, but that didn't happen."

Chief Jacobs was shocked when we told him who we believed had been sending letters and packages to L. C., not to mention the cigarette contraband.

"Dee knows better than to get involved with an inmate," he said. "She could technically lose her job just for fraternizing with him. And it's just that much worse that he used to work here and is charged with First Degree Murder."

"Well, out of professional courtesy, we wanted you to know what was going on. But when we approached her just a little while ago, she denied having mailed Underwood the contraband."

"She denied it?"

"Yeah, but I think we caught her really off-guard. She didn't know what to do or say, and she wanted her kids present when we talked with her. But we feel certain that she did it. Her post office box is listed on the return address, and the handwriting is remarkably similar to samples of her own handwriting."

Her supervisor asked, "Do you think it would mess up your investigation if I asked her about it myself? After all, it's a violation of our employment policy."

"Not at all. That's why we're letting you know, so you can take any action you feel you need to."

"Well I will certainly notify you as to any statement she makes to me. And I do appreciate your informing me about this. You know, I have had problems with her in the past, come to think of it. And I don't need these kinds of problems."

He apparently was not going to delve into whatever problems those were, so we did not ask. But I knew that his department was somewhat split already on those who knew L. C. had committed these murders and those who would never believe it. He asked that we keep him informed of what we learned, and we quickly agreed.

"She's gonna call," I predicted.

The next morning, Steve's pager went off. A short while later, Steve and I met Don and Terry at the Sheriff's Office, and we all waited for Dee to arrive. She walked into the office and looked even paler than she did the day before. She must have noticed that I was looking at her because the first thing she said was, "I know I don't look too good. I didn't get any sleep last night."

"Let's go in the conference room where we can talk privately," I said. Terry led us into an empty room and closed the door.

Once we sat down, she could not seem to wait to start talking.

"Yesterday, I was scared to tell you the truth. I want to tell you the truth now." I nodded, not about to chastise her for wasting our time the day before.

"I didn't want to tell you in front of my children, but I did send the tobacco, matches, and rolling paper to L. C.," Dee said. I nodded again.

"L. C. asked me to do it. In fact, he *begged* me to. He is so upset. And I didn't think about it being any kind of violation. I just thought it would either get through or it would get thrown away. L. C. said if anybody got in trouble, it would be him. He just wanted me to try. He was talking suicidal and so crazy. He said he couldn't bear thinking about the months ahead, knowing he was there for something he didn't do. His handwriting had gotten so shaky I could hardly read it. …I just thought the cigarettes would help calm him down." She looked down at her shoes and waited for one of us to speak.

"When did he first ask you to send him the cigarettes?" Terry asked.

"First, he told me to send the cigarettes in a shampoo bottle. But the jailer said he could only have a clear bottle with clear liquid. Then he told me how to hide them inside magazines. I wouldn't have never figured out how to do it on my own."

"How long have you known L.C?"

"I worked with him a lot. He saved my behind a few times. I had to let him know I believe in him. I feel bad for him."

"So you still don't believe L. C. committed either murder?" Steve asked her.

"No, I don't. But I'm sorry about how I treated ya'll yesterday. L. C. said so much about Paula May, that I was hostile to her from the beginning." Then she looked at me. "But I'm sorry about that now."

"It's okay," I assured her. "It wasn't the first time, and it sure won't be the last. ...So what did L. C. say about me?"

"He said you were the arresting officer, and he doesn't think you're being fair and above board. He said there must be something fishy going on because he was innocent. He said you made up evidence and just theorized about him instead of looking for real evidence. But I'm the one who was unreasonable, not you all. I just felt backed into a corner in front of my children."

Steve responded, "Well, ma'am, that's why we offered to talk to you alone. Outside the presence of your kids."

"I know. I know you did. I was just being silly. ...I had a nervous breakdown once. My boss made me see the department psychologist. I was in the hospital for a month, and I haven't really gotten over it. My daughter stayed with me when I was in the hospital, and she's very protective.

That's why she wanted to stay yesterday. But sometimes she makes poor decisions because she is so sensitive."

"Dee, did you tell your daughters the truth about what you did?"

She blushed and looked back down at her shoes again. "No. I guess I should, though."

"That's your prerogative," Steve told her.

She handed me a manila envelope and explained, "I brought you all the letters he's written. And there's also a picture he colored of you, Mrs. May."

I skimmed through the long letters and found a page torn out of a child's coloring book. It was a female monster labeled "Demona." He had colored the picture and written at the top of the page, "Paula May. The name fits her too." It was not a flattering rendering.

"Don," I said later, "I think I'm gaining on you in the popularity contest with L. C."

"Nah," he said, "You might be a close second but you'll never make the top of his list. That position belongs to me."

In the letters, L. C. gave very detailed instructions on how to smuggle cigarettes into the jail for him. She promised to stay in touch with us, and she promised to keep giving us copies of his future letters to her.

On January 12, 1996, Dee composed a memorandum to Sheriff Lyons, sending a copy also to her agency head, and to Steve and me. She apologized for her actions and stated that it would not happen again.

Dee maintained contact with Steve and me (mostly Steve) by phone. She even provided us with the letters L. C. had mailed to her since he had been incarcerated. I realized that if L. C. knew we were reading his letters, he would have had a conniption. The letters L. C. wrote were certainly enlightening about L. C.'s feelings toward me. I had no idea that a grown man would spend so much time in thought about me. I still was not flattered.

During one conversation between her and L. C., Dee happened to mention casually something L. C. had said to her on the phone. I think she was reluctant to mention it earlier because she did not want to be subpoenaed to testify against L. C. during the trial.

He kind of asked me to alibi him," she informed us nonchalantly.

"He what?" Steve asked.

"You know when all that stuff was going on during the first couple weeks of December in 1993?"

"Yes."

"Well, L. C. asked me… would I… could I say that he… that he and I were involved. In a relationship, you know, that we were seeing each other during that time."

"Do you know why he asked you to do that?"

"I guess so the police wouldn't think he was so obsessed with Kay Weden."

"And what did you tell L. C. when he asked you to do that?" Steve asked.

"No. I told him no, that I couldn't lie. And he said that was okay, and that he wasn't mad at me for not doing it," she explained.

CHAPTER TWENTY-SEVEN

*"Woe unto you, lawyers! for ye have
taken away the key of knowledge:
ye entered not in yourselves, and them that were
entering in ye hindered" (Luke 11:52)*

Tom Rusher, one of the best prosecutors in the state of North Carolina, was prepared. We had reviewed this case diligently for months. By this time, he had prosecuted over a hundred murder cases, several of them capital cases. A graduate of the University of the North Carolina School of Law, he began his career as an Assistant District Attorney in the 24th Judicial District in January of 1971. In 1982, he was elected to the office of District Attorney of the 24h Judicial District, and in every subsequent DA election since that time. Tom was a man of average build and above average abilities. He was intelligent, well-educated, and articulate, although we did not agree on every decision he made in every case.

His Assistant District Attorney, Gerald "Jerry" Wilson, a tall middle-aged man with a thick head of dark hair and a thick brown mustache, was neither thin nor heavy, and could frequently be seen wearing his favorite suspenders. Jerry earned a Bachelor of Science in History at the East Tennessee State University before earning his law degree at Wake Forest University in Winston Salem, North Carolina.

If it was morning, Jerry would be having a cup of coffee and two Little Debbie snack cakes, the breakfast of champions. He smoked like a freight train, all the while working intently on some case. I would usually find him reading case law through the half-lens reading glasses he wore down on his nose. Jerry was straightforward and to the point. He laughed occasionally at my dry sense of humor, and had always taken the time to discuss a case with me or answer a question. To a jury, he argued with common sense, which accompanied by his commanding presence and deep voice, conveyed confidence and conviction.

Together, Tom and Jerry (not to be confused with the animated cat and mouse duo of the same names) had proven themselves worthy opponents of any defense team I had ever observed in action. Tom and Jerry had prosecuted many of my other criminal cases in the past. I was comfortable with their style of questioning and knew how they tended to ask questions. In this case, I had already spent several hours on the stand defending the first search warrant we executed on L. C.'s house on February 1, 1994. Although I alone had sworn, or rather affirmed, to the affidavit of probable cause, Steve, Don, and Terry were present at the hearing. Well aware they were glad that it was me in the hot seat defending the search warrant, their presence and support allowed us to present a united front. Certainly, the application was a culmination of all the collective work we had accomplished both individually and jointly at that point. In the end, the search warrant was upheld, but the process was tedious and wearing. Every item seized pursuant to that search warrant was ruled admissible, including the electrical tape from L. C.'s utility room and the trunk mat from L. C.'s Monte Carlo where Agent Bendure found the human head hairs.

On Friday, June 27, 1997, the long-awaited trial began. I used the restroom one last time before entering the courtroom. My stomach churned as I realized that everything we had worked for in the past three and a half years was about to reach its zenith. I thought about the confidence the sheriff had placed in me, the countless hours we had worked each week, the extensive number of miles we had traveled, and the taxpayers' money that had been used to fund our investigative efforts. I even wondered briefly if I had done my very best. It was a grave responsibility, my role as lead detective in the Gunnarsson homicide. Years of rigorous work on this most solemn matter was about to end in either triumph or defeat; there was no middle ground. Nevertheless, it was not the score that concerned me so; it was the possibility that L. C. Underwood would go free... free to kill again.

The trial was presided over by the Honorable Forrest A. Ferrell, a 1963 cum laude graduate of the University of North Carolina School of Law in Chapel Hill, who had majored in History at High Point College from which he graduated in 1960. Judge Ferrell practiced law in the City of Hickory until he was elected as a Superior Court Judge in 1975. He had presided over countless criminal and civil proceedings for more than three years before I was born. A well-coiffed and distinguished southern gentleman with silver hair and a strong jawline, Judge Ferrell made for quite an imposing figure on the bench in his stately black robe. His quiet but confident supremacy was respected by both the State and the defense.

After the tedious process of jury selection was completed, opening arguments began. I sat on the front row between Don and Terry. Steve sat directly behind me. He leaned forward and whispered, "Stay tuned for the Tom and Jerry Show."

I glanced at my watch. It was 10:58 a.m. The jury was fully empaneled, and Tom Rusher, dressed in a conservative gray suit and navy tie, began making opening statements. He walked confidently over to the jury box, and without smiling, spoke with clarity and tenacity.

"Ladies and gentlemen, our purpose representing the State will be, insofar as we can, to produce before you a model of things that actually happened not only in this county but in Rowan County in the year 1993..."

Tom presented three and a half years of investigation into a chronological narrative that told the story of a jealous and pathological killer who robbed Kay Weden of her lover, her mother, and her peace of mind.

For the defense, Chester Whittle took his turn then, concluding with the following:

"...Thus our contention, ladies and gentlemen, our contention is that he's not guilty. And one thing they will never explain and *can* never be explained is how L. C. Underwood, with a known disability got up to the second floor of an apartment building, left no evidence there, got a nude man out, got him down the stairs, got him into the trunk of his car, got him up here to Boone, naked in the trunk of his car, somehow parks his car, gets him out, marches him up, because we know he couldn't carry him, and then shot him. There will never be an explanation for that. All anybody will ever be able to do is guess. We contend he's not guilty. Thank you."

It was high noon, and Court was adjourned for lunch until 1:30 p.m.

The first witness for the State was Dr. John Butts, Chief Medical Examiner for North Carolina. Dr. Butts testified to the results of Viktor Gunnarsson's autopsy. He estimated the date of Viktor's death to be in the vicinity of December 4, 1993. He further testified that Viktor's stomach contained identifiable bits of baked potato, which we knew was part of his last meal at Blue Bay Seafood Restaurant with Kay Weden and Catherine Miller. Then in spite of the defense's objections, Judge Ferrell allowed Dr. Butts to introduce the disturbing eight-by-ten-inch color photographs of Viktor's body, specifically the face and head area where the gunshot wounds were found. I watched the jurors' faces for signs of what they may be thinking, but they were unreadable.

Daniel Johansson, who had traveled all the way from Sweden for the trial, took the stand next. He alone represented Viktor's family and friends in Sweden, who could not afford to travel to the United States for the trial. Daniel cried aloud for the loss of his dear friend, and his pain was palpable. He glared at L. C., but L. C. would not meet his eye. Several jurors shed their own tears in sympathy for Daniel, Viktor's elderly parents and his sister.

"He was my very good friend. I loved him, and now I will never see him again. His mother and his father and his sister also loved him very much. But they will never, ever see him again. And all because of that man…" The defense attorneys objected, but Daniel had made his point.

As with most trials, there were both victories and disappointments along the way. Most discouraging to me was the fact that Judge Ferrell would not allow us to call as witnesses all the women who had been involved in personal relationships with L. C., even though they were victims of his pattern of violence. Crossed off our extensive witness list were L. C.'s former girlfriends Pam, Jeannie, Linda, and Monica, a significant victory for the defense. The petite brunette Victim-Witness Coordinator Sherry Wise and I had worked hard to persuade each of them to come to court. Once they had made up their minds to testify to all L. C. had put each of them through, these strong and successful women were ready to stand up for themselves. They left partly relieved; party disappointed.

The most significant victory for the State occurred when Judge Ferrell allowed us to introduce the Catherine Miller murder and all related evidence, despite the fact that L. C had not yet been charged with that offense. Judge Ferrell based his decision on North Carolina General Statute 8C-1, Rule 404(b), which states, "Evidence of other crimes, wrongs, or acts is not admissible to prove the character of a person in order to show that he acted in conformity therewith. It may, however, be admissible for other purposes, such as proof of motive, opportunity, intent, preparation, plan, knowledge, identity, or absence of mistake, entrapment, or accident." The Catherine Miller murder evidence was allowed for purposes of demonstrating proof of motive, plan, knowledge, and identity.

When Kay Weden began testifying, the jurors listened intently. As she conveyed the terror she suffered in the spring of 1993, the anonymous and threatening letters and phone calls, the shooting into Jason's bedroom, the ugly vandalism to her home and her car, L. C. remained expressionless and motionless. Kay cried tears of frustration when she described how often she had racked her brain trying to determine who would torment her and her son so. She described dysfunctionalities and struggles of her relationship with L. C. and his bizarre behavior. She cried tears of profound agony when she testified of her mother's death and then Viktor's disappearance and death. Occasionally L. C. whispered to his attorneys but mainly sat quietly, looking straight ahead or down at his notepad, never at Kay directly. Throughout the entire trial, L. C. never shed a single tear, this lack of feeling from a man who so often had sworn to love Kay Weden more than life itself.

When Kay finally stepped down from the witness stand several hours later, I met her at the door of the courtroom and accompanied her down the hall to the ladies' restroom. I hugged her and told her I was proud of her.

"I did not mean to get so emotional," she apologized. "It's just that after months – no years – of waiting to say what has been on my heart and mind for so long, well, it was all just so overwhelming."

"You have nothing to apologize for, Kay," I told her. "You held it together. You were articulate. And everyone in that courtroom could see that you were being honest. Your anguish was felt by everyone... well, everyone except L. C. That man has no conscience whatsoever."

"No he doesn't. And no matter what happens," she told me, "I feel somewhat cleansed just by being able to testify, to tell my story to the jury in front of L. C. Are you sure I did okay?"

"I'm sure. All you were asked to do was tell the truth, and that is what you did."

"L. C.'s attorneys tried to make me look bad," she added.

"That was par for the course, but they were not successful. You came across as a woman terrorized by a jealous man who robbed you of your family and of Viktor, and that's exactly what happened."

"But they tried to make me look like I had led him on, that I was toying with his feelings and dating every man I ever saw behind L. C.'s back."

"But they failed, Kay. You made it clear that you had repeatedly tried to break up with him, and he just refused to leave you alone."

"I hope the jurors don't think I'm some kind of floozy," she said, as she wiped a stray tear out from under her eye.

"If I had to guess, Kay, I would think that they likely are putting themselves into your shoes and thinking about how they would handle all the things L. C. put *you* through. They were tuned in to every word you said, and were visibly sympathetic, some even shedding tears with you."

"Paula, I want to thank you… for everything. I realize now just how much you and Steve and Don and Terry did on this case. I want you to know I will always be grateful." I walked with her back to the District Attorney's Office.

All witnesses, excluding Kay and the investigators, were sequestered at the request of the defense. The State's witnesses waited in the District Attorney's office until it was time for them to testify. Ironically, the circumstances were such that after Kay testified and just before Rex Keller was to testify, he and Kay were left alone in a small room in the DA's office for a short period of time. As I walked back into the office, it dawned on me that Kay had been left alone with the man who had made anonymous threatening phone calls to her during the spring of 1993.

"Oh good grief!" I said aloud. "I didn't know the two of you were alone in here!" But Kay seemed fine. She was relaxed on a small love seat, and Rex Keller was sitting in a straight-backed chair by the window."

"Oh, it's okay," Kay said. "We've already talked about things, and what happened was a long time ago."

"I apologized to Kay," Keller said, "and I really mean it. I'm sorry. I wish this whole thing had never happened."

Keller testified effectively. Although the defense attorneys brought up his criminal past at every opportunity, he was forthcoming about what he had done, and how L. C. had involved him in the entire case. The part of his testimony that set Bruce Kaplan and Chester Whittle squirming, however, was his telling about the cassette recording he had made at L. C.'s request, pretending to be L. C.'s stepbrothers acknowledging receipt of the guns. L. C.'s attorney Bruce Kaplan particularly lost his cool when Keller testified that L. C. said he gave the tape to his lawyers.

Judge Ferrell excused the jurors and proceeded to question Bruce and Chester concerning their knowledge of the tape. He pointed out, unnecessarily, that hiding or destroying evidence was a serious offense, particularly for attorneys to commit. One of them mumbled something about needing their own attorney for representation if they were being accused of something illegal. Judge Ferrell gave them less than forty-eight hours to be in Court with their own counsel and respond to the issue of the cassette recording in a hearing outside the jury's presence. Judge Ferrell ordered them to produce the cassette tape in question at the hearing if they had it.

It was nice to be a spectator in a court hearing for a change and merely observe. When the time arrived, local attorney Jeff Hedrick appeared to represent Bruce Kaplan and Chester Whittle, an ironic turn of events. Attorney Hedrick responded that neither Chester Whittle nor Bruce Kaplan currently had the cassette in question in their possession, nor do they know where it was at present. They would not admit or deny having had the tape in the past. Judge Ferrell would not compel them to say anything more than whether they had it at present. But there was no doubt that wherever the tape had been, it was now gone for good. Tom Rusher said the best we could hope for was that the jury believed Keller, and that such a tape did exist, once upon a time. I suspected that L. C. had given the tape to one of his attorneys in Salisbury prior to being arrested but had no way of knowing for certain. Regardless, I knew we would never see or hear that tape recording.

In spite of a few disappointments, there were brilliant moments during the trial. Jason Weden's testimony was one of them. While under cross-examination, Jason answered embarrassing questions about his use of alcohol and marijuana. The defense attorneys, in an attempt to discredit him as much as possible, asked Jason how much alcohol and illegal drugs he used and from whom he obtained them, bringing the subject up at every opportunity. I knew that Jason had experimented with alcohol and marijuana, but to my knowledge that was the extent of his use.

My closest friend Charlene, a skilled, experienced, and expressive prosecutor in District Court, had reminded me on multiple occasions that a lawyer should never ask a question to which he or she does not already know the answer.

"Isn't it true that you were the cause of most of the problems between L. C. and your mother?" Bruce Kaplan asked Jason accusingly.

"No, not that I know of," he said.

"Wasn't your drinking beer a disagreeable issue between your mom and L. C?"

Jason calmly answered, "No. L. C. is the one who bought me the beer." Bruce moved speedily on to another question, but the District Attorney brought it right back up for clarification on Redirect.

Tom Rusher asked Jason, "Son, did you testify earlier that L. C. Underwood, Master Police Officer and School

Resource Officer, purchased and provided alcoholic beer to you?"

Jason answered, "Yes sir, he did."

"And how old were you at that time, Jason?"

"Fifteen or sixteen." It was news to me as well as to Bruce and Chester.

"And did Master Police Officer L. C. Underwood know how old you were when he purchased and provided the beer to you?"

"Yes sir, he did."

Both Shirley Twitty and Wanda Hornbuckle were strong witnesses for the State as well. Each of them described in detail how L. C. had deliberately used them to stalk Kay. Again, the defense attorneys tried to make them look like immoral women who were either manipulated by the investigators or who outright lied about L. C. Underwood. Yet I trusted that the jurors could see the glaringly obvious truth.

Steve was the first of the four of us to testify. He stood facing the jury, talking easily, with his back to the defense. The jurors nodded and made eye contact with him as he distinctly described the crime scene in perfect detail, using large photographs, diagrams, maps, and extensive measurements.

"You were well prepared," Jerry told him during recess.

"Well, I've been preparing for over three years," he responded.

Terry testified to the various locations in Salisbury and Rowan County, which he also described thoroughly. Then Tom asked Terry how tall he was and how much he weighed. He asked him what Viktor's physical size was, according to the missing person police report. Terry was significantly taller and slightly heavier than Viktor. Then Tom introduced into evidence the various photographs of Terry inside the trunk of the Monte Carlo in Stacy Ward's junkyard. Although it was not quite as good as a physical demonstration of Terry in a real trunk in the courtroom, the photos were effective. It certainly prevented the defense from arguing to the jury against what they could see with their own eyes. A couple of the jurors squirmed in their seats as Terry described how miserable he was in the trunk of that Monte Carlo. Undoubtedly, they were imagining Viktor as he was likely bound and gagged in the freezing trunk for the two-and-a-half-hour haul to Deep Gap and the end of his life.

Don's testimony evoked a visible response from L. C. I knew when L. C. sat up straight in his chair and whispered intently to his attorneys that he wanted them to eviscerate Don on the stand. Although they did their best during cross-examination to make Don out to be an unprofessional, vindictive tyrant, Don remained as calm as always, even when accused of trying to frame L. C. and of manipulating every witness in the case, including Terry, Steve, and me. I watched L. C.'s facial muscles twitch as he glared at Don. I saw the perspiration bead at L. C.'s temple and trickle down his cheek. His hatred was palpable. Don was seemingly unaffected.

Although we did not have L. C.'s guns to analyze and introduce as evidence, witnesses did testify that L. C. owned the guns in question and had them in his possession prior to the homicides. One such witness was an elderly man who owned a pawn shop in Salisbury, specifically the pawn shop where L. C. purchased the Dan Wesson .22 caliber revolver. The shop owner did not intend to be funny. And yet…

"Sir, you've sold an awful lot of guns, haven't you?" the defense attorney asked.

"Yes sir," he replied.

"So… How it is possible that you could remember for certain every single person who has been in your pawn shop and purchased a gun?"

"Well, I don't think I *can* remember *every* person…" The defense attorneys were visibly pleased with his answer. They did not want us to put the weapon that had killed Viktor Gunnarsson's in L. C.'s hands at any given time.

"Then do you *really* specifically recall *exactly* who it was that came into your pawn shop way back in November of 1990 and bought a Dan Wesson .22 caliber revolver?"

"Oh yes sir, I remember that," the elderly man replied, trying to be helpful.

"You're one hundred percent certain about that?" he asked, skeptically.

"Yes sir. It was L. C. Underwood, my man on the beat. I'll never forget him. He was always just an awful nice person. And he told me when he bought that gun that if I ever needed anything, he'd be looking out for me." He went on and on about L. C. and how well he knew him. I thought the defense attorneys ought to have quit while they were just so far behind. But they did not.

"But you don't have any records to testify from, do you?" the defense attorney asked knowingly.

"No sir."

"Then how can you know exactly when Mr. Underwood purchased a gun from you? And how can you be sure it was Mr. Underwood who bought that specific gun at that specific time?"

"'Cause I did have my records till your private detective came and took 'em away from me." I actually heard giggles in the courtroom. We had obtained the same sales records, but had only made copies and left the pawn shop owner his originals.

"No further questions," the defense attorneys said simultaneously.

The State did prove through physical evidence and the testimony of the SBI crime laboratory analysts the matters that *should* have been proven in court in the spring of 1993: L. C. himself had perpetrated the terrorizing acts against Kay and Jason. Easily proven were the facts that L. C. authored the threatening letters, instigated the threatening phone calls, and stalked Kay relentlessly. Circumstantially, although L. C.'s .22 caliber rifle was unaccounted for, he undoubtedly used it to fire into Kay's house that night, knowingly near Jason's bed.

I could not help but wonder if L. C. had been charged with those offenses in 1993, would he have murdered Viktor Gunnarsson? Would he have murdered Catherine Miller still? Could Kay have dissociated herself from L. C. for good? I was reminded of a verse from the Old Testament, a verse I had contemplated since I first read the letter Kay wrote to the Salisbury Police Chief demanding that the investigation against L. C. cease, when she was so confident of L. C.'s innocence.

"Because sentence against an evil work is not executed speedily, therefore the heart of the sons of men is fully set in them to do evil" (Ecclesiastes 8:11). Perhaps the murders of Viktor Gunnarsson and Catherine Miller could have been prevented. But speculation at this point was moot.

It was my turn to testify. I stood at the witness stand and looked toward the clerk.

"Do you swear – I'm sorry, you wish to affirm, don't you, Detective Sergeant May?"

"Yes please." I took Matthew 5:34 literally. *Swear not at all...*

"Do you affirm that you will tell the truth, the whole truth, and nothing but the truth, so help you?"

I looked directly at the jury and answered, "I do."

My testimony began with the discovery of Viktor Gunnarsson's body on January 7, 1993, and ended with the statements L. C. had made in my presence up until the trial. I testified to the chain of custody on nearly every piece of evidence that was admitted. I testified to every significant interview I had conducted, every search, and every tactic we had employed during the investigation. Finally, I testified to the hair found in L. C.'s trunk mat, those hairs that had been submitted to the FBI for mitochondrial DNA analysis.

FBI Agent Joe Dizzino was one of the final witnesses. After the firearms experts testified to the gun and bullet evidence, after the latent experts testified, after the questioned documents experts testified, after the crime scene technicians testified, and after John Bendure testified to the microscopic hair match, Agent Joe Dizzino took the stand. Concisely and efficiently, Agent Dizzino explained how mitochondrial DNA from the hair found in L. C.'s trunk mat matched Viktor Gunnarsson's DNA, and how it could only be Viktor's hair since no other members of his family had ever been to the United States, much less to Salisbury, North Carolina.

"The State calls Beth Richardson to the stand," Tom announced. She was the last witness for the State. Her testimony ended with a point Tom wanted to drive home.

"Ms. Richardson, did L. C. make comments to you concerning the death of either or both Viktor Gunnarsson and/or Catherine Miller?"

"Yes he did," Beth responded.

"...What did he say to you, ma'am, concerning his arrest?"

"In November of 1994, he stated to me *that if he had not been such a good police officer,* he would have been arrested a long time ago."

"All right. Ma'am, was that the first time he had made that comment to you?"

"That was the first time."

"How many times thereafter did he make a similar comment to you?"

"Dozens of times."

"Thank you."

The jurors looked at L. C. One juror in particular looked at him with contempt in her eyes. I was encouraged to see that they were all paying attention.

At the close of State's evidence and outside the Jury's presence, Attorney Kaplan stood up and moved for a dismissal of the case. He argued that the State may have alleged a lot of things, but had failed to present evidence that L. C. kidnapped and murdered Viktor Gunnarsson.

"...Your honor, the State has alleged everything under the sun about my client. They claim he stole a gun from Lincoln County Sheriff's Office, that he committed assault by pointing a gun at Jason Weden, that he communicated threats to Kay Weden by phone and by letter, that he broke and entered Kay Weden's house without her permission, that he committed the offense of stalking, and that he even did something to his dog! But, your Honor, they have not charged him with any of that! They have charged Mr. Underwood with First Degree Kidnapping and First Degree Murder! They are labeling my client as a murderer, but they have not proven him to be a murderer. They have labeled him to be all those other things, and they have blamed my client for everything in the world!" Kaplan went on and on accusing us of unjustly making L. C. out to be a terrible person.

Finally, Tom Rusher was allowed to respond to Bruce's motion. Tom argued on behalf of the State that we had indeed presented more than enough evidence to let the Jury decide whether or not L. C. Underwood was guilty of kidnapping and murder. "I understand that the defendant doesn't like being labeled for *what he is*, but..." I could see the sting on L. C.'s face, but he continued to stare straight ahead. Tom continued, "We don't blame L. C. Underwood for *every*thing in the world, but we do blame him for *what he did*..." I saw the muscles twitching in L. C.'s jaw again as he continued to stare straight ahead.

Judge Ferrell denied the motions for a mistrial and dismissal. It was the defense team's turn to present evidence. I had waited a long time to see L. C. take the stand. Although he could exercise his Fifth Amendment rights and not testify, I could not see how a plausible defense could be created without him.

The defense, at 11:22 a.m. on July 18, 1997, requested that all the attorneys meet with Judge Ferrell in chambers. We were back in session at 11:26 a.m. I braced myself for the extensive hyperbole they were sure to claim in L. C.'s defense. So, I was shocked when, at 11:27 a.m., Attorney Kaplan stood and stated to the Court, "The defense rests." L. C. sat there with his head down and did not move a muscle. I could not believe they were not going to put L. C. on the stand. They were not going to present any evidence of any kind.

"What kind of a defensive strategy is that?" I asked Charlene in the DA's Office. She was adept at objective reasoning.

"They don't want to risk putting him on the stand," she said, "and I can understand that to a degree. He's unpredictable."

"But now he has no defense," I told her.

"Maybe they think we simply didn't prove our case," Don chimed in, having just walked through the door. "It's the State's burden. Sometimes that's enough of a defense."

"Well, if the jury can't find him guilty with all the testimony they've heard in *this* case, then no one can ever be found guilty," Charlene asserted. "It's true that juries are unpredictable. But the evidence in this case is overwhelming, and this jury is very attentive." Don did not appear quite as convinced.

"You're worried, Don, I can see that you are," I said to him.

Don looked at me with his big brown eyes and shrugged. I knew he was uptight. Don was making me doubt, despite Charlene's assessment.

At 11:30 a.m., Judge Ferrell took requests from the attorneys for specific jury instructions. The defense requested instructions be given to the jury for Second Degree Murder. The Judge declined, and announced that he would be instructing the jury only on First Degree Kidnapping, First

Degree Murder, Premeditation, Deliberation, and Felony Murder. At noon the jury was brought back in. Judge Ferrell informed them that closing arguments and deliberation would begin on Monday, July 21, and he recessed court. No matter what happened, I knew we had genuinely given it our best shot. I also knew that if L. C. was found not guilty, he would walk out of the courtroom empowered, energized, and vindicated. The aftermath would be horrific.

CHAPTER TWENTY-EIGHT

"And the judges shall make diligent inquisition" (Deuteronomy 19:18)

At 10:00 a.m. on Monday, we were back in the courtroom, and butterflies in my stomach were testing their wings once again. Chester Whittle began closing arguments for the defense.

"Folks, it's been a long trial. For three weeks ya'll have sat here and listened to a lot of evidence. I know it's been inconvenient for you. I know it's been difficult for you, and it's been a sacrifice... But at this point, L. C. Underwood is still presumed to be innocent... We'd ask that you keep at all times an open mind. The judge will tell you that under our system of justice when a defendant pleads not guilty, he is not required to prove his innocence. He is *presumed* to be innocent. So it's the burden and the duty of the prosecution, the State, to prove that Lamont Claxton Underwood is guilty beyond a reasonable doubt. And he doesn't have to prove anything. All of ya'll agreed with me during jury selection, that he's not required to prove anything, that the burden and the sole burden is on the State.

"...I'm one of those people that believes in history. Without knowing history, without having studied history, we don't know where we've been, we don't know where we are, and we can hardly know where we're going. And in this context I want to talk to you first about the jury system, which I hope you will find kind of interesting.

"Centuries ago in England the guilt or innocence of people was determined by one of three... ordeals. They had something called the ordeal of cold water, and what they would do with defendants or the accused is – they had bound them and they'd throw them in water. If the person floated, and hardly anybody swam at that time and they certainly would struggle to get to the surface, they were guilty. If they sank beyond the length of their hair, then they were deemed to be innocent...

"There's something also they had, another ordeal called the ordeal of hot iron. And what they would do in that instance is, they would take a red-hot iron and they'd put it in a defendant's bare hands and then they'd require the defendant to walk nine feet. At the end of the nine feet he could drop the iron. Then his hands were immediately bound up and they stayed bound up for three days. At the end of these three days these bandages would be taken off and if there was any unhealthy matter, that is corruption of the flesh or any kind of infectious process going on, the defendant was guilty. So everybody was guilty, of course.

"Then there was an ordeal of battle, and what the ordeal of battle was, was where they gave the opportunity to the accused to fight. If he won, he was innocent. If he lost, he was guilty. Now the crown or the king had champions to do this. The crown, the king himself, didn't go out and fight anybody, or the queen. As a matter of fact, these were the earliest forms of lawyers that there ever were. They didn't use law books and pens and paper. What they used were swords and maces and all the other implements of war that they had at that time.

"...So that's how things worked for many centuries up until 1215. In 1215...there was an evil king called King John, and a bunch of barons got together due to his excesses and his degradations and they made him sign a document known as the Magna Carta. The Magna Carta, among other things, guaranteed that the most a citizen would have taken was his life or property, except by a jury of his peers.

"Now, that was a fine idea and a noble cause, but things didn't work out that way because the crown did something else. If the crown did not like a jury verdict, they would impanel something called a jury of a taint, and the jury of a taint could go back, find the defendant nevertheless guilty, and also imprison and take away the lands of the jurors who had found the person innocent. ...This went on for almost 500 years. In 1670 in England there was a Quaker named William Penn, and I believe the state of Pennsylvania is named after him... He was on trial with another Quaker for some religious thing and the jury refused to find him guilty, and they refused to find the other person he was on trial with guilty as well. The trial judge, being an instrument of the crown in those days and not independent, scolded the jury, remonstrated with the jury, but the jury still refused to return a verdict of guilty. So the jurors were put in prison. And a Justice Vaughn came along, an English justice, and he freed them and he ruled that juries are independent... He ruled that juries stand between the accused and the crown...

"In the United States, as you know, our Declaration of Independence was written in 1776...And our Constitution, as you know, provides by trial, for trial by jury. And as Patrick Henry said... 'Give me liberty or give me death.' But he also asked this question, 'Why do we love this trial by jury?' And he answered his own question, 'Because it prevents the oppression, the hand of oppression, from cutting you off.'

"The reason I'm telling you these things is because you are an independent body of judges. This is how it's evolved over centuries. You and only you decide this case. I don't decide it. Mr. Rusher, Mr. Wilson, all the police, they don't decide it. Bruce [Kaplan] doesn't decide it. Judge Ferrell doesn't decide it. Just you and only you. You don't wear black robes and customarily we don't address you as Your Honors on the jury. But you are the judges of the facts. And

I'm sure that you would agree as anyone would agree that what we respect most from our judges is fairness, objectivity, and impartiality.

"The word 'verdict' itself comes from a Latin phrase, *verus dictum*, and that means in Latin "truth." The greatest danger... in his case or any case like it, ladies and gentlemen, is that as judges of the facts, you can decide that Lamont Claxton Underwood is a bad person, that he's a bad man and that he deserves punishment – even if he's not guilty of the charge for which he's actually on trial.... Now we're actually on trial here about whether L. C. Underwood kidnapped and murdered Viktor Gunnarsson. ...Now he's never been charged even, much less convicted, or anything as it relates to Catherine Miller. And if passion, prejudice, bias, any of these kinds of things enter into your deliberations, then you are no longer judges sitting as triers of fact. We would be getting into areas of vengeance and revenge, and we no longer will have a verdict which speaks the truth."

At 10:25 a.m., Assistant District Attorney Jerry Wilson began closing arguments for the State. "Ladies and gentlemen, some three weeks ago... Mr. Chester Whittle stood in front of you making an opening statement. He told you at that time what the defendant intended to show through his evidence, and he told you he was going to bring to you witnesses..."

"Your Honor, objection," said Chester. "We don't have to prove anything." Judge Ferrell overruled the objection.

Mr. Wilson continued. "Where are those people who will sit here in this chair in front of this microphone and tell you those things that the defendant's attorney said he would tell you? In fact, ladies and gentlemen, you heard nothing about any of those things that Mr. Whittle and Mr. Kaplan said they would bring to you. In fact, the State's case remains *uncontradicted*. In truth, Viktor Gunnarsson and Catherine Miller died at the hands of L. C. Underwood, overcome by a raging jealousy, an obsessive jealousy that led him to murder...

"Jealousy is an old, ancient emotion. We have all been subject to jealousy: a lost lover, the failing of an award that we wanted, we put in hard work to something and see someone else reap the benefits. It's normal. But what, ladies and gentlemen, do we say about the cold, hard jealousy of L. C. Underwood? What do we say about the premeditated, hateful, hate-filled, self-serving jealousy that led L. C. Underwood to murder? What do we say about jealousy based on obsessive selfishness? What do we say about jealousy based on hate, not on love? *What do we say about that type of jealousy?*

"What do we say about jealousy that made L. C. Underwood stalk the night? What do we say about jealousy that caused him to burst into a restaurant and to threaten physical harm to an innocent person sitting there? What do we say about jealousy that led him to fire a gun into an innocent child's bedroom? What do we say about jealousy that caused him to send these terrible, threatening, anonymous letters?" Jerry held up the letters as a reminder to the jury that they were indeed very real.

"What do we say about that cold, hard premeditated jealousy that caused him to bind Viktor Gunnarsson, that caused him to force Viktor Gunnarsson into the trunk of his automobile? What do we say about that terrible jealousy that caused him to take him to a lonely place and murder him, shoot him in the head twice?! What do we say about the cold, calculating jealousy that would cause a man to shoot an unarmed, helpless, shivering human being in the head?

"What do we say about the jealousy, the overcome, obsessive, hate-filled jealousy, that would cause a man then to strip that body, to strip it of its clothing, to strip it of its binding and leave it there in that lonely place to be devoured by animals? To be buffeted by the cold winter winds? To be covered by the ice and the snow?

"What do we say about the terrible, premeditated, steel-cold jealousy that causes a man to shoot an elderly woman in her home, again twice in the head? What do we say about the jealousy that would cause him to leave Catherine Miller lying there in her kitchen, as Agent Bill Lane said, below her halo of blood, at her meager meal cooked on the stove? What kind of jealousy is that?"

The mention of Kay's mother unlocked the tears that now were streaming freely down Kay's cheeks and into her open hands. Watching Kay brought tears to my own eyes.

"...What do we say about the jealousy, ladies and gentlemen, who renders the child motherless? ...That jealousy that renders the friend with no friend? What do we say about that kind of cold, hard, cruel jealousy? What do we say to this man who through the whole time whose eyes have not looked at you because they reflect in them the horrible crimes and deeds that he's done?" About three-fourths of the jurors looked at L. C. He continued to look at his notepad.

Chester objected. Judge Ferrell sustained the objection.

"I request an instruction, Your Honor," Chester stated. He did not like the fact that Jerry pointed out how L. C. had failed to look at any of the jurors.

Judge Ferrell addressed the jury. "Members of the jury, do not consider the contention of counsel that the defendant did not look at you or that his eyes reflected anything. Do not deliberate upon it, members of the jury."

The Assistant District Attorney continued. "I contend to you, ladies and gentlemen, what we say is, *'L. C. Underwood, you're guilty of terrible crimes! Mr. Defendant, you're guilty of kidnapping Viktor Gunnarsson! Mr. Defendant, you're guilty of the cold-blooded, premeditated murder of Viktor Gunnarsson! You're guilty of terrible crimes!'* That's what we say to him. It is what we say about that kind of cold jealousy!"

He continued in a solemn steady voice. "Over three years ago Viktor Gunnarsson and Catherine Miller were laid in their graves. Since then there has been no justice for either of them. There has been no jury convened to determine whether they should have died. On that cold hillside that late night of December 3rd or early morning of December 4th, there was no jury there to determine if Viktor Gunnarsson should have died. There was no jury in Catherine Miller's kitchen to determine if she should have died. There was no investigation for either of them. There was no chance for them to make a plea for their lives.

"But now, finally, ladies and gentlemen, the time has come, a time for you to stand up and bring, finally, to these two graves justice, a time to stand up and say, 'L. C. Underwood, we will not tolerate these terrible crimes that you have committed. We will not as a community countenance these things which you have done. L. C. Underwood, you must pay the price for your cold, hard, cruel jealousy!'

"I contend to you strongly that this man is guilty of the kidnapping of Viktor Gunnarsson, of binding him, of the terrible ordeal he must have gone through in the trunk of that vehicle. I contend to you strongly that this man is guilty of the cold-blooded, premeditated murder of Viktor Gunnarsson. And I contend to you this morning that you will return a verdict of guilty as to both charges. Thank you." Jerry Wilson sat down. It was 10:36 a.m.

District Attorney Tom Rusher stood up to address the Jury.

"...Ladies and gentlemen, I stand here now telling you that it's the contention of the State that this jury ought to be satisfied beyond a reasonable doubt that the defendant committed the crime of First Degree Murder of Viktor Gunnarsson, and that this jury ought to be satisfied beyond reasonable doubt that this defendant committed the crime of First Degree Kidnapping of Viktor Gunnarsson. And for the next few minutes I want to talk about some of those circumstances. ...We told you in our opening statement that we considered it significant, and we were going to prove it to be significant, that L. C. Underwood was a police officer trained in law enforcement and, beyond that, trained as being a detective. And one of the significant witnesses in that regard is the last witness who testified, Mrs. Beth Richardson, who told you that over and over again at least twelve times in a relationship that she developed with Mr. Underwood, after all of these events had happened, that he said over and over again, I would have been arrested a long time ago for the murder of Catherine Miller and for the murder of Viktor Gunnarsson *if I had not been such a good police officer.*

"What does that *mean*, ladies and gentlemen? That is precisely what I contend now, that the evidence shows beyond reasonable doubt. This crime, the murder and kidnapping of Viktor Gunnarsson, was *never intended to be solved!* It was undoubtedly thought that by taking this person to Watauga County, and murdering him in the woods in a lonely area near the Blue Ridge Parkway, that it would be a matter of mere chance if anyone ever discovered that body. But even so, if he were to be discovered, this defendant who has been trained in trace evidence knows how to *remove* trace evidence. Haven't we proved to you beyond reasonable doubt that there was more tape originally than that eighteen-inch segment, which was cut off at both ends and removed after it had been wrapped and wrapped and wrapped around something? And the reason you remove evidence is because there's a possibility that if you don't remove it, it can go to some laboratory where somebody will look through a microscope or dust it for fingerprints and find something revealing. Indeed, a scientist named John Bendure testified to that very thing. Can you imagine the painstaking effort that man has made over a period of month after month after month, where he tried to compare fibers from two cars, from two residences, and hair? Agent Bendure said during his testimony, 'I didn't have a lot to work with.' He said it twice. He did not have a lot to work with because all the clothing had been removed from this dead body. You see, if you're trained as a detective as L. C. Underwood was, you know that type of thing.

"...*This was a case that was never intended to be solved!* And if you look at the circumstances of the murder and the kidnapping, you realize that a more likely inference of the evidence is that at one time Viktor Gunnarsson had clothing on of some type, and that it was removed, obviously to conceal evidence. The tape was removed, *obviously to conceal evidence*. This man knew that within the trunk of his car there may be fibers left, some transfer of hair, and he did an extraordinary thing... Now, anybody who wants to in America can have the carpet in their trunk shampooed. There's nothing illegal about that. But have you ever known anyone in your life who *did*? Anyone who wants to can have the trunk of their car painted after the police have come in and started looking at the trunk of the car. There is nothing illegal about that. But it becomes a strand in the rope. Have you ever known anyone in your life who had the trunk of their car *painted*? This is a circumstance, ladies and gentlemen, a circumstance, and the beginning circumstances, as I told you some four weeks ago, was that this defendant is, number one, trained at public expense as a police officer and he has training in the area of detective work.

"When you consider the crime itself, how did this happen? A dog lived in the next-door apartment, a dog that you would ordinarily expect to bark. People live nearby, and apparently nothing was heard. Mr. Gunnarsson has been described to us by Daniel Johansson as being a cautious man, one who ordinarily did not open the door to anyone who approached. And yet from that residence a person was taken. And we know he had to be there, because his clothing, the clothing that he wore that night, was there. His car was there. The keys to his car were inside. We know he must have gotten home that night. And yet somehow, without any blood being spilled in his residence, without any blood in the trunk of the car, this person was taken somehow from that residence. And the same thing happened at Catherine Miller's house. Her door, her screen door, was unlocked.

"...According to her daughter and the testimony you have heard, when she was at home in her house, she kept that screen door locked. That's not unusual in our country. People tend to keep the door locked so that if some stranger knocks, they can open their door and still have the enclosure of the screen door locked in between them and that person. But it was *not* locked when Kay Weden was there. The main door was locked, and the officers had to kick it open. The other screen door was locked. But this one was not. It was out of habit for Mrs. Miller to leave it thus. How could this have happened except that the person approaching the residence of Viktor Gunnarsson or the person approaching the residence of Catherine Miller either was known by that person or presented an air of authority?

"Ladies and gentlemen, you would open your door to a person who is a police officer, would you not? And Master Policeman Lamont Claxton Underwood had all of his uniforms and all the paraphernalia that was associated with being a police officer. Detective May testified to seeing all those police uniform items in Underwood's home in February of 1994. Catherine Miller knew the person at her door the night of December 8, 1993. How else could this have happened? He went there under the guise of, the color of authority of, his office – that office that he formerly occupied as police officer... and Viktor Gunnarsson was taken the same way.

"Thus being a police officer is a circumstance, but it's also a circumstance, too, in that this crime could only have happened as it did *because* the defendant was a police officer. *You* don't have the legal right to call and ask a police computer to give you information about other people. But if you're a police officer, you do have that right. And we have shown you that Lamont Claxton Underwood uses people. Look at how he used Rick Hillard. Look at how he used Shirley Twitty. Look at how he used Wanda Hornbuckle. Look at how he used Danny Hillard and Rex Keller. Here is a man who uses people, and people who do that tend generally to start out by making them feel sorry for him. L. C. Underwood used his former wife to go, unbeknown to her, in her car yet again to Westcliff to see what Kay Weden was doing. He used the police, his fellow police officers in Salisbury, to get information that he should not have had. This is a circumstance that permeates this whole case. And the final witness, Mrs. Beth Richardson, who came forward and said, 'He told me he would have been arrested a long time ago'

"Ladies and gentlemen of the jury, this crime went unsolved from December 1993. The evidence is L. C. Underwood was arrested in October of 1995. He would have been arrested a long time ago *except for the fact that he was a good police officer*. That's a circumstance, ladies and gentlemen, that we put forth, that begins the strands of the rope that we have talked about.

"There are other circumstances as well. When given an opportunity to do so, he has not told the truth in the past on several occasions about his knowledge of Viktor Gunnarsson. He told Terry Agner he had *never heard of him*. And can you imagine that? The evidence shows clearly that he read that tag, called it in, was given his name by his friend Rick Hillard... And yet he's never heard of the name Viktor Gunnarsson, so he says to Detective Terry Agner.

"This man who is a police officer ...has not yet told the truth when he was given a chance to about why he called in that tag number. You have heard the witness who was his closest neighbor. He went to him and said, 'L. C., I've read in the paper about this tag you called in. Why did you do it?' L. C. answered, 'Well, it was suspicious. It was out in our neighborhood.' And you heard what he said to Rick Hillard. Rick Hillard recalls *three* different versions that L. C. gave him about why he had that tag number run. You heard what he said to Shirley Twitty herself, who obviously knew where he had gotten this tag because she was with him at the time, and she asked him about the house and he said, 'Well, it was my friend's house, not Kay's house, oh no,' when in fact it was indeed Kay Weden's house he was stalking. ... When he had a chance to do so on many occasions, he did not tell the truth. Telling the truth by L. C. Underwood is a matter of convenience. When he wanted to use somebody, he told them that his mother was dead, and he knew for a fact that was not true. She lives in California. Even if the person he referred to is another woman living in Ohio, he knew for a fact that she was not dead either."

Bruce Kaplan objected. The judge overruled it.

"...If you want to use somebody, you tell them whatever is convenient, and whether it's true or not is a matter of pure coincidence. He also said that his dog died by a virus. That's what he told Ms. Twitty. He told Kay Weden he choked to death by swallowing a coin. You will recall Danny Hillard's testimony that when Danny scolded him for kicking the dog cage with the dog inside, L. C. responded that the dog reminded him of Kay.

"When L. C. Underwood had a chance to do so, on so many occasions as shown by the evidence, he has not told the truth. And that becomes a circumstance that we contend is a strand in the rope. Standing alone, these circumstances might not prove guilt. But when you add them to the other circumstances as they begin to develop, the rope begins to have strength.

"L. C. had a motive, though not a good motive. There's never a *good* motive to kill anyone. But here's a person who really didn't like Kay Weden when he was with her; they quarreled and fussed. But when he was without her, he was obsessed by the thoughts of who she was with and so forth.

You have heard all of the evidence about how he used his cars, both of them, how he used other people's cars to go wherever he thought Kay might be. You heard how he and Wanda Hornbuckle went out looking for Kay that night on December 6, 1993...He told in the letter he wrote to Kay Weden on December 7 that it was a matter of mere accident that he had seen her the night before at Spencer's Restaurant when he clearly planned the outing with Wanda Hornbuckle for the sole purpose of making Kay jealous. I ask you, what kind of a person *is* he? I want to tell you something, ladies and gentlemen. You can put a uniform on a man. You can put a badge on him. But you don't put character there if it's not there already! And you don't make a man capable of handling his emotions if he doesn't have that capability otherwise. Every one of you, every person has at one time or another been rejected in your life. But you don't deal with it the way Lamont Claxton Underwood did, where you stalk and follow and where you create embarrassment and try to create pain, where you ask somebody to make anonymous threatening telephone calls, where you write and send such letters as these! And it is very interesting that counsel admitted that he did that, that he wrote these letters. And of course, he did. The evidence is there, proof beyond reasonable doubt that this man wrote these letters.

"In these letters he says he's concerned about Jason and he loves Kay. *What kind of a love is it?* It's *not* love that we're talking about, ladies and gentlemen. But it is an obsession, a possessive attitude that would prompt one to be on the one hand in a state of desperation and on the other hand in a state of malice towards a particular person. He wanted her and her adolescent son Jason harmed, bushwhacked. He wanted those who stood in their way harmed.

"...We have proved motive. Motive is not an element of these offenses. You don't have to find there existed a motive in order to find him guilty. But the fact that *a motive does exist* becomes a circumstance. He had an opportunity, ladies and gentlemen. He …had …an opportunity. He was three times that night out in Kay Weden's neighborhood some six or seven miles from where he lives. He was there at least three times, according to the evidence. Early on, he and Shirley Twitty went there in his Monte Carlo, right after she arrived. They later went *again* in her car. At that time, Ms. Twitty and Mr. Underwood would have already been through the neighborhood. But he saw this Monte Carlo that very night there in the neighborhood. We know that the stalker was out stalking on the night of December 3, 1993. An opportunity. He had the opportunity.

"...And then we consider the tape. You always hope, as I told you at the beginning, that a person who commits murder will somehow stub his toe. This was a crime that was never intended to be solved. It was committed by a person who never intended to be caught, and he knew how to manipulate and change the evidence so that the likelihood of his being caught was reduced. But in the darkness, in the haste, he left forth a piece of that tape. Now, you have heard about the tape. A scientist has said that he took it apart into the various layers, seven or eight layers of electrical tape and two or three layers of masking tape. This man Gunnarsson had been bound, and the tape wound and wound. And what we can say as a matter of science is, that tape is consistent in all respects to a piece of tape in the Lamont Claxton Underwood residence. Master Policeman Lamont Claxton Underwood had at some time made a repair or someone had made a repair in his residence using electrical tape, electrical tape that matched – in twenty-some scientifically measurable characteristics – the tape Viktor Gunnarsson was bound with. …We contend that it's a circumstance that, added together with the other strands, the strands and the strength of the rope continue to build.

"And then you consider the hair. Now, ladies and gentlemen, what is the probability that anyone is ever going to be in the trunk of your car so that their head hair is all the way to the extreme rear part of the car? What is the probability that that could ever happen? That is a rare event. But then you add to that two scientists who both come from a different perspective, and they render scientific analysis on it... So you have two scientists who are saying, number one, it's rare for the hair ever to have been way back in the rear part of the car. How could it happen in your experience in life that somebody's head hair would be way back in the rear part of your trunk, so deeply embedded that traditional means of trying to remove it had not worked, so deeply embedded, in fact, that a person who has shampooed the car had not extracted it. Probably some had been extracted, but these seventeen hairs remained. Have you ever heard of someone who came within a hair of getting away with a crime? And that's what we have here, ladies and gentlemen. Within a hair, he came that close. This crime that was never intended to be solved almost went unsolved. But I want to tell you something. These detectives from Rowan County and Watauga County, these SBI agents, the State of North Carolina needs to give them a standing applause. They have worked on this case from day one. They have worked with energy. They were determined not to overlook anything, and they have used much energy and many techniques throughout this period of time, and they came forth in the end in a rather miraculous situation." Tom picked up the trunk mat from L. C.'s Monte Carlo from the table where it had been admitted into evidence.

"...As Agent Bendure began to repackage this, he saw hair, so deeply embedded that a prior carpet shampoo had not removed it, so deeply embedded that his taping had not removed it. You always hope that somehow the offender will stub their toe. L. C. came within a hair of getting away with this crime. A scientist has said that head hair is microscopically in all respects consistent with the known head hair removed at autopsy from Viktor Gunnarsson.

"Now these lawyers... are extremely excellent. They're good lawyers. They're honorable people..." Steve adjusted his position in his seat. "The facts are there, ladies and gentlemen. Agent Bendure found telogen hairs near the rear of the trunk of that car, and those hairs microscopically are consistent with Viktor Gunnarsson ...and inconsistent with Lamont Claxton Underwood. If that were all, if there were nothing else, I would be standing here telling you that beyond reasonable doubt you ought to accept that evidence and find the defendant guilty. But there's more...The investigators in this case have subjected those seventeen hairs to the most scientific, the most advanced scientific techniques that currently exist in forensic laboratories. First, the traditional kind of nuclear DNA was tested, and it was not possible to get enough DNA extracted to make any kind of test. But then you heard the testimony about mitochondrial DNA testing. You have heard a scientist who came from the FBI laboratory. He did a testing, a comparison on the blood removed from the body of Viktor Gunnarsson and the hair found in the trunk of this car remotely to the rear, and according to his test results, the sequencing of the hair and the sequencing of the blood match. Now, he said ... maternal relatives all have the same type of mitochondrial DNA. Viktor Gunnarsson has a mother who lives in Sweden. He has a grandmother, the mother's mother. They all have the same type mitochondrial DNA, so the expert says. He has a sister who would have theoretically the same type of mitochondrial DNA, so the expert says, the same sequencing. His grandmother had three children, all of whom are maternal relatives, all of whom would have the same DNA. ...But they are thousands of miles from Salisbury, North Carolina. Across the ocean. They are thousands of miles away from Watauga County, North Carolina. Although they are expected to have the same DNA, how could their head hair ever have gotten in the trunk of Lamont Claxton Underwood's car?

"...We contend to you, ladies and gentlemen, scientifically beyond reasonable doubt that we have proved that Viktor Gunnarsson was in that trunk, and you don't put people in the trunk of your car if you have good will towards them.

"...And those scratch marks and that impression... We contend it's a circumstance along with the scratches. And I look at those scratches. Some metallic object somehow came into contact over and over with the trunk of that car. Not a very strong or forceful contact. You look at the scratches and they're not deeply impressed into the metal of that car. But consider a man bound and taped, consider that he may have found a lug wrench or a piece of metal in the trunk, doing his best. All of his energy was put forth in that rather minuscule effort, scratching, scratching, scratching for justice, justice that never came to Viktor Gunnarsson. It's a circumstance that we contend adds to all the other strands of the rope.

"...And then we consider three guns that are missing, missing, and an effort has been made to find them. You have heard of that effort made. You have heard of two searches at the defendant's house. You have heard of a trip to Ohio. You have heard of questions being asked. You have heard over and over about efforts made to find those three guns. And yet the evidence shows that they were at one time in the possession of Lamont Claxton Underwood. A .22 Ruger rifle, consistent with the rifle that fired the shot into Jason Weden's residence. *Where is that Ruger .22 rifle?* We know, we have shown you from the evidence that he at one time had it. A .22 caliber Dan Wesson that could have fired that shot into Kay Weden's residence. It's also missing. That's the type of weapon that could have been used... in the murder of Viktor Gunnarsson. *Where is it?!* ...And then you consider the .38 Colt [revolver] from Lincoln County. Do you have any reasonable doubt, ladies and gentlemen, but that somehow when he left Lincoln County he had it with him? He has told some people that he simply picked it up and walked away with it. That's what he told Keller. He's told other people that the former sheriff gave it to him. It doesn't matter how he came into possession of it. But a .38 nickel-plated Colt revolver is consistent in all respects with the weapon that fired those two terrible shots into the head of Catherine Miller. *And suddenly those guns that were in the possession of L. C. Underwood are no longer there!*

"There is witness after witness after witness who testified they saw them [the guns]. They knew he had them. Jason Weden even had the .38 pointed at him at one time...Jason saw that .38. Keller saw it. Hillard saw it. Jones saw it. His former wife Marcia saw it. He had a .38 nickel-plated Colt revolver. He doesn't have it now, seemingly, or at least it's been looked for and can't be found. The .22 Dan Wesson has been looked for and can't be found. The .22 Ruger rifle has been looked for and can't be found. How is it, ladies and gentlemen, that he had these weapons, so clearly, he had them up until the time of these terrible crimes, and suddenly they're not there? I suspect and I would contend that the evidence shows that they will never be found. And that becomes a circumstance, that he does not have what he *did* have, because they are linked to the commission of an awful crime, multiple crimes in fact!

"...And then we consider this man and the terrible thing that happened to Catherine Miller. ...I suppose they would tell you that her murder was simply a matter of coincidences, ladies and gentlemen. Is it a matter of coincidence that there had been no contact from the defendant to Kay Weden after that Bogarts incident, shortly after that, until December 4, 1993? He had tried, he had had his friends try, but she had finally had enough and put a call block on so he couldn't call her. No contact for a period of time immediately before December 3, 1993. But the very day after Gunnarsson is dead, the calls start again: 'Kay, it's time that you and I get this relationship back on track. I am going to come to your house and pick you up this very evening...'

"And then you will recall how he persisted over and over, as was his habit, after that date. Is that a mere coincidence, that only after Viktor Gunnarsson is dead in Watauga County that he tried again to resurrect this relationship? And then let me take you to Pearl Harbor Day, Jason Weden's birthday, December 7, 1993. She, Ms. Weden, gets a call: I've left a letter in your mailbox. She goes to get it. Before she can even read it, *he's there*. This man who is so impetuous, this man whose mind grows so quickly desperate, could not stand the anxiety of not knowing what her reaction was going to be!

"Look at that letter." Tom held up the letter L. C. wrote to Kay and hand-delivered on the 6th of December, 1993. "Something is very, very significant in that letter. Twice he says, 'Don't force me into something.' And the next day *her mother is dead, double-tapped as police officers are trained to do, shot twice in the head!* Viktor Gunnarsson was *also double-tapped, shot twice in the head area*. At Catherine Miller's a non-forcible entry somehow was made. The same had happened at Viktor Gunnarsson's. There is similarity between the events. There is proximity in time. It all fits into the overall motive that this defendant displays. It is, we contend, more circumstances tending to identify the defendant, Master Policeman Lamont Claxton Underwood, with having committed both offenses.

"Ladies and gentlemen, the defendant is accused of Kidnapping in the First Degree. Kidnapping in the First Degree occurs when there is a taking of a person without consent... The defendant was taken without consent and confined without consent. This defendant was confined and restrained, kidnapped, if you will. He was restrained by being taped, and he was carried from one place to another place. We would contend beyond reasonable doubt that the defendant ought to be found guilty of Kidnapping in the First Degree...

"...And then you will consider the charge of First Degree Murder. First Degree Murder ... can be committed in either one of two ways or perhaps both of them: number one, by way of premeditation and deliberation, a malicious killing of a human with premeditation and deliberation where there is an intent to kill. There is certainly evidence of that, and we would contend that beyond reasonable doubt, you ought to be satisfied that over this two-hour period, at least from Salisbury to Watauga County – and it could have been longer – the defendant had a fixed intent to do exactly what he did. *That's premeditation.*

"...And beyond that, our cases have held that when you leave a body recklessly out in an area where it is not likely ever to be found, and it's a matter of mere chance that it will be found, that is some evidence of premeditation and deliberation. So, we contend beyond reasonable doubt that the defendant is guilty of First Degree Murder *by way of premeditation and deliberation.*

"...But also, there is a second possibility. And either possibility constitutes First Degree Murder. But the second possibility is what is called the Felony Murder Rule, or a murder committed during the perpetration of a felony, such as kidnapping. If, during an act such as kidnapping, the defendant uses a deadly weapon and intentionally takes the life of another, then that is *Felony Murder.* It would be our contention that this jury ought to be satisfied beyond a reasonable doubt that the defendant is guilty of First Degree Murder on *both* theories, both the theory of premeditation and deliberation *and* Felony Murder.

"...Ladies and gentlemen, I've probably talked too long. I began to realize something as I have talked to you. For over three years, three and a half years, I've had an involvement in this case. Paula May has. Don Gale has. Steve Wilson has. A lot of people have. Suddenly our involvement has come to an end. And I totally will tell you candidly, I'm beginning to feel greatly relieved, because very quickly it's not going to be my decision anymore, but *your* decision." I personally felt no relief at all.

"...This case represents the very essence of America. Foreign people, people who live in foreign nations... want to live in America and they come here. They have throughout our history. We give our citizens great rights. We tell them that it's not enough for Paula May to say you may have committed a crime. It's not enough for Tom Rusher to say it. It's up to a jury of one's peers. How wonderful such a right is. How wonderful that in America we have this liberty.

"*But in America, who will speak for the dead*? Viktor Gunnarsson is not here!

"...There is, somewhere over in Sweden a mother who is old and a father who is old. And I am confident there, as here, there is tremendous feeling! It must be so. There is somewhere where Viktor Gunnarsson is remembered as Viktor Ake Lennart Gunnarsson, March 30, 1953 – December 4, 1993. That dash represents the life of Viktor Gunnarsson. ...Where was equal justice when it came to his life in America? Oh yes, we give magnificent rights and we're the envy of all the world. People come here because in America, in America we're free, and in America we're all entitled to the equal protection of the law.

"As I stand relieved that my role is over, I stand totally confident that you're going to do what is right. This is a case that you need to deliberate. If there is a reasonable doubt, then say so. Pick it apart. Deliberate on every aspect of it. I do not want you to convict an innocent person. But if after doing so, if after you have considered the things that I have tried to talk about and all the things that the defendant's attorneys talk about as well, if you are left of the opinion that I contend you ought to have, then come into this courtroom and stand proudly, stand tall, stand and say to the master policeman, the one who has taken an oath to enforce the law, Lamont Underwood, 'Thou shalt not kill!' ...Ladies and gentlemen, we contend that your verdict ought to be guilty. Guilty of First Degree Murder and guilty of First Degree Kidnapping. Thank you."

At 11:47 a.m., Chester Whittle stood and made further closing arguments to the jury. Basically, he argued against every point the District Attorney made. He also stated that Tom Rusher had referred to Viktor's father and mother in an attempt to gain sympathy from the jurors. He stated that the rank of L. C. Underwood was master patrolman, not master policeman. He argued that the bag the trunk mat was collected in was a grocery bag, not an evidence bag [although it was clearly marked as an evidence bag].

"...The prosecution has repeatedly tried to make you think that Viktor Gunnarsson was in that trunk struggling. And let me say this before going on. No one deserves a violent death... I am not without pity for anything that happened to Viktor Gunnarsson. No one, neither Bruce nor I have any kind of sense that this was okay. But that's not the issue." What victims have to suffer never seems to be an issue with defense attorneys.

"But the prosecution has repeatedly tried to show that there was a struggle in that trunk. They have tried through witness after witness and reference after reference to say there were scratches. Not only is there nothing on Viktor Gunnarsson's body to indicate any struggle; there's nothing under his fingernails. These little scratches, these little squiggles you saw in a very small area of the trunk, which they'd have you believe was behind him, could have been made by anything. Nobody knows how long they were there. They're inconsistent with fingernail scrapings because they're smaller and they're sharper." I wondered why, if Chester's arguments were true, would L. C. go to so much trouble to cover the scrapings with paint?

"...Now let me ask you to follow me on this. I'm going to tie these things together for you in just a minute. And I bet some of you already know where I'm heading, and I think some of you may have already figured this out. Where was everybody involved in this case on the night of December 3, 1993? Where was everybody? First of all, we got Rick

Hillard. Rick Hillard says, 'I got a call from L. C. between 11:00 and 11:30.' You remember that testimony..."Shirley Twitty... she heard the call to Rick Hillard. She also heard the call back... and she left twenty to thirty minutes later... So, if Rick Hillard called her at about 11:40 and she left twenty to thirty minutes later, she left at 12:00, 12:10, somewhere in that time frame.

"Let's talk about Kay Weden. She said that she, her mom, and Viktor Gunnarsson went to Blue Bay Restaurant, met at the Blue Bay Restaurant between 6:15 and 6:30. They left between 7:30 and 8:00. Between 9:00 and 10:00 they were alone. At 10:00 Jason showed up... Remember, all his friends showed up too. And at 11:30 Viktor Gunnarsson leaves... If Rick Hillard, the deputy, said he calls L. C. at 11:30 when Twitty was there, that means again she had to leave between... 12:00 and 12:10. And we know Viktor Gunnarsson left at 11:30... We know where everybody was within certain time frames.

"...The best estimate of distance is a hundred miles. That's from Salisbury up to Boone... If we know it's a two-hour drive... if at 11:30 L. C. Underwood suddenly rushed from his house, drove over to Viktor Gunnarsson's house, somehow got him in his car, somehow did all these things to him, it would take him two hours to get up here to find a place to put him and do all that other stuff. But just giving it two hours, that's 1:30. If in this two-hour drive – Ms. Twitty left at midnight, then we have – it takes till 2:00 in the morning for him to be up here...

"So, there's only one conclusion based upon what everybody says... and that is he was dead when he arrived up here. He could not have been alive. He could not have been alive objectively, psychologically, medically, nothing else. The man had to be dead on arrival." His arguments made no sense to me.

"...Now, how does L. C., who is retired at the age of forty-something, how does L. C., with a back injury serious enough to retire, get a man that's almost six feet tall, 206 pounds, into the car, out of the car, through the woods, a hundred and twenty feet from one direction, five hundred and some feet from the other direction, and something like a hundred feet from still a third direction, to the depression in the ground? Now these are the State's own witnesses, okay? So, you might say to yourselves, *Well, folks, maybe he figured out a way to do it.* No ladies and gentlemen, Viktor Gunnarsson was never in that trunk." Then Chester launches into an argument of how the head hair found in L. C.'s trunk mat must have belonged to the guy who worked at Sam's Car Wash. Chester had left out any references to the mitochondrial DNA analysis. Perhaps he hoped the jurors would forget about that.

At 12:31 p.m., Judge Ferrell interrupted Chester and took a lunch recess. Steve was called to another county for the afternoon to testify in another trial. Tom and Jerry were reviewing case law in the law library. I walked across the street to each lunch with Kay, the Victim-Witness Coordinator Sherry, Don, Terry, my husband, Randy, who had been able to escape his office to watch portions of the trial, and my best friend Charlene Norris. It was unusually hot, and no one seemed to have much appetite. We collectively drank sweet iced tea and sodas and talked about everything and nothing.

Court was back in session at 2:00 p.m., and Chester resumed his arguments. He made a big deal about the lack of blood in L. C.'s trunk. He talked about the fact that there were no other trace evidence matches of hair or fiber. Then he actually accused us of planting the evidence on the mat, but his argument was lame. Still it was offensive. It was probably a good thing for Chester that Steve was not present at the time.

Chester finally concluded, "...So ladies and gentlemen of the jury, I ask you in that context, has the State proven this case to you beyond a reasonable doubt, to a moral certainty, as the Supreme Court of this state has called it? I submit to you that no, it has not."

At 2:19 p.m., Bruce Kaplan addressed the jury for his final say before they began to deliberate on L. C.'s guilt. "…During the jury selection process, you said that you would not hold it against the defendant if he did not testify… I will ask you to remember two things when you go to deliberate. The State must prove its case beyond a reasonable doubt. And the State must prove to you beyond a reasonable doubt based on actual evidence of the crime of killing Viktor Gunnarsson and kidnapping him. Not bad acts, not other crimes, not things that were difficult to hear, but the evidence. And I will contend to you and show you that there is not sufficient evidence to convince you beyond a reasonable doubt that Mr. Underwood in fact killed Viktor Gunnarsson."

It was 3:03 p.m. Closing arguments to the jury were now complete. At the Judge's request, the bailiff handed copies of the instructions to each member of the jury. Judge Ferrell gave them verbal instructions, and at 3:26 p.m. they were handed the deliberation sheets.

"You will now return to the jury Room where you will begin your deliberations." Judge Ferrell had such a deep commanding voice. "The defendant is remanded to the custody of the Sheriff." It was 3:30 p.m.

We waited. When the courtroom was finally empty, Don, Terry, and I walked into the DA's office to wait it out. All the muscles in Don's body were visibly tense, though he was silent. Terry paced. I fidgeted. We took turns guessing how long it would take the jury to come back. No one thought the jury would be back before midday on Tuesday, the following day.

Yet at 4:35 that same Monday afternoon, the phone rang in Tom's inner office.

"Really?" he said to the caller. "We'll be right there." Turning to Don, Terry, and me, he said, "Let's go. The jury has reached a verdict."

I got a sick feeling in the pit of my stomach. Don looked at me and shook his head. "It's too soon, Paula; it's way too soon." Terry said nothing but led the way back to the seats we had occupied for the past three weeks.

I looked at L. C. Of course, I was not the one here with the most to lose. Judging by his facial expression, however, L. C. did not appear as worried as he should have been under the circumstances. It was no wonder that he could keep two murders a secret for four years, when he showed no visible concern whatsoever in a murder trial that could cost him his life.

The bailiff opened the door to the Jury Room, and the jurors filed in and took their seats in the jury box. Judge Ferrell did not waste time.

"Who is the foreman of this jury?" he asked.

Juror #7 raised her hand.

"Please stand," Judge Ferrell ordered. She stood.

"I understand that the jury has reached a verdict. Is that correct?"

"It is, your Honor."

"Very well. Bailiff, please take the verdict sheet from the jury foreman and bring it to me." The bailiff did so, and Judge Ferrell read it silently. He then handed he verdict sheet to the clerk, who stood to the right of the Judge. Sheriff Lyons got up from his seat and walked over to stand beside Clerk Deal, a petite redhead who was clearly uncomfortable with L. C. so near. I saw her mouth a 'thank you' to Sheriff Lyons. He nodded to her assuredly.

"Madam Clerk, please read the verdict aloud to the Court," the Judge ordered.

Clerk Deal's voice trembled only slightly as she read, "We, the jury, find the defendant Lamont Claxton Underwood *Guilty* of First Degree Kidnapping and *Guilty* of First Degree Murder." There were low key murmurings in the courtroom, but my eyes were glued to L. C.

I watched as L. C.'s stoic face finally crumbled. He lowered his head onto his hand, and both Chester and Bruce leaned over briefly to whisper something to him. Then they suddenly busied themselves rifling through paperwork on the table. Behind me and to my left, I heard L. C.'s pseudo-mother Barbara sob and then cry in earnest. Directly behind me, Kay Weden was crying and hugging her son, Jason, and her friend Anne.

Judge Ferrell turned to the defense table and asked, "What says the defendant regarding the form of the taking of the verdict?"

Bruce Kaplan responded, "We would ask that the jury be polled."

"Very well. Members of the jury, at this time the clerk, Mrs. Diane Deal will ask you and each one of you three separate questions. She will call your name and as she does, if you would please stand, listen carefully to the questions, and answer the same out loud. The foreperson will first be polled. Poll the jury, Madam Clark."

Beginning with the foreperson, Clerk Deal instructed separately to each juror, "Please stand. You have returned a verdict of Guilty of First Degree Kidnapping and First Degree Murder as to the defendant Lamont Claxton Underwood. Was this your verdict?" Each juror responded in the affirmative.

"Is this still your verdict?" Again, they responded yes.

"Do you still agree and assent thereto?" the clerk asked. Each juror responded yes. When jurors are polled, the possibility exists that when faced with the pressure of being called out into the open and in the immediate presence of the defendant, a jury may change their verdict. All it takes is one. But no one did.

Some days later, I learned exactly how much time it took for the jury to reach its verdict. They decided to take a vote first thing to see where they stood before they actually began deliberating. All twelve jurors voted "Guilty" within the first five minutes. They discussed some aspects of the case among themselves and took a fifteen-minute restroom break. There was no further deliberation.

CHAPTER TWENTY-NINE

"Let my sentence come forth from thy presence; let thine eyes behold the things that are equal. Thou has visited me in the night; thou hast tried me" (Psalms 17:2-3)

Court resumed for sentencing on Wednesday, July 23, 1997. In order to have the final arguments, the defense waived opening statements.

"We call Dr. Davis to the stand," Bruce said.

Dr. Davis was tendered an expert in clinical psychology. Judge Ferrell agreed.

"Dr. Davis, have you had the opportunity to meet and assess L. C. Underwood?"

"I have."

"And have you interviewed him?"

"Yes, I have."

"And administered psychological tests to him?"

"Yes. I interviewed him for approximately six hours, and I administered the MMPI, which is the Minnesota Multiphasic Personality Inventory, and the Rorschach inkblot test. In whole, I spent eight and a half hours or so with him across two days last month."

"And have you been able to reach a professional opinion as to his psychological status?"

"Yes, I have."

"What is your opinion as to his psychological status in December of 1993?"

"My opinion is at that point, and for about two months prior to that – so we're talking October, November, and December 1993 – that Mr. Underwood was suffering from his third bout of severe depression... Technically, the diagnosis is Major Depressive Disorder, Recurrent."

"How did you form that basis, and can you explain that basis?"

"The basis for my opinion is... I have several reasons to base that opinion on. Captain Belk, who worked with him in the Salisbury Police Department, told the police that he observed Mr. Underwood crying almost every day for a long period of time... Mr. Underwood was also speaking to acquaintances about his mother's illness. And by *mother*, he means Barbara Childress. He was also speaking to several witnesses about the wish to kill himself, or suicidal ideations as we would call them... Mr. Underwood was very frightened of losing his mother and his fear caused him to exaggerate the severity of her illness." *To the point of telling everyone she was dead? I thought that was more than mere exaggeration.*

Dr. Davis continued, "There's something else which was also present and which his police records reflected: a relative lack of meticulousness in his work. With the major depressive syndrome, people who are suffering from that sleep poorly... In other words, they rarely sleep soundly. They have a hard time falling asleep. They wake up a lot. They wake up and they think all the time about what's wrong and how things are going wrong and so on. In my judgment Mr. Underwood has suffered three such episodes at least – possibly more – but three that I feel are documented."

"And that began in 1976?"

"Right."

"Was Mr. Underwood given medication for depression?"

"Yes. He was given medication for depression in 1992. And in addition, he was having – well he was very upset specifically about his relationship with Kay Weden, which was very conflictual and... Mr. Underwood's dependency and desperation to get Kay Weden's attention..."

Dr. Davis was asked whether L. C.'s childhood was relevant to his depression.

"I think Mr. Underwood's childhood background is very relevant to developing the vulnerability to depression that we see in him as an adult... Prior to the age that Mr. Underwood has a conscious memory of his natural parents – both drinkers and violent in the household frequently – so this is from age zero to three, okay? He's the middle child of three. His older brother, Richard, who was age five at the time, recalls these incidents. There were frequent bloody fights, apparently, and L. C. who was three years old was crying and pleading with the parents to stop, stop fighting. Imagine a three-year-old observing the parents, getting themselves bloody, in a bloody fight and feeling helpless. And so, he would cry and wish for them to stop, but they did not stop.

"...Another story that Richard told me was that on a Christmas Eve when L. C. was three, their parents were again having a drunken argument, and for whatever reason that was apparently not explained to the children, he locked the children in the barn that Christmas Eve night while they continued their drunken argument in the house.... L. C.'s memory begins later than that, which again is typical."

"...How it affected Mr. Underwood is that it made him vulnerable to feeling abandoned, okay? He is pushed aside. ...His mother abandoned the children, and the father basically left the family not too long after this. Apparently, he was about three and a half, and then his father left the family about eighteen months later when he was about age five, leaving them with an aunt, and then the mother came back and then left again, okay? ...This was not within his conscious memory – but in his sense that he was not worthy of being loved."

Dr. Davis went on to discuss how L. C. was taken in by George and Delzia Underwood, when L. C. was age six to nine. During that time L. C. was subjected to his Uncle George's constant scrutiny for whether he was going to make a mistake at anything.

"For example," Dr. Davis shared, "L. C. recalled George standing over him and cuffing him on the head if he got a homework problem wrong. He also recalled that George would use any pretext, any minor transgression as an excuse for a reason to prompt a very severe punishment… including being forced to stand on one foot for hours at a time and being beaten if you fell over…"

Bruce asked, "Dr. Davis, based on this information you reviewed specifically as to his childhood, do you have an opinion on how these factors would affect your diagnosis or your opinion?"

"I do. The incidents that I described would affect the emotional status of a child in the sense of developing an overreaction to possible abandonment. In other words, the child would be often fearful and anxious – and possibly even expect that another abandonment would happen. In addition, the incidents of abuse and the sort of visual watchfulness that George Underwood subjected L. C. to also created in L. C. a great deal of anxiety about making a mistake. In other words, he grew into an adult who had a meticulous, careful way of making sure that everything was in order and in control…" I could not argue.

Dr. Davis spoke on, "In addition, the severity of the punishments that I feel Mr. Underwood was subjected to, created in him an anxiety about being helpless, okay? Imagine being small and being tied in a sack and so on… So I believe that he grew up as somebody who was very defensive, very unwilling to admit any vulnerability and weakness in himself, because in his mind, vulnerability and weakness is associated with extreme punishment."

"In your professional opinion, was Mr. Underwood suffering from major depressive disorder, recurrent, and was he under the influence of mental disturbance at this time of December 3, 1993?" Bruce asked.

Yes. I feel that Mr. Underwood was suffering from a concentration impairment that's typical of people with Major Depressive Disorder. I also feel that Mr. Underwood was suffering from a sense of desperation that clouded his judgment during that period of time."

Jerry Wilson began to cross-examine Dr. Davis. "Dr. Davis, I believe you said that you made your diagnosis before you interviewed certain people. Is that correct, sir?"

"That's correct."

"Did you interview Captain Belk?"

"No, and I also did not interview people from The Children's Home."

"Sir did you interview any of these officers? Did you interview Paula May with the Watauga County Sheriff's Department?"

"No."

"Did you interview Terry Agner with the Rowan County Sheriff's Department?"

"No."

"Did you interview Kay Weden, a primary witness in this case?"

"No."

"Did you interview Beth Richardson?"

"No."

"You interviewed the defendant?"

"Yes."

"And Barbara Childress."

"Yes."

"Dr. Davis, because someone saw L. C. crying, because he called his mother frequently and asked about her health, because he was upset about the fact that his mother might die, because he was not as meticulous in minor details, that he had some desperate feelings, and having some trouble sleeping, and therefore you decided he was severely depressed?"

Bruce objected.

"Overruled."

"Is that right, Dr. Davis?" Jerry asked.

"Well, uh… yes."

Jerry challenged Dr. Davis about a number of records he disregarded in forming his diagnosis of L. C.

"…Sir, when did you reach your diagnosis of severe depression?"

"After I completed my evaluation."

Jerry pressed, "Well give us a time frame."

"Well…"

"This morning or before that?"

"No. It was probably a week ago."

"A week ago?"

"That I came up with my final conclusions about this case."

"You spent a long time this morning justifying your diagnosis to the jury by anecdotes from the defendant's upbringing told you by Mr. Richard Underwood, didn't you?"

"…Yes."

"Sir, you did not interview Mr. Richard Underwood until this morning, did you?"

"That's correct."

"So you used for a basis of your diagnosis things that you did not know when you made your diagnosis, is that right?"

"No… When I spoke to Mr. Richard Underwood this morning, his anecdotes only confirmed what I had already expected to hear."

"Doctor, does depression cause a person to lie?"

Bruce objected.

"Overruled."

Jerry repeated the question.

"Not necessarily," answered the doctor.

"...Does depression cause people to go out and commit murder?"

"Objection."

Judge Ferrell sustained the objection. But Jerry's point was well made.

At 2:11 p.m., when the Judge gave him the go-ahead, Tom Rusher pushed his chair back, stood, and walked swiftly to the jury box.

"Ladies and gentlemen, can you be certain that Lamont Claxton Underwood will never kill again? The defendant is some forty-six years old. None of us know how many years may be allotted to us. But there's every reason to assume that he has many, many years remaining to live. Can you be certain that there will not be other funerals?"

Chester objected immediately. "Your Honor, I object to that, and I move to strike it and ask the jury to be instructed on it. He's already been convicted of First Degree Murder."

"Overruled. The motion is denied."

Tom continued. "Have you seen the defendant exhibit remorse for what he has done?" Tom reminded the jury of the recorded phone call Shirley Twitty made to L. C. in which she confronted him of taking her by Kay Weden's house, and L. C. denied that it was Kay's house.

"Has the defendant exhibited any remorse for what he did?" Tom reminded the jury of Rex Keller's testimony in which L. C. had him create a tape in which he pretended to be Underwood's brother receiving the Dan Wesson .22.

"Can you be certain that this manipulating person will not kill again? Can anyone be certain that there will not yet be other funerals? ...Why capital punishment, ladies and gentlemen? Because when some crimes are so aggravating and so heinous and so terrible, then the law must strike with its terrible swift sword. Why capital punishment? Because our citizens must know that when those who elect to commit crimes of such terrible aggravation, they must be aware that capital punishment does exist!"

Tom took a deep breath and slowed his speech. "He who was sworn to uphold the law, he who was sworn to be the benefactor of those in need, he whose duty as a master patrol officer, he who took this oath of office, he who had a better opportunity than anyone else to know what the consequences of his criminality were, he who took those oaths of office now stands before you, and I say to you, *Can you be certain that there will not be other funerals?*

"Ladies and gentlemen, this will be the last time I speak to you. This is not easy for you or anyone who's participated in this trial. But now you're going to be asked to find certain aggravating factors…There are three. One, the murder was committed while the defendant was engaged in the commission of, and then there are several felonies listed, but specifically kidnapping. The murder *was* committed while the defendant was engaged in kidnapping. …But we content beyond reasonable doubt that you have already found this aggravating factor in that you found the defendant guilty of murder; you found the defendant to have kidnapped the victim; and necessarily the murder would have occurred during the commission of the kidnapping.

"Two, the next aggravating factor says the murder was especially heinous, atrocious, or cruel. Now every murder is heinous, atrocious, and cruel. But the law recognizes those that are *especially* so. We contend that whenever one inflicts unnecessary torture, unnecessary dehumanizing and brutal conduct, onto his victim, if the case has some degree of torture and dehumanization and brutality not associated with ordinary murders, then the jury can find and assign the aggravating factor that the killing was *especially heinous, atrocious, and cruel.*

"Our contention is that Viktor was alive when and until they got to Watauga County. That's altogether different from what the defense told you. I don't seriously contend that he was carried – a dead body – carried and placed there. I would contend that he was marched or required to walk those final steps to the area where he was found dead.

"Another contention is the presence of luminol under the place where the body lay, indicating the probability that blood was spilled there, indicating the probability that Viktor Gunnarsson bled there to death. He bled *there*... nowhere else but where the body was found.

"We contend that the scratch marks and the print impression – whether it was a footprint, a shoeprint, a fabric print from an elbow, or a part of a body that had tape on it, and the hair, again, being so deeply ground into the carpet. We contend these things are evidence of a life in confinement in the trunk of that car. Our contention is that this is an especially heinous, atrocious, and cruel murder because of this terrible period of confinement, that Viktor Gunnarsson was *alive* in the trunk of that car on a winter night. Watauga County, as I recall, had a low temperature of 24 degrees the night of December 3, 1993.

"Is it not especially heinous, atrocious, and cruel to put a live person who was five feet eleven into the trunk of that car, undoubtedly bound severely, so that his movements were very greatly restricted, bound in that car without knowing where he was going, but surely being aware, too, that he was not going anyplace where he was going to be set free. Can you not imagine the terror, the fright, the concern that live person must have been enduring while he was confined, bound as he was in the trunk of that car! And for such a long time, at least two hours! And we contend as that man lay there – and you have seen how the defendant can be suddenly angered, and you can only imagine what he must have said to him during that time – and as that man continues to lie there, struggling as he could with a very limited capability to do anything but scratch, as he must have tried to do, and then after a while suddenly the car starts swerving around, and going up hills. Mr. Gunnarsson wasn't familiar with the terrain of Watauga County. As that car started going uphill, perhaps his ears started popping, as often is the case as the elevation ascends. Perhaps he began to be slung back and fro as the car went up a hill and around the curve... *Can you imagine the terror and the fright?!*

"Ladies and gentlemen, if L. C. Underwood had wanted him dead, he could have killed him in Rowan County where both of them resided. He could have killed him without all that torturous conduct that he put this poor man through. Can you imagine the agony, the dehumanizing conditions, the cold, the body stiffness as his body continued to be cramped in that position for so long a period of time, and then finally arriving in a place where he had no idea where he was, undoubtedly his mouth taped so that he could hardly speak, and then dragged or pulled or pushed five hundred and fifty feet or whatever distance, knowing all the while that he was going to be history in just a few minutes! The defendant could have killed him so less brutally, but this killing was especially heinous, atrocious, and cruel!

"...And then there's a third aggravating factor. The murder for which the defendant stands convicted was part of a course of conduct in which the defendant engaged and which included the commission by the defendant of some crimes of violence against another person or persons. Ladies and gentlemen, we contend that you ought to be satisfied beyond reasonable doubt that he confronted David Sumner in a restaurant after he sought out Kay Weden for some time. We contend that beyond reasonable doubt this jury ought to be of the opinion that David Sumner was one date, and maybe two dates away from himself becoming a victim...

"But that is paled in significance when you consider the death of Catherine Miller. Ladies and gentlemen, Catherine Miller was seventy-seven years of age. She was noted for her punctuality. She had stability in her life. Imagine, one job for forty years! And when she was a minute late, they were concerned because she had always been punctual. A cautious woman who ordinarily kept her door locked. No motive existed for anyone else to harm her except Lamont Claxton Underwood. Did he murder Catherine Miller? Of course, he did! And there is lots of evidence that points to that, and you will recall it all…

"L. C. Underwood, who so terribly loved Kay Weden, was so terribly calm and terribly indifferent when he feigned surprise, pretending that it was the first time he learned of Catherine Miller's murder, while he was in Charleston with another woman. Isn't that a circumstance that shows what was truly going on in this man's mind? How could anyone who had love for another person be so indifferent to the terrible murder of that person's mother?"

Tom stepped closer to the jurors, lowered his voice, lowered his brows, and said, "*Unless*, unless the unspeakable is true, ladies and gentlemen. No one else had any motive to do this. The Russians did not do this. It was not the act of robbers. What thief would not steal a gun? Jewelry? Televisions? All those things were not taken from Catherine Miller's home. You saw the photographs. This was the act of a person who had engaged in a course of conduct involving violence to more than one person. Lamont Claxton Underwood, Master Patrolman, murdered Catherine Miller." Tom turned around and looked directly at L. C. The jurors followed his gaze. L. C. appeared to be writing on his yellow legal pad, but from my vantage point, I could see that he was doodling.

"Ladies and gentlemen, those are the three aggravating circumstances that we contend exist in this case and which you ought to find beyond reasonable doubt…"

At 9:45 a.m. on July 24, 1997, after Don, Terry, Steve, and I were seated in front of the bar behind the prosecutors' table, the jury was brought into the courtroom and Chester Whittle began the final argument on sentencing for the defense. I braced myself for a heart-wrenching plea as Chester stood up and opened a big black leather-bound King James Bible.

"Look," I whispered, "I didn't know lawyers read the Bible," I whispered.

"Oh, they read it," Steve whispered back, "but they're just looking for loopholes."

I watched the jurors closely. I could see that Chester was getting to them. A couple of them had tears in their eyes before he was finished.

"Ladies and gentlemen," Chester began, "The decision you make is whether another human being spends the rest of his life in prison or whether he's put to death. I submit to you that that's a very important decision, and that hatred, fear, bias, prejudice should not enter into a decision like that. And clearly vengeance should not. While condemning L. C. Underwood for the things he's done, the State says for you to do the same thing…" I found it peculiar that all of a sudden, the defense attorneys were acknowledging the "things L. C. has done," when only a few days earlier they were adamantly professing his innocence.

"L. C. Underwood was not born the way he is today. He lived in fear with an abusive uncle, as told to you by his sister, an uncle who would hold him up by his feet and beat him with a belt, and her, until they bled, and then pour alcohol on them. An uncle who would make them stand for hours on one foot as he sat there and watched TV or read the paper, and if they faltered, more punishment, again, all verified by his sister. L. C. not only was beaten, but he was humiliated, for some infraction he was sent outside wearing his sister's dress so his friends could see him in a dress.

"L. C. got some help for himself, but not enough. And it affects different people in different ways. L. C. was so scared by those memories that he wouldn't even tell the woman that is his *mother-image* about it… It was so bad, he couldn't even keep a close relationship with his brothers and sisters, because it only reminded them and each other and him of what had gone before…

"Behind me sits a man that's been convicted of First Degree Murder and Kidnapping, and your verdict states that by his hand, he took the life of Viktor Gunnarsson, and by your hand the State asks you to take his life. And you will have a choice that will always be a decision that you're always going to remember. That's always going to be with you, the rest of your lives, no matter what you decide to do. It would be an easy decision for me, but I don't make the decision. The District Attorney doesn't make the decision. Nobody but you make this decision. And if you recommend death, that's an irretrievable act. You can't think about it next week or next month and wonder whether you should have done that or not. You cannot change your mind later.

"You have a responsibility for this man's life. We met him in 1995 after he was arrested, and my responsibility to him as a lawyer will soon end. And we will always wonder, Bruce and I, whether we could have done more. Maybe we should have done this, and maybe we should have done that. But the bottom line is that the decision is yours alone.

"The execution of L. C. Underwood is not going to bring back Viktor Gunnarsson. It will not bring him back. And statements by the prosecutors that he's crying from the grave and this sort of thing are just to inflame your emotions, to get you wound up, to make you feel vengeful. Mr. Rusher has stated to you that his execution will deter others. It won't. The sadness about it is, it won't. The sadness of any execution is that it doesn't deter anybody. A hundred years ago in England they used to hang pickpockets, hang them till they were dead. And these were public hangings and people would go watch, and while the crowds watched these pickpockets being hung, the pockets of the people in the crowd were picked.

"What I am saying is that those who kill *are* going to kill. These are even copycat killings. People learn about murder and they go copy it. And that's with or without a death penalty. Some states have no death penalty. Some countries have no death penalty. And the debate will always go on...

"The State says failing to kill L. C. Underwood would lessen the seriousness of his crime. And I would point out to you, does putting somebody behind bars for the rest of his natural life lessen the seriousness of his crime? How much does it lessen it? Does it diminish the seriousness of his crime when we know he will never sit under a Christmas tree again the rest of his life; he'll never hand out Christmas presents for the rest of his life; he'll never have a wife; he'll own nothing. He'll live a totally regimented life. He'll be told when to get up, when to get down and go to sleep. He'll be told when to eat, when to go to the bathroom, when to shower, when to shave, and he'll grow old and die in prison, separated from his beloved Barbara Childress, whom he calls Mom, and he'll never be able to go to her in a time of need or to be with her at a time of need. How is that diminishing his crime?

"There are some who would say that a convicted person should live his life with what he has done. He should think about it. He should be forced to think about it and live with it until in God's own time he's taken. And I submit to you that there's a lot of truth in that.

"The finality, ladies and gentlemen, of the death sentence is actually frightening when you think about it. It says that another human being is so worthless that they deserve to die, that his life should be forfeited like he's a rabid dog, that there's nothing ever that he can contribute to society or mankind, not even a letter to Barbara Childress or postcards or anything else, that he never will have the chance to redeem himself in some way, even if it's a small way, in the eyes of his fellow man.

"The District Attorney said 'He who showed no mercy now asks for mercy.' And I ask you to look into your own hearts. Are you angry at him? Do you feel hatred? Do you feel like you want to exact revenge, because that isn't the function of the jury. 'Vengeance is mine,' saith the Lord. The function of the jury is not vengeance. The function of the jury is to fairly and impartially, without fear and without hatred, decide this case.

"...Jesus brought to us two great commandments. The first was to love God. The second was to love your fellow man. It was a compilation and distillation of everything in the Old Testament. And where the Old Testament said, 'An eye for an eye and a tooth for a tooth, I say love thine enemies.' 'I say when your enemies are hungry, feed them. When they thirst, give them drink.' 'And when you're smitten upon the cheek, turn the other cheek.'

"Twice in Jesus's lifetime, the Bible tells us, He was confronted with a death. The first, you may remember, was the adulteress. In those days the punishment for an adulteress was to stone her to death. Literally what they would do is pick up rocks in a crowd and throw them at her until she was crushed, bleeding, and finally died. In coming upon a scene like this where this is about to go on, they asked Him, 'What should we do?' They were baiting Him again, as usual. And His response was, 'Let you who is without sin cast the first stone.' And those simple words stopped it all.

"The second time, ladies and gentlemen, when He was confronted with death, it was His own death. He had carried the instrument of His death, the cross, to the place of His death. The cross was put into the ground or put down. He was placed on it. He was nailed to it. He was lifted up. And while up for nine hours with a crown of thorns on His head, and as He was bleeding, He was handed drink by way of a sponge which had vinegar on it. He had been betrayed. He had been reviled. He had been spat upon. And as He was, He didn't cause a holocaust. He knew that His mortal life was coming to an end. He had the power to call forth a holocaust upon those that had done these things to Him and stabbed Him. And instead, He said, 'Forgive them Father, for they know not what they do.' He didn't hate sinners. He hated the sin. And I submit to you, you're being asked to hate the sinner and put him to death. The District Attorney said, 'He who had no mercy now wants mercy.'" Opening the Bible to Matthew, Chester read, "Blessed are the merciful, for they shall obtain mercy" from Jesus's Sermon on the Mount.

"The State contends there's something wrong with mercy. The State contends you can't be an alcoholic; you are a drunk. The State would have us go back to barbarism. Jesus also said, 'Whatsoever thou doest to the least of my brethren, thou also doest unto me.' And we can look around in this courtroom and we can find the least of our brethren without any problem at all, can't we?

"Showing him mercy, ladies and gentlemen, by sparing his life, by making him live with what he's done, isn't going to hurt you. It isn't going to hurt them. It isn't going to hurt society. It's not going to hurt anybody. But I'll tell you what. It's going to take courage for you to do that. That's what it's going to take: Courage. I hope you have that courage. The verdict to put him to death must be unanimous. I hope that all of you have the courage to say no. But I hope that if one of you, two of you, three of you can say, 'I can't do this.'"

Jerry objected.

"Sustained," Judge Ferrell ruled.

Chester concluded, "If you have a strong conviction, hold to it steadfastly. And finally, ladies and gentlemen, this is the last thing I'll say to you. When this trial is over, I hope that you will have an opportunity to see whomever it is that you most love and respect, and I would like to think that it would please you to say to that person whom you most love and respect, 'Today, I had the chance to recommend the death of another human being, but the choice I made was for *mercy*.' Thank you." Chester exhaled with finality and sat down. It was 10:43 a.m.

After a short break, at 11:01 a.m. Judge Ferrell read his final instructions to the jury and released them to deliberate on L. C.'s sentence. Again, we waited.

At 11:20 a.m., the court bailiff informed Judge Ferrell that the jurors had a question. Judge Ferrell had them brought back in, and asked them to write their question on a piece of paper. They did so, and Judge Ferrell read the question aloud.

"Regarding aggravating factor #2, do we have to find it especially heinous, atrocious, AND cruel, or just one of the three?"

Judge Ferrell informed the jurors that they needed to find the factor either heinous OR atrocious OR cruel in order to find the aggravating factor. I thought it was encouraging. Jerry Wilson thought it discouraging.

"Why is that?" I asked Jerry.

"Because if the jurors are having trouble finding that factor, then they are likely to have trouble finding others."

They sent out another question a few minutes later. This time they wanted to know if a life sentence actually meant that L. C. would never be paroled.

"He needs to tell them the truth," I said to Jerry.

"He isn't allowed to tell them the truth," Jerry said.

"That is not right," I replied.

"It's the law," Jerry said.

"It's a misleading law then," I responded.

Neither the Judge nor any of the attorneys were allowed to tell the jurors that life in prison means anything less than life imprisonment in the state's prison, per NCGS 15A-2002. When Judge Ferrell advised them of the mandatory response, the jurors returned to their deliberations erroneously believing that L. C. Underwood would never be able to walk out of the prison doors.

Though I did not know exactly what prompted the change, the law was modified slightly for crimes *occurring* on or after October 1, 1994, almost a year after Viktor and Catherine were murdered. NCGS 15A-2002 then allowed the judge to explain the wording of life in prison to mean life served in the state's prison *without parole*. This simply is not true. A life sentence in North Carolina equates to about twenty years in prison. I did not want to see L. C. Underwood walking out of a prison gate in twenty short years, or less.

At 12:15 p.m., the jury sent a message to the Judge that they wanted to go to lunch. Judge Ferrell looked perturbed but released them a few minutes later to go to lunch.

It was a bright sunny day, and Don, Terry, Steve, and I walked down the street to have a sandwich. Afterward, we ran into Chester Whittle right outside the restaurant.

"How can ya'll eat at a time like this?" Chester asked.

"Clean conscience," Steve replied. Everyone laughed except Chester.

"A clean conscience is typically just a sign of a bad memory," he responded and laughed.

At 2:00 p.m., the jurors resumed their deliberation, and we waited in the District Attorney's Office down the hall from the courtroom. Kay, Jason, and Kay's good friend Anne waited with Sherry, the Victims' Advocate, while Sheriff Lyons, Jerry Wilson, and the four of us sat in Tom Rusher's office.

"No matter what happens today," Sheriff Lyons stated, "you all have each done the best you could do. I don't know of any case that was investigated or prosecuted more thoroughly."

A chorus of "Thank you, Sheriff," followed.

"We appreciate your support throughout the whole investigation, Sheriff," Steve said.

"That boy ought to get the death penalty," Sheriff Lyons added.

"Yes, Sheriff, he ought to. But now I learned many years ago that trying to read a jury, or trying to predict what they will do in a given case is an exercise in futility," Tom replied. "There are those who make predictions based upon the length of deliberation, the expressions or subtle behaviors, nonverbal clues of the jurors during the trial, so on and so forth, but such predictions truly amount to little more than a guess."

"I do think Chester's closing argument impacted some of the jurors at least," I said.

"What do you mean, Paula?" Jerry asked.

"Chester made their decision more personal, causing each of them to think about their own accountability, not what L. C. did. Specifically, his comments were designed, I'd say, to think about their own lives. He wanted them to think long and hard about when, if given the choice between mercy and vengeance as he called it, they would be afraid to choose anything other than mercy. I think he made a powerful argument for choosing mercy. Most people do believe the Bible, and most people have been taught that same message from the Sermon on the Mount – that the merciful shall obtain mercy."

"If you were on the jury, Paula, would his arguments have made you choose Life over a Death Sentence?"

"No. I think in some cases the death penalty is *more* merciful to the offender than a life sentence."

"How is that?" Don asked. "Other than the fact that they won't have to sit in a prison cell for years and years, I mean."

"Because if a man is serving a life sentence, he spends all of that time still trying to get out and trying to convince other people that he is not guilty. But a man whose death is imminent and certain, who has exhausted his appeals and has nothing left but a set amount of time to think about eternity and judgment, is far more likely to confess to others and most importantly to God, to seek forgiveness and salvation. I can't think of anything that would be more humbling than knowing you are about to die."

"It is true that a person has to be humble – and often broken – before they can be sincere about getting things right with the Lord," Steve said.

"Well, Paula, I don't know if L. C. will ever humble himself to the degree that he confesses."

"Maybe not in the traditional manner, to an interrogator sitting across the table from him. But I can see him confessing in a more intimate setting, such as with his next love-interest-victim. He is so arrogant that I think he will eventually have to tell someone – and I think it will more likely be a female – how he had the guts to do it."

"I don't see him ever confessing under any circumstances," Steve said.

"Neither do I," Terry said.

I asked, "Don't you all remember what Beth Richardson said about L. C. having that picture of the Vietnamese man on his knees, and he told Beth that he killed him and then never felt sorry for it?"

"Yeah, okay maybe," Steve said.

"And wait till he gets settled in prison and makes a friend or two. He is an arrogant somebody, always bragging about himself. Like that stuff about himself on all of his walls at his house. But in prison he can't exactly brag about being a cop to a bunch of convicts. So, he will have to brag about what he did, or some version of it. I think he will confess to someone sooner or later. Now I don't think he will confess because he is humble; I think he will confess out of arrogance and pride. However, if he is given the death penalty and after all the hoops have been jumped through, and he has nothing left but time to think about death, I think he might legitimately confess. Anyway, he well deserves the death penalty for what he did to Viktor and to Catherine. The rage of that man…"

Steve said, "I do think the death penalty is appropriate, when properly applied. Even the Bible teaches a man to obey the law and the government or face the consequences. Where exactly does it say that?"

"Hebrews thirteen, and I think it is about verse 7, that says to obey those that rule over you," Sheriff Lyons stated.

I took a Bible from a shelf in Tom's office and turned to the book of Hebrews.

"You're right, Sheriff. Verse seven says, 'Remember them which have the rule over you, who have spoken unto you the word of God: whose faith follow, considering the end of their conversation.'" I flipped the pages back to Romans. "Also chapter thirteen, starting with verse one in Romans says, 'Let every soul be subject unto the higher powers… the powers that are ordained of God. Whosoever therefore resisteth the power, resisteth the ordinance of God: and they that resist shall receive to themselves damnation. For rulers are not a terror to good works, but to the evil. Wilt thou then not be afraid of the power? Do that which is good, and thou shalt have praise of the same: For he is the minister of God to thee for good. But if thou do that which is evil, be afraid; for he *beareth not the sword in vain:* for he is the minister of God, a revenger to execute wrath upon him that doeth evil…"

Nearly two hours had passed when we were instructed to go back into the courtroom. The jury, we were told, had reached a verdict. It was 4:10 p.m.

First, Judge Ferrell read aloud the aggravating and mitigating factors that the jury had decided upon. The responses were provided in writing and orally by the jury foreman.

"…Ladies and gentlemen of the jury, this is Issue Number One. Do you unanimously find from the evidence, beyond a reasonable doubt, the existence of one or more of the following *aggravating* circumstances?"

"Yes."

"Was this murder committed while the defendant was engaged in the commission of kidnapping?"

"Yes."

"Was this murder especially heinous, atrocious, or cruel?"

"No." *I looked at the jurors in disbelief. A stranger binding a grown man and throwing him in the trunk of a car to travel in the dead of winter to the mountains and into the woods in the middle of the night to be shot, stripped of his* clothing and left to die was neither heinous, atrocious, NOR cruel?

"Was this murder part of a course of conduct in which the defendant engaged, and did that course of conduct include the commission by the defendant of other crimes of violence against other persons?"

"No." *What? Were they even listening? Killing Viktor and Catherine was the culmination of all the years of L. C.'s pathological jealousy, stalking, and violence!*

"Issue Number Two... Do you find from the evidence the existence of one or more of the following *mitigating* circumstances?"

"Yes."

"Was this murder committed while the defendant was under the influence of mental or emotional disturbance?"

"Yes."

"Was the capacity of the defendant to conform his conduct to the requirements of the law impaired?"

"Yes."

"Was the defendant abandoned as a young child by his parents?"

"Yes."

"Did the defendant witness instances of bloody domestic violence between his parents?"

"Yes."

"Was the defendant ignored by his parents and forced to spend a Christmas Eve in a barn?"

"Yes."

"Was the defendant sent to reside with an uncle and aunt, and was he abused physically and emotionally by his uncle?"

"Yes."

"Did the defendant's parents provide no support, and did they not communicate with him nor his siblings after the abandonment?"

"Yes."

"The defendant, while growing up, did not know his mother's parents nor any of her brothers and sisters, and they provided no support to him or his siblings?"

"Yes."

"Was the defendant separated from his brother, who had been sent to reside with an aunt and grandmother, and did not live together after the defendant was five years old?"

"Yes."

"Was the defendant sent to reside in The Methodist Children's Home in Winston Salem and remained there nine years?"

"Yes."

At The Children's Home, did the defendant develop a loving relationship with a couple whom he came to regard as his mother and father, which relationship he maintained throughout his adult life?"

"Yes."

"Is the defendant greatly loved by the couple, who wished to adopt him but his parents could not be located for legal consent?"

"Yes."

"Did the defendant graduate from high school and maintain gainful employment since then?"

"Yes."

"The defendant has not seen his siblings in over twenty years?"

"No."

"Did the defendant serve active duty of six months in the National Guard, and was he honorably discharged?"

"Yes."

"Did the defendant serve the public as a police officer for nineteen years?"

"Yes."

"Did the defendant retire with a disability in 1993 after three back surgeries suffered in 1988 from a job-related injury, which caused him great pain?"

"Yes."

"Has the defendant suffered from depression throughout his adult life and was he diagnosed with depression in 1976 at age 25?"

"Yes."

"Has the defendant suffered three major depression episodes and was he diagnosed with Major Depression after separating from his wife in 1992?"

"Yes."

"Was the defendant disturbed by a series of serious illnesses his mother Barbara Childress suffered beginning in 1989, and did he fear she was suffering a life-threatening illness in 1993?"

"Yes."

"Did the defendant voluntarily seek psychological treatment in 1992 and 1993?

"Yes."

"Has the defendant expressed an intention on several occasions to commit suicide if anything happened to Barbara Childress?"

"Yes."

"Was the defendant severely depressed before and around the time of the killing of Viktor Gunnarsson?"

"Yes."

"Any other circumstance or circumstances arising from the evidence which one or more of you found is, or are, insufficient to outweigh the aggravating circumstance or circumstances found by one or more of you?"

"No."

"Issue Number Three. Do you unanimously find beyond a reasonable doubt that the mitigating circumstance or circumstances found is, or are, *in*sufficient to outweigh the aggravating circumstances found by one or more of you?"

"Yes."

"Issue Number Four. Do you unanimously find beyond a reasonable doubt that the aggravating circumstance or circumstances found is, or are, sufficiently substantial to call for the imposition of the death penalty when considered with the mitigating circumstance or circumstances found by one or more of you?"

"No."

The sentencing verdict, then, was read.

"WE, THE JURY, UNANIMOUSLY RECOMMEND THAT THE DEFENDANT, LAMONT CLAXTON UNDERWOOD, BE SENTENCED TO LIFE IMPRISONMENT. THIS 25TH DAY OF JULY, 1997."

The court erupted in noises, some cheering and some booing and everyone seemingly talking at once. Judge Ferrell tapped his gavel three times, and the bailiff called out, "Order in the Court, Order in the Court." The courtroom grew quiet again.

Judge Ferrell continued, "...The defendant is therefore sentenced to life imprisonment for First Degree Murder. He is also sentenced to Forty Years imprisonment for First Degree Kidnapping, the latter sentence to be served consecutively and not concurrently with the first."

I looked at L. C. but could not see his face. He was being tightly embraced by Barbara Childress. He did not seem to be returning her affection. Sheriff Lyons took hold of L. C.'s arm at the elbow then and drew him away from Mrs. Childress. Lieutenant Stout stepped up to assist him, but L. C. was not giving any trouble. Then I could not see L. C. any longer because I suddenly found myself surrounded by a sea of reporters.

Back in the District Attorney's Office the investigators and prosecutors were assembled together. Kay, Jason, and their friends had escaped the media throng as quickly as possible. Both Tom and Jerry tried to focus on the positive.

"It is just terribly, terribly difficult to get any jury these days to sentence a person to death. We gave it our best shot," Jerry commented. "We won the war. Sentencing was just a battle. We must not lose sight of that."

"And a life sentence plus forty years is certainly nothing to scoff at," added Tom.

I responded, "But we all know a life sentence is twenty years, *at best*. And as for the forty, once he gets in prison, he can be released in a fraction of that."

No one argued.

It seemed to me as if the jury had reduced the last three and a half years of our lives to mean something less than it ought to have meant. I felt like, more importantly, that we had somehow let Kay and Jason down. This sentencing decision had, as I saw it then, provided L. C. a list of excuses once again for his heinous, atrocious, and cruel conduct. I feared their decision delivered to him the wrong message, false justification for his actions, thereby destroying his ability to realize the condition of his doomed soul and his inherent need for a Savior. Holding to my earlier premise, I believed life imprisonment could damn his soul to hell.

It was several weeks later that I learned that the jury's sentencing vote count was 11-1 in favor of the death penalty. The unrelenting juror was a man who had a close relative serving time in prison for murder, a fact that was not disclosed during jury selection. Perhaps he could not disassociate himself and his relative from the case. Perhaps he did the best he could.

Still I attributed the decision of the jury to the fact that they were not informed that a life sentence was not a literal life sentence in prison. Had they known the truth, they might have called for a different sentence.

At this point we would be double-tapping ourselves, in a sense. The first shot at the death penalty failed to strike the right mark with this jury. Perhaps there would be one more shot at the death penalty in the case of Catherine Miller's murder. But it remained to be seen.

CHAPTER THIRTY

"Oh let the wickedness of the wicked come to an end; but establish the just: for the righteous God trieth the hearts and reins" (Psalms 7:9)

The late July day was unusually hot, and my sockless feet perspired inside my leather pumps. I slipped my feet out and wiggled my toes. The late morning sun was already stinging my bare arms, and I had only been sitting outside the jail for about thirty minutes. The sweltering heat was only relieved momentarily by the occasional light mountain breeze. Through the thin material of my pencil skirt I felt the radiant heat that the cement bench on which I sat had absorbed from the sun like a brick oven.

I studied the pale-pink nail polish on my toes. I had painted Katie's toenails to match mine the night before. She loved for me to paint her fingernails and toenails. I thought of Viktor's toes in the snow, five intact and five missing. I shifted my gaze slightly, frowning at the calluses beginning to form on the bottom of my feet, a telltale sign of my barefooting vice. The rubber on my shoe soles were softened from the scorching black pavement beneath them. I wondered if they would eventually melt away if I sat here in this heat long enough. I thought of the shoe print – it would always be a shoe print to me – in the dust on the underside of L. C.'s trunk lid. My scattered thoughts were interrupted by a familiar voice behind me.

"Hey there," Steve said.

"Hey yourself."

"Whatcha doing out here in this heat, taking a smoke break?" he joked.

"I'd walk a mile for a Camel," I responded with mixed cigarette brand slogans, "and I've come a long way, baby."

Steve chuckled. "We've all come a long way."

I had lost track of so many little things. "How long has it been now? Since you quit smoking, I mean."

"About two more weeks will make two years."

"And doesn't it feel good not to be coughing every other breath?"

"It does. But I didn't cough *that* much," he said.

"Okay then," I said. I had lectured him enough in the past. Except for the trial preparations and the trial itself, Steve had been busy in Avery County, an adjoining mountain county, where he was investigating another heinous murder. A forty-eight-year-old woman, Shelby Jean White, not only beat to death sixty-year-old Roberta Starr Charpentier whose home she wanted to purchase but could not afford, White buried her in the crawl space under the house. She then assumed Charpentier's identity, attempted to withdraw money from the victim's bank account, and lived in the house *as* the victim. She lived there several days until family members living across the country realized something bizarre was going on when a strange voice answered the phone insisting she was Charpentier, while at the same time neighbors began to complain about an awful smell emanating from the house.

"How is the murder investigation coming along in Avery County?" I asked.

"It's coming together. Unlike this one, it would be a strong case even without White's confession," he said. "The things that woman did... it's just... inconceivable."

"Except it *was* conceivable."

"Obviously. That's the point I guess."

The atrocities one person can exact upon another human being is, to most folks, unfathomable. But some are not afforded the luxury of blissful ignorance. Some of us are cursed with engrafted images of the unadulterated truth; that no act is so heinous, so outrageous, that it could not possibly be performed on one human being by another... no murder too cruel, no torture too unbearable, no person too invulnerable.

"It never ends does it?" I remarked.

"I don't think this *case* will ever end," he said. "By the way, reporters are calling. You have a stack of messages on your desk."

"Sheriff Lyons will handle most of them now."

"A couple calls came from Sweden."

I nodded. "They're chomping at the bit to find anything that would connect Viktor to the Prime Minister's assassination. So do you think Viktor could have done that?" I asked.

"Only the Lord knows," he said.

"Right... Well Viktor got the death penalty whether he deserved it or not," I commented.

"Yes, he got the death penalty instead of L. C. At least so far. Catherine Miller's murder will be a capital case too," he said.

"I would assume so."

"So... what is it you're doing, sitting out here in this heat?" he asked.

"I guess I am waiting for the transport deputy to bring L. C. outside. I want to see the face of a convicted policeman as he heads off to serve his first day of life plus forty."

"You've seen that face many times. Up close and personal."

"Yes, but I want to see it for Viktor's family, and for Catherine. I want to frame it in my mind in its own special place."

"Are you thinking he's going to say something else to you? You want to give him one more opportunity to confess? He's not going to do that, Paula. In fact, if he says anything, he'll tell you to go to hell."

"I am well aware, and I most certainly do not expect him to yell out a confession as he is hauled away. I just want to see him leave here in shackles and leg irons one last time, *post-conviction*."

"Alrighty then," he said, and put his sunglasses on.

I tried to explain. "It's like we've worked this case for so long. We were there at the beginning in that cold, cold place where Viktor was left, and I want to see it through, all the way to the end. I need closure – you know, the final chapter."

"Well, the trial is over, but I don't think it is going to end here. He is going to appeal till the cows come home, and he's going to be dragging us through the muck with him whenever he can. I am fairly confident we have not seen or heard the last of L. C. Underwood."

"Well, it's not like I'm going to miss him or anything, it's just that I have a fear deep down that he will get out. I can't imagine – well I don't *want* to imagine what will happen if he does."

"You can't live your life worrying about that though. It will make you old before your time. I think we'll see him again soon enough, hopefully in his next capital murder trial."

"Do you think Kennerly will indict him on Catherine's murder soon?"

"I would think so, in light of the fact that Tom and Jerry have already done all the hard work organizing all the evidence and witnesses, and since we have the witnesses all available and so forth. Plus, the jury in our case had no problem with finding him guilty of killing Viktor, and I believe they also know that he killed Catherine Miller. They would have convicted him on her murder too."

"I just have a bad feeling about it, that maybe Kennerly won't prosecute him."

"I guess we will find out soon enough."

"Do you think he knows how evil he is?"

"Bill Kennerly?" he joked. "That's not a very nice thing to say about an elected official."

"Ha, ha. Not Kennerly. L. C."

"I frankly don't think he cares, Paula. Regardless, L. C. has justified to himself every wrong thing he's ever done. Everything has always been someone else's fault."

"True. Well, for now, I can close this case finally, all twenty-four big fat voluminous notebooks of it. It feels weird."

"Well I for one am not going to miss traveling to Salisbury and back all the time."

"Me either. Salisbury is a beautiful old town, even if it does have some pretty mean people there. Like that guy who killed his wife, cut her up and set her on fire in the trash can in the middle of the highway down there. Remember that case was going on while we were down there working ours? Pure evil. But Salisbury does have its charm too. I will miss driving by all those stately old homes with the bright pink and fuchsia azaleas, and those lilac trees blooming in the spring. I've never seen color blooming like that all over an entire city."

"Right. And those tasty barbecue places on every corner."

"You're making fun," I accused.

"No, I'm serious. It's possible we could have missed eating at one," he said.

"I doubt it. Between the four of us grabbing barbecue on the run from every other block in Rowan County, I don't think we missed any. However, I wouldn't mind having another cheesesteak salad from Spencer's," I said. "But maybe now I can get home *before* dinner, most nights at least, hopefully."

He looked at me quizzically. "Are you glad they didn't sentence him to death?"

"No. Why, are you?"

"No. They should have."

"I still can't believe they didn't offer up a defense."

"Bruce and Chester kept arguing to the jury that he should be forgiven. But L. C. never once said he was sorry, or ever acted remorseful in any way. Don't you have to be repentant, remorseful to be forgiven? You know that verse, the one about God being close to those with a broken heart and a contrite spirit?"

"The Lord is nigh unto them that are of a broken heart; and saveth such as be of a contrite spirit. From Psalms."

"That's the one."

"But no, we are supposed to forgive whether a person is sorry or not. But the law, the criminal justice system, is responsible for handling criminal matters and offenders appropriately. It does not bear the sword in vain, you know. The law isn't made for the righteous, but for murderers..."

"Except in this case," he commented drily.

"I wonder if he will *ever* be sorry," I said, "in this life, I mean."

"L. C. doesn't have a conscience, Paula. You want him to have a conscience and be sorry, but he doesn't and he's not."

"I know. I do wish he had a conscience. And I know he must not have. I saw that that night in the jail cell when it was just him and me. I'll never forget those demonic black eyes and that coldness... But the little boy he used to be, with no one to love him, being abused and then just thrown away..." I squinted at the bright sun then, in case I needed an excuse for why my eyes were watering. I was probably the only cop within miles who did not own a pair of Raybans in the 1990s. Distractedly, I wondered if sunglasses would have prevented the tiny wrinkles around my eyes, which I had noticed of late. Stress and life experience in general were already affecting my body and my health, probably my mental health as well.

"I bet Randy's glad the case is over," Steve said.

"Yeah. He's put up with a lot of my being gone, and he's been a good dad to Katie."

"He's a good guy. And Katie will be glad to have her mama at home more."

"Yes, that girl is the love of my life. And totally a mama's girl. Tomorrow we are taking her and my little brother, Josh, to Tweetsie Railroad."

"She will love that."

"And I know Martha and Anna will be glad to have you done with this case and home more as well, and of course…" embarassed that I could not remember.

"Tim and Brian. I hope they will," he replied.

"I'm sure of it," I said. "And Sophie too," I added, remembering the family dog's name suddenly.

"Right." Steve propped one shiny Johnston & Murphy shoe, sans tassels, up on the edge of my bench and wiped his brow with the cuff of his long-sleeved dress shirt sleeve. "We may have a little reprieve from it for now, but like I said, this case really isn't over."

"Then why does it feel so… anticlimactic? I almost feel sad at the world all of a sudden, and that's ridiculous."

"Like you have no purpose and meaning in your life?" he asked.

"Yeah. Are you making fun of me?"

"Nah. I'm not. You shouldn't feel sad. You should feel good about it. Chalk one up for the good guys. We got our man. We won the case. The murderer is going to prison for a long time. Most importantly, he's not out stalking the night, as Tom said, and killing people."

"I hope Kay gets some justice for her mother," I said.

"As do I, but that's totally up to Kennerly."

"I know. …Kay deserves to see L. C. at least served with a warrant for killing her helpless little mama."

"At least she can take comfort in the fact that L. C. will be behind bars the rest of his life."

"True. Kay is a survivor, ya know? She lived a nightmare for so long, but she didn't let it destroy her."

"No, she didn't."

"Maybe one day she can be an advocate for women everywhere – for any kind of victim, really, domestic violence, stalking, etc. A public education campaign where she teaches people not to ignore the red flags, ya know?"

"Right."

"Kay would be great at it. She's articulate, genuine." Steve nodded.

Beads of sweat had formed at his temples. "Man, I can't ever remember it being so hot in the mountains," he said. I had also had about all the sun beating on my head as I wanted today as well.

He took his foot off the bench. "Well, Don and Terry have checked out of their hotel and are ready to go to lunch. Kay and Jason are going. Tom and Jerry can't go. They want to go to Blowing Rock and eat."

"Don't tell me they want barbecue?"

He nodded and grinned, "Woodlands." Woodlands had good smoked pork, but they also had very good southwest fare. I would have a beef burrito.

"The sheriff is coming. And Tom's Assistant Jason has already reserved us a table large enough for all of us. Charlene said to tell you to save her a seat. She's riding with Jason and Sherry. I invited Ray and Lieutenant Stout, but they ate already."

I slipped my feet all the way back inside my shoes. "Okay," I said, "I'm gonna walk over to Probation to meet Randy, and then we'll meet ya'll at Woodlands."

I never saw L. C. leave.

I said goodbye to Kay and Jason first, with mixed emotions, but I was fairly confident Kay would keep in touch with me. I hoped she would.

Then I turned to Don and Terry.

"Tell Joan we still have to plan that girls' trip," I told Don.

"I'll tell her," he said.

"And I still have to get her recipe for that pepper-steak she made us." Steve and I had dinner with them several times over the past three years.

"Well, until we meet again," Don said.

"Won't be long," Steve said.

"Hopefully soon," I said.

Don nodded and looked away. I know that wasn't a tear I saw gathering in his eye. Must be the heat.

"Terry, you're welcome to come back and stay at our house anytime you want to go hiking again."

"If your mom is making biscuits and gravy – and that chocolate gravy – I'll be right there!" he said.

"Almost every Saturday morning," Randy said.

"It's nice to have friends right by the Appalachian Trail," he said and added, "Just don't take me back to Stacy Ward's junkyard ever again." We all laughed.

"Keep an EpiPen handy, just in case," Charlene said, ever safety-conscious.

I knew I would see Don and Terry both again, and I was certain to be investigating new cases with Steve Wilson in the future, but it would not be the same as we would no longer be a team united by a specific common goal. My heart was heavy with a plethora of emotions. There were the same kinds of feelings one experiences at the end of an era, not unlike high school graduation.

Once a long sought-after goal has been reached, there is relief and some joy to be felt. But there is sadness as well. Sadness for a season in one's life that has reached an end. Sadness for the remembrance of days when the four of us shared a comradery, a common goal that no one else outside our circle shared with the same conviction. There was also a certain dread for those victims yet to come, those who would endure horrible crimes in the future, those I would meet and do my best to help in the days and months to follow.

Yet I also felt hope... hope that the memories we shared – the hard times, the challenges, and the way we overcame them and even had a few laughs along the way – would not fade quickly with time. I had hope that Kay and Jason could go on and enjoy a bright and peaceful future without the dread of L. C. Underwood in their lives. I had hope that the North Carolina Court of Appeals would affirm L. C.'s guilt in Viktor Gunnarsson's kidnapping and murder. Additionally, the hope remained that there would be justice for one kindhearted, beloved Catherine Louise H. Bentley Miller, that we would one day hold accountable Lamont Claxton Underwood for her heinous, atrocious, and cruel death. Perhaps, there was hope even for his soul.

"...for love is strong as death; jealousy is cruel as the grave: the coals thereof are coals of fire, which hath a most vehement flame"
(Song of Solomon 8:6)

PHOTOS

Viktor Gunnarsson and his favorite leather bomber jacket

Viktor Gunnarsson's car parked in his usual manner at his apartment complex.

Living area of Viktor Gunnarsson's apartment upon investigators' entry.

Catherine Miller, murder victim, mother of Kay Weden.

Catherine Miller and daughter Kay Weden

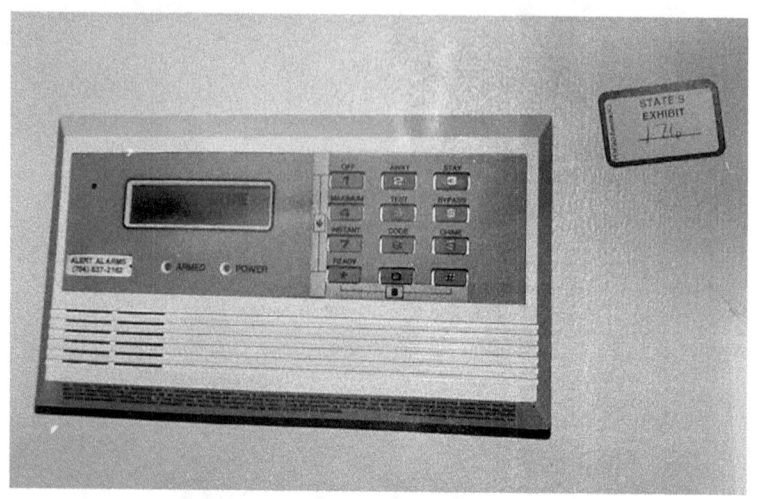

Alarm master panel from inside Catherine Miller's residence on December 9, 1993, showing that the home alarm was not armed at the time she was found murdered.

Crime scene as found on the morning of December 9, 1993. Catherine Miller, murder victim.

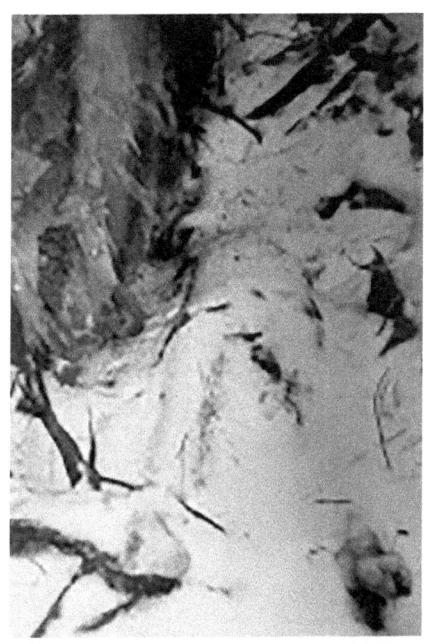

Body of Viktor Gunnarsson as discovered on January 7, 1994 in Watauga County, NC

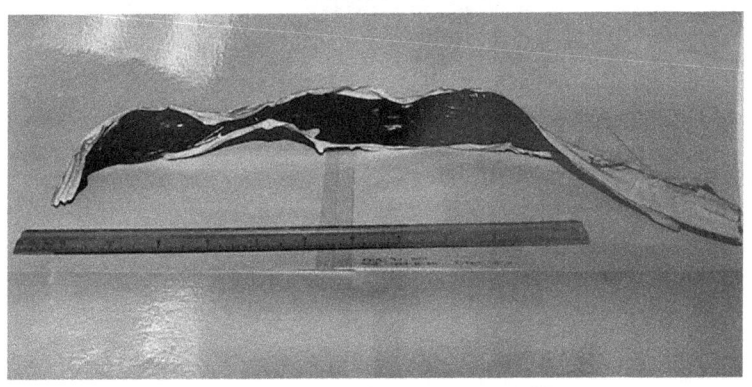

Length of tape found in the snow at mountain scene by Sheriff Lyons where Viktor Gunnarsson's body was discovered. Contains Gunnarsson's hair, blood and a gunshot hole.

*Master Police Officer L.C. Underwood,
Salisbury Police Department*

Residence of L.C. Underwood in Salisbury, NC at the time of the murders.

Officer L.C. Underwood and his beloved dog Misty given to him as a Christmas gift by Kay Weden.

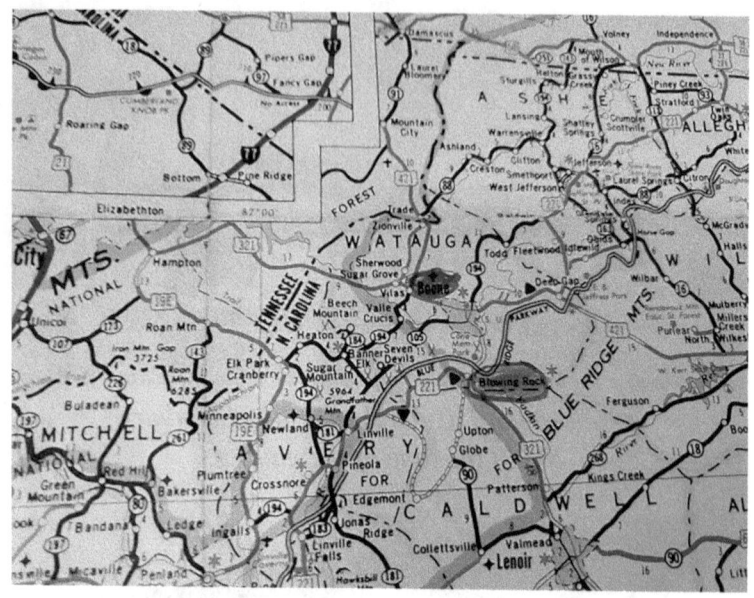

The North Carolina highway map found in Underwood's home with locations marked in the mountains near the site where Viktor Gunnarsson's body was found.

Methodist Children's Home in Winston Salem, NC where the Underwood children grew up after being abandoned by parents and given up by family.

*For More News About Paula May,
Signup For Our Newsletter:*

http://wbp.bz/newsletter

Word-of-mouth is critical to an author's long-term success. If you appreciated this book please leave a review on the Amazon sales page:

http://wbp.bz/fdra

AVAILABLE FROM MICHAEL FLEEMAN AND WILDBLUE PRESS!

MISSING... AND PRESUMED DEAD
by MICHAEL FLEEMAN

http://wbp.bz/mpda

AVAILABLE FROM MONIQUE FAISON ROSS AND WILDBLUE PRESS!

PLAYING DEAD by MONIQUE FAISON ROSS

http://wbp.bz/playingdeada

AVAILABLE FROM ROBERT DAVIDSON AND WILDBLUE PRESS!

THE BEAST I LOVED by ROBERT DAVIDSON

http://wbp.bz/tbila

See even more at:
http://wbp.bz/tc

More True Crime You'll Love From WildBlue Press

A MURDER IN MY HOMETOWN by Rebecca Morris
Nearly 50 years after the murder of seventeen year old Dick Kitchel, Rebecca Morris returned to her hometown to write about how the murder changed a town, a school, and the lives of his friends.

wbp.bz/hometowna

BETRAYAL IN BLUE by Burl Barer & Frank C. Girardot Jr.
Adapted from Ken Eurell's shocking personal memoir, plus hundreds of hours of exclusive interviews with the major players, including former international drug lord, Adam Diaz, and Dori Eurell, revealing the truth behind what you won't see in the hit documentary THE SEVEN FIVE.

wbp.bz/biba

SIDETRACKED by Richard Cahill
A murder investigation is complicated by the entrance of the Reverend Al Sharpton who insists that a racist killer is responsible. Amid a growing media circus, investigators must overcome the outside forces that repeatedly sidetrack their best efforts.

wbp.bz/sidetrackeda

BETTER OFF DEAD by Michael Fleeman
A frustrated, unhappy wife. Her much younger, attentive lover. A husband who degrades and ignores her. The stage is set for a love-triangle murder that shatters family illusions and lays bare a quiet family community's secret world of sex, sin and swinging.

wbp.bz/boda

www.ingramcontent.com/pod-product-compliance
Lightning Source LLC
Chambersburg PA
CBHW070801040426
42333CB00061B/1735